Computing in the Humanities

Computing in the Humanities

Proceedings of the Third International
Conference on Computing in the Humanities

Sponsored by the University of Montreal
and the University of Waterloo
August 2-6, 1977
at Waterloo, Ontario

Editors
Serge Lusignan and John S. North

The University of Waterloo Press

This book was typeset by the Mathematics Faculty Computing Facility, University of Waterloo, in New Times Roman on a Photon Econosetter. Manuscripts were entered and edited using the QED text editor, and formatted by the PROFF text formatter running on a Honeywell 66/60 computer system.

International Standard Book Number 0–88898–014–0

University of Waterloo Press
Waterloo, Ontario, Canada
N2L 3G1

1st Printing
Printed in Canada

Book Design, George W. Roth
Typography, UW Math Faculty Computing Facility
Printing and binding, Hunter Rose
Distributed in Great Britain by Edinburgh University Press
August, 1977

This volume is printed with the assistance of Honeywell Information Systems (Canada) Ltd.

Contents

Preface

Since the Cambridge conference of the Association for Literary and Linguistic Computing in 1970, scholars in the humanities have met regularly to discuss the use of the computer in their respective fields of study. They have now established a schedule of conferring annually, alternating one year in Europe, under the auspices of the Association for Literary and Linguistic Computing, with one year in North America, as the International Conference on Computing in the Humanities.

The Third International Conference on Computing in the Humanities was held August 2-5, 1977, in Canada, at Waterloo, Ontario, and was organized jointly by the University of Montreal and the University of Waterloo. More than one hundred papers were presented, dealing with various aspects of computer use in the humanities. This year our colleagues in music, ballet and the graphic arts contributed much more to ICCH/3 than in the past.

As with all academic conferences, the purpose of these meetings is to make known the results of the most recent work and to encourage discussion and an exchange of information in each subject. It is a truism to say that the process of discussion gives birth to new ideas and refines the results of intellectual labour. However, those using the computer in the humanities have unusual opportunities to benefit from conversations with colleagues in other disciplines, for they must consult with specialists in several areas: the humanities, mathematics, computing science and engineering. A final observation, even more prosaic but none-the-less useful, is that a conference such as ICCH/3 can be the occasion for the exchange of research material important for the satisfactory progress of our work, material such as computing programs and texts stored on magnetic tape.

In order to increase the influence of this international conference we have collected in one volume a selection of twenty-eight papers. The selection has been determined by the quality of the papers, of course, but also by the intention of demonstrating the diversity of applications of the computer to the humanities. This latter criterion has made it necessary to lay aside some papers which would have been included if excellence had been the sole consideration.

The editors bear the responsibility for the final choice of texts to be included in this volume. However, in our decisions we have been assisted by the editorial board listed on page 2. We warmly thank these people for their gracious and wise advice. We also express our gratitude to the technical team at the University of Waterloo: George Roth, the designer; Professor Richard Beach and his assistant Barry Chaffe, who handled the computer composition; Daphne Dalziel, who prepared the index; Grace Logan and Victor Neglia, our computer consultants. The efficiency and professionalism of this team, as well as the computerized publishing techniques used, have made it possible to publish the volume so promptly.

Serge Lusignan
John S. North

Previous Conferences on Computing in the Humanities

ALLC 1   (Cambridge, 1970)
ALLC 2   (Edinburgh, 1972)
ALLC 3   (Cardiff, 1974)
ALLC 4   (Oxford, 1976)
ICCH 1   (Minneapolis, 1973)
ICCH 2   (Los Angeles, 1975)

Published Proceedings

ALLC 1 – Cambridge
Wisbey, R. E., *The Computer in Literary and Linguistic Research.* Cambridge University Press, 1971.

ALLC 2 – Edinburgh
Aitken, A. J., R. W. Bailey, and N. Hamilton-Smith, *The Computer and Literary Studies.* Edinburgh University Press, 1973.

ICCH 1 – Minneapolis
Mitchell, J. L., *Computers in the Humanities.* University of Minnesota Press and Edinburgh University Press, 1974.

1
Stylometrics: Classical Literature

The Stylometric Study
of Aristotle's Ethics

A. Kenny

In the Aristotelian corpus there are two ethical treatises that scholars nowadays agree in attributing to Aristotle himself; the *Nicomachean Ethics* and the *Eudemean Ethics*. The manuscript tradition of these books presents a problem: three books make a double appearance in the manuscripts, once as books five, six, and seven of the *Nicomachean Ethics* and once as books four, five, and six of the *Eudemean Ethics*. Scholars have long since discussed the provenance of these books; but surprisingly no systematic study of their style or comparison with their rival *Nicomachean* and *Eudemean* contexts has been made.[1] The present paper contains the beginnings of such a study: it confines itself to a single aspect of style, vocabulary choice. In the paper I am not questioning the consensus of scholars that both the *Eudemean* and the *Nicomachean Ethics* are genuine works of Aristotle: nor am I putting forward any hypothesis about the fixity or fluidity of his style. I am simply attempting to discover whether the regularities which can be observed in the disputed books (which I shall call the *Aristotelian Ethics*, and abbreviate '*AE*', to contrast with *NE* and *EE*) resemble more closely those to be observed in the *Nicomachean* or those to be observed in the *Eudemean Ethics*.

The statistics given in the present paper are based on word-counts made on the Oxford ICL 1906A computer by the COCOA concordance and word-count program, from machine readable texts of the *Ethics* prepared by the *Thesaurus Linguae Graecae* of Irving, California; the editions used were *Bywater's Oxford Classical Text* for the *NE* and *AE*, and Susemihl's Teubner edition of the *EE*.[2]

Particles and Connectives

Table I gives the frequencies (with the associated standard error) for the thirty-six commonest particles in the three treatises.[3] The scores are the ratio of the number of occurrences of the word type in question to the total number of word-tokens in the text (these totals being 39,525 for the *NE*, 26,330 for the *EE*, and 17,041 for the *AE*). Thus, since *kai* occurs 994 times in the *AE*, its relative frequency is 0.0583, or 5.83 per cent, when expressed as a percentage to avoid a superfluity of zeros. As a rule of thumb, the statistics of two samples from a single population are unlikely to differ by chance from each other by more than twice the sum of their standard errors. According to this rule, it will be seen that in a majority of cases – twenty out of thirty-six – the difference between the AE and NE are too great to be attributable to chance; whereas the difference between the AE and the EE in every case but two are such as to require no explanation other than chance.

The significance of the differences between the pairs of sample proportions may be calculated more precisely as follows. First the value of a statistic z is calculated by dividing the observed difference between the proportions by the approximate standard error of the difference.[4] The theoretical probability of a z-value greater than 1.96 is 0.05 or one in twenty; the probability of a z-value greater than 2.58 is 0.01, so that the values above this figure show a difference significant at the 1% level.

Table II gives the z-values of the differences between the AE and the NE, and between the AE and the EE, for each particle. It will be seen that twenty-one of the differences between the AE and NE are statistically significant at the 1% level, some of them extremely significant. On the other hand, all but three of the differences between the AE and the EE are insignificant at the 1% level.

	Nicomachean		Aristotelian		Eudemean	
	Freq.	S.E.	Freq.	S.E.	Freq.	S.E.
alla	0.64	.04	1.26	.09	1.18	.07
an	0.92	.05	0.57	.06	0.69	.05
ara	0.09	.02	0.18	.03	0.12	.02
gar	2.56	.08	2.16	.11	2.19	.09
ge	0.19	.02	0.12	.03	0.14	.02
de	4.68	.11	4.24	.15	3.93	.12
dē	0.56	.04	0.27	.03	0.28	.04
dio	0.17	.02	0.26	.04	0.27	.03
ean	0.08	.01	0.10	.02	0.06	.01
ei	0.46	.03	0.66	.06	0.64	.05
eiper	0.06	.01	0.09	.02	0.02	.01
epei	0.05	.01	0.25	.04	0.23	.03
eti	0.14	.02	0.28	.04	0.17	.03
ē	1.13	.05	1.07	.08	1.21	.07
kathaper	0.18	.02	0.08	.02	0.04	.01
kai	6.66	.13	5.83	.18	6.20	.15
men	1.50	.06	1.91	.10	1.71	.08
mentoi	0.01	.00	0.04	.02	0.06	.02
mē	0.62	.04	0.85	.07	0.87	.06
mēn	0.06	.01	0.06	.02	0.07	.02
othen	0.09	.01	0.01	.01	0.03	.01
hoion	0.34	.03	0.41	.05	0.41	.04
hotan	0.09	.01	0.28	.04	0.19	.03
hote	0.09	.01	0.03	.01	0.11	.02
hoti	0.41	.03	0.78	.07	0.73	.05
ou	1.35	.06	1.69	.10	1.44	.07
oude	0.59	.04	0.46	.05	0.43	.04
oun	0.59	.04	0.54	.06	0.37	.04
oute	0.18	.02	0.43	.05	0.31	.03
poteron	0.06	.01	0.06	.02	0.08	.02
pōs	0.12	.02	0.10	.02	0.11	.02
te	0.41	.03	0.33	.04	0.35	.04
toinun	0.00	.00	0.02	.01	0.06	.02
hōs	0.51	.04	0.39	.05	0.54	.04
hōsper	0.25	.03	0.47	.05	0.47	.04
hōste	0.10	.02	0.36	.05	0.36	.04

Table I. *Particles in the* Aristotelian Ethical Treatises

Tables I and II deal with the *AE*, *NE*, and *EE* as wholes. We can consider also individual books in the treatise. We can take the twenty-four most frequent particles and calculate the frequency and the standard error of each particle in each book, and ask whether the characteristics of each book are those which would be expected of a sample drawn randomly from the population constituted by the whole treatise. Again we can use the standard errors as a standard unit to express the observed difference between the sample proportion and population proportion as a *z*-score: *z*-scores of 2.58 or more will reveal anomalies in usage.

When we make this calculation we discover that particle use in the ethical treatises is in general very regular. Of the 360 values recorded of frequencies in the seven books of the *NE*, five of the *EE*, and three of the *AE* only thirty-three (c.9%) are anomalous at the 1% level; in all other cases chance is an adequate account of differences observed. The *EE* turns out to be more homogeneous in respect of particle use than the *NE*: there are eight anomalies in 120 cases (6.7%) as against twenty-five anomalies in 168 cases (14.9%). Most regular of all the books are the books of the *AE*: no anomaly at all is found in any of the three books.

Particle	NE & AE Value of Z	EE & AE Value of Z
alla	7.39	0.69
an	4.24	1.51
ara	2.88	1.73
gar	2.82	0.22
ge	1.99	0.75
de	2.31	1.63
dē	4.67	0.29
dio	2.04	0.23
ean	0.80	1.60
ei	3.03	0.24
eiper	1.02	3.54
epei	6.46	0.39
eti	3.48	2.44
e	0.63	1.37
kathaper	2.69	1.91
kai	3.69	1.57
men	3.56	1.49
mentoi	3.12	1.02
mē	2.90	0.31
mēn	0.06	0.29
hothen	3.52	1.55
hoion	1.21	0.07
hotan	5.48	1.94
hote	2.36	2.84
hoti	5.57	0.60
ou	3.09	2.04
oude	1.82	0.53
oun	0.79	2.65
oute	5.35	2.09
poteron	0.40	0.57
pōs	0.62	0.21
te	1.43	0.30
toinun	2.43	1.90
hōs	1.91	2.10
hōsper	4.32	0.03
hōte	6.83	0.11

Table II. Significance of Difference between Proportions

This is a striking result since many scholars have claimed that the common books are a patchwork of material, some *Nicomachean* and some *Eudemean*. If patchwork, this is remarkable patchwork, more regular in pattern than the originals from which the pieces have been cut.

We may use the data to test the fit of the *AE* into its two rival contexts in the following manner. If we compute the mean proportion for the ten books made up of the *NE* plus the *AE* (that is, the traditional ten-book *Nicomachean Ethics*) we can again compute standard errors and z-scores for each of the frequencies of each of the ten books, and record anomalies as we did above; and similarily we can compute mean proportions for the eight books of the *EE+AE* and record anomalies. Tables III and IV show the anomalies revealed by this procedure. It will be seen that the effect is to make the *NE* considerably less homogeneous than it was (there are now fifty-one anomalies out of 240 cases, or 21.3%) while the *EE* becomes very slightly more homogeneous (with twelve anomalies in 192 cases, 6.25%). If we look in particular at disputed books, we find that in their *Nicomachean* context they display eighteen anomalies (25%), in their *Eudemean* context only two (2.8%). Once again, the common books appear much more at home in their *Eudemean* context.

Prepositions

Tokens of the nineteen commonest prepositions constitute roughly six per cent of the *NE*, *AE*, and *EE* text. In the majority of the cases the frequencies observed in the *AE* do not differ significantly from those in

Particles	Books as samples from a single population							
	1	2	3	4	5	6	7	8
alla	0	0	0	0	0	0	0	1
an	0	0	0	0	0	0	0	1
gar	0	0	0	0	0	0	0	0
ge	0	0	0	0	0	0	0	0
de	1	0	0	0	0	0	0	0
dē	0	0	0	0	0	0	0	1
dio	1	0	0	0	0	0	0	0
ei	0	0	0	0	0	0	0	0
epei	0	0	0	0	0	0	0	0
ē	0	1	0	0	1	0	1	0
kathaper	0	0	0	0	0	1	0	0
kai	1	0	0	0	0	0	0	0
men	0	0	0	0	0	0	0	0
mē	0	0	0	0	0	0	0	0
hoion	0	0	0	0	0	0	0	0
hoti	0	0	0	0	0	0	0	0
ou	0	0	1	0	0	0	0	0
oude	1	0	0	0	0	0	0	0
oun	0	0	0	0	0	0	0	0
oute	0	0	0	0	0	0	0	0
te	0	0	0	0	0	0	0	0
ōs	0	0	0	0	0	0	0	0
ōsper	0	0	0	0	0	0	0	0
ōste	0	0	0	0	0	0	0	0

A '0' denotes a z-score less than 2.58, a '1' denotes a z-score greater than 2.58 and therefore significant at the 1% level.

Table III. The Traditional Eudemean Ethics

the *NE* or those in the *EE*. But again, the difference which do exist display a closer similarity between the *AE* and the *EE* than between the *AE* and the *NE*. If we plot the occurrences of each of the prepositions in the *AE* against those in the *NE* we find the coefficient of correlation between *AE* occurrences and *NE* occurrences is 0.87 for the nineteen prepositions: the correlation between the *AE* and the *EE*, on the other hand, is 0.97. The favourite preposition in the *NE* is *en*; in the *AE* and *EE* it is *kata* with the accusative.

In sixteen out of nineteen cases the differences between the *EE* and *AE* do not exceed chance expectations; there is no non-chance difference between the EE and the *AE*. There are five cases where the *NE* differs significantly from the *AE* without a correspondingly significant difference between the *AE* and *EE*. This is the case of *aneu* (twice as frequent in *AE* and *EE* as in *NE*), *en* (very popular in *NE*) *epi* with the accusative (a *Nicomachean* favourite) *para* with the accusative (much less frequent in *NE*) and *peri* with the genitive (similarily rare in the *NE*).

Adverbs

Several adverbs and adverbial expressions exhibit striking differences between usage in the *NE* and in the *EE*. The *NE* is very fond of a group of adverbial modifiers of degree: *ekista* (least), *etton* (less), *ikanos* (enough), *lian* (too much), *mallon* (more), *malista* (most), *panu* (altogether). Tokens of these words make up over 1% of its entire text

Particles	Books as samples from a single population									
	1	2	3	4	5	6	7	8	9	10
alla	0	0	0	0	1	0	1	0	1	1
an	0	1	0	0	0	0	1	0	0	1
gar	0	1	0	0	0	0	0	1	0	0
ge	1	0	0	0	0	0	0	0	0	0
de	0	0	0	0	0	0	0	0	0	1
dē	0	0	0	0	1	0	1	0	0	1
dio	0	0	0	0	0	0	0	0	0	0
ei	0	0	0	1	1	0	0	1	0	0
epei	0	0	0	0	0	0	1	0	0	0
ē	0	0	1	0	0	0	0	0	0	0
kathaper	1	0	0	0	1	0	0	0	1	0
kai	1	0	0	1	0	0	0	0	0	0
men	0	1	0	0	0	0	1	0	0	1
mē	0	0	1	1	0	0	0	0	0	1
hoion	0	0	0	0	0	0	0	0	0	0
hoti	0	0	0	1	0	1	1	1	0	0
ou	1	0	0	1	0	0	0	0	0	0
oude	0	0	0	0	1	0	0	0	0	0
oun	0	0	0	0	0	0	0	0	0	0
oute	0	1	0	0	0	1	1	1	1	1
te	0	0	1	0	0	0	0	0	0	1
hōs	0	0	0	1	0	0	0	0	0	0
hōsper	0	0	0	0	0	0	1	1	0	0
hōste	0	0	0	0	1	1	1	0	0	0

A '0' denotes a *z*-score less than 2.58, and a '1' denotes a *z*-score greater than 2.58 and therefore significant at the 1% level.

Table IV. The Traditional Nicomachean Ethics

(as against 0.32% of the *AE* and 0.55% for the *EE*), and the difference can be observed throughout the various books of the treatises. When the *AE* is compared with either the *NE* or the *EE*, the differences, for the group of words as a whole, is greater than can be explained by sampling error (z for the *AE* and *EE* = 3.47; for the *AE* and *NE* = 8.81); but the differences between the *AE* and the *NE* are much greater than those between the *AE* and *EE*, and both diverge in the same direction.

Two adverbs which, by contrast, are *Eudemean* favourites are *monon* (only) and *aplos* (without qualification). The lowest scoring books of the *AE* and *EE* score approximately 0.2%, which is just below the highest scoring books of the *NE*. Just as the *AE* had more than *Eudemean* distaste for the *Nicomachean* favourite adverbs, so the *AE* has more than a *Eudemean* liking for the *EE* favourites.

The adverb *isos* (perhaps) is a *Nicomachean* favourite: it turns out to be one of a group of tentatitive expressions markedly more popular in the *NE* than in the *EE* or *AE*. The five commonest of these – *isos* (perhaps), *dokei* (seems), *doxeie* (would seem), *eoike* (seems likely), *phainetai* (appears) are studied in Table V, which gives their occurrence book by book. The expressions add up to over 1% of the *Nicomachean* text, but only 0.43% of the *EE* and 0.36% of the *AE*. Consistent with the hypothesis that the *EE* is less tentative than the *NE*, we find that expressions of certainty or clarity – *anagke* (necessarily), *delon* (clearly), *phaneron* (obviously) are about three times as popular in the *EE* as in the *NE*. The *AE*, in this respect, differs significantly from the *NE* but not from the *EE*.

Pronouns and Demonstratives

Among pronouns and pronominal adjectives we find three *Nicomachean* favourites: *hekastos* (each), *toioutos* (such), and *tosoutos*

Book	isos	dokei	dokeie	eioke	phainetai	Total 1-5	anagke	delon	phaneron	Total 6-8
Nicomachean										
1	16	14	5	10	29	74 (1.31)	0	18	0	18 (0.32)
2	2	2	0	0	4	8 (0.19)	0	2	2	4 (0.09)
3	13	18	6	16	15	68 (1.07)	1	7	1	8 (0.12)
4	1	18	5	11	8	43 (0.72)	0	7	0	7 (0.12)
8	8	24	3	25	10	70 (1.20)	0	5	1	6 (0.10)
9	15	10	13	18	12	68 (1.28)	0	5	0	5 (0.24)
19	15	28	10	11	9	73 (1.17)	0	14	1	15 (0.24)
Total	70	114	42	91	87	404 (1.02)	1	58	5	64 (0.16)
Aristotelian										
A	3	14	2	1	2	22 (0.34)	6	15	6	27 (0.42)
B	1	8	1	2	3	15 (0.35)	2	9	4	15 (0.35)
C	4	12	2	5	1	24 (0.37)	5	7	5	17 (0.27)
Total	8	34	5	8	6	61 (0.36)	13	31	15	59 (0.35)
Eudemean										
1	2	2	0	1	2	7 (0.21)	2	5	4	11 (0.32)
2	2	15	5	1	3	26 (0.37)	22	22	9	53 (0.75)
3	2	12	5	1	6	26 (0.56)	6	6	2	14 (0.30)
7	4	25	4	4	8	45 (0.52)	8	17	10	35 (0.41)
8	0	6	0	2	0	8 (0.31)	3	6	4	13 (0.50)
Total	10	60	14	9	19	112 (0.43)	41	56	29	126 (0.46)

Table V Expressions of Doubt and Certainty in the NE, AE, *and* EE

(so big). Taken together these three expressions account for over 1% of the *NE*, but in the case of the group as a whole, and *toioutos* singly, the differences betwen the *NE* and *AE* are significant at the 1% level. Five other words are more popular in the *EE* than in the *NE* and between them constitute 1.32% of the *EE* text but only 0.96% of the *NE*. The frequency of this group – *allelon* (each other), *allos* (other), *ekeinos* (that), *enioi* (some), and *heteros* (the other) – in the *AE* is much closer to its frequency in the *EE* than to its frequency in the *NE*.

Words concerned with multitude and magnitude, wholes, parts, and shares form a group which repays study. The *EE* is more interested in wholes and parts: the word *holos* (whole) and two words for part (*meros, morion*) make up 0.25% of its text as against 0.14% of the *NE*: in the *AE* the words account for no less than 0.45% of the text. The *NE* likes two words to do with parts and sharing – *koinos* (common) and *loipos* (rest) – but has a more general preference for words to do with multitude, such as *oligoi* (few) and *polloi* (many), and magnitude – such as *pleion* and *pleistos*, the comparative and superlative of *polus*, and *mikros* (small), and its comparative *elatton* and superlative *elachistos*. Together these words constitute 0.83% of the *NE* text, but only 0.61% of the *EE* and 0.56% of the *AE*.

The Definite Article

The distribution of the definite article is not as regular in the ethical treatises as one might have expected in advance. Between the *EE* and the *AE* we find statistically significant difference between the frequencies of the two cases of the article, and between the *NE* and the *AE* significant differences in seven cases. But the most striking feature which differentiates the use of the article in the *NE* from its use in the *EE* is the latter's more marked preference for the singular forms. The figures below give the proportion (in %) of each book constituted by (a) singular forms of the article; (b) plural forms of the article; (c) the sum total of both singular and plural forms.

	Nicomachean							Eudemean				
Book:	1	2	3	4	8	9	10	1	2	3	7	8
Sing.	7.26	9.31	7.51	8.32	7.86	7.96	8.14	9.25	9.54	9.73	9.98	7.97
Plur.	5.71	5.00	5.82	4.47	5.46	5.05	5.97	5.41	3.62	4.92	3.78	3.20
Total	12.97	14.31	13.33	12.79	13.32	13.01	14.11	14.66	13.16	14.65	13.76	11.17

Chart 1. Proportion of Articles.

It will be seen that four out of five of the *Eudemean* books have a portion of the singular forms of the article of more than five per cent. Only one of the *Nicomachean* books has a score in excess of this. If we take the plural forms, only the first of the *Eudemean* books has a score of more than 5% here; all except book 4 of the *Nicomachean* treatises score over 5%. Here, as so often, the disputed books display the *Eudemean* features in an accentuated form. The figures for these books are as follows:

	Aristotelian		
	A	B	C
Sing.	10.90	9.31	9.37
Plur.	2.72	4.10	4.04
Total	13.62	13.41	13.41

Chart 2. Proportion of Articles.

Altogether, the proportion of all occurrences of the article constituted by singular forms is 59.7% in the *NE*, 69.5% in the *EE*, and 75.5% in the *AE*.

Grouping Indicator Words

The words which we have so far studied amount to some fifty-three per cent of the entire treatises. In each treatise, roughly twenty-five per cent consists of particles and connectives, six per cent of prepositions, nine per cent of adverbs, pronouns and similar words, and thirteen per cent of the definite article. In respect of every feature so far in which there was a significant difference between *Nicomachean* and *Eudemean* usage, the common books resembled the *Eudemean* pattern more than the *Nicomachean*. Undeniably, the results so far presented amount to a substantial argument in favour of assigning these disputed books taken as a whole to an original *Eudemean* context.

We will now take our argument a step further and see whether the data we have collected enables us to assign a context, not just to the *AE* as a whole, but to the small sections within it. We may divide it for this purpose into seventeen samples of approximately 1,000 words each. The samples are listed in Table VI.

The *Aristotelian Ethics* divided into seventeen samples of c.1000 words.
1)   1129a1−1130b8; book V chapters I−II; general and particular justice.
2)   1130b8−1132a15; book V chapters II−IV; distributive justice.
3)   1132a15−1133a22; book V chapters IV−V; corrective justice and reciprocity.
4)   1133a22−1134a26; book V chapters V−VIII; justice as mean; political justice, nature and law.
5)   1134a26−1136b32; book V chapters VIII−IX; justice, voluntariness and involuntariness.
6)   1136b32−1138b1; book V chapters IX−XI; equity, *aporiai* about justice.
7)   1138b1−1140a1; end of book V, book VI chapters I−III; intellectual virtues, man as agent.
8)   1140a1−1141b2; book VI chapters IV−VII; art, wisdom, and learning.
9)   1141b2−1143a5; book VI chapters VII−X; wisdom and its parts and satellites.
10)   1143a5−1144b5; book VI chapters X−XIII; wisdom in relation to learning and intellect.
11)   1144b5−1146a6; book VI chapters XIII, VII, I−II; wisdom and virtues; opinions on *akrasia*.
12)   1146a6−1147b8; book VII, chapters II−III; *akrasia* and knowledge.
13)   1147b8−1149a12 book VII, chapters III−IV; the sphere of *akrasia*.
14)   1149a12−1150b12 book VII, chapters V−VII; different kinds of *akrasia*.
15)   1150b12−1152a13 book VII, chapters VII−X; continence, incontinence, intemperance.

Table VI

What we must do is to take words together in groups and count not the occurrence of single words, but the occurrence of a group, the occurrence of any word in the group counting as an occurrence of the group. To serve our purposes, a group must satisfy two conditions. First, the group must be one which is characteristic either of the *Nicomachean* or *Eudemean* ethics: it must consist in general of words which are either *Nicomachean* favourites or *Eudemean* favourites; the occurrence of the group as a whole must be substantially more frequent in one of the treatises than in the other.

We can ensure that our groups satisfy the former condition by calculating, for each word and group, a *distinctiveness ratio*.[5] Let us express the distinctiveness ratio of an expression occurring in the ethical treatises as its *Nicomachean* frequency divided by its *Eudemean* frequency. Thus, a word which occurs more frequently in the *Nicomachean Ethics* will have a distinctiveness ratio greater than unity, a *Eudemean* favourite will have one between zero and one, and word which is used with the same relative frequency in each will have a distinctiveness ratio of one.

We may expect the distinctiveness ratio of many words, in two treatises by the same author, to be very close to one: words with such a distinctiveness ratio will obviously be worthless as discriminators. For our purposes we must look for words, or groups of words, whose distinctiveness ratio is some distance from unity – say more than 1.4 or less than 0.7; words, that is, which occur about three times or more in one treatise for every twice they appear in the other.

To ensure that our group enables predictions to be made of its occurrence in samples as small as 1,000 words it is necessary to insist on an absolute minimum frequency as well as a characteristic relative frequency. In practice, we need groups which will enable us to predict an absolute occurrence of not less than ten in each sample of 1,000 words. Since the *Nicomachean Ethics* is 39,525 words long, this means that we can make predictions based on *Nicomachean* frequencies of 400 and above: for if a word or group occurs 400 times in a text of about 40,000 words it can be expected to occur 10 times in a 1,000 word sample homogeneous with it. The *Eudemean Ethics* is 26,330 words long, and so for predictions based on *Eudemean* frequencies we need words or groups occurring at least 260 times in the *EE*.

We whall look, therefore, for groups of words with the following characteristics. They should be either a *Nicomachean* favourite group with at least 400 occurrences in the *NE* and a distinctiveness ratio of at least 1.4; or they should be a *Eudemean* favourite with at least 260 occurrences in the *EE* and a distinctiveness ratio of less than 0.7. On the basis of the *Nicomachean* favourite groups we can calculate a *Nicomachean* expectation for each of our seventeen samples of the *AE*, and on the basis of the *Eudemean* favourite groups we can calculate a *Eudemean* expectation. By comparing the expected number of occurrences of each group in each case with the actual occurrences, we can determine for each sample in turn whether it resembles the *Nicomachean Ethics* more than the *Eudemean*. Any substantial patching, say, of an original *Eudemean* text with *Nicomachean* material should display itself in a fluctuation between one sample and another in respect of comparative resemblance.

It turns out that it is possible, from the data that we have already recorded, to assemble six *Nicomachean* and six *Eudemean* groups

answering to these specifications. The first *Nicomachean* group is formed by taking together five particles popular in the *NE*; *Dē*, *eiper*,
kathaper, *othen*, and *oun*. Taken as a whole the group has a D.R. of
2.00 and occurs 587 times in the *NE*, so that words from the group
could be expected to occur 14.85, that is, 15 times, in a 1,000 word sample homogeneous with the *NE*. The second group consists of the single
participle *en*, with a distinctiveness ratio (D.R.) of 1.44 and a total of
482 occurrences in the *NE*. The third group has already been studied as
a group: the qualifying adverbs *ēkista*, *etton*, *ikanōs*, *lian*, *mallon*,
malista, *panu* occur altogether 418 times in the *NE*, and the group as a
whole has a D.R. of 1.93. Even more distinctive is the group of expressions of tentatitiveness already studied: *isōs*, *dokei*, *doxeie*, *eoike*,
phainetai. This group occurs 404 times and has a D.R. of 2.37. Three
Nicomachean favourite pronouns and demonstratives – *ekastos*,
toioutos, and *tosoutos* – form another group with a D.R. of 1.56 and
407 occurrences in the *NE*. The final *Nicomachean* group is made by
putting together the two *Nicomachean* favourites *koinos* and *loipos*
with the 'multitude and magnitude' group of *oligos* with *mikros* and
polus and their comparatives and superlatives. This group has a total
occurrence in the *NE* of 417 and a D.R. of 1.51.

The six *Eudemean* groups are made up as follows. The conjunction
alla is popular enough to constitute a group of its own, with 311 occurrences in the *EE* and a D.R. of 0.54. The two connectives *dio* and *oti*
form a group occurring 263 times with a D.R. of 0.58. A third group
can be made up from three more *Eudemean* connectives, *ōsper*, *ōste*,
and *epei*: this highly characteristic group has a D.R. of 0.38 and occurs
279 times in the *EE*. We have already seen that *anagkē*, *dēlon*, and
phaneron form a characteristically *Eudemean* set of expressions, but as
they make up only 0.48% of the *Eudemean* text they are not by
themselves frequent enough to make up one of our test groups. The
group remains too small if we add it to the 0.38% of the text made up by
the characteristically *Eudemean* adverbs, *aplōs* and *monon*. We may
add further two particles, *mentoi* and *toinun*, which we saw earlier to be
Eudemean favourites. This brings our group to a total of 256 occurrences, near enough to 260 occurrences to predict an expectation in
1,000 words approximating 10. The D.R. of the group so formed is
0.30: it is thus an extremely characteristic *Eudemean* group. For the
next group we take four prepositions popular in the *EE* – *aneu*, *eneka*,
para with the accusative and *pari* with the genitive – and add them to
the popular adverb *ama*. This gives us a group with D.R. 0.48 which occurs 267 times in the *EE*. The pronouns and pronomial adjectives which
we noticed characteristic of the *EE* – *allhlōn*, *allos*, *ekeinos*, *enioi*,
eteros – will make up a sixth and final group, as they occur in total no
less than 380 times. But the group is not as distinctive as the others,
with a D.R. as high as 0.73.

Table VII compares the expected frequency per 1,000 words of the
Nicomachean groups with the actual frequencies in the seventeen
approximately 1,000-word samples of the *AE*, and Table VIII compares the expected frequency of the *Eudemean* favourites with the actual occurrences in the same samples. The final line of each table gives
the mean occurrence per sample. The results are strikingly uniform in
their tendency. In none of the samples does the actual occurrence of the
Nicomachean indicator words reach higher than 80% of the
Nicomachean expectatiòn; in most of them the actual occurrence is

about half the expectation, and the mean is exactly 0.51 of the expectation. If we turn to the *Eudemean* favourites we find that in nine of the sixteen samples the actual occurrence surpasses the *Eudemean* expectation, and the mean of the actual occurrence is 0.99 of the expectation. In every single sample the *Eudemean* expectation is approximated better than the *Nicomachean* one: once again there is no sign of patchwork.

It is possible to construct twelve other groups of test-words, six of the *Nicomachean* favourites and six of the *Eudemean* favourites, by studying the metaphysical, psychological, and logical terminology of the treatises, certain technical terms of *Aristotelian ethics*, and evaluative expressions. Space forbids the reproduction here of the results of these tests: it must suffice to say that in all but one case the tests confirmed the results here presented, showing the *AE* to resemble the *EE* much more closely than the *NE*. (The one exception was a group of *EE*-favourite evaluative expressions). Altogether the twelve groups of *Nicomachean* favourites and the twelve groups of *Eudemean* favourites provide twenty-four independent tests to apply to the disputed books. Twenty-three of the twenty-four tests give an unambiguous answer that the common books, considered as a whole, resemble the *EE* more than the *NE*. When we take the twenty-four tests together and apply them as

	1	2	*Nicomachean* Groups 3	4	5	6	Total
NE Total	587	482	418	404	407	417	2715
D.R.	2.00	1.44	1.93	2.37	1.56	1.51	
Expect. in 1000	14.85	12.19	10.58	10.22	10.30	10.55	68.69

Actual Occurrences in Samples

	1	2	3	4	5	6	Total
1	8	10	3	9	4	8	42
2	8	20	2	2	3	20	55
3	10	5	2	2	6	12	37
4	7	6	2	2	8	12	37
5	7	5	1	1	2	5	21
6	7	9	5	4	5	6	36
7	19	11	2	2	2	5	41
8	9	6	1	3	7	2	28
9	9	4	5	5	9	5	37
10	10	5	3	4	8	2	32
11	12	7	4	2	7	2	34
12	10	6	3	2	7	0	27
13	10	3	3	1	11	2	30
14	12	6	6	2	2	8	36
15	8	6	3	4	8	7	36
16	10	2	6	3	5	7	33
17	12	5	2	8	1	3	31
Mean	9.9	6.8	3.2	3.2	5.5	6.2	34.8

Groups
1: (dē, eiper, katheper, orthen, oun)
2: (en)
3: (ekista, ēton, ikanōs, lian, mallon, maliste, panu)
4: (isōs, dokei, doxei, eoike, phainetai)
5: (ekastos, toioutos, tosoutos)
6: (oligos, polus, pleōn, koinos, lopos)

Table VII Nicomachean *Favourites in Seventeen Samples of the* AE

a group to each of the seventeen 1,000 word samples of the *AE*, they indicate in the case of each individual sample that it is closer to the *EE* than to the *NE*. None of these tests gives any support to the theory that the *AE* is a patchwork. The conclusions are confirmed by other independent tests (such as a study of the definite article).

Altogether the tests, which cover some sixty per cent of the total word-usage of the treatises, present an overwhelming weight of evidence for the view that the common books resemble the *Eudemean Ethics* more than the *Nicomachean*. The most economical explanation of the evidence presented in this paper is that the common books, as they now stand, belonged originally to the *Eudemean Ethics*. It would no doubt be rash to claim that stylometric methods have solved a problem which has occupied scholars for centuries: but certainly the stylometric results will have to be taken into account in any future scholarly study of the problem.

	1	2	3	*Eudemean* Groups 4	5	6	Total
EE Total	311	263	279	256	267	380	1756
D.R.	0.54	0.58	0.38	0.30	0.48	0.73	
Expect. in 1000	11.81	9.99	10.60	9.72	10.14	14.43	66.69

Actual Occurrences in Samples

1	13	15	6	14	9	17	74
2	11	3	8	12	6	12	62
3	7	11	11	5	2	16	52
4	15	13	8	13	7	17	73
5	17	6	12	10	16	10	71
6	18	11	9	13	10	11	72
7	10	8	5	6	13	12	54
8	8	13	13	7	14	23	79
9	15	17	8	12	13	10	75
10	8	8	8	4	16	9	51
11	14	15	10	6	17	13	75
12	16	7	8	9	12	13	65
13	15	8	13	13	16	12	67
14	7	13	16	16	6	8	66
15	11	4	20	7	9	8	59
16	13	15	15	11	5	13	72
17	13	10	12	5	6	6	52
Mean	13.8	9.8	11.4	9.6	10.8	12.4	65.8

Groups
1: (alla)
2: (oti, dio)
3: (ōsper, ōste, epei)
4: (anagkē, dhlon, phaneron, monon, aplōs, mentoi, toinun)
5: (eneu, eneka, para A, peri G, ama)
6: (ekeinos, eteros, allos, enioi, allhlōn)

Table VIII   Eudemean *Favourites in Seventeen Samples of the* AE

L'analyse de dépendance et
l'etude des variations libres

B. Moreux, J. Renaud

A la suite des travaux de Ch. Muller,[1] on a assez souvent utilisé des tests statistiques, et en particulier le χ^2, pour étudier les variations libres[2,3]. On démontre par exemple que telle variable contextuelle est en relation significative avec la forme de la variation libre: ainsi, dans l'article cité dans la note 3, MM. Martin et Muller constatent (p. 220-221) que la variété de l'aspect du verbe (imperfectif ou perfectif) est en corrélation significative avec l'emploi des temps (Plus-que-parfait ou Passé antérieur) dans *La Mort le Roi Artu.* Ils peuvent alors supposer que le choix de l'aspect influence le choix du temps.

Des recherches de ce genre apportent un peu de rigueur dans un domaine où les intuitions se donnent trop souvent libre cours. Elles sont cependant exposées à deux dangers. Tout d'abord, il est rare qu'elles expliquent d'un point de vue linguistique les influences postulées à partir des tests statistiques: pour comprendre pourquoi, en français, l'aspect influe sur le temps et, plus particulièrement, quelle est la nature de l'affinité constatée entre l'aspect imperfectif et le Plus-que-parfait, il faudrait étudier l'ensemble du système verbal du français. C'est qu'a du reste fait R. Martin dans un remarquable ouvrage paru ensuite (voir note 4). Il est bien évident que, si MM. Martin et Muller ont choisi d'étudier la relation entre l'aspect et le temps plutôt que celle qui peut exister par exemple entre la présence d'un complément et le temps, c'est parce que la première leur paraissait linguistiquement plus intéressante que la seconde; toutefois, apparement ils ne faisaient aucune hypothèse linguistique précise sur cette relation, ils ne préjugeaient même pas de son sens, c'est-à-dire qu'ils ne s'attendaient pas plus à observer une liaison entre l'aspect imperfectif et le Plus-que-parfait que la liaison inverse; du reste, même après la mise en évidence de la corrélation, ils ne cherchent pas, dans cet article, à la justifier linguistiquement.[4] Au contraire, pour que l'on puisse passer de l'observation d'associations à l'hypothèse d'influences, il faut, selon nous, justifier celle-ci à l'intérieur de cadres linguistiques plus vastes, d'hypothèses linguistiques plus générales.

Cette lacune est d'autant plus fâcheuse que, dans ce genre de recherche, il est rare que l'on ne puisse dégager plusieurs corrélations significatives entre la variable à expliquer (la variation libre) et différentes variables contextuelles. Ainsi MM. Martin et Muller dégagent successivement sept variables en corrélation significative avec la variation libre qu'ils cherchent à expliquer. Ils sont ainsi amenés à poser l'existence de plusieurs facteurs influant indépendamment sur la variation libre; la justification linguistique s'en trouve compliquée, d'autant plus que l'on peut supposer que certaines de ces variables explicatives sont reliées entre elles par des liens de cause à effet.[5] Ce dernier point complique aussi l'analyse quantitative, car, on le verra, l'existence de telles influences peut modifier la mesure de l'influence de chaque variable sur la variable à expliquer.[6]

Dans les situations de ce genre, on doit utiliser, pour aboutir à un modèle d'ensemble cohérent, une démarche qui, sans renoncer à l'induction, fasse également appel à la déduction, à une déduction dont on contrôlera les résultats en les comparant aux données numériques. On partira d'hypothèses concernant le fonctionnement de la variation libre; on posera donc un modèle causal comprenant différentes variables explicatives et la variable à expliquer, les variables explicatives pouvant elles-mêmes être reliées par des liens de cause à effet. Ce modèle peut bien entendu être partiellement suggéré par l'observation, appuyée sur des tests statistiques, de la fréquence des cooccurrences entre tels élément du contexte et telle variante libre, mais il doit surtout se fonder sur des considérations théoriques concernant la nature de la variation libre étudiée et sa place dans le système linguistique dont elle fait partie.

Il faut évidemment soumettre ce modèle, d'une manière ou d'une autre, à l'épreuve des faits. On utilisera pour cela une procédure mathématique, l'analyse de dépendance *(path analysis)*, facilement praticable à l'aide de l'ordinateur; elle permet de voir si le réseau causal ainsi posé est compatible avec les données numériques; dans l'affirmative, elle permet aussi de mesurer l'impact relatif, tant direct qu'indirect, de chacune des variables explicatives sur la variable à expliquer. Si l'analyse de dépendance montre que le modèle est incompatible avec les données, on peut retoucher ce modèle autant qu'on le veut, dans la mesure où cela est possible dans le cadre des hypothèses linguistiques sur lesquelles il est fondé, et le soumettre à chaque fois à l'analyse de dépendance. Si toutes ces retouches s'avèrent vaines, c'est donc que ces hypothèses de base sont fausses; le chercheur devra alors attaquer le problème sur des bases entièrement nouvelles ou bien ... laisser cette tâche à d'autres.

L'alternance entre cas et tours prépositionnels avec les verbes ablatifs de l'attique

Nous exposerons les principes et les modalités d'application de l'analyse de dépendance en montrant comment nous l'avons utilisée pour l'étude d'une variation libre du grec ancien: l'alternance entre cas et tours prépositionnels avec les verbes ablatifs dans les oeuvres des Orateurs attiques.[7] Nous appelons ainsi les verbes qui indiquent le point de départ d'un mouvement, réel ou figuré: par exemple $\phi\epsilon\acute{v}\gamma\omega$ ("fuir"), $\dot{\alpha}\pi\alpha\lambda\lambda\acute{\alpha}\tau\tau\omega$ ("débarrasser de", "quitter"); avec certains de ces verbes, le complément indiquant le point de départ du mouvement est marqué soit d'un cas (accusatif ou génitif) soit d'un tour prépositionnel à valeur ablative ($\dot{\alpha}\pi\acute{o}$, $\dot{\epsilon}\kappa$ ou $\pi\alpha\rho\acute{\alpha}$ + gén.): $\ddot{\epsilon}\phi\epsilon\nu\gamma\epsilon$ $\tau\grave{\eta}\nu$ $\dot{\epsilon}\alpha\nu\tauο\tilde{v}$ $\pi\acute{o}\lambda\iota\nu$ ("il fuyait sa propre cité", LYS. 6. 28) mais $\phi\epsilon\acute{v}\gamma o\nu\tau\epsilon\varsigma$ $\dot{\epsilon}\kappa$ $\tau\tilde{\eta}\varsigma$ $\pi\acute{o}\lambda\epsilon\omega\varsigma$ ("fuyant la cité", HYP. 3. 2). Voici la liste des verbes étudiés, avec le nombre d'exemples casuels et prépositionnels relevés pour chacun d'eux:[8]
$\dot{\alpha}\pi\alpha\lambda\lambda\acute{\alpha}\tau\tau\omega$: 125 gén./ 2 $\dot{\alpha}\pi\acute{o}$, 10 $\dot{\epsilon}\kappa$, 3 $\pi\alpha\rho\acute{\alpha}$. $\dot{\prime}A\pi\alpha\lambda\lambda o\tau\rho\iota\tilde{\omega}$: 1 gén.; $\dot{\alpha}\lambda\lambda o\tau\rho\iota\tilde{\omega}$: 1 $\dot{\alpha}\pi\acute{o}$. $\dot{\prime}A\pi\epsilon\lambda\alpha\acute{v}\nu\omega$: 7 gén./ 8 $\dot{\alpha}\pi\acute{o}$. $\dot{\prime}A\pi o\delta\iota\delta\rho\acute{\alpha}\sigma\kappa\omega$: 5 acc./ 1$\dot{\alpha}\pi\acute{o}$, 11 $\dot{\epsilon}\kappa$; 1 ex. avec acc. et $\dot{\epsilon}\kappa$. $\dot{\prime}A\pi o\lambda\acute{v}\omega$: 12 gén. / 1 $\dot{\alpha}\pi\acute{o}$; $\dot{\epsilon}\kappa\lambda\acute{v}\omega$: 1 gén. $\dot{\prime}A\pi o\pi\lambda\alpha\nu\tilde{\omega}$: 1 gén./2 $\dot{\epsilon}\kappa$. $\dot{\prime}A\phi\acute{\iota}\sigma\tau\eta\mu\iota$: 109 gén./ 5 $\dot{\alpha}\pi\acute{o}$. $\Delta\iota\acute{\iota}\sigma\tau\eta\mu\iota$: 1 gén./2 $\dot{\alpha}\pi\acute{o}$. $E\ddot{\prime}\rho\gamma\omega$ et composés (sans les exemples influencés par des

textes de loi). εἴργω: 3 gén.; ἀπείργω: 2 gén./ 1 ἀπό; ἐξείργω: 3 ἐκ. Ἐκβάλλω: 1 gén./ 29 ἐκ, 1 ἔξω. Ἐκπίπτω: 1 gén./ 25 ἐκ. Ἐκφορῶ: 1 gén./ 4 ἐκ. Ἐλευθερῶ: 1 gén./ 2 ἀπό, 1 ἐκ. Ἐξαρτῶ: 1 gén./ 1 ἐκ. Ἐξελαύνω: 1 gén./ 24 ἐκ. Ἐξορίζω: 1 gén./ 2 ἐκ, 1 ἔξω. Φεύγω (fuir):[9] 115 acc./ 18 ἐκ; ἀποφεύγω (fuir): 1 acc.; διαφεύγω: 30 acc.; διαφυγγάνω: 1 ἐκ; ἐκφεύγω: 10 acc./ 2 ἐκ. Χωρίζω: 7 gén./ 2 ἀπό.[10]

Corrélations entre la variable à expliquer et chacune des autres variables

En principe, l'étude que nous voulons mener pourrait se passer d'une étape préliminaire constituée par l'application de tests statistiques; en effet, l'influence d'une variable sur la variable à expliquer peut s'exercer par l'intermédiaire d'autres variables et, dans ce cas, sa relation avec la variable à expliquer peut être faible et non significative. Une variable ne devrait donc être exclue du modèle à tester que pour des raisons linguistiques. Cependant, si l'on appliquait ce principe au problème que nous étudions, on se trouverait devant des modèles extrêmement complexes, car nombreuses sont les variables dont on pourrait supposer une influence sur la forme du complément alternant dans le cadre des hypothèses que nous présenterons plus loin (de plus, ces variables pourraient souvent être reliées entre elles). L'application préalable des tests vise à simplifier l'analyse multivariée qui la suivra.[11]

Quatre variables se sont révélées être en relation significative avec la variable à expliquer. Nous appellerons celle-ci f (= forme du complément alternant), ses deux catégories étant F_1 (cas) et F_2 (tour prépositionnel). Les quatre autres variables seront:

p: nature du préverbe, $P_1 = \varnothing$ ou ἀπο-, $P_2 = $ ἐκ-.

s: sens figuré (S_1) ou matériel (S_2) du syntagme. S_0: sens douteux.

l: valeur abstraite (L_1) ou non (L_2) du lexème. L_0: valeur douteuse.

v: valeur figurée (V_1) ou matérielle (V_2) du verbe. V_0: valeur douteuse.

Plutôt que de donner les quatre tableaux à partir desquels sont calculées les corrélations entre chacune des quatre variables explicatives et f, nous donnons tout de suite le tableau à partir duquel s'effectuera l'analyse de dépendance, tableau qui donne la distribution (en effectifs) des exemples selon les cinq variables. Nous définirons ensuite plus précisément chacune des variables explicatives et indiquerons le χ^2 et le ϕ (coefficient d'association) obtenu pour sa corrélation avec la variable à expliquer.

	P_1							P_2						
	S_1			S_2		S_0		S_1			S_2			S_0
	V_1			V_2		V_0		V_1			V_2	V_2		V_0
	L_1	L_2	L_0	L_2	L_0	L_2	L_0	L_1	L_2	L_0	L_1	L_2	L_0	L_0
F_1	333	53	5	15	1	0	5	5	7	1	1	0	0	0
F_2	18	15	1	22	8	3	5	7	3	0	18	35	23	5

Tableau 1. Distribution (en effectifs) des exemples selon les cinq variables.
Les exemples appartenant aux catégories 0 (S_0, V_0, et L_0) sont ambigus et seront exclus de l'analyse.

1) Nature du préverbe (p).
Les verbes à préverbes ἐκ- sont le plus souvent accompagnés d'un tour prépositionnel, tandis que les verbes à préverbe ἀπο- ou sans préverbe sont généralement accompagnés du cas. Nous regrouperons les verbes simples ou composés à l'aide d'autres préverbes que ἀπο- ou ἐκ- (nous appellerons cette catégorie verbes à préverbe $\emptyset$) et les verbes à préverbe ἀπο-; ce regroupement peut surprendre mais les données numériques l'imposent (cf. tableau 2) ainsi du reste, on le verra plus loin, que des raisons linguistiques.

La relation entre l'opposition *préverbe $\emptyset$ / préverbe ἀπο-* et *f* est faible ($\phi = -0,01$; $\phi^{min.} = -0,55$) et non significative ($\chi^2 = 0,02$ soit P > 0,80). Si l'on réunit ces deux catégories, la relation entre la nature du préverbe et *f* est forte ($\phi = 0,61$, $\phi^{max.} = 0,75$) et significative ($\chi^2 = 222,71$, soit P < 0,001).

2) Sens figuré ou matériel du syntagme (s).
Le mouvement exprimé par le syntagme *verbe ablatif + complément alternant* est soit figuré, soit matériel (ou physique). On opposera par exemple ἀπαλλαγῆναι τοῦ πολέμου (AE. 2.13; "mettre fin à la guerre") à ἀν...ἀπαλλαγῇμὲν ἐκ Θρᾴκης (D. 23.57; "s'il quitte la Thrace"). L'intuition du sens du syntagme (variable que nous appelons s) est le seul critère qui permette de distinguer ces deux sens; aussi aux catégories S_1 (sens figuré) et S_2 (sens matériel), nous avons adjoint une catégorie S_0 réservée aux exemples de sens douteux. Si on laisse de côté ces exemples S_0, on voit que la relation entre *s* et *f* est forte ($\phi = 0,63$; $\phi^{max.} = 0,79$) et significative ($\chi^2 = 223,50$ soit P < 0,001).

3) Valeur du lexème complément (l).
Un nom comme πόλεμος ("la guerre"), dans l'exemple d'Eschine qu'on vient de citer, peut être qualifié d'abstrait. Si l'on regroupe tous les noms abstraits, on s'aperçoit que, dans les syntagmes que nous étudions, ils sont généralement casuels. A cette catégorie L_1, on opposera la catégorie L_2, composée de tous les autres noms sauf ceux (catégorie L_0) qui ont un sens tantôt abstrait tantôt non abstrait (local par exemple).[12] La relation entre *l* et *f* est forte ($\phi = 0,43$, $\phi^{max.} = 0,85$) et significative ($\chi^2 = 98,50$, soit P < 0,001).

4) Valeur figurée ou matérielle du verbe (v).
Il est nécessaire de distinguer *v* et *s*. En effet, certains exemples de sens figuré comprennent des verbes ablatifs qui, ailleurs, et en particulier hors des exemples alternants, ne sont jamais employés dans les syntagmes de sens figuré; cf. ἐκβεβληκέναι δὲ τῆς ἀρχῆς Κερσοβλέπτην (littéralement: "avoir expulsé Kersobléptès de son pouvoir"). Nous admettrons que les exemples de ce genre sont métaphoriques: le verbe y

---

Tableau 2. Relation entre la nature du préverbe et la forme du complément.

Forme du complément	Préverbe			
	$\emptyset$	ἀπο-	ἐκ-	Total
Cas	85%	85%	13%	72%
Tour prépositionnel	15%	15%	87%	28%
Total	100%(178)	100%(306)	100%(195)	100%(589)

a une valeur matérielle (V_2) mais le caractère abstrait du lexème complément (L_1) rend nécessaire l'interprétation figurée du syntagme (S_1). Il y a donc ici discordance entre la valeur du verbe et le sens du syntagme: $S_1 = V_2 + L_1$.[13] Pour repérer ces exemples, il faut faire la liste des verbes qui, comme ἐκπίπτω, n'ont jamais de valeur figurée dans les exemples non alternants ainsi que dans les exemples alternants où le lexème est L_2 ou L_0.[14] Il s'avère alors que les exemples métaphoriques sont peu nombreux. La relation entre v et f est donc peu différente de la relation entre s et f;[15] elle est forte ($\phi = 0,71$; $\phi^{max.} = 0,88$) et significative ($\chi^2 = 290,50$ soit P < 001).

Etablissement d'un Modèle Théorique

Comment interpréter les quatre relations, significatives et fortes, ainsi mises en évidence? C'est ici qu'il est nécessaire de poser des hypothèses sur le fonctionnement de l'alternance considérée, ou même les alternances en général, et également sur les relations que peuvent entretenir les variables explicatives: il est évident que la plupart d'entre elles sont fortement reliées les unes aux autres.[16]

Nos hypothèses sur le fonctionnement des alternances entre cas et tours prépositionnels, avec les verbes ablatifs mais aussi avec d'autres types de verbes,[17] nous ont été fournies par E. Spang-Hanssen, qui a étudié la concurrence entre prépositions 'incolores' et prépositions fortes en français moderne.[18] Selon lui, à la faiblesse ou à la force du morphème alternant correspond respectivement la force ou la faiblesse de la cohésion du syntagme qu'il constitue avec le verbe. Ainsi, en français, *discuter de quelque chose* constituerait un syntagme plus cohérent que *discuter au sujet de quelque chose,* où le complément tend à devenir circonstanciel ou 'éloigné'. Spang-Hanssen montre de plus que la cohésion du syntagme peut être affectée par la présence de certains éléments qui se trouvent soit dans le syntagme considéré, soit hors de lui. C'est ainsi qu'en français, la présence d'un élément déterminant le complément augmente le poids de celui-ci, déséquilibre ainsi le syntagme à son profit et, finalement, affaiblit la cohésion de ce syntagme. D'une manière générale, la cohésion du syntagme s'affaiblit quand le poids sémantique de l'un de ses deux éléments constitutifs se trouve, pour une raison ou une autre, augmenté.

Cette étude de Spang-Hanssen peut fournir l'hypothèse de départ pour une étude des alternances de l'attique: le cas est bien, morphologiquement et sémantiquement, faible par rapport au tour prépositionnel. Il reste à trouver les variables qui ont pu influer sur la cohésion du syntagme et entraîner l'emploi de l'une ou de l'autre forme du complément alternant. La valeur, figurée ou matérielle, du verbe, ainsi que le sens, figuré ou matériel, du syntagme peuvent constituer de telles variables: la valeur et le sens matériels peuvent bien être considérés comme forts par rapport à la valeur et au sens figurés; leur apparition doit donc déséquilibrer le syntagme, en compromettre la cohésion; de fait, le complément est plus souvent prépositionnel, on l'a vu, quand la valeur du verbe et le sens du syntagme sont matériels (nous préciserons plus loin nos hypothèses concernant les causes sous-jacentes à ces relations).

L'influence de la variable *préverbe* pourrait s'expliquer de la même manière. Nous admettons que ἐκ- caractérise comme précis le mouvement exprimé par le verbe ablatif; si ἐκ- n'est pas employé, le mouvement reste non caractérisé du point de vue de sa précision.[19] Les verbes composés à l'aide de ἐκ- contiennent donc un élément sémantique absent des autres verbes ablatifs; la cohésion du syntagme qu'ils constituent avec leur complément est plus faible, ce qui favorise l'emploi d'un tour prépositionnel.

En revanche, notre hypothèse générale expliquerait moins bien une influence de *l* sur *f*: peut-on vraiment dire que les noms abstraits sont sémantiquement faibles par rapport aux autres? Plutôt que de poser ce postulat, nous préférons supposer que la relation *lf* ne correspond pas à une influence de *l* sur *f*, qu'elle est simplement l'effet indirect des influences (ou de certaines des influences) que nous venons de supposer, et de quelques autres: on peut ainsi admettre que la valeur du verbe influe sur le choix du lexème, un verbe à valeur figurée admettant plus facilement un complément abstrait. Ainsi, si un lexème abstrait apparaît plus souvent dans un syntagme casuel; ce pourrait être parce que la valeur figurée du verbe favorise d'une part l'emploi d'un tel lexème, d'autre part l'apparition du morphème casuel (cf. schéma 1).

Par ailleurs, on peut admettre que le sens, figuré ou matériel, du syntagme résulte de la valeur, figurée ou matérielle, du verbe et de celle, abstraite ou non, du lexème: la concordance entre *v* et *s* n'est rompue que dans la métaphore, qui est rendue possible par la valeur abstraite du lexème complément. L'hypothèse de deux influences, d'une part de *v* sur *f*, et d'autre part de *s* sur *f*, paraît peu économique, étant donné que la plupart des exemples sont classés de la même façon par rapport à *s* et à *v*; on essaiera donc de se passer de l'influence de *s* sur *f*.[20]

Il faut enfin supposer une influence de *p* sur *v*: le préverbe fait partie de ce que nous appelons le verbe et l'on attend qu'il contribue à sa valeur.

On arrive ainsi à un modèle causal qu'on peut représenter par la figure suivante:[21]

Schéma 1. Hypothèses concernant les relations entre les variables.

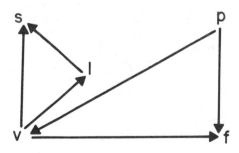

L'adéquation de ce modèle à nos données va être contrôlée par l'analyse de dépendance.

Vérification du modèle: l'analyse de dépendance.

Initialement utilisée dans les années 20 en biologie,[22] l'analyse de dépendance (ou *path analysis*) s'est par la suite diffusée à un grand nombre de disciplines, dont la sociologie.[23] La prolifération des utilisations de ce modèle d'analyse tient d'une part à ce qu'il permet de systématiser là où l'accumulation des tests et mesures statistiques bivariés crée souvent plus de confusion que de clarté et, d'autre part, à ce que cette systématisation se fait en des termes facilement transposables au niveau du discours théorique. Formellement, l'analyse de dépendance est un sous-ensemble du modèle linéaire général, sous-ensemble qui se caractérise par ceci qu'il constitue une épreuve non pas de la probabilité qu'une relation, simple ou partielle, soit significative mais bien une épreuve de la *cohérence générale d'un réseau d'influences* posé par l'hypothèse.

Avant de présenter le modèle, il importe de distinguer deux notions: celle d'association et celle d'influence ou d'effet. La notion d'association entre deux variables (ou deux ensembles de variables) correspond à un constat descriptif élémentaire: x et y covarient ensemble. Mais rien dans cette notion ne permet de spécifier pourquoi, en vertu de quel processus, x et y sont associés. Si on désire dépasser cette constatation, il faut alors recourir à la notion d'influence: au contraire de la notion d'association qui pose la symétrie d'une relation, la notion d'influence pose l'asymétrie de cette relation. On dira par exemple que y est fonction de x ($y = f(x)$) ou que y est causé par x, ce qui est équivalent. La notion d'influence est donc une sous-partie spécifique de la notion d'association.

Une association entre deux variables peut donc provenir de ce que l'une des variables influe sur l'autre directement. Mais deux autres cas sont également possibles. Deux variables peuvent être associées en l'absence d'influence de l'une sur l'autre (pseudo-influence: 'spurious correlation') si ces deux variables sont elles-même 'causées' par une même troisième. C'est ce que représente le schéma 2 où aucun lien asymétrique ne relie y et z.

Schéma 2. Cas de pseudo-influence.

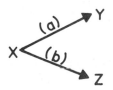

Dans ce cas, l'association entre y et z est égale au produit des influences de x sur y (a) et de x sur z (b) et la simple connaissance de l'association entre y et z ne permet aucune interprétation.

Une autre possibilité dont il faut tenir compte pour interpréter l'association entre deux variables en l'absence d'influence directe de l'une sur l'autre, est représentée au schéma 3.

Schéma 3. Relation entre x et z médiatisée par x (influence indirecte ou médiatisée).

$$Y \xrightarrow{\text{(a)}} X \xrightarrow{\text{(b)}} Z$$

Dans ce schéma, y influence x qui, à son tour, influence z. L'association entre y et z vient donc de ce que y est une *cause indirecte* de z, y étant médiatisé par x. Dans ce cas, l'association entre y et z est égale au produit des influences de y sur x et de x sur y.

Enfin, l'association entre deux variables peut être le fruit de la combinaison entre les trois types de structures d'influence: influence directe, pseudo-influence et influence indirecte (ou médiatisée). C'est ce que représente le schéma 4, où l'association entre x et z se décompose en deux parties: une partie qui est l'influence directe de x sur z et une partie qui provient de ce que x et z ont une cause commune: y.

Schéma 4. Combinaison entre trois types de structures d'influence.

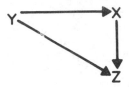

La décomposition de l'association entre les variables en termes des structures d'influence constitue la trame de fond de l'analyse de dépendance: le schéma flèché représente la structure globale des influences. Chacune de ces influences (ou effets) peut être mesurée et, par la suite, on peut recomposer à partir de ces seules influences l'association entre les variables qui ne sont pas explicitement reliées dans le schéma,[24] et comparer ces associations estimées aux associations effectivement observées pour tester si le modèle posé par l'hypothèse rend compte de toutes les variations observées.

A un niveau plus formel, on peut démontrer que, dans le cas de variables métriques ou de variables dichotomiques, les coefficients de dépendance qui mesurent l'influence d'une variable sur une autre sont identiques aux coefficients de régression partiels standardisés: on aura donc recours à la régression pour estimer ces coefficients de dépendance.

L'estimation de l'association entre deux variables non explicitement reliées dans le schéma flèché se fait par l'application itérative de l'équation:

$$\hat{r}_{ij} = \sum_k d_{ik}\, r_{kj}$$

où: r_{ij} et r_{kj} sont des coefficients de corrélation, d_{ik} est un coefficient de dépendance, et k représente toutes les variables ayant un effet direct sur i.

Cette équation permet d'isoler chacune des chaînes d'influence qui contribuent à l'association entre les variables i et j. Il faut dire ici que cette phase du calcul, à cause des procédures itératives qu'elle comporte, a tout avantage à être faite à l'aide de l'ordinateur[25].

Une fois connue la valeur numérique des $\hat{r}_{ij}$, on les compare aux r_{ij} observés. Si l'écart dans tous les cas est nul ou très faible, on pourra conclure que le modèle, et conséquemment les hypothèses qu'il représente, est valide: la structure générale des influences posées par le chercheur est compatible avec les données observées.

C'est ce qui se passe pour le modèle présenté dans le schéma 1 et les données numériques du tableau 1: les relations observées et les relations déduites des influences supposées sont très proches les unes des autres, comme le montre le tableau suivant où, à chaque couple de variables correspondent trois lignes; la première donne le ϕ (relation observée); la seconde la relation déduite du modèle; la troisième l'écart entre les deux premiers chiffres.

	s	v	l	f
p	0,48	0,62	0,28	0,61
	0,56	0,62	0,32	0,61
	−0,08	0,00	−0,04	0,00
s			0,90	0,63	0,63
		0,90	0,63	0,63
		0,90	0,63	0,64
		0,00	0,00	− 0,01
v			0,51	0,71
			0,51	0,71
			0,00	0,00
l				0,43
				0,37
				0,06

Tableau 3. Comparaison entre les relations observées et les relations déduites du modèle.

Pour juger de la validité du modèle, on observe les écarts, là où ils peuvent être différents de zéro, c'est-à-dire lorsque les deux variables concernées ne sont pas reliées directement par une flèche. Ici les quatre écarts observés ne s'éloignent pas sensiblement de zéro; aucun d'eux n'atteint la limite (arbitraire mais fréquemment utilisée) de 0,1[26].

On voit ainsi que les fortes corrélations mises en évidence plus haut entre la forme du complément (*f*) et d'une part la valeur du lexème (*l*), d'autre part le sens du syntagme (*s*), peuvent fort bien être presque uniquement dues aux effets indirects des autres facteurs: 1) *v* influe à la fois sur *l* et sur *f* (structure du schéma 2), et *p* influe à la fois sur *l* par l'intermédiaire de *v* et sur *f* (directement et indirectement). 2) *p* et *v* influent à la fois (directement et indirectement) sur *s* et sur *f*.

On ne peut cependant dire que notre modèle est vérifié par l'analyse de dépendance; il serait plus exact de dire qu'il n'est pas falsifié par elle; d'autres modèles (faisant intervenir ou non d'autres variables) pourraient peut-être rendre compte des mêmes données. Mais cette réserve, qu'on doit apporter dans l'interprétation de toute analyse de dépendance, n'est-elle pas valable pour toute théorie scientifique?

Le schéma 5 présente le modèle avec les coefficients de dépendance.

Schéma 5. Relations entre les variables.

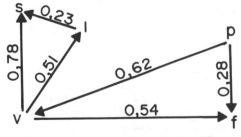

On constate que la variation libre subit beaucoup plus fortement l'influence de la valeur du verbe (0,54) que celle du préverbe (0,28).

Nous avons appliqué le modèle ci-dessus à deux autres corpus:
1) aux exemples fournis dans le *Corpus Platonicum* par les verbes cités;[27] le modèle n'est pas infirmé par l'analyse de dépendance, même si la force des coefficients de dépendance est parfois sensiblement différente.

2) aux exemples fournis, chez les Orateurs attiques, par les verbes
ablatifs à construction obligatoire.
En effet, certains verbes ablatifs se construisent toujours avec un cas
(accusatif ou génitif; cf. ἀπέχω, ἀπογιγνώσκω etc.), d'autres toujours
avec un tour prépositionnel à valeur ablative (ἀπάγω, ἀφικνοῦμαι etc.);
on peut comparer les contextes des exemples casuels et des exemples
prépositionnels ainsi fournis; or ces contextes s'opposent presque de la
même façon que les contextes des exemples casuels et prépositionnels
fournis par les verbes à construction facultative: on retrouve les quatre
corrélations significatives que nous avons signalées plus haut. Il faut
donc admettre que les facteurs qu'elles reflétent jouent avant le choix
des valeurs particulières à ces verbes, choix qui entraîne le caractère
obligatoire et non plus facultatif de la construction favorisée par les
facteurs. Le modèle causal établi pour les verbes à construction
facultative s'applique aussi aux verbes à construction obligatoire, à condition cependant de renoncer à l'une des hypothèses faites plus haut[28].

References

[1] *Essai de statistique lexicale. L'illusion comique de Pierre Corneille*
(Paris, 1964). *Initiation à la statistique linguistique* (Paris, 1968).

[2]Lorsque ce test du χ^2 n'est pas valide, par exemple lorsque l'un des
effectifs théoriques est inférieur à 5, on peut utiliser le test de Fisher: cf.
H.M. Blalock, *Social Statistics* (New York, 1960), 212-221; S. Siegel,
Nonparametric Statistics for the Behavioral Sciences (New York,
1956), 98-99; D.J. Finney, "The Fisher-Yates test of significance in 2×2
contingency tables," *Biometrika, 35,* 145-156.

[3]Cf. R. Martin et Ch. Muller, "Syntaxe et analyse statistique: la
concurrence entre le Passé antérieur et le plus-que-parfait dans 'La
mort le roi artu', *Travaux de linguistique et de littérature,* II, 1 (1964),
207-233; M. Hug, "L'adjectif épithète et le complément du nom dans la
langue des journalistes. 1968 et 1928. Etude statistique comparative",
Etudes de linguistique appliquée, NS 1 (1971), 58-100; J. Schmidely,
"Grammaire et statistique: l'alternance *le/lo* dans l'expression de l'objet 'direct' en espagnol", *Etudes de linguistique appliquée,* NS 6 (1972),
37- 58.

[4]Il en va de même pour les autres corrélations significatives qu'ils
retiennent, à l'exception de celle qui unit le temps à la variété de l'aspect
accompli ("le Passé antérieur est, déjà en langue, orienté vers l'expression de l'accompli concomitant, le Plus-que-parfait vers l'accompli
d'antériorité; *op. cit.,* p. 228; cf. aussi *infra* ref. 5 et R. Martin, *Temps
et aspect. Essai sur l'emploi des temps narratifs en moyen français*
(Paris, 1971)). Notre critique vise aussi les corrélations mises en
évidence par J. Schmidely dans l'article cité dans la note 3.

[5]Ils ne retiennent finalement (p.228-232) que quatre de ces variables;
deux sont éliminées apparamment parce que les corrélations qui les un-
issent à la variable à expliquer sont moins fortes que les autres (p. 226).
Le raisonnement qui écarte l'influence de l'emploi de l'auxiliaire fait in-

tervenir une hypothèse concernant les relations entre les variables explicatives: la corrélation entre l'emploi de l'auxiliaire et l'emploi des temps est "secondaire ou médiate" (p. 225); c'est le type de raisonnement que nous chercherons à étendre à l'ensemble des variables jouant un rôle dans le fonctionnement de la variation libre que nous étudierons; l'utilisation de l'analyse de dépendance nous permettra d'appuyer les hypothèses de ce genre sur les données numériques. MM. Martin et Muller mettent bien en évidence un autre type de relation entre les variables: ils montrent (p. 223) que l'influence du cadre syntaxique (proposition temporelle ou non) renforce les influences de l'aspect accompli et de l'aspect du sémantème; ils supposent en somme l'existence de deux influences conjonctives, mais ils traitent ensuite le cadre syntaxique comme un facteur n'exerçant qu'une influence disjonctive sur la variable à expliquer. Dans le modèle que nous présenterons plus loin, nous n'avons fait entrer que des influences disjonctives.

[6]C'est pourquoi la comparaison des pesées respectives des différents facteurs à l'aide de leurs coefficients d'association, et l'étude de leurs conjonctions (cf. Martin et Muller, *op. cit.*, p. 228-232) ne peuvent remplacer une analyse multivariée du type de celle que nous allons présenter.

[7]Le corpus comprend les oeuvres qui ont été transmises sous les noms d'Andocide, Antiphon, Démade, Démosthène, Dinarque, Eschine, Hypéride, Isée, Isocrate, Lycurgue et Lysias, excepté les *Tétralogies* attribuées à Antiphon, les soi-disant *Lettres* d'Eschine et les fragments d'Isocrate. Nous avons donc admis dans le corpus des oeuvres qui peuvent être des falsifications postérieures au IVème siècle mais, dans tous ces cas, l'hypothèse d'une rédaction au IVème siècle est possible et parfois même probable. Nous avons suivi le texte de la collection Budé. Le dépouillement de ces oeuvres a été facilité par l'existence d'index complets pour presque tous les Orateurs.

[8]On n'a pas tenu compte ici de quelques exemples où l'influence d'un facteur non sémantique est probable et possible (l'une des deux formes du complément alternant peut ainsi, dans certains contextes, avoir été choisie par certains Orateurs parce qu'elle permettait d'éviter un hiatus).

[9]On a exclu les exemples où $\phi\epsilon\acute{u}\gamma\omega$ et $\dot{\alpha}\pi o\phi\epsilon\acute{u}\gamma\omega$ signifient respectivement, avec un complément comme $\delta\acute{\iota}\kappa\eta\nu$, "être accusé" et "être acquitté."

[10]On n'a pas étudié ici les composés de $\alpha\acute{\iota}\rho\tilde{\omega}$ signifiant "enlever"; ces verbes présentent certaines particularités par rapport à ceux qu'on vient de citer; ils seront étudiés dans B. Moreux, *Les alternances entre cas et tours prépositionnels dans la langue des Orateurs attiques. Etude sur la cohésion des syntagmes verbaux* (en préparation).

[11]Nous laissons de côté ici deux facteurs qui sont étudiés dans l'ouvrage cité dans la note précédente, mais dont l'influence est faible: 1) facteur stylistique: tel auteur peut avoir une certaine prédilection pour l'une ou l'autre des deux constructions; 2) la valeur particulière de chaque verbe: un verbe peut être employé plus souvent qu'un autre avec telle con-

struction sans que cette différence soit complètement expliquée par le jeu des autres facteurs.

[12]C'est πόλις ("la cité") qui fournit le plus grand nombre d'exemples de cette catégorie; la cité est envisagée soit comme une entité abstraite soit comme une entité géographique. La catégorie L_2 comprend, outre quelques noms concrets, des noms de lieu et des noms animés, ceux-ci étant moins souvent prépositionnels que ceux-là. On aurait pu constituer les noms animés en une catégorie indépendante; nous ne l'avons pas fait car, en étudiant d'autres corpus, nous avons constaté que le comportement de ces noms par rapport à l'alternance est peu constant, contrairement à ce qu'on peut observer pour les autres catégories de lexèmes et pour les catégories des autres variables. Il nous a donc semblé préférable de les étudier en tant que non abstraits.

[13]En revanche, on ne note pas d'exemple de la métaphore inverse, qui correspondrait à la formule $S_2 = V_1 + L_2$.

[14]On admettra qu'un verbe ayant les valeurs V_1 et V_2 ne peut être employé métaphoriquement, c'est-à-dire avec sa valeur V_2, dans des syntagmes S_1 L_1. Dans une première étape de notre travail, nous avions admis ce type de métaphore et classé ces exemples comme V_0; nous perdions beaucoup d'information, car ces exemples sont nombreux; toutefois l'analyse de dépendance donnait des résultats presque identiques à ceux que nous obtenons en considérant ces exemples comme V_1. Nous serons du reste obligés de renoncer à cette hypothèse quand nous chercherons à expliquer les exemples fournis par un autre corpus (cf. ref. 28).

[15]Les exemples S_0 seront classés V_0 et laissés hors des calculs.

[16]La valeur des ϕ correspondant à ces relations est donnée, dans le tableau 3, sur la première des trois lignes concernant chaque couple de variables.

[17]Ces autres alternances seront étudiées dans l'ouvrage cité dans la note 10.

[18] *Les prépositions incolores du francais moderne* (Copenhague, 1963).

[19] Sauf si c'est la préposition ἐκ qui est employée. Notre interprétation de l'opposition entre ἐκ- et ἀπο- s'appuie sur la possibilité de leur cooccurrence avec les prépositions homonymes. 'Εκ, dans notre corpus, est toujours employé avec la préposition ἐκ; ἀπο- peut être employé avec les prépositions ἐκ ou ἀπό. 'Εκ et ἐκ- peuvent donc être considérés comme marqués par rapport à ἀπό et à ἀπό- lorsqu'un mouvement a été décrit comme précis par l'emploi de ἐκ-, il ne peut plus être considéré comme non marqué de ce point de vue, c'est-à-dire qu'on ne peut employer ἀπό (la présence du cas dans cette situation s'explique par le caractère probabiliste de l'influence du préverbe sur la forme du complément). Au contraire, un mouvement non marqué comme précis au niveau du verbe (verbe sans ἐκ-) peut toujours être marqué comme tel au niveau du complément, par l'emploi de la préposition ἐκ; il peut aussi rester non marqué, par l'emploi de ἀπό ou du cas.

[20]Nous choisissons cette hypothèse plutôt que l'hypothèse inverse (influence de s sur f et non de v sur f) parce que nous plaçons le verbe au point de départ de l'analyse sémantique de la phrase. Le sens des flèches entre s, v et l a aussi été déterminé en fonction de ce postulat.

[21]Cette figure ne représente pourtant pas un aspect important de nos hypothèses: les variables v et p agissent sur f par l'intermédiaire d'une autre variable, la cohésion du syntagme. Cependant, cette dernière variable n'est pas mesurable et nous n'en tiendrons pas compte dans l'analyse de dépendance. On pourra supposer que le rapport entre la cohésion du syntagme et f est égal à l.

[22]S. Wright, "Correlation and Causation," *Journal of Agricultural Research,* 20 (1921), 557-585.

[23]Boudon, R., "A Method of Linear Causal Analysis: Dependance Analysis," *American Sociological Review* 30 (Juin 1965), 365-374.
Boudon, R., *L'analyse mathématique des faits sociaux* (Paris, 1967), 88-134.
Duncan, O.D. "Path analysis: Sociological Examples," *American Journal of Sociology,* 72 (Juil. 1966), 1-16.
Blalock, H.M. (ed.), *Causal models for the Social Sciences,* (Chicago/New York: Aldine-Atherton, 1971).
Land, K.C., "Principles of Path Analysis," in Borgatta, E.F. (ed.), *Sociological Methodology 1969* (San Francisco: Josey-Bass, 1969), 3-37.

[24]Un modèle saturé, c'est-à-dire où toutes les influences entre les variables prises deux à deux sont présentes, n'est pas testable.

[25]Un bon nombre d'Universités, principalement dans les Départements d'Economie, de Biologie et de Sociologie, possèdent un programme permettant d'effectuer ces calculs.

[26]Si l'on veut utiliser une procédure plus précise, on peut calculer la corrélation entre les facteurs implicites (facteurs, non posés dans le modèle, influant sur chacune des variables) à l'aide de la formule $r_{uv} = (r_{ij} - \hat{r}_{ij})/(r_{iu} r_{jv})$, où u et v sont respectivement les facteurs implicites de i et j. Cette corrélation tendra à s'approcher de zéro dans la mesure où le modèle sera compatible avec les données. Dans notre cas on obtient $r_{be} = -0,05$, $r_{ad} = -0,06$, $r_{de} = -0,11$ et $r_{ab} = -0,22$, où a, b, c, d et e représentent respectivement les facteurs implicites influant sur s, p, v, f et l. Seul le dernier de ces coefficents s'éloigne sensiblement de zéro, mais sans remettre en question l'ensemble du modèle.

[27]Grâce à l'obligeance de L. Brandwood, nous avons pu utiliser son index de Platon avant qu'il ne soit publié.

[28]Il s'agit de l'hypothèse présentée dans la note 14.

Homer and IMPRESS:
Application to Greek Metrics of a
Social-Science Analysis Package

S.V.F. Waite

Metrics form a fundamental part of poetry; the tension caused by forc-ing natural language into a more or less constrained rhythm heightens the effect of a poem. Nonetheless, getting specific information about a poet's metrical practices has been tedious; it has normally entailed careful reading of his works. The investigator has had to note each occurrence of the feature or features being studied, and always lurked the possibility of overlooking some occurrences through carelessness or simple fatigue. Worse yet, collecting data on another metrical feature required a complete rereading of the poem with the same care.

Further, metrics and their effect are made up not only of isolated features but also of their interrelationships, which can grow quite com-plex when several items are considered simultaneously. In Homer, even as fundamental an investigation as O'Neill's, on localization of words of a particular metrical form within a line, considered only the first 1,000 lines each (omitting repeated passages) out of the 27,792 lines total in the *Iliad* and the *Odyssey*.[1] Porter, who expanded somewhat on O'Neill's work, still considered only 1,000-line samples from the two Homeric poems.[2] In a more extensive study, Schmiel investigated the relationship of word accent and verse stress in 6,705 lines of Homer, looking at lines as a whole.[3] Still unknown is the influence of the presence of a word accent in one position in a line upon its presence elsewhere in the same line.

Faced with the problem of handling such questions for a nearly overwhelming amount of data, William C. Scott in the Classics Department at Dartmouth and I determined to develop and experiment in conjunction with an upper-level Greek course. Scott already had available a specially prepared concordance to the *Iliad* and the *Odyssey* combined. This concordance, as those for many other authors now do, lists words occurring more than once in the alphabetical order of their following contexts so that repeated phrases or formulae are evident from a simple inspection of the bulky pages. Still, the concordance, which was prepared from a text originally put into machine-readable form by Andrew Q. Morton, did very little to answer metrical questions.

There was available at Dartmouth, however, a program to scan Greek dactyllic hexameters; this program was initially prepared as an aid in proofreading texts in the American Philological Association's Repository of Greek and Latin Texts in Machine-Readable Form. Like other programs for scanning Greek and Latin hexameters, this program works from the end of a line backwards, determining the nature of as many syllables in the line as possible.[4] It then takes the known syllables and matches them against the templates of the allowable scansions.

Since the number of possible scansions is relatively small (32, if the nature of the final syllable in the line is ignored), the process can work efficiently.

The program was refined to take into account additional features beyond the simple nature of the syllables and applied to Morton's text, which was based on the Oxford Classical Text of Allen for the *Iliad* and on the Editiones Helveticae version of von der Muhll for the *Odyssey;* this text had in the meantime been enhanced by the addition of accents and breathing marks from a tape prepared by the Thesaurus Linguae Graecae at the University of California, Irvine. A student assistant, Cynthia Doenges, was hired with funds provided by the Sloan Foundation through Dartmouth's Office of Instructional Services and Educational Research; she actually ran the programs to scan the texts, supplying information for the lines which had doubtful syllables or caused the program to be unable to reach an acceptable result, as well as doing most of the verification of those results.

The output was quite massive. For each line, the book and line number were given, as well as indication of whether it was bracketed as spurious by the editor. The decision was made to provide the remaining data on a syllable-by-syllable basis, since Greek dactyllic hexameters are determined by the nature of each syllable, and this approach allowed more flexibility in considering various metrical features. The basic pattern of the meter is a dactyl (long, short, short or – ..), but a spondee (– –) can be substituted for the dactyl, reducing the normal foot of three syllables to a foot of two. Every line contains six feet, each either a dactyl or a spondee; the last foot is an exception. If this foot is a dactyl, the second short syllable is omitted to help provide a break in the otherwise regular pattern; thus, this foot has only two syllables in all lines and is either – . or – – in shape. In order to allow the programs which analyzed the results to be able to consider each foot as starting and ending at determined positions in the line, spondaic feet were treated as if they had an absent middle syllable, thus keeping the count to three. An exception was made for the last foot, which always has just two syllables; since there can be only two syllables in this foot, it is considered as ending at position 17 in the line instead of 18.

In addition to this information about the length of each syllable, other data were prepared by the scanning program. These included the position and nature of word accents. Also provided were indications of word endings and, if they were present, separate information about the presence of punctuation and possible loss of the final syllable through elision, about irregular shortening or lengthening of the final syllable in the word, both of which occur frequently, and about hiatus. Further, since an elided monosyllable can occur and does so frequently, the possibility of two word ends after a single syllable was allowed for, and information about punctuation and the nature of the word ending was repeated for the possible second word end after each position in the line. Finally, Homer sometimes coalesces two syllables into one through synizesis or, conversely, separates two vowels normally united in a diphthong through diaeresis, which was indicated only where it was specifically marked in the text. The kinds of information and their categories are given in Table 1.

Table 1   Types of Metrical Information and Categories

I) For entire line
   A) Book number
   B) Line number
   C) Narrative or Dialogue
      0) Narrative   (i. NRRTIV)
      1) Dialogue   (ii. QUOTE)
      2) Quoted Dialogue   (ii. QUOTE)
   D) Bracketed by Editor as Spurious
      0) No   (i. NO)
      1) Yes   (ii. YES)
II) For Each Syllable
   A) Nature of Syllable
      0) Not Present   (x)
      1) Short   (i. SHORT)
      2) Irregularly Shortened to Preserve Meter (i. SHORT)
      3) Irregularly Lengthened to Preserve Meter (ii. LONG)
      4) Long   (ii. LONG)
   B) Word Accent
      0) No Syllable Present   (x)
      1) No accent   (i. NOACC)
      2) Grave Accent   (i. NOACC)
      3) Acute Accent   (ii. ACCENT)
      4) Circumflex Accent   (ii. ACCENT)
   C) Word Ending and Punctuation
        (Twice for each syllable)
      0) No Syllable Present   (x)
      1) No Word End   (i. NOEND)
      2) Word End without Punctuation (ii. END)
      3) Word End with Comma   (ii. END)
      4) Word End with Dash   (ii. END)
      5) Word End with Colon   (ii. END)
      6) Word End with Question Mark (ii. END)
      7) Word End With Period   (ii. END)
   D) Nature of Word Ending
        (Twice for each syllable)
      0) No Sylllable Present   (x)
      1) No Word End   (i. NO-REG)
      2) Normal Word End   (i. NO-REG)
      3) Word End with Elision   (ii. IRREG)
      4) Word End with Semi-hiatus (ii. IRREG)
      5) Word End with Hiatus   (ii. IRREG)
      6) Word End with Lengthened Final Syllable (ii. IRREG)
   E) Presence of Synizesis or Diaeresis
      0) No Syllable Present   (x)
      1) Normal Syllable   (i. NORMAL)
      2) Synizesis of Two Short Syllables (ii. SYNDIR)
      3) Synizesis of Short and Long Syllable (ii. SYNDIR)
      4) Synizesis of Long and Short Syllable (ii. SYNDIR)
      5) Synizesis of Two Long Syllables (ii. SYNDIR)
      6) Diaeresis (When marked in text) (ii. SYNDIR)

Note
In the right hand column are indicated categories used for the standard dichotomies.
'x' indicates that the answer is excluded from consideration.
'i.' and 'ii.' indicate the two groupings for the standard dichotomies, with the title used.

These data are presented with the full realization that they only partially cover a single aspect of poetry, leaving out such obvious features as
assonance and alliteration, not to mention special poetic and rhetorical

figures of speech. Nonetheless, many of the questions often proposed by philologists can be extracted from the features listed.

Altogether, 123 data are provided for each line, or over 60,000 for a single book of average length in the *Odyssey*. Clearly, the amount of information is at once massive and complex. Indeed, it approaches the quantities acquired by social scientists in their surveys. Further, since both raw counts and interrelationships are desired, just as in the social sciences, the packages prepared for analysis in these disciplines could be applied quite readily.

Probably the most famous of these packages is SPSS. Since Dartmouth has a Honeywell computer, SPSS was not available, so a similar suite of programs intended for interactive use, IMPRESS, was developed. This system, which offers extensive guidance to the user, allows for predefined groupings and dichotomies of the data. Since the number of categories remained relatively limited for each specific question, the groupings were simply assigned to the raw categories; obviously, an exception was made for the line numbers, where no groupings were provided. The dichotomies are indicated by the signals (i.) and (ii.) in Table 1, where (x) marks data excluded from consideration in the dichotomized state. Once the first few books had been prepared and put into the full format for the IMPRESS program, I wrote additional driver programs which essentially automate the process of assigning labels as well.

Such, then, is the package which has been available to Scott and his students during the winter term of 1977. By the end of the term, 11 books of the *Odyssey* numbers 1, 2, 3, 4, 5, 6, 9, 11, 19, 23, and 24, were available; they comprise 5,776 lines, slightly under 50% of the 12,110 lines in the *Odyssey* and almost exactly 20% of the lines in the two Homeric poems combined. The choice of the books was dictated in part by the reading assignments of the students who were using the material during the winter term of 1977, and a systematic effort will be made to complete the work for the entire Homeric corpus. Students were able to use the programs after a single hour's demonstration, and several in the relatively small class started their own analyses, as did their professor. I shall now suggest some of the kinds of questions which are being answered with the material, on the principle that the work can be justified only if the results gained from it can help in understanding Homer and, by extension, poetry and literature.

The Homeric poems were handed down orally for a period of several hundred years, gradually undergoing modification, expansion, and addition of new material. Some scholars have suggested that the narrative portions of the poem became relatively standardized only some time after the dialogue had been fixed; the dialogue might be considered as more suitable for an oral presentation and more crucial for the development of the ideas in the story. What evidence is there in the meter of the *Odyssey* for such an assertion?

The first example shows the differences between narrative and dialogue when the presence of absence of an accent in the first syllable of a line in Book 1 of the *Odyssey* is considered. Throughout, the IMPRESS program asks questions which are answered at the terminal; if a user makes a mistake or does not know what the possible answers are, the program corrects him or provides a list of the possibilities. Here, the variable QUOTED, which indicates whether a line is narrative, dialogue, or quoted dialogue, and the variable ACC01, which shows the presence and nature of an accent in the first position in a line, are treated together. The mode of analysis is discrete, and the standard dichotomy is chosen as mapping; in this, quoted dialogue and normal dialogue are grouped together, while a syllable with a grave accent is considered as if it lacked any accent, leaving those with acute and circumflex accents to be treated as accented.[5] A cross-tabulation of the

---

Table 2   Narrative/Dialogue and Accent in the First Foot in Odyssey 1

IMPRESS, Last modified on 03 JAN 76.

CROSS-NATIONAL DATA ANALYSTS: SOCPOL 2 IS HERE !! LIST IMPNEWS***

Privacy Warning.

Do you want user's instructions? NO

Enter name of study? HOMERLIB***:OD01

Metrical Information for Odyssey Book 01
N = 444 on 123 variables.

Enter names of 2 to 20 variables to be run
? QUOTED, ACC01

Analysis mode? DISC

Enter mapping option? SD

ENTER COMMAND
? XTAB:QUOTED,ACC01;FREQ,%A,CHI

QUOTED BY ACC01

DOWN: LINE IS NARRATIVE OR DIALOGUE OR QUOTED DIALOGUE
ACROSS: FIRST FOOT FIRST SYLLABLE ACCENT

PERCENTAGES ACROSS

	NOACC	ACCENT	TOTAL
NRRTIV	59.1%	40.9%	159
	94	65	
QUOTE	48.4%	51.6%	285
	138	147	
TOTAL	52.3%	47.7%	444
	232	212	

CHI SQUARE = 4.682 WITH 1 D.F.
THE PROBABILITY OF CHI SQUARE IS 0.029

Exclusion analysis:
Table total: 444
Excluded: 0
Sample size: 444

ENTER COMMAND
? STOP

two variables, giving their absolute frequencies, has been chosen. Also produced are the percentages of narrative lines with an accent in the first syllable and those without; similar percentages are provided for dialogue. Finally, a chi-square test is requested. The latter shows that, while differences do exist between narrative and dialogue, they are not significant at the 1% level, that often chosen for determining significance in literary studies. Thus, in this one instance, the two divisions of the poem probably should not be considered as different.

Figure 1 shows graphs of the results for every position in the line in the first, twenty-third, and twenty-fourth books of the *Odyssey*. Noteworthy in this graph is the generally close correspondence between the two divisions of the first book, particularly in the middle of the line and towards its end. The general pattern of this graph is echoed in those for Books 23 and 24, with some divergence toward the beginning of the line but close correspondence at the middle and the end. The general similarity of the graphs for the different books is of some interest, since the authenticity of the last book of the *Odyssey* has sometimes been questioned. Some differences between narrative and dialogue in this feature are found towards the beginning of the line, but, in general, the two kinds of presentation of the story appear closely similar.[6]

Figure 1 Location of Word Accents in Narrative and Dialogue

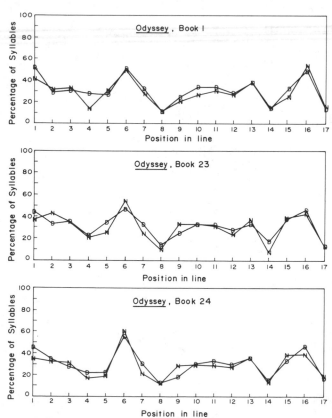

When the chi-square values for the differences between narrative and dialogue are checked for each position in the line, the results bear out the similarity shown in the graphs. In Book 1, the difference between narrative and dialogue is significant at the 1% level only for the first syllable of the second foot (10.710 on one degree of freedom, probability 0.001). In the other two books, the values found for this position are markedly different (Book 23, 0.172, probability 0.682; Book 24, 1.192, probability 0.163, both on one degree of freedom, as will be all other chi-square values presented in the paper). In Book 23, no position yields a chi-square value significant at the 1% level; the closest is found for the second syllable of the fifth foot (6.106, probability 0.013); this position definitely shows no significance in the other two books considered (Book 1, 0.261, probability 0.616; Book 24, 0.557, probability 0.538). Book 24 shows two positions where the narrative and dialogue apparently differ significantly in the number of accents: the first syllable in the line (7.065, probability 0.008) and the last syllable of the third foot (8.397, probability 0.004). Once more, these positions yield different values in the other two books being considered (for the first syllable: Book 1, 4.682, probability 0.029; Book 23, 2.188, probability 0.135; for the last syllable of the third foot: Book 1, 0.704, probability 0.594; Book 23, 2.892, probability 0.085). The suggestion is that there may be some variation among the books, but no fixed pattern has been obtained. While there is some hint that Book 24 may differ slightly from the other books, any statement asserting such a difference would have to depend on far more evidence that is presented here.

A second example shows how the relationship between accents in two or more positions can be explored. First, the cross-tabulation for accents in the first and second positions in the lines is given (Table 3).

Table 3   Accents in First Two Syllables in Odyssey 1

ACC01 BY ACC02

DOWN: FIRST FOOT FIRST SYLLABLE ACCENT
ACROSS: FIRST FOOT MIDDLE SYLLABLE ACCENT

PERCENTAGES ACROSS

	NOACC	ACCENT	TOTAL
NOACCC	52.0%	48.0%	125
	65	60	
ACCENT	87.2%	12.8%	133
	116	17	
TOTAL	70.2%	29.8%	258
	181	77	

CHI SQUARE = 38.172 WITH 1 D.F.
THE PROBABILITY OF CHI SQUARE IS < .001

Exclusion analysis:
Table total: 258
Exluded: 186
Sample size: 444

Here, the chi-square value is high, with a probability of getting a higher value by chance less than 0.001.

Before any shouts of exultation over a great discovery are raised, the nature of the Greek language itself must be considered. Under normal circumstances, each word has only one accent. Most exceptions arise when a word is followed by an enclitic, which has no accent but is treated as part of the preceding word; then, according to a rather complex set of rules, two accents may occur in the earlier word. Even then, however, they will be on consecutive accent. Thus, serveral conditions must be met for accents to come on two succeeding syllables in one word. The possibility remains, however, that the last syllable of one word and the first of the next could both have an accent. True, but if the first word has an acute accent on its final syllable and does not precede a major sense break in the text, the acute is automatically changed to a grave accent, which is counted as no accent at all in the rules by which the standard dichotomies have been defined. Thus the possibilities under which two accents can occur on successive syllables are restricted even when the two syllables are in different words. Here, the analysis programs have done nothing but point out what would be evident to any well-trained elementary Greek student who exercised a modicum of thought.

The possibility exists that there still might be a relationship between accents in different parts of a line, even when these parts are too far apart to fall into a single word or even adjoining words under all but extreme conditions. Until all the possibilities have been investigated, no definite statement can be made. When, however, the accents in the first syllable of the first foot and in the last syllable of the third foot are treated together in Book 1, the resulting cross-tabulation yields a chi-square value which would be exceeded 68% of the time, as the data in Table 4 show.

Table 4   Accents in First Foot and Third Foot in Odyssey *1*

ACC01 TO ACC09

DOWN: FIRST FOOT FIRST SYLLABLE ACCENT
ACROSS: THIRD FOOT LAST SYLLABLE ACCENT

	PERCENTAGES ACROSS		
	NOACC	ACCENT	TOTAL
NOACC	77.2%	22.8%	232
	179	53	
ACCENT	75.5%	24.5%	212
	160	52	
TOTAL	76.4%	23.6%	444
	339	105	

CHI SQUARE = 0.174 WITH 1 D.F.
THE PROBABILITY OF CHI SQUARE IS 0.680

Exclusion analysis:
Table total: 444
Excluded: 0
Sample size: 444

In this instance, at least, no relationship is shown. Still, an extensive study would be required before all possibilities should be ruled out, and such a study has not yet been made.

In the same manner that graphs were produced showing the differences between occurrences of word accents in narrative and dialogue, so were they also produced for locations of word ends in narrative and dialogue. These are reproduced in Figure 2. In general, it is immediately evident that the shape of the graphs is very much similar from book to book, although there are some variations. As one would hope, the graphs show that there is a word ending at the end of every line. What variations exist between books seem to be found primarily at the beginning of the line.

Figure 2 *Location of Word Ends in Narrative and Dialogue*

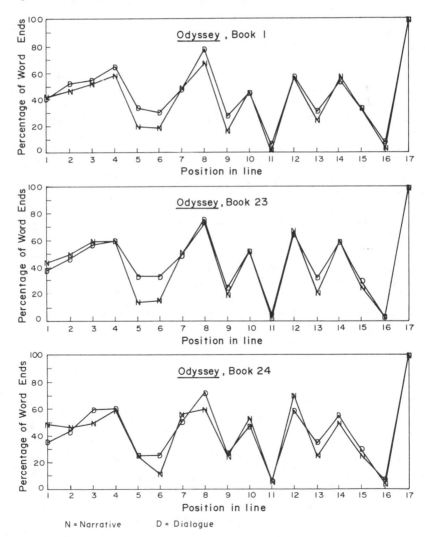

N = Narrative   D = Dialogue

Also similar are the percentages of occurrences of word endings in individual positions in the line for narrative and dialogue, although again some variation is found. For the most part, this variation seems greatest towards the end of the second foot, where there are markedly fewer word ends in narrative than in dialogue. This observation is confirmed by checking the chi-square values where they can be obtained (for some positions in some books, the expected values for either narrative or dialogue fall below 5 for one of the choices, and the chi-square value is not supplied); all the values are given for one degree of freedom. In Book 1, the only values significant at the 1% level are those for the last syllable in the second foot (7.148, probability 0.008) and the last syllable of the third foot (6.905, probability 0.08). In Book 23, the two locations producing chi-square values significant at the 1% level are the middle syllable of the second foot (11.211, probability 0.001) and the last syllable of the second foot (15.368, probability < 0.001). In Book 24, three positions yield significant chi-square values; they are the first syllable of the first foot, where there are more word endings in narrative than dialogue (9.151, probability 0.003), the last syllable of the second foot (17.532, and the probability < 0.001), and the middle syllable of the third foot (7.518, probability 0.006). With the exception noted, in every case, the narrative has fewer word ends than the dialogue in the particular position. Most interesting is that in at least these three books narrative and dialogue differ significantly in the percentages of word ends in one position, the end of the second foot; the suggestion is that this phenomenon might be investigated further.

Fortunately, with IMPRESS*** or a similar system, and in less then 20 minutes, it was possible to obtain information about the word endings in narrative and dialogue for the remaining eight books available at the time of writing. The results are summarized in Table 5. In all of the eight books, the material classified as narrative has fewer word endings at the end of the second foot than dialogue. Further, in four of the eight books, the results support the suggestion reached on the basis of Books 1, 23, and 24. Two of the remaining books deserve special attention. Books 9 and 11 are both part of Odysseus' long narration of his wanderings to the Phaeacians; these are purely dialogue, strictly considered, except for two lines in Book 9 (neither of which has a word ending). Chi-square values could not be obtained. When Odysseus' own narration of his travels is treated as narrative and the material he is quoting is taken as dialogue, the results are those given in Table 5. For these books, however, the distinction between narrative and dialogue has been blurred in producing figures. Books 5 and 6 remain to indicate

Table 5   Chi-Square Values for End Words at End of Second Foot in Narrative and Dialogue

Book	Chi-Square Value	Probability
2	6.981	0.008
3	13.817	<0.001
4	18.755	<0.001
5	4.899	0.025
6	2.419	0.116
9	1.947	0.159
11	1.162	0.281
19	19.001	<0.001

that all the books of the *Odyssey*, and perhaps also those of the *Iliad* should be studied before attempting to reach any definite conclusion. The additional evidence rather tends to support the initial hyppothesis of a difference, but it also suggests that this question, like many, is complex. Further, while a possible temporal difference in the fixing of the form of the dialogue and narrative was alluded to earlier, other explanations of the possible difference are at least equally likely. The results here at most point out a possible difference between narrative and dialogue; they do nothing to suggest its cause.

Worthy of comment is the fact that both graphs presented, that for percentages of accents in a given position and that for percentages of word ends, show greater apparent variety at the beginning of the line than at the end. For the word ends in particular, there may be a tendency to stabilize in the third foot and again toward the end of the line. Such a finding, if confirmed by further work, would support other arguments which have been advanced on the nature of the Homeric line and its construction, as for instance in Allen.[7]

These examples have been presented to give some idea of the kinds of questions which have been asked and answered by this combination of literary studies and the social sciences; not shown have been the features of IMPRESS*** which allow divisions of the material into categories different from those provided at the initial entry of the material into the data base for the program. This feature has proven particularly interesting to Scott in his work; frequently he divides books into sections based on criteria suggested by non-metrical grounds and then proceeds to see if differences also appear in the metrics. Obviously the possibilities are nearly infinite.

The examples mentioned provide some idea of the possibilities afforded by a marriage of literature and the analytic methods of the social sciences. They should also serve as a caution to indicate that the offspring of such a union have their limitations; sometimes the elaborate tool produces results which should be evident upon a moment's reflection. Nonetheless, the combination provides an additional tool which can be used fruitfully by literary scholars interested in metrics, if employed with discretion. By facilitating the answering of questions, these methods also put an additional imposition on the literary critic: he must be prepared to frame more questions and to follow up the leads which are suggested by initial results. In this way, he can, if he wishes, make the fullest use of the techniques which are now becoming available to provide data for him. To at least two classicists, Scott and myself, the investigations are becoming increasingly interesting, even when the results merely provide suggestions of what kind of things to look for in the text itself. Ultimately, the judgment of the value of a result suggested by the computer must be decided by the scholar who returns to the text with a keener eye and a greater awareness.

References

[1]Eugene G. O'Neill, Jr., "The Localization of Metrical Word-types in the Greek Hexameter: Homer, Hesiod, and the Alexandrians," *Yale Classical Studies,* 8 (1942), pp. 103-178.

[2]H. N. Porter, "The Early Greek Hexameter," *Yale Classical Studies,* 12 (1951), pp. 1-63.

[3]Robert Charles Schmiel, *Rhythm and Accent in Homer* (PH.D. Dissertation, University of Washington, 1968; abstract in *Dissertation Abstracts,* 23, 3 [September 1968], pg. 886A).

[4]See particularly Wilhelm Ott, "Metrical Analysis of Latin Hexameter by Computer," *Revue* of the Organisation Internationale pour l'Etude des Langues Anciennes par Ordinateur, 1966:4, pp. 7-24 and 1967:1, pp. 39-64, with 32 pages of appendices; and Nathan A. Greenburg, "Scansion purement automatique de l'hexametre," *Revue* of the Organisation Internationale pour l'Etude des Langues Anciennes par Ordinateur, 1967:3, pp. 1-30 (in English).

[5]Schmiel (*op. cit.*) makes the same division between accented and unaccented syllables.

[6]Schmiel (*op. cit.*) finds differences significant at the 1% level between narrative and dialogue when the coincidence of word accent and verse stress throughout the line is considered.

[7]W. Sidney Allen, *Accent and Rhythm: Prosodic Features of Latin and Greek: a Study in Theory and Reconstruction* [Cambridge Studies in Linguistics, 12] (Cambridge, England: Cambridge University Press, 1973).

2
Stylometrics: Modern Literature

Authorial Privilege in Joseph Conrad

T.K Bender

The complete works of the novelist Joseph Conrad are in the process of analysis by computational techniques in a multi-institutional project based at the University of Wisconsin-Madison.[1] From this data bank, two sets of literary indexes of an experimental nature have been published: *Concordance to Heart of Darkness* and *A Concordance to Conrad's Lord Jim*.[2] A basic position in our work is that it is not an adequate aim for a literary scholar to imitate the structure of traditional handmade concordances, which was developed in primitive times: he must try to develop systems of indexing and reference which explore more flexible organizations of research materials. Using the recently published *A Concordance to Conrad's Lord Jim*, we wish to look at ways in which elementary regrouping of verbal indexes provides a new understanding of Conrad's use of limited narration and of the processes required of the reader of his fictional narratives.

Conrad's fiction is remarkable for its use of limited or 'unreliable' narration. That is, the story is often told through the limitations of a character so that what the storyteller says does not agree with the reader's understanding of the total discourse. For example, a story might be set up so that a thief tells you of his crime and asserts that he is a terribly clever fellow. At the end of the work, however, he is arrested and imprisoned. This kind of story sets up a contrast between showing and telling; the limited intelligence of the speaker *tells* us that he is clever, but the work as a whole *shows* us that he is not. Because the speaker in such a case is limited, obtuse, or 'unreliable', we say that he is not so privileged as the author's own voice might be. Literary critics speak of the degree of privilege a speaker has in fictional narrative, meaning the degree of divergence the reader perceives between the ideas and attitudes the speaker expresses and the 'authorial intention' or normative judgment implied in the total work. Conrad's *Lord Jim* is a particularly interesting example of limited narration. The central affair, Jim's disgraceful abandonment of the ship Patna, of which he was an officer, is organized into a story by Conrad's limited narrator Marlow. The narrative is therefore a twice-told tale. Various witnesses tell Marlow; Marlow tells the story as he sees it to a group of listeners on a veranda on a certain evening; one member of that audience presumably tells us the words which make up the total text of the novel. The narrative is a series of nested 'unreliable' statements. Can we trust the individual witnesses, or can we trust Marlow, or can we trust the first narrator who speaks to us more nearly in an authorial voice?

Lord Jim is written as an 'impressionist affair'. The core of the story is a scandalous event which has already taken place when the narrative opens: the British officer Jim has disgracefully abandoned his ship and

passengers through fear following an accident at sea. The craven
officers plan to tell authorities that their ship has sunk without trace,
but a French ship comes upon the derelict, places a French lieutenant
on board, and takes the wreck in tow safely to port. The narrative
proceeds by evergrowing circles of complexity as the reader tries to un-

---

Figure 1. Simplified Scheme of 'Nested Unreliable' or 'Twice-Told' Narration in Lord
Jim.

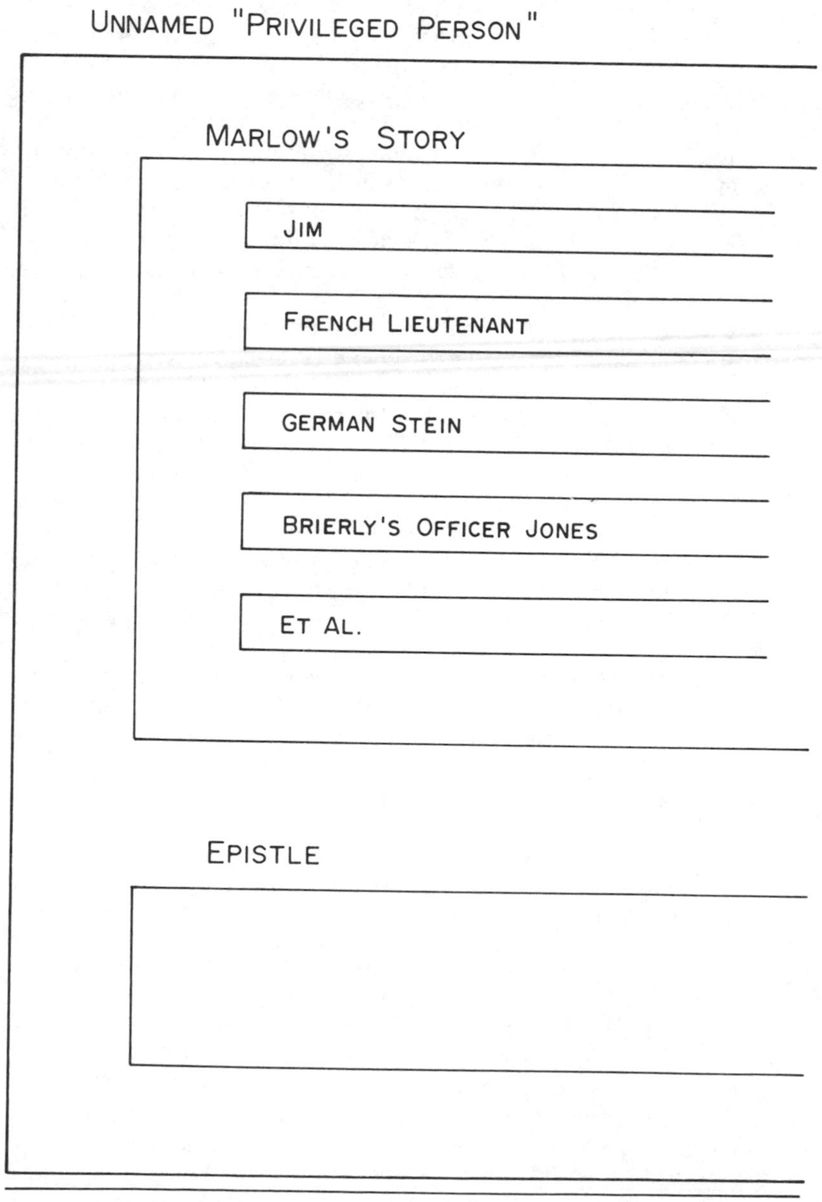

UNNAMED "PRIVILEGED PERSON"

MARLOW'S STORY

JIM

FRENCH LIEUTENANT

GERMAN STEIN

BRIERLY'S OFFICER JONES

ET AL.

EPISTLE

derstand Jim's character. The reader's initial guess that he is a simple coward, or simply irresponsible, is not nearly adequate to explain the affair. The dramatic tension of this story lies not in the events, but in the contrast between the various observers' impressions of those events: the French lieutenant's mind contrasted to Jim's; Marlow the storyteller's impression played against the privileged person in his audience who relays the story to us. We might visualize a simplified scheme of the 'nested unreliable' or twice-told narration in *Lord Jim* as in Figure I. Here Marlow the storyteller collects information from informants and his own eyewitness, quotes these sources and shapes them into a story which he tells to an audience on a certain evening, a member of that audience reports his tale and adds information to which he alone is privy from a letter and other sources and thus shapes the total fiction as we have it, making a data string of 516 'pages' of thirty 'lines' each.

Figure 2. French Vocabulary in Conrad's Lord Jim.

allez	178.17	lachez	178.26
au	176.04	la	178.20
autour	169.14	les	169.28, 177.16
autres	177.16	marins	173.10
bien	170.29, 171.20, 178.21	menagements	169.29
	178.22, 174.12	merci	168.23, 170.27, 171.21
bosse	178.14	metier	178.20
c'est	171.20	mon	174.07
ca	171.20, 178.20, 181.02	monde	173.08
cadavre	167.12, 173.11	monsieur	180.27, 181.03, 181.15
cassis	169.04		181.24
ce	167.21, 169.14, 171.04	ne	179.24, 180.24
	173.08	notez	170.29
cet	173.11, 173.21	ouvrir	171.28
comprendre	169.06	parbleu	169.17, 179.08, 179.25
concevez	169.06	pas	180.24
coquet	175.22	peut	171.05
d'hote	243.02	qu'on	171.04
dans	173.21	qualite	170.16
de	169.06, 169.14, 170.16	que	173.20, 179.03
	172.20, 173.10, 173.20	s'en	171.20
diable	179.03	s'est	177.16
dieu	170.27, 174.07	sans	170.15
doute	170.15	serviteur	181.23
enfin	172.03	seul	180.24
enfue	177.16	sorte	173.20
entendue	178.23	tout	173.08, 178.26, 180.24
epouvantable	178.29	toute	169.22
est	179.24	tres	175.22
etat	173.10	triste	175.24
exigeait	169.28	va	171.20
fait	171.04	veux	178.20
finis	215.03, 215.11	vie	173.22
juste	176.04	vient	180.24
l'	173.10	ville	175.24
l'eau	169.04	voila	179.27
l'homme	179.24	votre	170.16
l'oeil	171.28	vous	169.06, 178.25

Conrad was Polish by birth, spent much of his childhood in a Russian penal settlement, and served in the French merchant navy, before beginning laboriously in his twenties to use English as his tongue. We might expect to find a high proportion of foreign words in his novels. In fact, Conrad seems very careful to keep non-English words segregated for special uses in his text. If we scan the 516 pages of *Lord Jim* for words which are not standard English, we discover that Conrad has a rather extensive vocabulary in French and German (see Figures 2 and 3). Note that with the trivial exception of *d'hote* and *finis*, all the French words fall between pages 168 and 181 of the text, or in 13 out of 516 pages. The German vocabulary falls almost entirely in three sections: pp. 122-133, 241-268, and 428-433. Readers of *Lord Jim* do not need a computer to tell them that Conrad uses foreign words to differentiate character, so that the French words are used entirely in connection with the French lieutenant, the German words with connection to the four German characters in the story: on pp. 122-133 in connection with the cowardly captain of the ship Patna which Jim deserts; pp. 241-268 in connection with the businessman Siegmund Yucker, the hotelkeeper Schomberg, and the butterfly collector Stein who arranges for Jim's final and fatal job as agent in Patusan; and in the final section pp. 428-433, which is related entirely to Stein.

The French lieutenant views Jim's desertion quite differently from Marlow. The French officer is not able to imagine how the Patna was abandoned by her officers:

Glancing with one eye into the tumbler, [the French lieutenant] shook his head slightly. "Impossible de comprendre – vous concevez," he said with a curious mixture of unconcern and thoughtfulness. I could very easily conceive how impossible it had been for them to understand. (169.04-169-09)

Throughout this passage, the *I voice* is Marlow, who imagines all too well how Jim was compelled against all his training to jump from the wrecked ship. The French officer's mind is of a completely different quality, incapable of sharing Marlow's impression of Jim's act. The use of French differentiates the characters and separates their conflicting views of Jim's conduct. Likewise, the German words, used by the despicable captain of the Patna, indicate that he differs completely from Marlow in the respect he has for a seaman's certificate of competency. The captain and Jim lose their papers entitling them to serve as ship's officers as a result of their conduct, which is a terrible disgrace in Marlow's eyes. The German captain says,

"A man like me don't want your *verfluchte* certificate. I shpit on it." He spat. "I vill an Amerigan citizen begome." (49.13-49.15)

Here, not only the German word *verfluchte*, but also the phonetic representation of dialect, *shpit*, *vill*, *Amerigan*, and *begome*, differentiate the German mind from the British seaman Marlow. Apparently an important element or convention in Conrad's narrative is that *authority is granted more readily to a speaker who uses standard or formal English than to one who deviates from it.* When linguistic verisimilitude appears in the text, using slang, phonetic spelling, non-standard or informal discourse, the reader conventionally does not take the values so stated with the same authority as when the language follows formal, standard usage.

Figure 3. German Vocabulary in Conrad's Lord Jim.

Ach	241.17, 258.09, 259.17	ich's	257.03
	428.19, 433.21	ist	241.21, 241.22
Bleibt	256.04	Ja	259.14, 260.19
denn	257.03	mein	125.01, 133.29, 257.04
ein	241.21, 241.22	meinen	257.03
endlich	257.03	nenn'	257.04
ewig	261.29	nicht	260.29
ewigheit	55.25	residenz'	254.04
ganz	256.04	ruhig	256.05
gelungen	255.17	schon	268.02
gewiss	263.21	schrecklich	432.30
gewissen	257.04	schwein	27.04
gott, etc.	122.15, 125.01, 133.30	sehen	429.02
	260.21	sie	429.02
halt'	257.03	sinne	257.04
himmel	260.21	und	257.04
idee	241.21, 241.22	verfluchte	49.13

Dialect (like *cap'n* or *gabasidy*), slang (like *b'gosh* or *crakee*), phonetic representation (like *d-d-die* or *g-g-glad*), ejaculations (like *oh* or *pah*) all seem to call into question the authority of the speaker, inviting the reader to judge for himself what he sees happening. Often such forms indicate a highly 'dramatized' scene, depicted as if unrolling right before our eyes rather than at a distance in past time. Likewise the use of the apostrophe creating forms such as *hadn't* for *had not* or *haven't* for *have not* can be graphed in the text of *Lord Jim* and will be found to cluster, so that the apostrophe occurs in groups in those segments of the text which are dramatic, those which imitate speech ways directly, but the apostrophe disappears almost entirely when the persona speaking approaches an authorial voice. When apostrophes occur thickly, in general, the reader *judges* the values of the speaker. When language becomes more formal, the reader *accepts* less critically what the text says.

Linguistic verisimilitude and dialect are means by which the author controls the reader's response to the language, the degree to which the reader accepts the ideas and values of the speaker. The shifting degrees of formality in the language cause the reader to move in and out of sympathy with the speaker as he progresses 'horizontally' from beginning to end of the text. But these fluctuations of formality can also occur in the 'vertical' dimension of the work, in layers of drafts, revisions, and proof corrections standing behind the printed text. Professor Daniel Tynan in *A Computer Concordance to the Red Badge of Courage* discusses Stephen Crane's use of dialect.[3] Crane made extensive dialect revisions in at least two stages of the second draft manuscript, States I and II. In State III he began more revisions, but was not consistent throughout the novel. These inconsistencies remain in the 1895 text. The quality of the intellectual problem for the reader seems similar on the 'vertical' and on the 'horizontal' axis. As we pass from the dramatized persona of the French lieutenant to that of Marlow, subtle shifts in language call on the reader to judge, to resist accepting too readily the speaker's attitudes. Likewise as we follow Crane through layers of revisions of his text we can see the author shifting on the 'vertical' axis the linguistic verisimilitude, hesitating about what expressions should bear his own 'authority' or be disavowed dramatically as ideas and attitudes of some 'other' mind.

A mediocre joke of the mid-sixties concerned the Lone Ranger and his faithful companion Tonto. Finding themselves surrounded by fierce Apaches in overwhelming numbers, the Lone Ranger said to Tonto, "Well, we are certainly in a tight spot this time." As the arrows whizzed past them, Tonto replied, "What you mean *we*, White Man?" The nub of this story lies in the surprising regrouping of characters' allegiances. Under what conditions will a character show allegiance to or violate a community of attitudes? Conrad has said in his prefaces that his novels are all concerned with simple virtues like *fidelity* and *honor,* and so they are. Marlow says that he must explore Jim's conduct because they both belong to

an obscure body of men held together by a community of inglorious toil and by fidelity to a certain standard of conduct ... (59.15-17).

But Conrad's fiction is not like *Tom Brown's School Days,* merely propaganda for the prescribed set of values such as 'playing the game fairly'. Conrad inquires how a community of values is formed, what is the basis for elementary social groupings: "What you mean *we*, White Man?"

In Conrad's *Lord Jim* the word *we* is used 189 times. There are some quite obvious subgroupings possible among occurrences of *we*. First, we can divide *we* into those cases in which a group of characters including the speaker *act* together, as opposed to those cases in which a group including the speaker *agree* in ideas or feelings or shared experience. For example, the first use of *we* in *Lord Jim* occurs when one of the boys on Jim's training ship tells of how they had rescued a sailor in an adventure which Jim had failed to join. The lad says,

... the other, the big one with the beard. When *we* pulled him in he groaned (8.12).

Here the speaker uses *we* to indicate that he is part of a group which has *acted* together. Jim listens, eaten with envy and remorse, because he is not part of this group. *We* includes the co-agents, but excludes Jim.

Contrast this usage of *we* to that which occurs at 24.23. Jim is described as replying to the "odious and fleshy figure" of his skipper, which

fixed itself in his memory forever as the incarnation of everything vile and base that lurks in the world *we* love: in our own hearts *we* trust for our salvation in the men that surround us (24.23-25).

In this second passage, the *we* group is formed by a community of feelings, not of action, and the speaker reaches into the story to include Jim and outward from the story to include the implied reader in his community, while excluding the skipper. The use of *we* in such cases draws the implied reader into the community of values created by the speaker. If the real reader is hesitant about accepting that community or adopting those feelings as his own, there is a turbulence set up between the sets of values created in the fiction and those of the reader.

The activity of reading *Lord Jim* sets up a struggle between the speakers and their audiences to find an acceptable community of values.

When we look at Jim's version of what happened after he had abandoned the Patna at the urging of the other cowardly crew members, we see that the novel is primarily a consideration of what constitutes a community. The other officers are afraid that Jim will tell the truth, if they are rescued, and their story about abandoning a sinking ship will be revealed as a lie. They ask one another, "What can he do?" and Jim reports that he thought, "What could I do? Weren't *we* all in the same boat?" (152.16). The central question of the novel is: even though Jim jumped into the same boat as these men, does he share in the community values of these men? When Marlow first sees Jim he expects that they belong to the same community.

I liked his appearance; I knew his appearance; he came from the right place; he was one of us. He stood there for all the parentage of his kind, for men or women by no means clever or amusing, but whose very existence is based upon honest faith, and upon the instinct of courage (50.20-26).

The central issue of the novel is whether or not Jim belongs to this community or some other.

A main topic in *Lord Jim* is sometimes called 'pseudo-speciation' by sociologists.[4] Briefly stated, a community's values become ritualized in religion, games, and art. Education frequently consists of acquiring familiarity with those rituals and accepting them. This fortifies one's sense of belonging, but has the sinister effect of excluding from the community that part of mankind which does not know the proper rituals of behaviour. In its extreme, 'pseudo-speciation' allows cowboys to kill Indians without paining the feelings of children at a Saturday cinema matinee, or marines to 'waste gooks'. When Jim abandons the Patna with its crowd of pilgrims, Conrad explores for us a paradox of 'pseudo-speciation'. The more firmly he belongs to the community of Marlow's White Men, the more inhuman his pilgrim cargo seems to him; but the key to belonging to Marlow's community is fidelity to protecting that despised group.

A main topic of the novel is the formation of elementary communities of value. The language of the novel reinforces that topic because it engages the reader in the activity of forming such communities. In the dramatic situation the reader must judge whether to 'join' the community of Marlow, or of the French lieutenant, or some other group. Repeatedly the persona reaches out of the story and includes the reader in a set of values:

We wander in our thousands over the face of the earth, the illustrious and the obscure, earning beyond the seas our fame, our money, or only a crust of bread; but it seems to me that for each of us going home must be like going to render an account. We return to face our superiors, our kindred, our friends – Those whom we obey, and those whom we love (270.28-271.05).

The reader has to ask the same question that Jim does, "What you mean *we*, White Man?" The fiction is so constructed that the reader is forced to enact the same process in reading that the character Jim enacts in the plot.

References

[1]T.K. Bender, "Literary Texts in Electronic Storage: The Editorial Potential," *Computers and the Humanities*, 10, pp. 193-9.

[2]T.K. Bender, Sybyl C. Jacobson and Robert J. Dilligan, *Concordance to Heart of Darkness* (Carbondale: Southern Illinois University Press, 1973) and T.K. Bender and others, *A Concordance to Conrad's Lord Jim* (New York: Garland Pub., 1975).

[3]Daniel Tynan, *A Concordance to The Red Badge of Courage, 1895 Edition, With an Introductory Essay* (University of Wisconsin diss., 1972).

[4]See Erik H. Erikson, *Childhood and Society* (New York: Norton, 1951).

SPAN: A Lexicostatistical Measure and Some Applications

J.A. Leavitt, J.L. Mitchell

For several years we have been investigating aspects of the complex problem of how to characterize and discriminate among texts. Text discrimination is a fundamental issue in such apparently diverse areas as authorship attribution,[1] the characterization of individual and period styles,[2] and the distinction between pathological and normal language, such as aphasic vs. non-aphasic and schizophrenic vs. non-schizophrenic speech.[3]

Most attempts at text discrimination have traditionally involved the measurement of the distribution of morphemes or words in a text or part thereof (a sub-text) in terms of frequency of occurrence. However, there exists another important distributional variable, hitherto sadly neglected, which we will label clustering. We claim that the incorporation of clustering into a lexical measure provides an important addition to the discriminatory arsenal, once it is recognized that words with the same frequency in texts of the same size may differ in the manner of their distribution (that is, in their clustering). An analogy may prove helpful here. Say we were interested in the wolf population in two national forests of exactly the same size – four hundred square miles. We might compute the number of wolves per square mile, and discover that in each forest there was one wolf per square mile, that is, four hundred per forest. Yet there might be gross differences in the actual distribution of the wolf population in the two forests: in one forest all the wolves might cluster in a single, one hundred square mile area, whereas in the other the wolves might be uniformly distributed throught the entire forest. Clearly, our perception of the identity or difference of the two forests is a function of the specific measure used.

Thus our judgement about the identity of two texts (were they, for example, written by the same man?) or about the integrity of a single text (does it, for example, contain interpolated passages?) should be based at least upon a measure which incorporates both frequency and clustering as parameters.

We have, therefore, developed a multi-dimensional tool which we call SPAN (SPan ANalysis). In it, we

  i) retain a frequency measure (log TTR),
  ii) employ a lexical filter which enhances stability yet permits flexibility, and
  iii) add a clustering component.

In this paper, we describe and evaluate SPAN, and show its application to lexicostatistical problems in Old (OE) and Modern (NE) English.

Description of SPAN

When we employ SPAN to examine a text we do the following:
  i) restrict entities to those that satisfy a category requirement (for ex-
     ample, all words in a text that are categorized as verbs).
  ii) restrict entities to those that occur at least p times (for example, all
      words that are verbs that occur at least three times). We call a string
      of p-consecutive occurrences of an entity a 'token', and consider the
      location of the first element in the string as the location of the token.
      We measure the distance of the token from its defined location to
      the location of the first element after the token (for example, the
      'span' of p+1 consecutive occurrences of a given word). If the token
      has no successor, we define the measured distance as infinity.
  iii) utilizing the union of the measured distances of the admissible en-
       tities, we construct a function which is the cumulative relative fre-
       quency of these measurements. We parameterize this function in
       terms of two values: the log TTR and what we call the 'clustering'
       factor. The relationship of these parameters to the function is
       described below. Each text now enjoys a unique position in the plane
       of the two parameters. The plot of these positions allows us to dis-
       criminate among texts. Furthermore, the location of the texts within
       this plane allows us to determine properties of each text. For ex-
       ample, we can determine whether the tokens are widely distributed
       or clustered within the text.

Herdan discusses the problem of the dependence of Yule's K upon
sample size.[4] Specifically, the issue is the instability of the 'long tail' of
low frequency words. The solution proposed was the truncation of the
tail in order to nullify the effect of unstable low-frequency words.
Herdan tested the hypothesis by arbitrarily excluding from the
calculation words of frequency less than one hundred, and
demonstrated that such arbitrary truncation simply would not work.
From our point of view, this study is important because it highlights the
negative effect of low-frequency entities upon a measure, as well as the
absence to date of any satisfactory solution.

However, the incorporation of the p-parameter into our measure
provides an orderly way of controlling the effects of low frequency entities in statistical analysis. Thus we resolve the well-known problem of
the contamination of statistical results by low-frequency entities. Since
we automatically measure over a range of values for p (which thereby
functions as a truncation device), it is possible to determine empirically
rather than arbitrarily, the optimal p-values for a given statistical population.

SPAN Algorithm

In our analysis, we employ two procedures. One imposes an admissibility condition upon the types, which leads to special definitions
of tokens and distance. This is discussed below. The other procedure ex-
amines the distribution of these types.

Let t_i, $i=1,2,...N$ be a set of types which occur at the locations $L_{i,j}$,
$j=1,2,...M_i$. We associate with the jth token of t_i a distance $d_{i,j}$ (for
example, $d_{i,j} = L_{i,j+1} - L_{i,j}$). If this token has no successor ($j = M_i$),
then we define $d_{i,j} = \infty$. The total number of distances under

consideration is $M = M_1 + M_2 + ... + M_N$. We define a relative cumulative frequency function by

$$Y(r) = [\text{number of distances } d_{i,j} \leqslant r] / M$$

where r indicates a gap size. $Y(r)$ is a non-decreasing function; $Y(0 = 0$; and $1 \geqslant Y(r+1) \geqslant Y(r)$. Furthermore, for r sufficiently large (possibly equal to the text length), $Y(r)$ reaches a maximum value, say $\bar{v}$. It is easy to show that this value of $\bar{v} = 1 - [N/M]$. This formula shows that $\bar{v}$ is related to the type-token ratio N/M. This result is due to our inclusion of ∞ in the definition of $d_{i,j}$.

We shall characterize the function $Y(r)$ in terms of two parameters, V and H. V will reflect the behaviour of Y for large values of r; H will indicate the behaviour of Y near the origin. To the right (r large) we could use $\bar{v}$ as the parameter. However, we shall employ the more stable measure

$$V = \text{Log TTR} = [\text{Log } N]/[\text{Log } M].$$

V is always in the range (0,1). If V is close to 0 then Y is close to 1, and vice versa.

We shall choose H so that it will describe how the curve Y rises out of the origin. We avoid approximating the slope of the curve in our calculations because such measures are numerically unstable (small changes in the data can produce large changes in the measure). Instead, we shall consider a rectangle in the (r, Y) plane defined by $(0,0)$, $(R, 0)$, $(R, Y(R))$, $(0, Y(R))$. We set

$$H = [\text{area below Y in this rectangle}] / [\text{area of this rectangle}]$$
$$(= RY(R)).$$

In Figure 2, $R = 500$ and the numerator of H is the area of the shaded region. H is always in the range (0,1). When the text contains types appearing in clusters, the curve Y will rise rapidly near the origin (Figure 1, i) 1nd H will be large. A small value of H will indicate that the tokens corresponding to each type will tend to be widely spread across the text (Figure 1, iii). Clearly H depends on the choice of R. However, since we are comparing texts with one another, it is sufficient to keep R constant for all texts. This does not cause any great problems providing R is small compared with the text size. Our texts are about 2000 words long, the smallest being I, with length 1372. After experimenting with several values of R we finally settled on $R = 500$ throughout. We produced our graphs with various sizes of R until the relative positions of the texts did not change appreciably. This happened for R in the range 450-550.

Figure 1. Contrasting Examples of Y

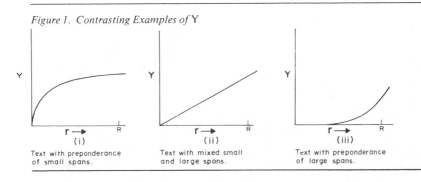

(i)	(ii)	(iii)
Text with preponderance of small spans.	Text with mixed small and large spans.	Text with preponderance of large spans.

In our studies of texts we have been concerned with the adverse effects upon lexical statistics of low frequency types. This has led us to modify our definitions of types, tokens, and distances. In order to be admissable, a type must occur at least p times. A token is considered a string of p-consecutive occurrences of the type. Our distance is defined as the span of p+1 consecutive occurrences of a type. If a token has no successor the distance is considered infinite. Thus $d_{i,j} = L_{i,j+1} - L_{i,j-p+1}$ for $p \leqslant j < M_i$
and

$$d_{i,M_i} = \infty.$$

The total number of distances under consideration is

$$M = \sum_{i=1}^{N} (M_i - p + 1 = N(1-p) + M_1 + M_2 + \ldots + M_N$$

where N is the number of admissable types; each $M_i \geqslant p$. We employ the measures defined above without further modification. For p = 1, Y is similar to the Spang-Hanssen gap distribution function.[5]

Implementation of SPAN

We extract (by means of the COT program, described below) from a sample text the conjugations along with their locations. The results are contained in Table 1. We shall form Y(r) for p=3. In order to do this, we need to form a table of span distances. The only types which are admissable are those which occur at least three times. Thus we admit the types: 'and', 'as', 'but', 'or', 'which', and 'while'. There are 21 tokens, $M_1 = 5, M_2 = 4, M_3 = 2, M_4 = 5, M_5 = 4, M_6 = 1$. From these tokens, we form the span distances. For example, $d_{4,5} = L_{4,6} - L_{4,3} = 1004 - 361 = 643$; $d_{4,7} = \infty$ since there are no occurrences of the word 'or' in the text after the one located at 1095. The full set of span distances is found in Table 3.

Figure 2. Cumulative Relative Frequency Function Y(r) Based on Tables 1 and 2. P=3

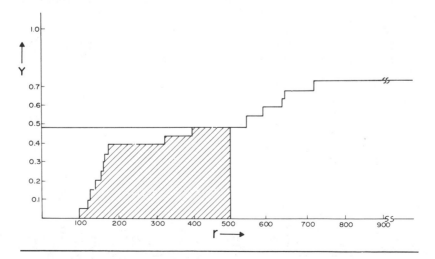

Let us consider the formation of Y(r) with M = 21 (the number of entries in Table 2). There are 8 distances less than or equal to 200. Thus Y(200) = 8/21. Y(r) is given explicitly below.

$$
Y(r) = \begin{cases}
0/21 & 0 \leqslant r < 103 \\
1/21 & 103 \leqslant r < 128 \\
2/21 & 128 \leqslant r < 134 \\
3/21 & 134 \leqslant r < 150 \\
4/21 & 150 \leqslant r < 163 \\
5/21 & 163 \leqslant r < 165 \\
6/21 & 165 \leqslant r < 171 \\
7/21 & 171 \leqslant r < 182 \\
8/21 & 182 \leqslant r < 329 \\
9/21 & 329 \leqslant r < 405 \\
10/21 & 405 \leqslant r < 547 \\
11/21 & 547 \leqslant r < 588 \\
12/21 & 588 \leqslant r < 642 \\
13/21 & 642 \leqslant r < 643 \\
14/21 & 643 \leqslant r < 720 \\
15/21 & 720 \leqslant r < \infty
\end{cases}
$$

The graph of Y(r) is shown in Figure 2. Note that the last value of Y (15/21) is related to the type token ratio: TTR = 6/21 = 1 − 15/21. Clearly, the number of types refers only to admissible ones (the number of types in Table 2). The number of tokens equals the number of span distances in Table 2. Thus V = Log 6/Log 21 = .5885. The area of the shaded region of Figure 2 must be calculated for the numerator of H. The denominator is given by 500Y(500). Thus

H = [.5Y(0)+Y(1)+Y(2)+...+Y(499)+.5Y(500)]/[500Y(500)]

  = [.50/21+1020/21+251/21+62/21+...+.510/21]/[50010/21]

  = .6150

The DAN program takes Table 1 as input, forms Table 2 as an intermediate step, calculates V and H, and displays the results in a graph.

We can see from the graph of Y that there are no span distances less than 100, that there are many span distances in the range 100 to 185, and that relatively few distances are greater than 185. The rapid rise of Y is indicated by the value of H, .6150. Since H>.5 we will expect to find more small spans represented in the rectangle than large ones. In Figure 1, there are texts where H is dramatically larger or smaller than .5. These extreme values indicate relatively large variation among texts in the number of small spans compared to large ones.

The Programs: COT and DAN

We wrote two major programs, COT (Create Occurrence Table) which creates a KWOC concordance of the text by category, and DAN (Distribution ANalysis) which analyzes the distribution of the tokens in the concordance and displays the results graphically. Both programs are written in FORTRAN and PASCAL.

The COT program acts on one or more files which contain texts in tagged dictionary format. Initially, the program requests a Designated Category Marker, DCM, eg. A, +, /, *, ... It then extracts from the indicated files tokens with matching category markers, CM, and appends a location to each token. If the DCM is an A (for All),

Table 1.

	Description of Corpus			
Text Symbol	Text	Tokens	% Interpolation	Language
A	P.C.	2008	<10%	O.E.
B	P.C.	1987	40%	O.E.
C	P.C.	1997	75%	O.E.
D	P.C.	2003	<10%	O.E.
E	P.C.	2021	10%	O.E.
F	P.C.	1977	<10%	O.E.
G	P.C.	2013	<10%	O.E.
H	P.C.	1994	40%	O.E.
K	P.C. (Amalgam)	2000	100%	O.E.
J	Orosius	1758	N.A.	O.E.
L	Orosius	2002	N.A.	O.E.
M	Journal of George Sturt	2025	N.A.	N.E.
I	Minnesota Daily Article	1372	N.A.	N.E.
total		25,157		

Designated Category Markers

Symbol	Category
-	Noun
.	Verb
(	Adverb
$	Pronoun
)	Preposition
+	Conjunction
=	Determiner
*	Auxiliary
/	Adjective
]	Cover Symbol
A	All (i.e. ignore category)

Table 2.   TOC (Table of Occurrences) for a sample text. DCM (Designated Category Marker) conjunctions.

AND	18	73	153	183	207	256	354
AS	90	272	480	495	601	1122	
BECAUSE	105	1137					
BOTH	265						
BUT	589	836	1081	1136			
HOWEVER	972	1284					
IF	402						
OR	225	359	361	945	947	1004	1095
SINCE	679						
THAN	424						
THOUGH	346						
WHICH	53	129	196	235	292	324	
WHILE	320	924	1189				

Table 3.   SPAN distances derived from Table 2 for p=3

AND	165	134	103	171	∞
AS	405	329	642	∞	
BUT	547	∞			
OR	720	588	643	150	∞
WHICH	182	163	128	∞	
WHILE	∞				

Figure 3.

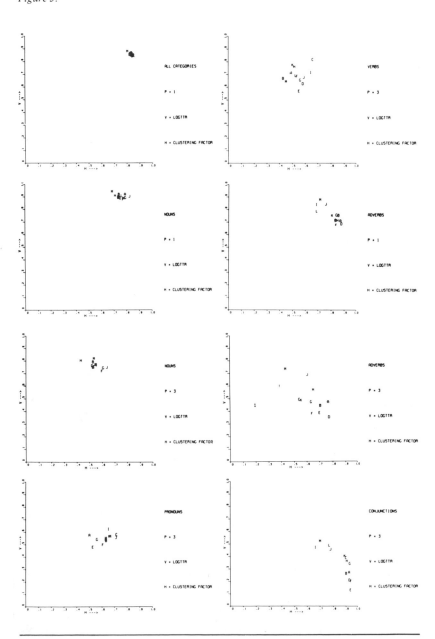

category matching is ignored. These tokens, with their locations, are
finally sorted to create an occurrence table and the product is stored in a
file called TOC (Table of OCcurrences). We have the option of having
the TOC ordered alphabetically or by descending order of frequency,
with the 'hapax legomena' alphabetized. The values from the TOC
serve as input to DAN, a program which computes span distances for a
given value of p. The program forms a table of span distances from the
location of the admissible types. While the table is being formed, a
count is kept on the number of admissible types and tokens. Next the
table $Y(r)$ is formed for $r=1,2,...,500$. Higher values of r are not considered since we have already calculated the number of types and
tokens. The area under Y is calculated for this range of r by the
Trapezoidal Rule, which is exact for this type of function. DAN finally
outputs the types N, the tokens M, $V=Log\ M$, and $H=$(area under
Y)/$[500Y(500)]$ along with a graph locating the text in the H-V plane.

Corpus

As a data-base for the refinement of SPAN, we have utilized some -
21,760 words of OE and 3,397 words of NE. Our choice of texts was influenced by a number of factors. First of all, we wanted to choose texts
which contained substantive textual problems amenable to our in-
vestigative techniques. Secondly, we thought it desirable to focus upon
text in which at least one investigator had some professional expertise – so that his knowledge of the nature of these texts might profitably
be tapped. Not least in importance was the availability of texts in
computer-readable form. The Peterborough version (Bodleian ms.
Laud 636) of the *Anglo-Saxon Chronicle* seemed an ideal text for our
purposes. Already in computer form, this early twelfth-century version
of a Northern recension has a complex textual history, but includes interpolations recognizable by their local (Peterborough or
Medeshamstede) allusions.[6] We arbitrarily divided the first sixteen
thousand of the 51,069-word text of PC into eight sub-texts (A-H) of
approximately two thousand words each (divisions were made wherever
possible at the end of annals and/or sentences).

The OE translation of Orosius' *Historiae adversum Paganos* was
chosen in part because it is, like PC, Alfredian in origin, and in part
because unlike PC, it is not an annal, and is largely a translation from
Latin. The translated portion is represented by sub-text L (beginning
Book II, Chapter 1), and the Alfredian additions by the famous
'Ohthere and Wulfstan' passage (sub-text J), which has been the object
of scholarly interest since the sixteenth century. Additions such as J are
naturally of special interest; though the product of the same hand as the
translated material, they may well be structurally different, being
'natural' OE. Yet, they are not exactly interpolations in the same sense
as the additions in PC.

One other OE sub-text (K) requires special mention. It is an
amalgam of the interpolated material at the end of B and that at the
beginning of C, and, thus, being 100% interpolation, provides a useful
control.

The modern English (NE) pieces were selected for different reasons.
The Journals of George Sturt, 1890-1927 (sub-text M) is indented to
reflect the same kind of periodic entry as PC, yet differs in being written

in the first person, and being compact and elliptical in style. The article from the *Minnesota Daily* (sub-text I) was chosen more or less at random.

Discussion of Results

On the basis of our preliminary investigation, we have excluded three of the original ten grammatical categories from further analysis: Auxiliary, Adjective, and Particle. The existence of both inflectional ('waes'~'waeron') and orthographic ('waes'~'wes'~'was') variation precludes there being enough tokens of any one type within these categories for valid analysis. After lemmatisation of the texts is completed, however, we will re-examine the data.

In our discussion of the programs, we referred briefly to an option which allows COT to ignore grammatical categories altogether in the compilation of the tables of occurrence. The inclusion of this feature in COT reflected our interest in testing the discriminatory power of SPAN, should it be applied to unparsed texts. The evidence of ALL on Figure 1 is conclusive, though hardly surprising: none of the texts are distinguishable from one another, either in Log TTR or in clustering. This finding casts doubt upon the validity of investigations which do not use parsed text, and upon the confidence assertion of Herdan, in his discussion of "whether to use all words or just certain categories," that "the basic distribution laws of vocabulary remain on the whole, valid, no matter whether the partial distributions are studied separately or compounded into one overall distribution."[7]

When we imposed an admissibility condition upon word types, looking only at words of a single category, our results were dramatically different. We successfully distinguished among our texts in the first significant place. That is, the range of the values returned by SPAN is from 0-1, and we separated texts by as much as .5 (see Figure 1). McKinnon and Webster, by comparison, claim to have achieved discrimination in their work – yet only do so in terms of the second and third place. In their study of Kierkegaard they set out to prove that the pseudonymous (PS) selections were significantly different from the acknowledged (SK) selections. Their results show that "The average for the PS set is .845, while that for SK is .825, or deleting the synthetic SK8, .819. In brief, the PS authors have a much richer vocabulary than SK."[8]

If we use the range between peripheries (highest – lowest for V; rightmost – leftmost for H) as a criterion, we can also determine the relative discriminatory power of each parameter. In five out of seven categories (Noun, Adverb, Pronoun, Preposition, Determiner), clustering (H) is demonstrably the better measure. [Preposition and Determiner are omitted from Figure 1 for lack of space.] Only in the case of Verb and Conjugation does Log TTR seem to function better, and then only marginally. But it is most important to observe that both H and V contribute to the 'spread' of the texts on the graphs. That is, both provide information. However, H is typically a more effective discriminator than V. Even for nouns (see Figure 1) where the H-range is smaller than in any other category (.2027) H nonetheless contributes significantly to the separation of texts J-A-B-H. Conjugations provide an interesting and all but unique contrast. Here the sub-texts of the PC show almost no distinction in clustering, but differ widely in their Log TTR. The fact that A-H are all highly clustered can almost certainly be attributed to the structure of the PC itself: it is paratactic. The single most frequent word in the PC is the coordinating conjunction 'and', which occurs - 4,131 times, and by itself represents 8.33% of the text. But although all of the PC texts have considerable conjoining, some of them also have a certain amount of subordination. Since subordination is rarely repetitive, those sub-texts with the most subordination will be isolated from the rest by Log TTR, a measure of diversity. As it happens, the sub-texts with the most subordination are those that are least like the PC as a whole – the texts with twelfth century interpolations. K, an artificially constructed merger of the interpolated passages in B and C, is least like the PC as a whole, and is appropriately highest on the scale of diversity (V). Of the untampered-with sub-texts, C happens to contain the longest interpolated passage (about 75% of the text), and predictably appears just below K. H has the next most interpolation (about 40% of the text) and is just below C. The *Orosius* is, of course, generically quite unlike the PC – and is characterized by much more subordination. Therefore, it is not surprising to find that J and L are clearly separated from A-H.

The introduction of a third parameter, p, into SPAN dramatically enhances the discriminatory power of the measure. When p=3, (that is, when only words of frequency $\geqslant$ 3 are included in the computations), the Log TTR drops for every category in every text because of the exclusion of low-frequency words. For example, in I, with p=1, there are 83 pronoun tokens drawn from 24 types; but with p=3, there are only 46 tokens drawn from 11 types. Thus the Log TTR for pronouns in I drops from .7192 to .6263. At the same time, the p-filter generally moves the text locations leftward on the H axis, away from clustering. The combined effect of the two kinds of movement is to distribute sub-texts more widely accross the graphs, obviously a desirable effect in text discrimination. However, the single optimal value for p may well vary with text and genre, and should therefore be determined empirically. For the future, we plan to incorporate several values of p into a single measure in order to determine whether we can thereby further increase the discriminatory power of p. We have already discovered that the clustering factor (H) changes smoothly with p, whereas Log TTR (V) is less well-behaved. This fact is attributed to the irregular behaviour of the lower end or 'tail' of a vocabulary frequency-distribution – a phenomenon which has much vexed previous investigators, and prompted a variety of ingenious remedies, none of which really solves the fundamental problem (see Muller, for a lucid account of the Waring-Herdan formula).[9] We merely raise the issue here to point out the merit of using clustering as well as Log TTR, since clustering is not effected by the 'tail'.

Of all the categories we examined, the best across-the-board discriminator was Adverb. Figure 1 shows that every sub-text is clearly distinguished from every other sub-text, on at least one parameter. The contiguity of C and K does not contradict this claim, given that K is 100% interpolated, an artificially created amalgam of the interpolations in B and C, while C itself is the text containing most interpolated material. We are not yet prepared to assert that Adverb is invariably a good discriminator, any more than we are prepared to commit ourselves entirely to the rejection of Noun. But, Adverb shows the two

NE texts to be very different, and best separates the sub-texts of the PC. As with Conjugations, there are easily demonstrable structural properties of the PC which account both for the difference of the whole from the *Orosius* and from the NE texts, and for the internal differences. To wit, almost every annal begins with the adverb 'her', (here), with the result that this word is high on the ranking list (17th with 442 occurrences). We can predict, then, that sub-texts which contain short annals will show more adverb clustering, primarily because of the repetition of 'her', whilst sub-texts with long annals, and therefore fewer, more widely spaced occurrences of 'her', will show less adverb clustering. Furthermore, we can predict that, since interpolations are long unified entries within a single annal, the more interpolated a sub-text, the less clustered it will be in adverb-distribution. A and D, the sub-texts with most clustering in Figure 1, are perfect examples: A contains more 'her'-tokens (73) than any of the other sub-texts, and has no interpolations at all, whilst D follows A in 'her'-tokens (56), and has but seven lines of interpolation. In contrast, C, the sub-text lowest in clustering, has fewest 'her'-tokens, and is the most heavily interpolated. Adverb, then, seems to pattern like Conjugation in separating M-I-J-L from the PC as a whole, and in revealing the internal differences of the sub-texts of the PC. Moreover, the two categories compliment one another, in that Adverb separates in terms of clustering and Conjugation in terms of Log TTR.

Let us now look more closely at Noun, which, as we have already observed, appears to be the weakest discriminator on both parameters. None of the sub-texts is located far from the mean. The range is .2027, with J = .6333 and H = .4306. Yet in the PC, F (= .5971) and G (= .6061) are most unlike the contiguous H (= .4306). Scrutiny of our alphabetized word-lists arranged by category reveals why this is the case. All three texts share the same high-frequency nouns (over 10), but H has fewer nouns in the high-frequency range (H=4, F=6, G=7) with fewer tokens. Another way of comparing the data is to compute the percentage of the noun-tokens represented by the high-frequency words with p=3, which can be taken as an index of the dominance of high-frequency nouns in each subtext. Nouns of frequency $\geqslant$ 10 constitute 52% of all nouns when p=3 for F, 61% for G and only 36% for H. These figures appear to be a good reflection of the relative positions of F, G and H in Figure 1. The next problem is to account for the differences we have identified. Analysis of the alphabetized word-list for nouns in H, which includes the location of each token, reveals anomalies in the distribution of three out of the four high-frequency words: 'here' (10), 'geare' (15), and 'cyng' (10). These words appear to be restricted almost exlusively to the latter part of H (the sole exception is 'cyng' which occurs once early on). Closer examination shows this distribution to correspond precisely to the non-interpolated portion of H. In other words, H has two distinct vocabularies which reflect the different concerns of the interpolated and non-interpolated passages. The interpolation is an account of the restoration of Peterborough, which had been reduced to "ealde Weallas, wilde wuda" by the heathen. It includes details of the alleged grants originally made by King Wulfhere, documentary evidence of which was conveniently discovered "idde in pe ealde wealle." The non-interpolated passages include a panegyric on the death of King Edgar, but are otherwise much taken up with the constant incursions by the Scandinavian forces (*se here*).

In summary, we claim to have developed a new lexicostatistical measure, SPAN, the unique feature of which is a clustering parameter. Clustering appears to be both more stable and of greater discriminatory power than Log TTR, the other parameter of SPAN. Application of SPAN to data from OE and NE suggests that the examination of each grammatical category may be profitable. This finding is at odds with those investigators who have relied solely upon one category, or who assert the superiority of function words over content words or vice-versa. Herdan and Williams, for example, argue that the relative usage of function words is essentially fixed by the structure of the language, and that therefore, only context words are stylistically significant.[10] Herdan goes on to argue that "style differences are best brought out by nouns, less so by adjectives, and least of all by verbs and grammar forms." Such categorical statements seem unwise both in light of the conflicting evidence and of what seems to us the obvious fact that differences in result reflect differences in methodology.[11]

References

[1]G. Yule, *A Statistical Study of Literary Vocabulary* (Cambridge, 1944); A. Ellegard, "A Statistical Method for Determining Authorship: The Junius Letters, 1769-1772," *Gothenburg Studies in English* (Gothenburg, 1962, no. 13); F. Mosteller and D. Wallace, "Inference in an Authorship Problem," *Journal of the American Statistical Association), LVIII (1963),*275-309; "Inference and Disputed Authorship: The Federalist," *Reading,* (Mass., 1964).

[2]J. Miles, *Eras and Modes in English Poetry,* 2nd. ed., (Berkley, 1964) and *Style and Proportion: The Language of Prose and Poetry* (Boston, 1967); L. Milic, "Old English as an SVO Language: Evidence from the Auxiliary," *Papers in the Linguistics 5:* 2 (1972), 183-201; D. Mansell, "The Old Man and the Sea and the Computer," *Computers and the Humanities* V I (1974), N 4.

[3]S. Baker, "Ontogenetic Evidence of a Correlation between the Form and Frequency of Use of Words," *The Journal of General Psychology* XLIV (1951), 235-251; B. Skinner, "The Alliteration in Shakespeare's Sonnets: A Study in Literary Behaviour," *The Psychological Record,* 3 (1939), pp. 186-192; R. Wachal and O. Spreen, *A Computer Aided Investigation of Linguistic Performance: Normal and Pathological Language* (THEMIS-UI-TR-29 Contract N000 14-68-A-05000, 1970).

[4]G. Herdan, *Type Token Mathematics* (The Hague: Mouton, 1960), sect. 5.6.

[5]H. Spang-Hanssen, "Typological and Statistical Aspects of Distribution as a Criterion in Linguistic Analysis," *Proceedings of the Eighth International Congress of Linguistics* (Oslo, 1956).

[6]L. Mitchell, "A Computer-Based Analysis of an Old English Manuscript: The First Stages." *Mid America Linguistics Conference Papers* (Stillwater: Oklahoma State University Press, 1972), and "The Language of the Peterborough Chronicle," *Computers in the Humanities* (Edinborough University Press, 1974).

[7]Herdan, p. 169.

[8]A. McKinnon and R. Webster, "A Method for Author Identification," in Wisbey, R.A., *The Computer in Literary and Linguistic Research* (Cambridge, 1971).

[9]C. Muller, "Lexical Distribution Reconsidered: The Waring-Herdan Formula," *Cahiers de Lexicologie,* VI (1969).

[10]Herdan, p. 171, and C. Williams, *Literary Style and Vocabulary: Numerical Studies* (London: C. Griffin and Co., 1970), p. 72.

[11]Mosteller and Wallace; and A. Morton and A. Winspear, *Its Greek to the Computer* (Montreal: Harvest House, 1971).

Dialogue and Narration in Joyce's "Ulysses"

M.B. Pringle, D. Ross, Jr.

This study's impetus was an observation about dialogue in *Ulysses*. While reading the novel, we noticed that in the 'Eumaeus' episode (Chapter 16) Bloom speaks to Stephen in an uncharacteristic way. One example of his peculiar speech occurs as the two grope their way toward the cabman's shelter after an evening's revelry in Dublin's nighttown. Bloom, leading Stephen, offers verbose and cliched advice about Stephen's friendship with Buck Mulligan:

No ... I wouldn't personally repose much trust in that boon companion of yours, who contributes the humorous element, Dr. Mulligan, as a guide, philosopher and friend ... it wouldn't occasion me the least surprise to learn that a pinch of tobacco or some narcotic was put in your drink for some ulterior object (*U*, p. 620).[1]

This remark is typical of Bloom's elevated dialogue that occurs throughout the episode, yet it is stylistically inconsistent with his talking elsewhere in the novel. On all but one previous occasion, he speaks simply and clearly.[2] His first quoted words, for example, are a colloquial, dialectal address to his cat:

O, there you are ... Milk for the pussens ... Afraid of the chickens she is ... Afraid of the chookchooks. I never saw such a stupid pussens as the pussens (*U*, p. 55).

Even in conversations on abstract topics he speaks directly – he answers Molly's question about rebirth:

Metempsychosis ... is what the ancient Greeks called it. They used to believe you could be changed into an animal or a tree, for instance. What they call nymphs, for example (*U*, p. 65).

It is not enough to say that Bloom's speech in the Eumaeus alters because he talks to Stephen. Besides, his dialogue sounds remarkably like the stilted *narrative* style of the episode. To explore more fully the relation between narrative and dialogue styles in *Ulysses*, from chapter to chapter, a computer-assisted survey of language features was conducted. The primary data for the project came from samples of the text which were analyzed using the 'EYEBALL' program (Ross and Rasche, 1972 and 1976). The passages comprise nearly all the directly-quoted dialogue, and 500-word random samples of narration from each chapter (7,300 and 8,900 words, respectively). EYEBALL uses a combination of automatic and manual procedures to annotate each word for features such as length-in-syllables, part of speech, grammatical function, and location in sentence and clause. The program gives statistical output for each passage on the distribution of word-clauses, average word and clause lengths, repetition of vocabulary, and so on. Additional computer programs combine data of several samples to describe other features such as the correlation of adjectives as a function of nouns, and the relation of type-token ratios to text length, or to compare features between groups of samples. To a limited extent we augmented the data from *Ulysses* with a study of stage drama, one on narration in Hardy, and another which combines narration and dialogue from Conrad's *Heart of Darkness*.

As a result of the project, we drew two conclusions. First, Bloom's speech from the Eumaeus exemplifies a situation where the narration style dominates the style of directly quoted dialogue, much as is the case of paraphrased or reported speech. This finding calls into question whether dialogue always is a means of revealing either the manner of speaking or content of speech of a character. Incidentally, we found that Stephen's dialogue tends to retain its integrity; that is, it seems unaffected by the narrative environment.

The second finding of the study of *Ulysses* is that, despite narrative filtering and Joyce's use of a diversity of narrative modes, characters' quoted words and narration are consistently unlike each other in many significant respects. This finding shows the advantage, perhaps the necessity, of distinguishing between dialogue and narration before an accurate description of a novel's style is possible. This paper will present evidence that supports this finding, but we need first to discuss the rhetorical function of dialogue in the novel.

On Dialogue

In *Narrative Modes in Czech Literature*, Lubomir Dolezel recalls that the ancient critics distinguish among novels, poetry, and drama by means of the interplay between two discourses, narration and characters' speech: Diomedes (in the fourth century AD) singled out this property as the main distinguishing feature of the narrative genre:

the narrative genre (epopee) is *genus commune*, combining two differentiated discourses – the poet's speech (*modus enarativum*) and the characters' speech (*modus imitativum*). On the contrary, lyric and drama are 'simple' genres, lyric characterized by *modus enarativum* only and drama by *modus imitativum*.[3]

Since the fourth century, critics have evolved more "complex and detailed schemes of the plurality of narrative discourses."[4] Many influential books and articles focus on the subtleties of narrations, but by contrast, dialogue has been virtually neglected.

As one might expect, the function and nature of dialogue in stage drama have been treated, since characters' speech is the sole discourse (beside stage directions). Eric Bentley's list, from *Playwright as Thinker*, is fairly comprehensive:

[Dialogue] sheds light on the character speaking [1], on the character spoken to [2], on the character spoken about [3]; it furthers the plot [4]; it functions ironically in conveying to the audience a meaning different from that conveyed to the characters [5] ... finally ... [it] is part of the rhythmic pattern which constitutes the whole act [6].[5]

Bentley's specific discussion is about Ibsen, the first to exploit the full potential of prose dialogue. The effect of Ibsen's success has dominated modern drama. Most literary critics assume, often silently, that dialogue in the novel functions as it does in Ibsen's plays. This assumption may be incorrect, since novels use narration and dialogue to accomplish what the latter must do alone in drama.

James Joyce was, in Bentley's view, a "zealous Ibsenite."[6] Few general readers know that he wrote in dramatic form, other than in the Circe episode of *Ulysses*. However, in 1914, between *A Portrait of the Artist As a Young Man* and *Ulysses*, he wrote the play *Exiles*. It is "more lyric than play" in Tindall's estimation, and Tindall joins others who find the work an imitation of Ibsen, and a failure.[7] The major flaw is its tedious, didactic, unrealistic, and overburdened dialogue; in other words, it narrates events and themes, and it does not resemble the rhythm or content of speech. The poor execution is despite his early interest in play construction – at eighteen, in "Ibsen's New Drama", he praised the "apparently easy dialogue," and Ibsen's "ability to differentiate" characters.[8]

Dialogue in *Ulysses* is more skillfully wrought. Stephen's speeches perform the six functions enumerated by Bentley. Bloom's only do the last three – they further the plot, create irony, and contribute to the rhythmic patterns of the book. Because of the narrative filters in the Eumaeus (and perhaps the Cyclops episode), however, dialogue does not reveal the character of the speaker (Bloom himself), or the immediate audience, or those spoken about. The two most consistent functions of both characters' dialogue – and those we will focus on – are the plot development and 'rhythmic action.'

Dialogue can further a plot in two ways. First, it can present a novel's central themes or images. While the methodology need not detain us at this time, it is first important to recognize that five of *Ulysses'* eighteen chapters have most of their narration attributed to Stephen, that is, they are narrated through his physical and psychological perspective.[9] These are the first three chapters, plus the second half of "Aeolus" (7), and "Scylla and Charybdis" (9). In these, dialogue, especially Stephen's, presents more central themes and images than does dialogue in chapters attributed to Bloom or Molly (18), or those with an external narrative stance (14,16, and 17), or the masque in "Circe" (15). While the first three episodes are dominated by the narration, dialogue also contains important material. In Stephen's "Telemachus" (1), three important themes of the book are talked about: Stephen's relation to his country ("It is a symbol of Irish art. The cracked looking-glass of a servant" [*U*, p.6]), his mother and family ("You said ... O, it's only Dedalus whose mother is beastly dead" [*U*, p. 8]), and the Church ("I am the servant of two masters ... And a third there is who wants me for odd jobs ... The imperial British state ... and the holy roman Catholic and apostolic church" [*U*, p. 20]). In the Nestor episode (2) he discusses history and God, in Scylla and Charybdis (9) his speeches treat the relation between life and art, and give his views on paternity.

None of the five full and two half episodes which are attributed to Bloom contains dialogue with important thematic issues.

Dialogue also furthers the plot by establishing tension. According to Ibsen, good dialogue should force action from another character.[10] In drama, the speeches create suspense, arouse questions not about what *will* happen, but *how* it will come about. It often leads to peaks of emotional intensity (for both audience and characters) and, eventually, is central to the drama's climax. Dialogue in most of *Ulysses* follows this precept. Each episode works like a little play; in the majority, tension is established between the chief protagonists (Stephen, Bloom or both), and another individual or a group. Although narration adds to this tension, in at least half the chapters the tension depends heavily on the speeches. This list summarizes the complexity:

Episode	Protagonist(s)	Antagonist(s)	Importance of Dialogue to Tension
Telemachus	Stephen Dedalus	Mulligan/Haines	strong
Nestor	Stephen Dedalus	Students/Mr. Deasy	strong
Proteus	Stephen Dedalus		little
Calypso	Leopold Bloom	Cat/Molly	strong
Lotus Eaters	Leopold Bloom	M'Coy	weak but present
Hades	Leopold Bloom	Simon Dedalus/ Mr. Power/ Martin Cunningham	strong
Aeolus	Bloom/Stephen	Newspapermen	strong
Lestrygonians	Leopold Bloom	Nosey Flynn/	weak but present
Scylla and Charybdis	Stephen Dedalus	Eglinton/Best/ Russell/Lyster	strong
Wandering Rocks	various narrators		little
Sirens	Leopold Bloom	Richie Goulding,	little
Cyclops	Leopold Bloom	men in bar	strong
Nausicaa	Gerty/Bloom	Bloom/Gerty (situation not developed)	little
Oxen of the Sun	Bloom	Stephen and friends	weak
Circe	Bloom	characters in his imagination	strong
Eumaeus	Bloom/Stephen	men on the street	strong
	Bloom	Stephen	
Ithaca	Bloom	Stephen	little
Penelope	Molly Bloom	various suitors	little

Chart 1.

The list shows that dialogue is more important in creating tension in the first nine episodes than in the latter nine, where only three episodes have a strong relation. In all important cases, dialogue exchanges are terse and are near each other, with little intervening narrative comment. The 'stage directions' for the situations have the protagonists and antagonists standing in one place, as if they were framed by a procenium arch.

In the second half of the novel, however, Joyce relies more on unquoted material to establish tension. Nevertheless, he uses that narration much as he had used dialogue – to establish a dialectic. For example, Molly's interior monologue (formally a narrated section) in Penelope responds to Stephen's interior monologue in Proteus (3). The Nausicaa (13) is in two balanced parts: the first gives Gerty MacDowell's interior monologue, the second, Bloom's response. Seen in this context, the catechism (17) fits in a broader pattern. Here Joyce sustains the dialectic format he has used throughout the book. The dramatic form of Circe fits into the total pattern, perhaps more easily than has commonly been thought.

According to what we have established about the theories of the novel and the drama, and Joyce's general attitudes toward those theories, we can test a hypothesis concerning the relation between the novel's dialogue and stage drama, and another concerning the distance between dialogue and narration. Because of the current state of data collection for literary works, the latter case has proven easier to establish than the former.

General Differences Between Narration and Dialogue

The most obvious and most expected difference between the two parts of a novel is that dialogue has more pronouns. The explicit references to speaker and hearer comprise most of the pronouns in a dialogue, but other people ('he' and 'she') and even things ('it') will add to the effect. The same general difference appears when stage drama ('pure' dialogue) is contrasted to essays ('pure' narration). After observing this difference, we thought to test whether pronouns were the only difference between the two elements in *Ulysses*. To do this, we recomputed the word-category distributions with the pronouns deleted (see Table 1). The constituents of nominal phrases (nouns, determiners, and prepositions) are a bit closer with these pronouns out, while differences in verbal-phrase constituents (main and auxiliary verbs) are intensified. Pronouns do not make all the difference.

The comparison between narration and dialogue can be improved when we use measures which are statistically independent and which reflect linguistic relations within nominal and verbal phrases. Simply listing word class proportions is not the best way to present the data, and no satisfactory way exists to compare such distributions through *t*-test or X^2 tests. To overcome the difficulties, several ratios and combinations are computed, and their average results (among the chapters of *Ulysses*) are compared with the *t*-test (Table 2). The ratios concern options (the choice of noun versus pronoun) or the relation of modifier to head (adjective to noun).

Table 1.   *Word categories for narration and dialogue, differences and ratios; values recomputed with pronouns removed from the distribution.*

| | All Categories | | | | Pronouns Removed | | | |
	Narr %	Dial %	Dif: N-D %	Ratio N/D	Narr %	Dial %	Dif: N-D %	Ratio N/D
Noun	23.9	21.4	2.5	1.12	26.0	24.5	1.5	1.06
Verb,inf.	14.5	16.1	−1.6	0.90	15.8	18.5	−2.7	0.85
Adj.	12.5	7.7	4.8	1.62	13.6	8.9	4.7	1.53
Advb.	3.9	3.7	0.2	1.05	4.3	4.3	0	1.00
Pron.	8.1	12.7	−16.9	0.64	−	−	−	−
Det.	12.5	11.9	0.6	1.05	13.7	13.6	0.1	1.01
Prep.	12.7	10.6	2.1	1.20	13.8	12.1	1.7	1.14
Aux. Vb.	2.5	3.8	−1.3	0.66	2.7	4.4	−1.7	0.61
Subor.	2.9	3.3	−0.4	0.88	3.1	3.8	−0.7	0.82
Coor.	3.6	3.2	0.4	1.13	3.9	3.6	0.3	1.08
Misc.	2.9	5.6	−2.7	0.52	3.2	6.4	−3.2	0.50
Words	8864	7341			8147	6406		

The largest significant difference in nominal phrases is in the proportion with nouns as heads (Measure 2 on Table 2): about 75% of phrases in narration have nouns, and 57% in dialogue. This is matched by the larger proportion of all nominal groups in dialogue – 34% of all words are heads of such phrases, as against 32% in narration. This difference, like the others which will be commented on, is statistically significant at the 0.01 level. No large differences show up in the ratios of determiners to nouns or prepositions to nouns. Narration has a higher ratio of adjectives to nouns – about half the adjectives in narration, but only a bit more than a third (36.2%) in dialogue. This last measure is not obviously or directly related to linguistic necessities of dialogue, but it does seem to follow the pattern of other genres, as we will show. The overall proportion of prepositional-phrase words is higher in narration (Measure 13).

Word-class Measures	Narration		Dialogue		Difference of Means	
	Av.	SD	Av.	SD	t	level
Consituents						
Heads of noun phrases (noun+pronoun)	.320	.025	.343	.020	2.81	.01
Portion of heads which are nouns	.749	.090	.570	.108	4.76	.01
Ratio of determiners to nouns (articles, "his", etc.)	.534	.111	.561	.102	.68	n.s.
Ratio of adjectives to nouns	.516	.135	.362	.134	3.07	.01
Ratio of prepositions to nouns	.494	.080	.439	.097	1.64	n.s.
Verbal Phrase Consituents						
Heads of verbal phrases (main verb+infin+participle)	.145	.027	.169	.016	3.09	.01
Ratio of auxiliary verbs to verbal phrase heads	.179	.143	.296	.128	2.35	.05
Other Category Measures						
Adverb proportion	.039	.010	.036	.011	.88	n.s.
Conjunctions (coordinator + subord.+rel. & interrog. pn.)	.064	.025	.059	.013	.74	n.s.
Proportion of conjunctions which are coordinators	.583	.138	.454	.184	2.07	.05
Miscellaneous: clause and phrase signals, 'not', interjections	.029	.012	.069	.032	4.06	.01
Verbal Generalization						
Portion of nominal+verbal classes which are nominal	81.5%		75.6%			
Word Function Measures						
Prepositional-phrase words	.343	.058	.225	.060	5.20	.01
Predicate part of major clause elements (including subj & comp)	.335	.063	.361	.029	1.52	n.s.
Portion of subj+comp that is subject	.368	.109	.404	.060	1.16	n.s.

Table 2. Word-class measures and comparisons for Ulysses *narration and dialogue*

The proportion of verbal-phrase heads, that is, main verbs, plus the rankshifted infinitives and participles, is significantly larger in dialogue. All verbs (including auxiliaries) are also more frequent in dialogue (21.9% compared to 16.9%). The ratio of auxiliaries to head verbs follows the same – 0.30 to 1 in dialogue and 0.18 to 1 in narration. None of these measures, and certainly not the the ratio of auxiliaries, seems linguistically related to the greater use of pronouns. The conclusion that narration is more 'nominal' than dialogue is compelling.

For no obvious reason, coordinators are a greater portion of all conjunctions in narration.

It is difficult to get other sets of word-class data which are compatible with that gathered for *Ulysses;* some hints are instructive. The best comparison for dialogue is that gathered by Baillie from Shakespeare, Fletcher, and *Henry VIII.* by means of EYEBALL.[12] Less complete is the information given out at a lecture by J. Mackay for narrative samples from Hardy and several other novelists.[13] We use these as tentative controls; the values are in Table 3.

First, the proportion of nominal-phrase heads is greater in both parts of *Ulysses* than in either of the controls. The pronoun measure is nicely paralleled by the controls: the proportion of noun heads is 57% in Shakespeare, 59% in Fletcher, and 62% in *Henry VIII.*, while it is 74% in the narration samples. *Ulysses*, again perversely, has lower determiner-to-noun ratios than either control, whose values go from

Word-class Measures	Elizabethan Drama Flet. Hen. &Shake.			*Ulysses* Dial. Narr.		Novels Hardy Conrad	
Constituents							
Heads of noun phrases (noun+pronoun)	.321	.315	.311	.343	.320	.282	.298
Portion of heads which are nouns	.585	.621	.571	.570	.749	.737	.625
Ratio of determiners to nouns(articles,'his,'etc.)	.654	.717	.757	.561	.534	.740	.787
Ratio of adjectives to nouns	.339	.310	.308	.362	.516	.461	.439
Ratio of prepositions to nouns	.374	.439	.441	.439	.494	.600	.625
Verbal Phrase Constituents							
Heads of verbal phrases (main vb+infin+participle)	.171	.160	.170	.169	.145	n.a.	.157
Ratio of auxiliary verbs to verbal phrase heads	.307	.339	.355	.296	.179	n.a.	.254
Other Category Measures							
Adverb proportion	.043	.043	.037	.036	.039	.038	.043
Conjunctions (coordinator+subord)	.101	.090	.096	.059	.064	.101	.064
Portion of conjunctions which are coordinators	.468	.428	.389	.454	.583	.560	.537
Miscellaneous: clause and phrase signals, 'not', interjections	.051	.044	.053	.069	.029	.073	.043
Verbal Generalization							
Portion of nominal+verbal classes which are nominal	72.2%	73.9%	71.7%	75.6%	81.5%	83.4%	76.8%

Table 3.

0.65/1-to-0.76/l. The adjective-to-noun ratios follow the pattern of *Ulysses*: 0.46/1 in narration and 0.32/1 in drama. Differences in the preposition to noun ratios are significant in the controls: 0.60/1 in the narration and about 0.42/1 in drama.

Because Mackay did not separate various sub-groups of verbs, we have no separate measure of verbal phrases in narration. However, the proportion of verbal phrase heads in drama is about 17%, which is quite close to the dialogue of *Ulysses*. A lower general proportion of all verbs in narration is suggested, since its control has 13%, while the drama control is 22%. The ratio of auxiliaries to heads is even higher in the drama sample than in the dialogue of *Ulysses*. The converse of the statement about narration's being 'nominal' seems valid – dialogue, whether in drama or in novels, is 'verbal'.

Lengths of Words and Phrases

While interpretations are not obvious, word lengths and prepositional phrase lengths differ markedly between the two parts of *Ulysses*. The data for word lengths can be summarized by the percentage of monosyllables.[14] The comparison with data on essays and drama is not surprising:

	Shakesp.	*Ulysses* Dialogue	*Ulysses* Narration	Carlyle	Gibbon
Monosyllable	79%	75%	70%	70%	62%
Av. word length(syllables)	1.27	1.35	1.42	1.48	1.63

Chart 2.

The rank within *Ulysses* is what is expected, since the narration uses shorter words. If we reasonably assume that nearly all pronouns are monosyllables, and subtract the number of pronouns from the two parts, the differences are smaller (71.6% for dialogue and 67.3% for narration), but are still significant.

Prepositional phrases are shorter in dialogue than in narration, which probably makes sense if we think that conversation might have simpler phrases, although the use of such shorter phrases is by no means an intrinsic property of the English language.

	Ulysses Dialogue	*Ulysses* Narration
Av. length (words)	2.79	3.03
S.D.	.85	.92
Number of phrases	528	936
% of words	25.6%	34.2%

Chart 3.

Data from credible control texts has not been gathered, so far as we know.

Specific Differences Among the Chapters of Ulysses

Even casual readers of *Ulysses* know that the novel has more stylistic variety than most. Some caution is needed in using the purely statistical data of word-classes as the only way to account for the variability. One 'control' exists in the data from Conrad's *Heart of Darkness*, gathered by Sikes with the use of EYEBALL.[15] The average coefficient of variation (the mean divided by the standard deviation) for categories is 0.31 for narration and 0.28 for dialogue in *Ulysses*, while it is 0.20 for Conrad. The variability for Joyce is high, but not outrageous – Keat's sonnets have 0.38 and Blake's *Songs* have 0.49 (See Table 4).

Title	No. of Samples	Average Coefficient of Variation (10 Catagories)
Ulysses – Narration	18	.314
Ulysses – Dialogue	12	.283
Blake, *Songs*	45	.493
Keats, sonnets	66	.379
Heart of Darkness	51	.201
Shakespeare (from 3 plays)	16	.157

Table 4. *Variability of word-category proportions in Ulysses, groups of poems, Heart of Darkness (from Sikes), and plays (from Baillie).*

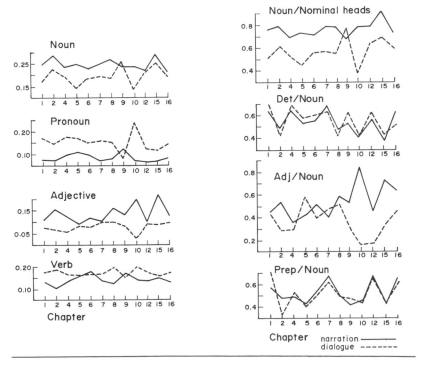

Figure 1. *Word-category proportions and ratios by chapter*

	Noun/head	Det/noun	Adj/noun	Prep/noun
Measure for Narration				
Avg.	.762	.545	.532	.522
S.D.	.064	.091	.138	.096
Range	(.698−.826)	(.454−.636)	(.394−.670)	(.426−.618)
Measure for Dialogue				
Avg.	.570	.560	.362	.510
S.D.	.103	.097	.128	.105
Range	(.467−.673)	(.463−.657)	(.234−.490)	(.405−.615)
Correlation and regression				
r coeff.	.10	.78	−.38	.78
sig.	n.s.	**	n.s.	**
slope	.169	.830	−.346	.850
intercept	.441	.108	.547	.066
Chap. 10 out				
r coeff.	.20	.73	−.04	.84
sig.	n.s.	**	n.s.	**

Figure 1.   Parameters for chapter-by-chapter ratios

Of the eighteen chapters of *Ulysses*, twelve contain a large enough sample of quoted dialogue to make comparisons profitable. Two chapters have fewer than twenty words of dialogue; four have none. Various measures were compared for the dozen chapters – the proportions of nouns, pronouns, adjectives and verbs, and the nominal-group ratios concerning heads, prepositions, determiners, and adjectives. The graphs on Figure 1 show the results.

We have already seen that the determiner/noun and preposition/noun ratios are statistically similar for both parts of the novel. The chapter-by-chapter picture shows that these values tend to work in harmony – with a few exceptions (mostly preposition/noun in the first two chapters), they go up and down to roughly the same places and change at roughly the same rates. The correlation coefficients are 0.78 for both measures, and that value is significantly large. These are not, obviously, fruitful for additional, closer scrutiny.

The ratios of nouns to nominal-phrase heads, and that of adjectives to nouns are not significantly correlated when dialogue and narration are compared. The correlation coefficient for the former is 0.10, and it is -0.38 for the latter. Since Chapter 10, "Wandering Rocks", had the largest difference between the two parts, the correlation was computed a second time with that chapter removed, with no appreciable change in the result (0.20 and -.038, respectively). The distance and direction of difference for the noun measure is fairly uniform, with the obvious exceptions being the ninth ("Scylla and Charybdis") and tenth chapters: in the former, pronouns are actually less frequent in dialogue than in narration because narration contains more interior monologue. Also, Stephen presents his theory about paternity in this episode. Since ideas and not their originators are the focus of the discussion, "he", "she" and "they" pronouns occur infrequently. In Chapter 10, the highest relative use of pronouns in all samples of dialogue is observed because Stephen's and Bloom's consist of short sentences about themselves ("That I had" [*U*, p. 235]) and questions ("What are you doing? What have you there?" [*U.*, p.243]). As the latter examples illustrate, short sentences such as these contain 50% pronouns.

Not surprising is the general lack of a pattern in Joyce's use of adjectives – the distances are larger on average than differences in the measure of choices for heads, and the variability is larger. The ratio is larger in dialogue for Chapter 5 ("Lotus Eaters") and Chapter 7 ("Aeolus"), although the middle chapters which contain both narration and dialogue have the ratio at the closest, while the chapters at the ends, in decreasing order, Chapters 10, 15 ("Circe"), 12 ("Cyclops"), 2 ("Nestor"), 9, and so on, have the largest differences. The ratio is tied to the simple proportion of adjectives (as shown on Figure 1), but it better describes the way Joyce used language.

The generally closer ratio of adjectives to nouns in episodes 4 - 8 may reflect Bloom's roles as both narrator and speaker. In the later episodes, because the simple attributed narration mode occurs less frequently, the ratios are larger. Probably the reason that adjectives occur more frequently than nouns in the "Lotus Eaters" (5) is Bloom's transitory, information-gathering activities in this chapter. Bloom strolls along the quay, stopping at the post office and drug store and greeting friends. In a visit with M'Coy, Bloom uses adjectives to describe the state of his health, the death of Dignam, and forthcoming events in Molly's career. At the druggist's, Bloom uses adjectives to describe Molly's skin lotion and the soap that he wants. In the Aeolus episode, he describes the Keyes advertisement that he wishes to place in the *Telegraph*. Stephen, on the other hand, speaks in parables in his section of the Aeolus, using such long adjective phrases as "one and fourpenceworth" and "in a red tin letterbox moneybox" [*U*, p. 145].

What the preceding discussion has shown is the dissimilarity between dialogue and narration styles in *Ulysses*, and, with certain exceptions, the similarity between dialogue in the novel and dramatic dialogue. Whether similar observations can be made about dialogue and narration in other novels is, as yet, undetermined. In any case, some more specific conclusions about these two discourses in *Ulysses* should be noted. First, only Bloom's dialogue (and two speeches by Bob Doran in the Cyclops episode [12]) are affected by the local narrative style. Stephen's dialogue seems unaffected by narrative style, but there may be an explanation for this possibility. Stephen speaks in only one episode in the second half of *Ulysses* (excluding his dramatic dialogue in the Circe episode [15]), whereas only in the second half of the novel does Bloom's dialogue style change. In fact, *Ulysses* seems stylistically to fall into two halves, Chapters 1-9 and 10-18. In chapters 1-9, even Bloom's talking seems reasonably consistent across episodes.

Perhaps, during the long process of composing *Ulysses*, Joyce may have subscribed completely to Ibsen's theory of dialogue. In composing the novel's second half, he evidently had in mind another role for character speech. Perhaps he had begun to ponder the way in which one person's speech is reported by another: that the report is often an inaccurate representation of the speech as it was transmitted.

This possibility has far-ranging implications for *Ulysses*. If the reader cannot accurately determine *how* a remark was stated, how can he determine *what* was said? Since the style and content of Bloom's speeches have been called into question, can one safely assume the accuracy of the narrative modes that report Stephen's dialogue? Does an attributed narrator more accurately report his own speech than an external narrator reports another character's speech? These are questions that need answering. For now, our theory that dialogue only tentatively and in certain cases reveals character in *Ulysses* is a conservative observation indeed.

References

[1] James Joyce, *Ulysses* (New York: Vintage Books, 1961). References to *Ulysses* will be marked *"U"* and will appear in the text.

[2] One short speech in the Cyclops episode (12).

[3] Lubomir Dolezel, *Narrative Modes in Czech Literature* (Toronto: University of Toronto Press, 1973), p. 3.

[4] Dolezel, p. 3.

[5] Eric Bentley, *The Playwright as Thinker* (New York: Meridian Books, 1946), p. 97.

[6] Bentley, p. 102.

[7] William York Tindall, *A Reader's Guide to James Joyce* (New York: Farrar, Strauss, and Geroux, 1959), p. 106.

[8] *The Critical Writings of James Joyce,* ed. Ellsworth Mason and Richard Ellman (New York: The Viking Press, 1964), pp. 49 and 63, respectively.

[9] For a general discussion of the ways narration is attributed to a character see Donald Ross, *Who's Talking? How Characters Become Narrators in Fiction,* MLN, 91 (1976), 1222-42; for attribution in *Ulysses* see Chapter 2 of "A Stylistic Analysis of Dialogue and Narrative Modes in James Joyce's *Ulysses*" (Pringle), an unpublished dissertation.

[10] These remarks about Ibsen's dialogue are from an interview with Alan Yaffe of the Theatre Department, Wright State University, April 10, 1977.

[11] Donald Ross, "The Use of Word-Class Distribution Data for Stylistics: Keat's Sonnets and Chicken Soup," *Poetics,* 6 (1977), forthcoming.

[12] W.M. Baillie, "Authorship Attribution in Jacobean Dramatic Texts" in J.L. Mitchell, ed., *Computers in the Humanities* (Edinburgh: University Press, 1974), pp. 73-81.

[13] J. Mackay, "A Stylistic Analysis of Thomas Hardy's novels," (mimeo) delivered at the Symposium on the Use of Computers in Literary and Linguistic Research (Oxford, April, 1976).

[14] S. Keith Lee and Donald Ross, "Statistical Models of the Distribution of Monosyllabic and Polysyllabic English Words," *SMIL* (1975), 51-63.

[15] Elizabeth A. Sikes, "Conrad's Conscious Artistry: A Computer-Assisted Exploration of Style in *Heart of Darkness,*" unpublished Ph.D. dissertation (South Carolina), 1976.

Style in Syntax:
A Computer Aided Quantitative Study

D. Srinivasan

Syntactic analysis of random samples of sentences from three novels of Thomas Mann, *Buddenbrooks, Doktor Faustus,* and *Felix Krull* and statistical rank correlation tests show that Thomas Mann's preferences amongst the rules for generating a complex sentence from a basic nucleus have remained the same over the years in the three novels under study. The paper suggests an interpretation for the statistical indices developed.[1]

If it is not possible to define what an image is, what a motif, what a metaphor, it is equally difficult to define what style is. Discussions on stylistic analyses tend to end up with the question: What is style? Statistical studies of language data have perforce concerned themselves with quantifiable features of language such as the frequency distribution of lexical items in a corpus, or mean number of syllables per sentence. Implicit in this approach is the idea that style is the aggregate set of all linguistic features in the text under study. Krallmann has traced the historical development of statistical studies of language.[2]

Extensive studies have been undertaken by Fucks and his collaborators with the syllable as unit.[3] Lauter investigated the fit of Poisson distribution and came to the conclusion that the sequence of words with respect to their length in terms of syllable follows randomly, but the sequence of sentence length is not random: generally long sentences tend to stand near long sentences and short sentences near short ones.[4] With the help of frequency polygons, mean and standard deviation, Fucks shows how far politicians use similar styles and how it is with modern prosaists.[5] He represents a text of an author as a point in the co-ordinate space by taking on the x-axis the mean number of words per sentence, and on the y-axis the mean number of syllables per word. Weiss has shown that there exists a correlation between the mean word length in syllables and mean sentence length in terms of words. In other words, shorter sentences tend to have shorter words and longer sentences tend to have longer words also.[6]

In the current study the scope of the statistical approach has been extended by subjecting syntactic analysis to quantification. The fundamental question to which we seek an answer is: Is the phrase structure exhibited by an author in his works an 'invariant' characteristic?[7] In developing his sentences from a basic nucleus does the author display any hidden constancy in the preferences which he shows for the various rules of production by which he has expanded his sentence?

For our methodology we have assumed that in writing a complex sentence an author proceeds from a basic nucleus. We have further assumed that a basic nucleus consists of slots of three categories: noun, verb, and an adjective/adverb:

$$S = (N_1)(N_2)..(N_r)(V(r))(Adj/Adv),$$

r representing the number of noun slots which the valence of the verb permits. One adverbial or adjectival slot, whether bound or free, is regarded as part of the core structure.

The length of the sentence has been considered along two dimensions, one which may be termed horizontal and the other vertical. A horizontal expansion is said to take place when the writer chooses in the place of one slot several slots of equivalent grammatical status. A transitive verb, for instance, is followed by a noun. If the author chooses to use several noun phrases instead of just one, then he has expanded the phrase horizontally. Grammatically a single noun phrase would have satisfied the valence of the verb. All production rules of the type N – NN are of this category.

A vertical expansion takes place when within the same slot the author uses other grammatical categories to expand the phrase. A noun phrase 'the man' can be expanded into 'the old man with the child' where 'old' and 'with the child' are modifiers of the same rank introduced by the production rule: N – N(A) and N – N(P) and P – P(N).

In transcribing phrase structure we therefore first of all determine what slots are to be considered basic to the verb in the main sentence. Once the number of basic slots has been determined the sentence is further analyzed to see how each slot has been expanded and filled. A noun slot, for instance, needs a noun and often a determiner for filling up the slot. All other additions alone are considered expansions. At each depth a finite number of rules constitute the possibilities of expanding a slot by means of a modifier. Below are given some production rules by way of illustration. The initial number denotes the code number assigned to the rule.

  1 A – A(A) an adjective expanded by an adverb
  2 A – A(O) an adjective modified by a clause
  5 G – G(G) a genitive noun modified by a genitive noun
10 N – N(O) a noun by a minor clause other than relative
15 N – N(R) a noun by a relative clause
20 I – I(P) infinitive by a prepositional phrase
21 O – O(O) a minor clause by a minor clause
33 A – AA doubling the adjective
34 G – GG doubling the genitive

In all there were forty rules of production, rules 33 to 40 representing horizontal expansion, that is, duplication of the same category. Adjectives and adverbs were treated as belonging to the same class of modifiers.

The depth of each expansion was determined according to the level of dependency. The first depth was reserved for the reduplication rules:

     A – AA, N – NN, etc.

For instance 'He walked out slowly and calmly' would give us the adverbial expansion 'slowly and calmly.' The adverbial slot has been doubled and then filled by two adverbs. At deeper levels reduplication was counted on a par, with the dependent attributes filling up the duplicated slots. For instance the phrase: 'in a fit of anger and frustration' will give the expansion:

```
in a fit  P  (   N
   of anger          (   G
   and frustration        G )   )
   =  P  (   N  (   G  G  )   )
           1      2          1  0
depths:  1  2      3
rule no.:  -  26   11          34
```

The first depth is vacant because there is only one adverbial slot, without duplication. At the second depth the rule applied is $P - P(N)$ i.e. No. 26. At the third depth the noun phrase is expanded by two genitives. Hence we have two rules, $N - N(G)$ and $G - GG$, which are accorded the same depth.

The syntactic analysis was based on the operational grammar developed by Glinz, making use of substitution tests, displacement tests and transformation tests, to verify intuitive grammatical analysis.[8] Glinz's technique has been used, not because any claim to its theoretical superiority is made here, but because it was found adequate for the empirical study. The approach is pragmatic in the sense that intermediary grammatical categories were dispensed with and the production rules reflected the concern of authors usually with lexical items as they develop their sentences, and not with grammatical categories.

As in the grammars of other natural languages, problems of uncertainty arise also in the syntactic resolution of sentences in German. In particular they apply to quasi-parenthetical expressions, certain adverbials of circumstance, and participal constructions. Duden (1966, sect. 6100) gives for instance the following examples as a case where the absolute construction is related to the object:

... indem sie (die Blutung) *ihn* zwang, ... sich wieder flach auf den Brettersitz hinzustrecken, *das feuchte Tuch auf der Nase* (Th. Mann)
(in that the bleeding compelled him, ... to stretch himself again flat on the wooden seat, the wet cloth on his nose).

Here, actually, a recursion has taken place:

die Blutung zwang ihn
(the bleeding compelled him)
er streckte sich auf den Brettersitz
(he stretched himself on the wooden seat)
er hielt das feuchte Tuch auf der Nase
(he held the wet cloth on his nose)

The last sentence is embedded in the second sentence and not the first one, since a combination of first and third will generate:

die Blutung zwang ihn, das feuchte Tuch auf der Nase zu halten,
(the bleeding compelled him, to hold the wet cloth on his nose)

and not:

die Blutung zwang ihn, das feuchte Tuch auf der Nase,
(the bleeding compelled him, the wet cloth on his nose)

whereas we can have:

er streckte sich auf den Brettersitz, das feuchte Tuch auf der Nase.
(he stretched himself on the wooden seat, the wet cloth on his nose)

Thus the absolute construction is not really 'objektberzogen' but related to the subject of the verb 'hinstrecken.' Apart from absolute constructions also adverbials such as 'eigentlich,' 'im Gegenteil,' 'andererseits,' pose problems in syntactic analysis.

Das Vergnuegen, oder eigentlich, die Heiterkeit, die ihre herrschaftlilche Schoenheit mir erregt, ... *(Felix Krull)*
(The pleasure, or actually, the exhilaration, which their majestic beauty excited in me, ...)

Arguments could be advanced both for treating 'eigentlich' in the above sentence as quasi-parenthetical or else as modifier to 'Heiterkeit.' In many cases transposition test or case markers sometimes add weight to one argument so that decision is facilitated.

The computer was utilized for resolving the formulae back into rules, the main reason for the use of the computer being avoidance of errors.[9] The program checked first the number of left and right parentheses. The analysis of the rules started with the innermost bracket. Once the subroutine had compared the signs with the rules and stored the relevant information the left parenthesis was changed into a right parenthesis by another subroutine. For instance, in the formula:

```
    1     2     3     4     3   2   1   0
  P  (  N  (  P  (  N  (  A  )  )  )  )
  1  2  3  4  5  6  7  8  9  10 11 12 13
```

the subroutine would start with the portion:

```
       4     3
     N  (  A  )
     7  8  9  10
```

and after storage of rule, change the left parenthesis at position 8 into a right parenthesis, thus giving:

```
  P  (  N  (  P  (  N  )  A  )  )  )  )
  1  2  3  4  5  6  7  8  9  10 11 12 13
```

so that innermost bracket now becomes positions 5,6,7,8. The program also arranged to rules according to depth and increasing order of magnitude.

The sizes of the samples were as follows:

Buddenbrooks – I   sample (sequential)   – 708 rules
Buddenbrooks – II   sample (sequential)   – 608 rules
Buddenbrooks – III   sample (random)   – 1125 rules
Felix Krull – IV   sample (random)   – 782 rules
Doktor Faustus – V   sample (random)   – 1501 rules

In all, 484 sentences were analyzed.

Table 1 gives the ranks of the high frequency rules as found in the samples from the three novels. The most striking result is that the ranks of *Felix Krull* and *Doktor Faustus* are exactly the same, revealing 100% positive correlation. The rho values for the sequential samples I and II from *Buddenbrooks* show the least correlation, which is in conformity with the expectation that the same novel would show heterogeneity in parts.

Table 18 shows that among the grammar categories the prepositions occur with the highest frequency. As P – P(N), the prepositional expansion, is the only rule in the list which deals with a functional word, one may not be much surprised that this rule, No. 26, tops the list each time, nor that N – N(A) (the expansion of a noun by a modifier) figures as the second most frequent. But there is no particular reason why the other rules should occur in a particular order. Even assuming that the rules are likely to vary by not more than one rank either way, the number of permutations possible with the remaining nine rules is 55, so that the probability of a particular arrangement is 1/55 only. This is the calculation under the stringent restriction that there are unknown stabilizing factors in language by reason of which the rank of each rule does not vary beyond a very narrow limit. The results can therefore be taken as significant.

What conclusions can we derive from the statistical results with regard to the style of Thomas Mann? The high correlation between those from *Buddenbrooks* and *Felix Krull* and between those from *Buddenbrooks* and *Faustus* shows that the generative structure of the novels are the same. That is, the apparently highly complicated sentence structure of *Doktor Faustus*, where the periodic construction is longer than in *Buddenbrooks*, has fundamentally the same syntactic structure. Wherein lies then the difference? Let us take a look at the mean number of syllables per sentence and the mean number of rules applied per sentence in the three novels:

	i	j
Buddenbrooks (1901)	35.3	9.78
Felix Krull (1954)	38.7	12.01
Doktor Faustus (1947)	50.8	18.08[10]

These figures show that the sentence length has increased from *Buddenbrooks* to *Faustus*, and also that the number of applications of the rules has consequently registered an increase. This means that the author has expanded the width of the sentence without altering his preference for and among the dominant rules. Variation in style has therefore to take into consideration both quantity as well as quality of change. The method provides a quantitative index for defining the texture of a passage. The sequential samples I and II and the random sample III from *Buddenbrooks* have, for the 11 dominant rules, the following mean and standard deviations:

	mean	s.d.
Sample I	6.33	7.22
Sample II	5.98	5.32
Sample III	7.71	6.70

Taking the random sample as norm, we find that the mean of the first sample is less than the norm mean, but the dispersion is less. The smaller means denote that the eleven dominant rules do not cover a large percentage of the rules and that a larger number of rules have been employed in the text. The dispersion indicates how the values of the various rules are distributed around the mean. The higher the dispersion, the greater are the differences among the various values. The lower the dispersion, the lesser the marked preference which the author shows for any particular rule or rules. The density of a text moves along two dimensions.

One of the minor interesting results of the investigation concerns the application of rule 38, P – PP. Although rule 26 P – P(N) has the highest frequency, 38 comes at the bottom of the table. This means that Thomas Mann prefers to develop the phrase from one node. An adverbial phrase can be developed from a preposition, and if at the start two or three prepositions are taken and their nouns developed, a complicated structure will ensue wherein the top rule would have been P – PP. But Mann avoids this. On the other hand rule 36, N – NN (duplication of the noun slot) occurs with high frequency. We may describe this graphically:

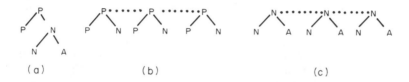

(a)   (b)   (c)

A possible criticism of the method could follow the line that no subcategories have been taken into account and that the grammatical analysis tends to concern itself more with features of surface structure. It may be pointed out in defence that a writer like Thomas Mann is extremely conscious of so called surface structure, as can be discerned from the innumerable plays on patterns of construction which he exhibits:

geradlinigen, weisslackierten und mit einem Loewenkopf verzierten Sofa
(Straight-backed, white enamelled sofa, decorated with a golden lion's head)

N (A A A (P (N (A))))

breit, doppelt und mit einem Ausdruck von Behaglichkeit
(broad, doubled and with an expression of ease)

A A P (N (P (N)))

hoch, steil, und mit ploetzlichem Drucke
(high, steep and with sudden pressure)

A A P (N (A))

starke, aschblonde, mit weissen Faeden durchsetzte Kotelletten
(Strong ashblond side-burns interspersed with white threads)

N (A A A (P (N (A))))

The utility of the statistical technique lies in evening out the effect of syntactic ambiguities inherent in language. A fruitful application of the method would lie in investigating the syntax of works belonging to a particular genre, say the novellas.

References

[1]Valuable guidance received from Prof. D.D. Mahulkar of the Department of Linguistics, M.S.University of Baroda, is acknowledged with pleasure.

[2]D. Krallman, *Statistische Methoden in der stilistischen Textanalyse* (Ph.D. Dissertation, Bonn 1966).

[3]W. Fucks, *Mathematische Analyse von Sprachelementen, Sprachstil und Sprachen, Arbeitsgemeinschaft fuer Forschung d.Landes NRW*, Heft 34a(1953), Westdentsdur, Verlag.

[4]J. Lauter, *Untersuchungen zur Sprache von Kants Kritik der* Reinen Vernunft") (Ph.D. Dissertation, Bonn 1966).

[5]W. Fucks, *Nach allen Regeln der Kunst, Deutsche Verlags-Anstalt,* (Stuttgart, 1968).

[6]H. Weiss, *Statistische Untersuchungen ueber Satzlaenge und Satzgliederung als autorspezifische Stilmerkmale* (Ph.D. Dissertation, Aachen, 1967).

[7]The term 'invariant characteristics' has been used by Sol Saporta in "The Application of Linguistics to the study of Poetic Language," T.A. Sebeok (Ed.), New York, 1960.

[8]H. Glinz, *Die Innere Form des Deutschen* (Francke Verlag, Bern, 1968).

[9]I am indebted to Mr. H.M. Dannhauer of I.Physics Institute of Technical University, Aachen and Dr. S. Ramani, T.I.F.R., Bombay, for assistance in programming.

[10]Data on Syllable count from Weiss (1967).

Rule	Bud.I	Bud.II	Bud.III	Felix K.IV	Faustus V
26 P(N)	1	1	1	1	1
10 N(A)	2	2	2	2	2
36 N N	9	4	3	3	3
1 A(A)	4	5	5	4	4
33 AA	10.5	3	4	5	5
11 N(G)	7	7	8	6	6
16 N(P)	5	6	7	7	7
15 N(R)	6	8	6	8	8
3 A(P)	8	10	10	9	9
38 PP	10.5	9	9	10	10
34 GG	3	11	11	11	11

Note: *Buddenbrooks* I, II are sequential samples, the rest are random samples. Rho values for rank difference in frequency of rules between pairs of samples:

$$(= 1 - 6 \sum D^2/(N(N^2 - 1)))$$

	I & II	I & III	II & III	III & IV
Rho	0.23	0.30	0.96	0.93

Table 1. Ranks of rules according to their frequency in the various samples

	26	10	34	1	16	36
I	–	–	3.67	–	–	1.41
II	12.99	6.49	1.55	1.69	3.10	0.84
III	6.22	5.36	1.55	1.55	1.27	0.14
IV	2.26	3.95	0.14	0.99	0.56	0.14
V	1.27	0.42	0.14	0.70	0.14	–
VI	0.28	0.28	–	0.42	0.14	–
VII	0.14	–	–	–	–	–
VIII	0.14	–	–	–	–	–
IX	–	0.14	–	–	–	–
Total	23.30	16.64	7.05	5.35	5.21	2.53

High frequency rules arranged according to rank – Sample I (*Buddenbrooks*)

26	P(N)	23.30
10	N(A)	16.64
34	GG	7.05
1	A(A)	5.35
16	N(P)	5.21
15	N(R)	3.37
11	N(G)	3.10
3	A(P)	3.09
36	NN	2.53
33	AA	0.00
38	PP	0.00
total		69.64

Table 2. Relative frequencies of the high frequency rules in Sample I (Buddenbrooks)

3	15	11	33	38
–	–	–	–	–
1.55	1.41	0.99	–	–
0.70	0.84	1.55	–	–
0.56	0.70	0.28	–	–
0.14	0.28	0.14	–	–
–	0.14	0.14	–	–
0.14	–	–	–	–
–	–	–	–	–
–	–	–	–	–
3.09	3.37	3.10	–	–

Table 2 continued

	26	10	34	1	16	36
I	–	–	–	–	–	2.79
II	10.36	6.56	0.16	1.81	2.63	3.12
III	4.61	3.28	–	1.64	0.82	0.49
IV	1.48	1.97	–	0.82	0.32	0.32
V	0.82	–	–	0.82	0.16	0.16
VI	0.49	0.49	–	0.65	0.16	–
VII	–	–	–	–	–	–
VIII	–	–	–	–	–	–
Total	17.76	12.30	0.16	5.74	4.09	6.88

High frequency rules arranged according to rank – Sample II *(Buddenbrooks)*

26	P(N)	17.76
10	N(A)	12.30
33	AA	9.39
36	NN	6.88
1	A(A)	5.74
16	N(P)	4.09
11	N(G)	3.12
15	N(R)	2.95
38	PP	2.12
3	A(P)	1.30
34	GG	0.16
	Total	65.81

Table 3. Relative frequencies of the high frequency rules in Sample II (Buddenbrooks)

	26	10	34	33	1	16
I	–	–	–	1.69	–	–
II	12.44	12.09	–	4.26	3.38	3.82
III	6.22	3.91	0.09	0.98	2.58	0.89
IV	1.78	2.31	0.09	0.89	0.73	0.71
V	0.73	0.09	–	0.09	0.27	–
VI	0.09	0.27	0.09	0.09	0.09	–
Total	21.26	18.67	0.27	8.00	7.05	5.42

High frequency rules arranged according to rank – Sample III *(Buddenbrooks)*

26	P(N)	21.26
10	N(A)	18.67
36	NN	9.77
33	AA	8.00
1	A(A)	7.05
15	N(R)	5.60
16	N(P)	5.42
11	N(G)	4.90
38	PP	2.31
3	A(P)	1.51
34	GG	0.27
	Total	84.76

Table 4. Relative frequencies of the high frequency rules in Random Sample III (Buddenbrooks)

33	3	15	11	38
2.31	–	–	–	1.64
3.45	–	1.97	1.81	0.32
2.31	0.49	0.49	0.99	0.16
1.32	0.65	0.49	0.16	–
–	0.16	–	0.16	–
–	–	–	–	–
–	–	–	–	–
9.39	1.30	2.95	3.12	2.12

Table 3 continued

36	3	15	11	38
6.22	–	–	–	1.42
0.62	0.80	4.00	2.76	0.89
2.13	0.62	0.89	1.16	–
0.62	–	0.62	0.71	–
0.18	0.18	0.09	–	–
–	–	0.09	0.18	–
9.77	1.51	5.60	4.90	2.31

Table 4 continued

	26	10	34	33	1	16
I	–	–	–	1.66	–	–
II	10.36	9.97	0.64	2.17	1.91	2.30
III	4.48	4.73	0.52	0.90	2.04	1.41
IV	3.32	2.30	–	0.52	1.15	0.64
V	0.90	1.41	–	0.39	0.39	0.39
VI	1.02	0.52	–	–	0.39	0.13
VII	0.13	0.52	0.52	0.26	–	0.13
VIII	0.13	–	–	–	0.13	–
Total	20.34	19.45	1.68	5.90	6.01	5.00

High frequency rules arranged according to rank – Sample IV *(Felix Krull)*

26	P(N)	20.34
10	N(A)	19.45
36	NN	9.50
1	A(A)	6.01
33	AA	5.90
11	N(G)	5.75
16	N(P)	5.00
15	N(R)	4.24
3	A(P)	2.21
38	PP	2.05
34	GG	1.68
Total		82.13

Table 5. Relative frequencies of the high frequency rules in Random Sample IV (Felix Krull)

	26	10	34	33	1	16
I	–	–	–	2.86	–	–
II	9.86	7.40	0.27	2.07	2.47	2.73
III	7.40	4.33	–	1.53	2.33	1.07
IV	2.53	1.93	0.33	0.73	1.93	0.67
V	1.73	0.87	0.20	0.20	0.67	0.40
VI	0.67	0.87	–	0.13	0.33	–
VII	0.07	0.33	–	0.07	0.20	–
VIII	–	0.07	0.07	–	0.07	–
IX	–	–	–	–	–	–
X	0.07	–	–	–	–	–
Total	22.33	15.80	0.87	7.59	8.00	4.87

High frequency rules arranged according to rank – Random Sample V *(Doktor Faustus)*

26	P(N)	22.33
10	N(A)	15.80
36	NN	8.46
1	A(A)	8.00
33	AA	7.59
11	N(G)	6.06
16	N(P)	4.87
15	N(R)	3.28
3	A(P)	2.94
38	PP	2.93
34	GG	0.87
Total		83.13

Table 6. Relative frequencies of the high frequency rules in Random Sample V (Doktor Faustus)

36	3	15	11	38
5.64	–	–	–	1.66
2.82	0.65	2.69	3.32	–
0.52	0.78	0.90	1.91	0.26
0.26	0.26	0.13	0.26	–
0.13	0.52	0.26	0.13	0.13
0.13	–	0.13	–	–
–	–	0.13	–	–
–	–	–	–	–
9.50	2.21	4.24	5.75	2.05

Table 5 continued

36	3	15	11	38
5.73	–	–	–	2.13
1.53	1.00	1.67	2.73	0.53
0.60	1.00	0.80	1.73	–
0.53	0.87	0.67	1.07	–
0.07	–	–	0.40	0.07
–	–	–	0.13	0.20
–	–	0.07	–	–
–	–	0.07	–	–
–	0.07	–	–	–
–	–	–	–	–
8.46	2.94	3.28	6.06	2.93

Table 6 continued

25	Prepositions	119.56 (per mille)
15	Determiners	132.75 (per mille)
23	Pronouns	77.42 (per mille)
27	Other Particles	98.60 (per mille)
1	Noun	1.33 (per mille)
		429.66

Table 7.   Relative frequency of 91 most frequent words from Keating's list

3
Lexicography

The Dictionary of Old English and the Computer

A. Cameron

From its very beginning, the *Dictionary of Old English* project has been planned with computer-processing in mind. If our plans carry through it will be one of the first dictionaries to use the computer at all stages of its compilation from the inputting of texts at the beginning to the type-setting of the actual volumes at the end. At present we are half-way through our work, and the computer has served us well. I would like to give an account of the project, outlining its brief history and emphasizing the part that computers and computer programmers have played in it.[1] I would especially like to draw attention to the places where either our planning has worked out well, or the realities have differed from our expectations.

My realisation that a new dictionary of Old English was a scholarly necessity dates from the mid-60's when I made a semantic study of a small group of Old English nouns and adjectives for my dissertation. Sheer frustration brought me to it. The present scholars' dictionary of Old English, *An Anglo-Saxon Dictionary,* published by the Clarendon Press, is a pair of large quarto volumes totalling 2123 pages of closely packed print. It is an accretive dictionary. The traditions of Old English lexicography begin in the 16th century with the work of Laurence Nowell and continue in the 17th and 18th centuries with the dictionaries of Somner, Lye and Manning; each editor builds on his predecessors' work. The involvement of Dr. Joseph Bosworth (1789-1876), the first editor of the present dictionary, began in 1838 when he published his *Dictionary of the Anglo-Saxon Language.* He spent the remainder of his life revising and improving this dictionary. At the time of his death he was at work on a final recension; the letters A to F were in print, and he had revised the text to page 288. The task of editing his huge mass of material was given to Professor T. Northcote Toller (1844-1930) of the University of Manchester. Professor Toller brought out the dictionary in four parts between 1882 and 1898 and then set to work on a supplement (which for the first letters of the alphabet from A to F is fuller than the original dictionary). This appeared in three parts between 1908 and 1921. In its biography of Bosworth, the *Dictionary of National Biography* tersely notes, "The work was received with general dissatisfaction."[2]

The dictionary has been reprinted several times in the twentieth century, most recently in 1972 with revised addenda of 68 pages by the late Professor Alistair Campbell. It now causes even more dissatisfaction. The main difficulties stem from the fact that Bosworth's own work predates the revolution in historical English lexicography brought about by Sir James Murray and the *New* or *Oxford English Dictionary,* while Toller makes use of the new techniques. The two editors employ very different systems of setting up entries and different systems of headwords. This means that for any one word, the user must check in at least two, often three, and sometimes as many as ten or twelve places in the dictionary before the possibilities are exhausted.

Without the computer, our best hope for an improved Old English dictionary would have been a revision, a bringing up to date of Bosworth and Toller's work. However, with the possibility of computer sorting, we had the rarest of opportunities in lexicography, a fresh start. The other factor which made a fresh start possible is the great deal of recent useful work on Old English texts. The corpus has been beautifully defined and catalogued by N.R. Ker (1957), H. Marquardt (1961), Peter Sawyer (1968), and Elisabeth Okasha (1971).[3] Using their information, the best way to begin on an Old English dictionary seemed to be to put the entire corpus of texts in Old English into computer-readable form, to concord it, and base a new dictionary on the results, comparing them all the while with the citations and entries of Bosworth and Toller.

My own interest in using computers to handle texts also goes back to my days as a graduate student, when in Oxford I attended classes given by Dr. Trevor Howard-Hill on his concordances to individual plays by Shakespeare. In the *Dictionary of Old English,* we are of the second generation in our use of the computer, and much of our success has been a result of being able to talk to those who have gone before us. By the time we began to plan our project in 1969 there were already 4 or 5 scholars active in preparing concordances of Old English texts, and they were generous in sharing their successes, as well as warning us of their failures. As a subject, the use of computers in the humanities is extraordinarily well served with guides to work in progress and directories of scholars active, so that it is possible to learn rapidly from the works of others.

Major work on the *Dictionary of Old English* is going on in three places, the University of Toronto, the University of Wisconsin at Madison, and the Université de Montréal. The work has been funded by the Canada Council at the two Canadian universities, and by the *National Science Foundation* at the University of Wisconsin. All three universities have also been generous in their support of the work going on within them. I and a staff of 5 are taking care of editorial work in Toronto. Until last year my co-editor was Mr. Christopher Ball of Lincoln College, Oxford, but he has had to withdraw because of the pressure of administrative duties. The first stage of computer-processing, up to a set of concordances organized under dictionary headwords, is directed by Professor Richard L. Venezky, now of the University of Delaware, and his research team at the University of Wisconsin. The second stage of computer processing, the editing process for the dictionary and the photo-composition of the final volumes, is directed by Professor Paul Bratley and Dr. Serge Lusignan at the Université de Montréal. As we get into the editing of the dictionary itself, we hope that editorial consultation and perhaps some writing of entries will be shared among scholars of the universities of North America, Britain and Western Europe.

As well as a large scholars' dictionary, we also hope to produce our concordance materials by microfiche, as well as a student's dictionary and a series of volumes which will get into print all the previously unedited Old English texts, together with the vocabulary studies and bibliographies which are essential to the project. This series is well under way, first under the direction of Dr. Malcolm Godden of Exeter College, Oxford, and more recently under that of Professor Roberta Frank of the University of Toronto.

In all these endeavours we are guided by an international advisory committee with members from Canadian, American, British and German universities. In the beginning, we planned the dictionary as a fifteen year project, allowing five years for collection of materials, five years for putting them in computer readable form and five years for editing the dictionary. I now realize that the proportions of time were wrong. After seven years of serious work, the collecting process is complete, the texts are all in computer-readable form, their proofreading and concording is well advanced. We are beginning to build up slip files in Toronto; but the editing of the dictionary itself looms much larger than it did in 1970. All in all, I would say that we are slightly ahead of schedule, and I still hope to have the dictionary out by 1985.

I now would like to give you an account of the project in greater detail, showing how we met various problems and how the computer has been of use to us.

The project began with two international conferences held in Toronto to discuss its feasibility. At the first of these in March 1969 we specifically discussed questions of handling Old English texts by computer and heard reports from scholars active in the field. At the second, in September 1970, the dictionary team presented a plan of work, including a first sketch of the computer system by Professor Venezky, a set of specimen entries, and a textual bibliography of the corpus. We received much helpful criticism of these from the assembled scholars and were on our way.

In the first two years of the project, most of our attention went into the collection of materials, microfilms of the manuscripts containing Old English texts, and printed editions. From the point of view of computer application, it was a time of experimentation. At the 1970 conference, Professors Bessinger and Smith had very generously given us a copy of their concordance to the *Anglo-Saxon Poetic Records,* so we were able to go through it in detail. In addition, Professor Smith and I prepared two Ælfric concordances, to the *Lives of Saints,* and to Pope's edition of the homilies, in a keyword-in-context format (KWIC).[4] Our conclusion from these exercises was that for lexical work we would need a concordance with a variable field rather than a fixed field format, so that our concordance citations would be semantic units determined by editorial punctuation, rather than arbitrary ones. It has been reassuring to see that the Dutch lexicographer de Tollenaere has come to similar conclusions.[5] During this time Professor Venezky was able to visit historical dictionaries using the computer in Italy and Israel, and was able to get much useful comparative information. In 1972-73, he began to develop the Lexico system and we began the preparation of texts for it.

Our idea in publishing Professor Venezky's preliminary sketch of the computer system was that scholars in various universities could help with the inputting of texts if they knew the conventions we followed. With one important exception this help did not come forward. The exception was the text of Ælfric's First and Second Series of Catholic Homilies prepared from their forthcoming editions by Professor Peter Clemoes and Dr. Malcolm Godden at Cambridge University. For this work Clemoes and Godden used a format similar to ours and we were able to enter the text in our collection without much difficulty.

However, once we put our minds to it, the problem of inputting the corpus of Old English texts was possible. Between autumn of 1972 and the autumn of 1976, with the help of a splendid typist, Mrs. Elaine Quanz, we edited, checked, and typed the three million or so words of text which constitute the corpus of Old English.

We gave a great deal of thought to the problem of inputting our text, and the problems of error rates with punch cards, and after reading about Professor Ben Schneider's work with the *London Stage Project,* we decided to type on sheets for optical scanning machines. We found a company in Toronto with Scan-Data equipment, so, after purchasing an OCR-B typing element and doing some test runs, we began to work through our texts.

We found that the system for identifying texts which I had used in the list of texts presented to the 1970 conference worked very well for entering and keeping track of texts in a computer corpus. This system has an initial letter identifying genre (A – poetry, B – prose, C – interlinear glosses, D – glossaries, E – runic texts, F – non-runic inscriptions), and numbers indicating sub-divisions by kind of text or author within the genre. We found that this system could be very easily expanded if any text had natural divisions in its lineation system, or if we wished to type in a second manuscript version or lexical variants of a text, by simply adding a decimal point and a new range of numbers. In the dictionary itself a corrected and updated list of texts showing these amplifications will be printed.

In preparing texts for the computer we checked printed editions against the facsimile of the manuscript used. For unedited texts we made transcripts from our facsimiles to be updated as proper editions appear. Any discrepancies between the manuscript facsimile and the printed edition were marked with a diagonal slash. We soon found that the simplest marking system was the best, and set up a filing system where the xeroxed, marked copy was filed together with any notes on special problems or conventions in the text. We tried to keep the text lineation systems as simple as possible, with a continuous line, or chapter and verse reference wherever possible. Sometimes, however, we have kept page and line references of particular editions, when these seemed easiest to use.

For the three Old English characters not available on IBM typewriters and keypunches we used the substitute characters suggested by Professor Venezky. In addition we marked with a dash the hooked e found in manuscripts, so that we could check its distribution. We found that we had no difficulty with the substitute characters, and came very quickly to think of 'æ', 'þ' and 'ð' as '$', '*' and '+', respectively. In the meantime, the University of Toronto Computer Centre has obtained a Library of Congress print chain, so that for proofreading we have the original characters.

The scanner worked well for the most part, although we found that it was more prone to errors than our typist. In particular it had difficulty recognizing the descenders of letters, so that "p's" often became "q's" or "g's". Because of this we have left our major proofreading until after the scanning stage. Even with the scanning errors, our error rate has been quite manageable, and probably averages between 10 and 15 errors per 100 lines of text. If we were beginning again now, I think we would use a display screen terminal with the text running on to a floppy disc or tape cartridge, as a method of inputting our text. However, the sheets typed for optical scanners worked well for us. It was reasonably economical and it allowed us to collect batches of text, which could be sent to the scanners at our own convenience.

Our first arrangement was to send our scanner tapes to Madison, Wisconsin, where they were divided into citation units (editorial sentences) and the new tapes returned to us for printing and proofreading. However, because of difficulties with errors in the systems of reference, particularly with mis-scanned brackets, we have taken to proofreading and editing the scanner tapes in Toronto and then sending them to Madison to be divided into citation units and concorded.

The editing system in Lexico allows us to call up the citation wanted. The correction is then typed in, and the corrected citation is verified. The errors which get through this proofreading and editing process are very few, perhaps one in two hundred lines of text. Most of these turn up in the first concording process and can be corrected then.

After correction, the texts are concorded in the Old English collating system worked out by Professor Venezky. We then take this first-stage concordance and the list of alphabetized keywords which follows it and, in a system which employs both editors and computers, each doing the kinds of classification he best can, the editor begins to match the keywords against the headwords under which they will appear in the dictionary. In this way all morphological and phonological variants will be 'lemmatized' or gathered under the appropriate headwords. If the match is an obvious or unambiguous one, then the editor can mark it so that it is made automatically in all subsequent texts. If there is a chance of homograph confusion, then the assignations are left for the editor to make, and he tags each citation.

We have begun work on this matching process and now have a file of about 10,000 matching rules. In recent first-stage concordances between 60 and 70% of the matches have been automatic, and we hope to get to between 70 and 80% when the system is fully in operation.

At either the first or the second concordance stage, slips can be generated for use in the dictionary office and for setting up a hand file. At present we have generated a large number of slips for the works of AElfric and the poetry at the first concordance stage and are using these to set up our headword list and our basic matching rules.

When all our texts have been concorded through the second stage, our work with the Lexico system will be finished. We hope that the resulting concordance can be issued in microfiche for the use of scholars and are presently working out ways and means for this.

When our editors have worked on this concorded material and have written drafts of entries, and in some cases have sent these drafts for comment and improvement to specialist consultants, we will begin the composition of the dictionary itself by computer. The system for this has already been sketched in its first form by Professor Bratley and Dr. Lusignan, and for the past two years we have been working with their research team.[6] The great advantage of their system, which consists of a display-screen terminal, a mini-computer and a photocomposer, is that it is self-contained and can be used for the life of the project without the disruptions and reprogrammings caused by changes in university computing equipment.

If all of this comes to pass, I hope that the University of Toronto Press will publish the *Dictionary of Old English* in four or five stout volumes around the year 1985. I now imagine it will be between 5000 and 6000 pages long, will have about 40,000 headwords and a rather more generous selection of citations than its predecessor. I hope it will be easier to use.

References

[1]The early progress of the project is given in:
A. Cameron, R. Frank and J. Leyerle, *Computers and Old English Concordances* (Toronto, 1970);
J. Leyerle, "'The Dictionary of Old English': A Progress Report," *CHum*, 5 (1971), 279-83;
R. Frank and A. Cameron, *A Plan for the Dictionary of Old English* (Toronto, 1973);
H. Gneuss, "Vorarbeiten und Vorüberlegungen zu einem neuen Wörterbuch des Altenglischen," in *Festschrift Prof. Dr. Herbert Koziol* (Wiener Beiträge zur englischen Philologie 75, Vienna, 1973), 105-15;
R.I. Page, "'The Proper Toil of Artless Industry': Toronto's Plan for an Old English Dictionary," *Notes and Queries,* 215 (1975), 146-55.

[2]L. Stephen and S. Lee, *Dictionary of National Biography* (London 1885-1901), reprinted in 22 vols., 1921-22, II, 902-04.

[3]N.R. Ker, *Catalogue of Manuscripts Containing Anglo-Saxon* (Oxford, 1957);
N.R. Ker, A Supplement to *Catalogue of Manuscripts Containing Anglo-Saxon, ASE,* 5 (1976), 121-131;
P.H. Sawyer, *Anglo-Saxon Charters: An Annotated List and Bibliography* (London, 1968);
H. Marquardt, *Bibliographie der Runeninschriften nach Fundorten I: Die Runeninschriften der Britischen Inseln* (Göttingen, 1961);
E. Okasha, *Handlist of Anglo-Saxon Non-runic Inscriptions* (Cambridge, 1971).

[4]W.W. Skeat, *AElfric's Lives of Saints* (EETS, 76, 82, 94, 114, London, 1881-1900); reprinted as 2 vols., 1966;
J.C. Pope, *Homilies of AElfric: A Supplementary Collection* (EETS, 259, 260, London, 1967-68).
Permission to run these concordances has been received from the Early English Text Society.

[5]F. de Tollenaere, "The Problem of the Context in Computer-Aided Lexicography," in A.J. Aitken, R.W. Bailey and N. Hamilton-Smith, *The Computer and Literary Studies* (Edinburgh, 1973, 25-35).

[6]P. Bratley and S. Lusignan, "Information Processing in Dictionary Making: Some Technical Guidelines," *CHum,* 10 (1976), 133-143.

SHAD (A Shakespeare Dictionary): Toward a Taxonomic Classification of the Shakespeare Corpus

M. Spevack

The International Conference on Computing in the Humanities (ICCH) has had a special role in the history of the Shakespeare Dictionary (SHAD), having served as platform and forum for the developing SHAD. In 1973, at ICCH-1, SHAD was introduced: its scope and aims were outlined, and the lemmatization process described.[1] In 1975, at ICCH-2, the lemmatization of the Shakespeare corpus well underway, some preliminaries for a semantic description were presented.[2] In the interim the Shakepeare corpus – some 900,000 word-tokens – has been fully lemmatized, the material analyzed and evaluated, and the boundaries of the first volume staked out. Since the outlines were suggested only recently at a meeting of the Association for Literary and Linguistic Computing, perhaps a glance at some of the material distributed in London will best serve as a general orientation and as an introduction to the question of the taxonomic classification of the Shakespeare corpus.[3] Figure 1 presents some of the possibilities for the first volume of SHAD: a sample morphological analysis and suitable statistical and distributional information.

1) HORSE is the lemma.
2) It is a noun.
3) It first appeared in the Old English period.
4) It is Germanic in rough etymology.
5) It appears in the word-forms 'horse' (s.), 'horse' (pl.), 'horses', 'horse's', 'horses','
6) Whose inflections indicate the singular form, the plural, the genitive singular, and the genitive plural, respectively, and
7) Whose frequencies are 235, 63, 4, 4.
8) The morphological family of which 'horse' is both head and member may be arranged alphabetically according to its morphemic structure for ease of reference. The members given first are monomorphemic, followed by those consisting of a prefix plus 'horse', followed by those consisting of a compound with 'horse' as the first element, followed by those consisting of a compound with 'horse' as the second element.
9) The word-class is given for each member.
10) The first recorded appearance in print is given for each member.
11) A play abbreviation after a date indicates that the member's first appearance in print is attributed to Shakespeare by the *OED*.
12) The statistics for 'horse' are given.
13) The morphological family structure is given. Horizontal edges represent compounding, the vertical edge conversion (zero derivation). Branching off from these are prefixations and suffixations.

14) The chronological distribution over Shakespeare's career is given.
15) Remarks are given. In this case, one instance of 'hobby-horse'
    (*WT* 1.2.276) is derived from the edition of Nicholas Rowe, who
    emends the First Folio reading 'Holy-Horse'.

A final decision as to the exact nature of the material and the format
in which it is best presented can only be made when the blocs of data
have been processed, evaluated, and compared against each other. That
is one of the first 'laws' of computer linguistics. It is also the experience
of SHAD with a taxonomic classification, a complementary body of information which, together with the morphological analysis, will make
up the first volume.

1	2	3	4	5	6	7	
Horse	n.	OE	Germ.	horse	s.	} 235	
				horse	pl.		
				horses	pl.	63	
				horse's	gen.s.	4	
				horses'	gen.pl.	4	

8		9	10	11	
horse				n.	OE
horse				v.	OE
fore-horse				n.	1483
unhorse				v.	LME
horse-back				n.	ME
horse-back-breaker				n.	1596	1H4
horse-drench				n.	1607	COR
horsehair				n.	ME
horse-leech				n.	ME
horseman				n.	ME
horsemanship				n.	1565
horse-piss				n.	1611	TMP
horseshoe				n.	ME
horse-stealer				n.	1599	AYL
horse-tail				n.	ME
horse-way				n.	985
fill-horse				n.	1596	MV
hobby-horse				n.	1557
malt-horse				n.	1561
pack-horse				n.	1475
post-horse				n.	1527
stalking-horse				n.	1519
trotting-horse				n.	1425

12	
family members:	23
word forms:	33
word-tokens:	366

Figure 1. (continued next page)

13

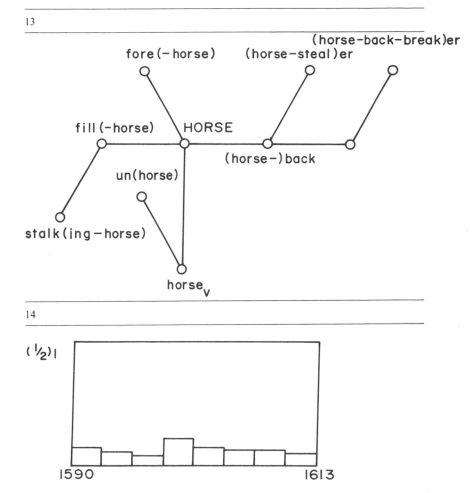

14

15

hobby-horse (WT 1.2.276)] Rowe; Holy-Horse F1

Figure 1.

Attempts at classification have been numerous. They antedate computers, of course, and must be viewed as more than an academic or
technological exercise, as more even than a lexicographic or linguistic
Schemazwang. Indeed, the aim of Francis Bacon – no newcomer to the
field – was to build "in the human understanding a true model of the
world, such as it is in fact, not such as a man's own reason would have it
to be."[4] The advancement of learning was synonymous with the pursuit
of the truth about the natural world, the regaining of the lost paradise of
knowledge. Like Milton, Bacon and other systematists were – *mutatis
mutandis* – interested in but showing the ways of God to man.

And since God moves in mysterious ways, it is not surprising that the
numerous attempts at delineating those ways constitute a maze of interests and purposes. Although Bacon believed that "truth ... and utility
are ... the very same things,"[5] it is admittedly a far cry from the

intention of the opening of Genesis, with its systematic classification of
the created universe, to that of Comenius' *Orbis Sensualium Pictus,
Hoc est, Omnium fundamentalium in Mundo Rerum, & in vita Ac-
tionem, Pictura & Nomenclatura,* which, as his English translator saw
it, was "to entice witty Children to it, that they may not conceit a
torment to be in the School, but dainty-fare,"[6] or to the aim of Roget's
Thesaurus of English Words and Phrases, which (so the subtitle) is "to
Facilitate the Expression of Ideas and to Assist in Literary Composition." Or perhaps these works are not so very far apart. For all
these attempts at classification presuppose or indeed picture 'the' or 'a'
world. Lists of vocabularies, collections of 'synonyma', bi- and
polylingual dictionaries, preparations for a universal and philosophical
language that would be adapted to "the exact and perfect representation
of things"[7] – whatever form of function the various works take, they all
attempt to hold a mirror up to nature. Swift's scorn of projectors, his
singling out of tinkers with language in Part III, Chapter 6 of *Gulliver's
Travels,* could just as well be a jeremiad against the blasphemy of
perverting the true identity given to words and things by God, after the
manner of the early encyclopaedists, like Isidore of Seville, whose com-
pendium *Etymologiarum sive Originum libri XX* (622-633) was not
simply utilitarian. Or, put the opposite way, John Wilkins sought truth
in his *Essay Towards a Real Character, and a Philosophical Language*
(1668), which he regarded as a "remedy ... against the Curse of the Confusion" and as an aid in "the clearing of some of our Modern differences
in Religion, by unmasking many wild errors, that shelter themselves under the disguise of affected phrases."[8] Language reformers may well
have to be taken as seriously as they take themselves: George Orwell
was not the first recorder of this fact. It is perhaps not a coincidence
that Wilkins, a particular butt of Swift's attack, was a founder and first
Secretary of the Royal Society, a post held 160 or so years later by
another of the 'projecting species,' Peter Mark Roget.

Politics or philosophy or vocabulary or whatever aside, the question
is how one perceives, conceives, organizes the world. Not surprisingly,
all systems accept the created universe as outlined in Genesis, whether
God is placed at the pinnacle of the world, as in the earlier systems and
even as in Wilkins, or tacked on at the very end, as in Roget. Whatever
their aims, whatever their names, the systems classify according to
things and words, the concrete and the abstract. The agreement about
the large outlines is inevitable: the world is, after all, the world. In this
respect, even avowedly different systems are similar: the countless
revisions and enlargements of Roget's *Thesaurus,* for example, do not
differ essentially from the Hallig/Wartburg *Begriffssystem als
Grundlage für die Lexikographie.*[9] Where they mainly differ is not in
where God is, but where the devil is, that is, as the German expression
goes, in the detail, in the constitution and inner arrangement of the
categories, where the difference may at times be like that between a
landscape produced by a camera and by a cubist.

The nature of the problem is obvious if we examine the relatively simple taxonomic classification of 'horse', for which there are two main
and interrelated questions to be dealt with. The first is the position or
niche of this information within the world which the corpus presents;
the second is the particular character of each grouping in itself. The
answers to these questions are not merely of theoretical importance;
without them, the 'raison d'etre' of a reference work, the locating of a

particular item, as well as the relationship of the items to each other, could not be realized.

It may – or may not – be surprising that there is no complete agreement in the most widely known lexica about the place of 'horse' in the world. Even systems governed by the same principles and with the same aims may differ. Thus one well-known versione of Roget, *Roget's International Thesaurus*, based on the work of C.O. Sylvester Mawson, classifies information for the generic 'horse' under Class Four: Matter; Division III: Organic Matter; Section D: Animal Life; Number 413: Animals; Paragraphs 12-21: horses, and 58: breeds of horses.[10] Roget's *Thesaurus of English Words and Phrases*, in the 'authorized' version, classifies 'horse' under Class Two: Space; Section IV: Motion; Subdivision 1°: Motion in General; Number 271: Carrier."[11] These and other works of this kind differ not only in macrostructure but also in microstructure, for they are neither pure nor even without inherent contradictions. Despite their avowed systematic structure – be it according to ideas, concepts, notions, titles, pictures – they tend to be adaptive and expediential. Hallig/Wartburg, for example, treats 'abstracta' in practically the same way as Roget, as is evidenced in the arrangement according to such 'markers' as the pairing of synonyms and antonyms. In the treatment of 'concreta' the tendency is toward a mixture of this with function and something resembling the 'picture vocabularies' of Comenius, the Duden system, and countless primers: the kind of scenic approach apostrophized in that mighty period "La plume de ma tante est sur la table."

The approach, in other words, is pragmatic, the result of a direct experience with language an acknowledgement of response to reality and complexity, semantic and otherwise. It is 'per definitionem' experimental, the outcome of a process of sorting and re-sorting until something 'reasonable' emerges. This seems to have been the procedure of all major attempts after Genesis. But if it is pragmatic, it is not unimpressionistic, occupied more with the conceptual and relativistic aspects than with the structure of language. And it is exactly here that computer linguistics and a lemmatized corpus can combine to help provide clear and clean ways of dealing with the intricate taxonomic data.

Since it is impossible to review our entire experience in the maze – unfortunately so, because the experience has produced a myriad of useful details – I should like to suggest the tactics for an initial assault on the general problems of classification. It involves the role of the morphological information in the establishment and delineation of taxonomic groups. The computer-produced morphological family (Figure 2.1) can in turn be used to provide automatically what might be called a provisional taxonomic family and some of its core members as well. In this case, the family head and also member would be the simplex 'horse' and, assuming a normal morphological situation, those items consisting of a prefix plus 'horse' and those consisting of a compound with 'horse' as the second element. In other words, although not yet further evaluated, the core taxonomic family would thus be composed of members in which 'horse' is the determinant: 'horse' (n.), 'horse' (v.), 'fore-horse', 'unhorse', 'fill-horse', 'hobby-horse', 'malt-horse', 'pack-horse', 'post-horse', 'stalking-horse', 'trotting-horse' (Figure 2.2). The remaining members of the morphological family, in this case those consisting of a compound with 'horse' as the first element – that is, where 'horse' is the determinatum – would, on the basis of regular rules for compounding, provide both new tentative taxonomic families and some of their core members (Figure 2.3). 'Horse-way', for example, would be grouped with those members of the morphological family consisting of the simplex 'way', those consisting of a prefix plus 'way', and those consisting of a compound with 'way' as the last element: 'way', 'away', 'alway', 'always', 'castaway', 'church-way', 'crossway', 'highway', 'horse-way', 'midway', 'Norway', 'pathway', 'roadway', 'runaway', 'straightway' (Figure 2.4). Applied to all the lemmas, this formal process of constituting taxonomic families in the basis of morphological determinants would produce not only the tentative

1. Morphological Family	2. Core Taxonomic Family (*horse* as determinant)	3. Core Taxonomic Family (*horse* as determinatum)
horse (n.)	*horse*	
horse (v.)	*horse*	
fore-horse	*fore-horse*	
unhorse	*unhorse*	
fill-horse	*fill-horse*	
hobby-horse	*hobby-horse*	
malt-horse	*malt-horse*	
pack-horse	*pack-horse*	
post-horse	*post-horse*	
stalking-horse	*stalking-horse*	
trotting-horse	*trotting-horse*	
horse-back		*horse-back*
horse-back-breaker		*horse-back-breaker*
horse-drench		*horse-drench*
horsehair		*horsehair*
horse-leech		*horse-leech*
horseman		*horseman*
horsemanship		*horsemanship*
horse-piss		*horse-piss*
horseshoe		*horseshoe*
horse-stealer		*horse-stealer*
horse-tail		*horse-tail*
horse-way		*horse-way*

4. Core Taxonomic Family (*way* as determinant)	5. Taxonomic Expansion			
way	*road*	*path (n.)*	*street*	*etc.*
away	*inroad*	*path (v.)*		
alway		*unpathed*		
always		*by-path*		
castaway		*foot-path*		
church-way				
crossway				
highway				
horse-way				
midway				
Norway				
pathway				
road-way				
runaway				
straightway				

Figure 2.

microstructure consisting of the core families themselves but also the provisional network of families which might be the taxonomic macrostructure.

It would produce problems as well. For one thing, it is obvious that a purely formal solution is inadequate, for it would merely reproduce but not complement the morphological information, and, of course, according to purely morphological criteria. Thus evaluation is needed to differentiate, for the purpose of the taxonomic classification, between 'horse-back' and 'giving-back', or between 'way' and 'Norway'. This evaluative process serves both to 'purify' the group and to suggest ways of solving a second problem, the expansion of families, a situation which emerges from the fact that in the Shakespeare corpus the average morphological family is fairly small and the percentage of lemmas consisting of only one word-type is unusually high. The most obvious means for automatically expanding families would be through the combining taxonomically of roughly compatible morphological families. The possibilities for combination may at this point be suggested not merely by common observation but also by the morphological structure of the family members, as in the implicit cross-referencing in such forms as 'pathway' to 'path' and to 'way'; or 'road-way' to 'road' and to 'way'. Thus the core taxonomic family *way* would be combined with similarly constituted families for 'path', 'road', 'sheet', and the like. The result (Figure 2.5) would be a preliminary intermediate-sized clan.

This process – automatic production of a taxonomic core based on an interplay with morphological data, followed by repeated evaluation and expanding synthesis – would continue 'ad libitum' until the blend seemed satisfactory, the right combinations had been found, and the special imperatives of an author dictionary (like accounting for the specific contours of Shakespeare, as in the case of the preliminaries for a semantic description discussed at ICCH-2) and of this volume of SHAD in particular (like the necessity of keeping all the complementary morphological and taxonomic information at a fairly uniform level of compatibility) had been taken into consideration. The process is, of course, simple and is not without obvious limitations. But it has considerable advantages: it is objective and self-evident; it does not insist unduly upon 'a priori' schemes or impressions; it develops from fixed points by means of structural nexus; it produces a network which is logical and predictable; it generates a system which is elastic and modifiable at every stage.

It is admittedly a start. And although the attempt has been made to shun what Bacon called "a dream of our own imagination for a pattern of the world"[12] it is apparent that, dealing with a very large corpus, we will have to do a lot of stumbling before we can walk. And the steps we take, however careful, can only be tentative and exploratory. For what is involved is not just the avoidance of "foolish and apish images of worlds which fancies of men have created," but nothing less than what Bacon saw as its correlate: "a very diligent dissection and anatomy of the world."[13]

References

[1]M. Spevack, H.J. Neuhaus, T. Finkenstaedt, "SHAD: A Shakespeare Dictionary," in *Computers in the Humanities,* ed. J.L. Mitchell (Edinburgh, 1974), pp. 111-123.

[2]H. Joachim Neuhaus and M. Spevack, "A Shakespeare Dictionary (SHAD): Some preliminaries for a Semantic Description," *Computers and the Humanities,* 9:6 (November 1975), 263-270.

[3]M. Spevack and H. Joachim Neuhaus, "SHAD (A Shakespeare Dictionary): Toward Volume One," *Bulletin of the Association for Literary and Linguistic Computing,* forthcoming in 1977.

[4]Francis Bacon, *Novum Organum,* in *The Works of Francis Bacon,* ed. James Spedding, Robert Leslie Ellis and Douglas Denon Heath, IV (1860; facs. rpt. Stuttgart - Bad Canstatt, 1962), 110.

[5]*Ibid.*

[6]Joh. Amos Comenius, *Orbis Sensualium Pictus,* trans. Charles Hoole (1659; facs. rpt. Menston, England: The Scolar Press Limited, 1970), sig. A4.

[7]For a convenient historical survey of such attempts, see Franz Dornseiff, *Der deutsche Wortschatz nach Sachgruppen,* 5th ed. (Berlin, 1959), pp. 29 ff. ˙

[8]John Wilkins, *An Essay Towards a Real Character, and a Philosophical Language* (1668; facs. rpt. Menston, England: The Scolar Press Limited, 1968), sig. b.

[9]Rudolf Hallig and Walther von Wartburg, *Begriffssystem als Grundlage für die Lexicographie. Versuch eines Ordnungsschemas,* 2nd ed., rev. and enl. (Berlin, 1963).

[10]*Roget's International Thesaurus,* 3rd ed. (1963; rpt. London, 1973).

[11]Peter Mark Roget, *Thesaurus of English Words and Phrases,* auth. ed. rev. to 1941 (London, 1947).

[12]Bacon, pp. 32-33.

[13]*Ibid.,* p. 110.

4
Oral Literature

Solutions to Classic Problems in the Study of Oral Literature[1]

M.J. Preston

The study of oral texts may seem to be the vaguest endeavor imaginable. One oral text is not necessarily more definitive than another. Printed versions generally contain numerous emendations and may well contain substantive changes. Modern versions may well have been affected by the various media and popular versions of folklorists' theories. The pitfalls are so many and so great that it is tempting to ignore problems of textual reliability and avoid detailed work with the texts altogether.

In the nineteenth century it was commonly held that the folk plays were "probably the remnant of some ancient 'mystery' play, which time and the memories of ... folk have considerably altered."[2] E.K. Chambers discarded the mystery play notion and argued for a later source: "It cannot ... be earlier than the end of the sixteenth century, and may may been composed a good deal later. It has only come down to us in corrupt forms, and although the general resemblance of these, widespread as they are, points to a single archetype, it remains doubtful what the exact outline of this may have been."[3] Both of these positions are now generally discredited among folklorists because they overemphasize possible literary origins and are rather contemptuous of 'the folk'.

Of a later date is the curious history of folk play theory among folklorists. T.F. Ordish, the first editor of *The Revesby Sword Play*, published two articles both heavily indebted to his earlier commentary on the Revesby text. "What is of first consequence," he wrote, "is the action and the characters represented; the dialogue is of secondary importance altogether."[4] Sixty years later, in an article laying down "certain definitive facts," Margaret Dean-Smith stated her "first proposition" that "the Play and any significance it may have, resides in the action: the text is a local accretion, often both superfluous and irrelevant. The Play can exist in action alone, without a word spoken."[5] The key word in these two definitions is 'action,' and it was later repeated in Alex Helm's statement that "the Play is best considered an action, that it has its origins in primitive religious beliefs."[6] Exactly what this 'action' was has been explained variously: Ordish maintained that it was "in the tradition of Summer and Winter champions."[7] C.R. Baskerville maintained that the wooing plays are "forms no doubt of the 'sacred marriage.'"[8] Dean-Smith's 'second proposition' tied all the forms of folk drama together: "in England, practically all the examples we have of the Play are fragments of a single entity."[9] This 'single entity' is the so-called Life-Cycle Play.

If one restricted one's reading to the commonly cited studies of the folk plays, it would be easy to assume that the question of the origin and nature of this tradition was settled, but this is not the situation. There seem always to have been those unhappy with an explanation based on selected evidence.[10] Seven years ago, in a splendid formulation of one argument against established theory, Roger Abrahams wrote:

There does not seem to be any evidence for the existence of any 'original folk drama' involving this total life-cycle perspective; rather, there is a great deal of evidence to the contrary. We have reports from a great many peasant communities indicating that the 'ragtag ends' which we have now are just the sorts of dramas that have always existed. And this conforms with what we know of the agrarian world view: that the progression of seasons is not viewed as a totality, but that the passing of each season is embraced and celebrated individually.[11]

After years of debate about the origin of the folk plays, it seems best to look at the evidence we have and set aside, at least for the present, the theories which seem to have been an obstruction to a rigorous examination of this evidence. It seems beneficial to develop some means of determining the reliability of the texts, many of which were recorded in the nineteenth century, and then proceed towards some kind of rigorous analysis.[12]

Two folk play texts which one might expect to be quite alike are the twin recordings of the 1824 performance at Keynsham, Somerset.[13] Collating James Cantle's text (BM. Add. MS 24,546) with the other text in Hunter's papers (BM. Add. MS 24,542) produces a lengthy list of variants. Most are of a minor nature: simple inflectional variants – 'run' and 'runs' (7) and 'who' and 'whom' (30); substitutions – 'which' for 'that' (18); and contractions – 'man's' and 'man is' (44). There are additions and deletions, the most extensive of which occurs after the second line. But none of this tells us *how much* they differ, and it is to this question that I propose a computer-aided quantitative approach – a text-matching method by which similarities among texts are measured. This differs in direction from the study of textual differences which is the aim of traditional collating. It is analogous in method to that developed by Professor S. Michaelson, I.A. Moir and A.Q. Morton, for identifying fragments of the Dead Sea Scrolls.[14]

The Keynsham text edited by Baskerville begins:

In come I, Old Father Christmas, Welcome or welcome not
I hope old Father Christmas will never be forgot.

If we divide the first line into overlapping units, each beginning with a word and continuing for fifteen spaces without regard for punctuation of word boundaries, we have the following overlapping snatches of text:

In come I, Old F
come I, Old Fath
I, Old Father Ch
Old Father Chri
Father Christma
Christmas Welco
Welcome or welc
or welcome not
welcome not / I h
not / I hope old

Because words are usually short in oral texts – 'Christmas' is unusually long – four words or more may be included in a given group. Thus the fragments are more than just isolated words, often approaching phrases. If these are compared with the other text from Keynsham, one will find exact equivalents except for the first two units, where the difference between *come* and *comes* points up some of the difficulties of working with oral texts.

But demanding an exact match when one is working with oral texts seems to be more rigid than is reasonable. It is for this reason that conventional collation of oral texts is inadequate, when not impossible. In ordinary speech we find a great freedom in the use of 'who' and 'whom,' and it seems appropriate to allow a similar low level variation in working with oral texts. Thus I consider a valid match has been made when thirteen of fifteen consecutive alphabetic characters and spaces are identical and in sequence, assuming that the first word in each sequence is identical or an inflectional variant. If we apply the fifteen-character matching method to the two Somerset texts, we find that 592 or 659 possible matches are made (89.8%).

Upon close inspection, however, one would notice that a disproportionate number of units which end a line do not match, and this finding differs from the general idea that the rhyme end of a line in oral verse tends to be more stable. The problem here is not in the line, but in the fifteen character unit which must run over the end of the line and thus depend on the following line's stability for a match to be made. It is obvious that this method is only of partial use in studying the stability of the extreme end of each line. However, the concept of the fifteen-character unit may be turned about so that each unit of fifteen characters *ends* with a word, rather than begins with a word. Thus one would be checking the stability of a word and what precedes it, as opposed to the stability of a word and what follows it. By this reverse process we find that seventy-six of eighty rhyme units match (95%). The method, then, is no longer at odds with the idea of stable line endings, but has supported it.

Clearly there is a great similarity between the two Keynsham texts and an even greater similarity between rhyme units. These percentages of similarity may, I think, be considered highly unusual, and any plays related to this degree almost without a doubt bear a closer relationship to each other than simply belonging to the same general play tradition.

Expanding this method of mechanical matching to the body of recorded folk play texts presents a series of possibilities. One could continue texts presents one play to another, but the large body of quite similar material suggests other possibilities. Several years ago I produced a concordance to one hundred fifty-six complete texts and thirty-eight fragments.[15] With this as an aid, it was not difficult to compare all phrases of one play with all similar phrases in other plays. The text of the play from Cinderford, Gloucestershire, appears as Appendix I.[16] It was selected because it was both short and readily available. The frequency of matches made is indicated; matches of rhyme units are indicated in parentheses. In the Cinderford text, there are 348 units, of which 234 are matched with equivalent phrases in other folk plays (67.2%). Rhyme units are matched forty of forty-nine times (81.6%). Again, the rhyme portion of the line is more consistent than the line as a whole, but the majority of phrases are to be found among the plays concorded.

Upon inspecting the Cinderford text, one might note that there is considerable variation in the number of times a unit is matched. Many of the radical deviations within the same line can be explained easily as internal change, such as the corruption from 'courageous' to 'creeagus' in line thirteen. The substitution of 'King George' for 'Jamaica' upsets line fifteen considerably. 'King George' appears in many plays, but, as is obvious by the complete lack of matches for the preceding and following, 'King George' occurs in this context in no other play. Another example of change is to be found in line forty-four, in which the more common "I carry my club" appears as "carries a nub." If only one of the four changes had taken place, the various units concerned would have been successfully matched, but the extent of the change is made manifest by none of the final three units being matched even once.

The reverse rhyme unit is of more value than simply to indicate the relatively conservative qualities of the end portion of a line. By contrasting the reverse rhyme unit with the final unit of the line which runs over into the following line, one can determine which lines traditionally follow each other.

I would cut him and hew him as small as flies
And send him to King George to make mince pies (14-15)

is sufficiently illustrative. The number of times the two rhyme units are matched is forty-five and forty-four respectively; this indicates the relative consistency of the end of each line. However, the end units of these lines are matched twenty-eight times in line fourteen, but none at all in line fifteen. The obvious conclusion may be drawn that line fifteen traditionally follows line fourteen, but either line fifteen does not precede line sixteen in any other text or line sixteen is itself corrupted or untraditional. A glance at the number of times each unit is matched in line sixteen indicates that the line itself is relatively traditional. The final conclusion is that in no other play does line sixteen follow line fifteen. This, of course, lends support for the theory that individual speeches remain quite stable within themselves but may float considerably within the context of the play performance.

Another aspect of matching that is of value may be readily illustrated by line eight: "In comes I, the Royal Prussian King." The number of matches for the first unit is eighty-nine, but there is a distinct falling off in frequency of units matched for the remainder of the line. The frequency of matching for the first unit is accounted for by the relatively formulaic nature of many introductory lines in the folk play texts; "In comes I" is one of these formulas, which has among its regional variants "Here comes I." The falling off for the remainder of the line is accounted for by the Royal Prussian King's being a highly regional character, occurring in a few Gloucestershire and Oxfordshire texts.

More distinctions may be made on the basis of the frequency with which units are matched. First of all, the general observation that verse is more resistant to change than prose is made obvious. A great falling off in the frequency of matches occurs in the prose portions of the doctor episode, as, for example, in lines twenty-five through thirty. Even though this episode is present in almost all play texts, the number of matches is minimal, with the exception of certain phrases. Turning to the speech of the doctor in lines thirty-three through thirty-seven, we find that one line contains units which are matched quite frequently, while the units in the other lines average considerably lower. This speech appears in a number of variant forms throughout England, but the one line that is almost always present is "the itch, the pitch, the palsy and the gout." The same kind of explanation accounts for the variation in frequency of the 'Big Head' speech in lines thirty-eight through forty-one. The first three lines of the speech remain extremely constant throughout most of England, but the last line – which tells the audience just what kind of entertaining Big Head will do – differs from region to region, and almost from play to play, though still retaining its final rhyme. Thus we find that a mechanical matching of text units indicates the relative stability of certain aspects of the texts and aids in determining how broadly traditional a particular verse passage is. It also points out words which are distinctly non-traditional or are corruptions of the traditional.

The application of the process of mechanical matching to texts which are for some reason suspect, although verbally related to traditional texts, is revealing. Thomas Hardy's *The Play of St. George*[17] is unusual in that the speeches of the doctor are wholly in verse, there are none of the usual functionless characters (not even the one who collects the money at the end), and the curing of the champions takes place at the end of the play even though the doctor was called in earlier. However, the characters, with the single exception of the Saracen, are highly traditional, and parts of many speeches are widespread. This obvious kinship to the traditional plays accounts for the general acceptance of Hardy's version as authentic.

Hardy's play (see Appendix II for the first thirty-six lines) manifests the same general relationship to the concorded body of folk plays that the text from Cinderford does in that some units are matched many times and some not at all. Likewise there are some in which not a single is matched with other folk plays, and some lines contain units matched many times. But out of 1205 fifteen-character units, only 571 are matched even once (47.8%). This is a significant falling off from the 67.2% of units matched in the Cinderford text. The rhyme units also show this same decline. Of 151 units, only eight-four are matched (55.6%) as opposed to 81.6% in the Cinderford play. This difference in the number of matched units indicates something distinctly odd about Hardy's St. George play and warrants further discussion.

If one looks at the individual speeches of Hardy's play, what is at least a partial explanation for the difference presents itself. In the initial speech of Father Christmas, what is interesting is the contrast between the first four lines and the last eight. The first four lines are highly traditional, but the others are matched infrequently. In fact, lines six, eleven, and twelve contain individual units that are not matched at all.

The Valiant Soldier's speech (11. 13-22) manifests the same tendency revealed in the speech of Father Christmas. The first four lines are frequently matched and, like the first four lines of Father Christmas, are obviously tied together because of the relative frequency of terminal matches. Without a doubt these four lines are traditional and are preserved in their traditional order. The last six lines of the Valiant Soldier's speech are another matter. Here the average number of matches per unit drops considerably. Line twenty-one is the only line matched frequently.

The key to understanding how Hardy put this text together is in the Turkish Knight's first speech (ll. 23-28). Line twenty-six is never matched, while the other five are quite frequently matched. From the total lack of matching, it would seem that Hardy added the last half of line twenty-five, all of twenty-six, and the first half of twenty-seven. External confirmation may be found in *Return of the Native*.[18] In the novel the Turkish Knight's speech is four lines long, and those four lines correspond closely with the matched portions of his six-line speech in the play. I have no doubt that Hardy inserted:

> ... Saint George and all his crew,
> Aye, countryfolk and warriors too.
> Who is ...

The remainder of the play follows a similar pattern.

That Hardy's play is not traditional in any strict sense seems a reasonable conclusion.[19] Although traditional speeches were used, they were expanded or rewritten to make a complete, coherent verse text. This coherence should have made Hardy's text immediately suspect. This is no condemnation of Hardy – he worked for his own purposes – but it does give us a crucial insight into the way in which nineteenth-century authors treated oral folk play texts.

Turning to *The Revesby Sword Play*, a text which has been of direct interest to medievalists, one finds that only a small percentage of lines bears a close resemblance to the folk plays as a whole, but those lines are of extreme importance in understanding the nature of this play. Among these traditional lines are to be found speeches which are restricted to Lincolnshire as well as speeches common throughout England. To illustrate the Revesby play's relationship to the folk play traditions, one need only consider the Big Head speech.[20]   At Clayworth, Nottinghampshire, the speech goes:

> In comes I that's never been yit
> With my big head and little wit
> My head's so great and my wit's so small
> I can act the fool as well as you all.

and at Sapperton, Gloucestershire:

> In comes I as ain't been yet
> With my big head and little wet
> My head is so big and my wits so small
> I' play you a tune as will please you all.

At Revesby the speech is distinctly similar, but contains a most uncharacteristic 'witty' line:

> Here comes I that never come yet,
>   Since last Time lovy
> I have a great Head but little wit
> Tho' my Head be great & my Wits be small
> I can play the Fool for a While as well as best of y[m] all (274-278).

Despite my conviction that the Revesby play is a literary product, it is still related to the tradition as a whole, and the method of which I have been speaking worked adequately to isolate this and the other traditional speeches.

The *Shetland Sword Dance*, reprinted by E.K. Chambers[21] from Sir Walter Scott's *The Pirate*, and the *Ampleforth Play*, printed in two quite different versions by Cecil J. Sharp[22] and E. K. Chambers,[23] have been extremely influential. In fact, Dean-Smith's theory is based directly on a consideration of the *Shetland Sword Dance*. The play from Ampleforth bears approximately the same relationship to other folk plays that the play from Revesby does – probably that of adaptation or expansion – but there is no textual relationship whatever between the Shetland play and any other known folk play. Fortunately the manuscript sent to Scott survives, as do both manuscripts of the Ampleford play. Although all the evidence has not yet been assembled, the conclusion that these plays are literary compilations intended to replace the more disjointed traditional plays (if there ever was a traditional play in Shetland) seems inescapable. What all of this indicates is that there was a widespread tradition of adapting and imitating folk plays throughout the eighteenth and nineteenth centuries. Those interested in folk plays have been drawn to the longer, more complex, and better-written plays – in short, those which are different. I am convinced that the several hundred 'typical' plays and the thousands of fragments are more indicative of the tradition as a whole than any of the commonly anthologized anomalies.

Alan Brody began his book on the folk plays with the statement: "Trying to deal with the study of the mummers' play is like trying to sort out hundreds of different sets of fingerprints."[24] Brody's statement is correct, and I believe that the bewildering textual snarl is what lured scholars into seeking methods which avoided detailed textual work. But the folk plays, like fingerprints, can be classified and identified. Appendix III shows the distribution of Father Christmas and Dame Jane, both regional characters. Appendix IV displays the geographic distribution of the Big Head speech – two distinct clusters and the inevitable exception. These illustrate the tendency of the various aspects of the folk plays to follow geographic patterns. This is best explained by a statement of M. W. Barley: "There was no constant play, but rather a fund of speeches, steadily maintained, or even enlarged by borrowing, and shrinking only in the past century."[25] This statement gets us beyond plot or structure or 'action' and into the chaotic rag-tag world of oral texts. A 'fund of speeches' can readily differ from area to area, as can the sequence in which they are assembled to form a play. Barley's statement was formulated after a detailed study of scores of plough plays, many of which he recorded himself. Although Barley restricted himself to the East Midlands, his ideas are generally valid for the play tradition on the whole, particularly if allowance is made for a tendency of the order in which the variable 'fund of speeches' appears to crystalize in particular places.

There is much more evidence concerning the folk plays than is generally known. *English Ritual Drama*[26] contains a bibliography which must be the starting point for any study of folk plays, however it will be expanded substantially before long. Nearly one hundred additional chapbooks – one a good number of years older than any previously known – have been located in the last five years, as have several important collections of folk play manuscripts and a number of textually related broadsides, such as *The Infallible Doctor*. This additional information is reducing the surface chaos of the folk plays.[27] Printing histories have been worked out for various groups of chap-

books, and the broadsides are being worked on. We know now that the
chapbooks and the oral texts existed side by side, and only under special
circumstances did the chapbooks exert any influence on the oral texts;
there is evidence of some influence of the oral texts on the chapbooks.
We know that in some areas there were traditions of manuscript
prompt books, handed down in a manner distinctly paralleling the
romantic idea of oral transmission. What we are coming to realize is
that what we call 'the British folk play' might better be perceived of as a
complex set of intertwined semi-dramatic traditions which relate to still
other traditions, such as T'Owd Tup, which historically have been excluded from consideration because they did not follow the prescribed
ritual pattern. In all of this we find traditional costuming, the motive of
money raising at holiday time, and the so-called functionless characters
of the folk plays – Big Head, Beelzebub, and the others. Sometimes we
find the doctor and the doctor's helper. If we are interested in isolating
any elements of considerable antiquity which might bear some
relationship to Middle English or Tudor drama, then a systematic study
of the plays and the related traditions must be carried out in considerable detail.

References

[1] I wish to thank the American Council of Learned Societies for a
Grant-in-Aid and the National Endowment in the Humanities for a
Younger Humanist Fellowship which allowed me to complete the
groundwork for this essay. Two Grants-in-Aid from the University of
Colorado Council on Research and Creative Work have enabled me to
continue since.

[2] P.H. Ditchfield, *Old English Customs* (London, 1901), 9.

[3] E. K. Chambers, *The English Folk-Play* (Oxford, 1933), 16.

[4] T. F. Ordish, "Folk-Drama," *Folk-Lore*, II (1891), 333-334.

[5] Margaret Dean-Smith, "The Life-Cycle Play or Folk Play: Some
Conclusions Following the Examination of the Ordish Papers and
Other Sources," *Folk-Lore*, LXIX (1958), 244.

[6] Alex Helm, "In Comes I," *Folk-Lore*, LXXVI (1965), 118.

[7] T. F. Ordish, "Folk-Drama, II," *Folk-Lore*, IV (1893), 173.

[8] C. R. Baskerville, "Mummers' Wooing Plays in England," *Modern
Philology*, XXI (1924), 226.

[9] Dean-Smith, p. 225.

[10] A parallel objection to the traditional explanation of the origin of
Greek drama appears in Gerald F. Else, *The Origin and Early Form of
Greek Drama* (New York, 1972), 1-31.

[11]Roger D. Abrahams, "British West Indian Folk Drama and the 'Life Cycle' Problem," *Folk-Lore*, 81 (1970), 241-242.

[12]See my article, "The British Folk Plays and Thomas Hardy," forthcoming in *Southern Folklore Quarterly*, for a fuller treatment of the methods employed in this paper.

[13]C. R. Baskerville, 250-258. Compare the passages from *Wily Beguiled* in this play with those in *Recruiting Sergeant,* also published by Baskerville, 259-262, and in my edition of *The Revesby Sword Play*, University Monographs LD00058, Ann Arbor, 1975.

[14]S. Michaelson, I. A. Moir, and A. Q. Morton, "Search the Scriptures: The use of computers for fragment location," *Zeitschrift für Papyrologie und Epigraphik*, Band 17, Heft 2 (1975), 119-124.

[15]This concordance was produced in the KWIC (Key Word In Context) format. The concorded word is centered in eighty characters of context. Further, each entry is alphabetized on twenty characters and spaces so that the word boundaries are overcome and the most closely related phrases drawn together. The plays are identified in the concordance by country, county, town, Ordinance Survey grid reference, and date of recording or publication. Microfilm copies are stored in the Norlin Library at the University of Colorado at Boulder, with the Folklore Society in London, and in the Archives of Cultural Tradition, Sheffield University.

[16]R. J. E. Tiddy, *The Mummers' Play* (Oxford, 1923), 160-161.

[17]Thomas Hardy, *The Play of St. George* (London, 1928). The title page describes the play "as aforetime acted by the Dorsetshire Christmas Mummers" and "based on the version in *The Return of the Native* and completed from other versions and local tradition."

[18]Thomas Hardy, *The Return of the Native* (New York, 1969), 106. It is interesting that none of the editions of this novel published during Hardy's life contain variant readings of the folk play text or of the descriptions of the performance, even though much of the novel was rewritten. The portion of the *Return* which contains folk play fragments was written while Hardy's father was staying with him at Bath. It seems plausible that Hardy's father, who is known to have taken part in various Christmas activities, was the direct source of Hardy's information about the folk play and that Hardy himself is considerably removed from this tradition.

[19]See Ruth Firor, *Folkways in Thomas Hardy* (Philadelphia, 1931), 197-207. She treats the folk play in *Return of the Native* at length, but not in *The Play of St. George*. For revealing comments on Hardy's knowledge of folk plays, see J. S. Udal, *Dorsetshire Folk-lore* (Hertford, 1922) 98-100.

[20]See my article, "The Revesby Sword Play," *The Journal of American Folklore*, 85 (1972), 51-57.

[21]E. K. Chambers, *The Mediaeval Stage* (Oxford, repr. 1967), Vol. II, 271-276.

[22]Cecil J. Sharp, *The Sword Dances of Northern England, III)*, (London, 1913), 132-149.

[23]E. K. Chambers, *The English Folk-Play* (Oxford, 1933), 132-149.

[24]Alan Brody, *The English Mummers and Their Plays* (Philadelphia, 1969), 3.

[25]M. W. Barley, "Plough Plays in the East Midlands," *Journal of the English Folk Dance and Song Society*, VII (1953), 74.

[26]E. C. Cawte, and others, *English Ritual Drama*, Publications of the Folk-lore Society [CXXVII] (London,1967), 95-132.

[27]See M. J. Preston, M. G. Smith, and P. S. Smith, *An Interim Checklist of Chapbooks Containing Traditional Play Texts*, History of the Book Trade of the North (Newcastle, 1976). Related publications are in press.

Appendix I

```
                         27   13 25   30   9        3 (9)
Old Father Christmas:    Room a  Room brave gallants all,

7     42  9  22   2  2 (20)
Pray give me room to rhyme;

18 3  25   5  3   4   9 (4)
I  am come to show you activity

20   53   59       8 (59)
This merry Christmas Time:

12       9 11     13       0  0 (12)
Activity of youth, activity of age                          5

3 7   3   1  8   4 (8)
I will show you such activity

13   0    1  1    2   2 4     1 (4)
that never was acted upon a common stage.

                        89 15   0 1   1    1      1 (8)
Royal Prussian King:    In comes I the Royal Prussian King:

13   8 9    5   0 0   0 (9)
Many a battle have I been in,

4 0   4    0   3    4 4   0   0 (4)
I have fought this battle at home and abroad;           10

6 7   0    1  1    2    0  0 (0)
I have brought the truth upon my sword.

5      41 21  7   5    6 10  3  2 (10)
Where's the man that dares to bid me stand?

2 3    29 23 22   0   0  0      0 (0)
I would cut him down with my creeagus hand,
```

```
2 3     5    3    1    2    23 37 43    29 28 (45)
I would cut him and hew him as small as flies

22  0    0   0  64   0      51 51   0      0 (54)
And send him to King George to make mince pies.                        15

                 7    13 8    0 (14)
[Father Christmas:]   Walk in Jack Vinney.

                 1  5     1 2    0 (1)
[Jack Vinney:]   In comes I Jack Vinney.

5       41 21  9    4    6  10  0   0 (10)
Where's the man that dare to bid me stand?

0   0    0    1   2 2    0    0    0        0 (0)
He said he'd cut me down with his creeagus hand.

9 9      3 0     3    0  1 1    6 (0)
A battle, a battle with him I will try,                                20

35 36  25    8   3   2    0      0 (2)
To see which on the floor shall lie.

                 30  70     18 14 4    2      5  5  0   0   0 (5)
Father Christmas:   Ten pounds for a good doctor if he was but here:

0        0  14 1      0 (14)
Doctor, do no longer stay

0   0    0    0    0   0    1 (0)
But mount your horse and ride away.

              11   12 1      1 (12)
Doctor:   Hold my horse, Jack.                                         25

          0    0    0 0    0  6    0   0    0 (6)
Jack:   Yes, Sir, I have it fast by the tail.

              3  5     0  0       0 (0)
Doctor:   In comes I, Doctor Hero.

1 0   0      0  1 (0)
I was bornd at home:

15 16   2        0    0    7  0    4 (10)
I  have travelled many parts of the country

0   0 0 0     0      0  0 (0)
and I am well known at home.                                           30

              0     19      60   74  0    0 (75)
Father Christmas:   Pray, Doctor, what can you cure?

          0   12  9     3  4 (9)
Doctor:   Oh, all sorts of diseases,

0        2  2       0 (2)
Whatever my physick pleases,

0  0    43 39    7   5      48 59    75  12  2 (75)
If it's the itch, the pitch, the palsy and the gout,

13 11  0     0  1   5 4   0      0   0 (13)
If the devil is in, I can fetch him out.                               35

0    0   0    2   4  12  2      2 (14)
Now if this man is not quite dead,

7     1   4    2      46 13    7 (45)
Rise up, bold fellow, and fight again.
```

```
              11 9     8 1 1     7    6 (7)
[Tom Fool:]  In comes I as an't been it

26   26 35 50   45 30     18 (48)
With my big head and little wit:

11 12   12 14  29 13  2  6 (29)
My head so big my wit so small,                          40

0 0    0    0 0   71 77    0   0 (76)
I will dance a jig to please you all.

              0    2  13  3 (20)
Father Christmas:  Walk in old Beelzebub.

          82 17    16 14  24 (20)
Beelzebub:  In comes I old Beelzebub

10  44 50 6      0        0 0 (0)
and on my should carries a nub

27  47 25 26   34 42        0 (48)
and in my hand a dripping pan.                          45

11 31  0    0   0   58 59    1   2 (60)
Do you think I'm not a  jolly old man?

                  18    18 20   16  23    19 19 (24)
[Unknown Speaker:]  . . . Money I  want and money I  crave:

37 32  1    3    1  0    3 (2)
If you don't give us some money

1 1   24   6  8  9          (10)
I will sweep you all to the grave.
```

Appendix II

```
              40   52   51 130 138    39 (138)
Father Christmas:  Here come I, old Father Christmas;

    33      40 33     43 (40)
    Welcome or welcome not,

42 44   130 138    50 (138)
I  hope old Father Christmas

56   57   2 2 (57)
Will never be forgot:--

1     0   138   0       0   15 6    6   0 0 (6)
Although it's Father Christmas I've a  short time to stay,      5

0  11  26  1 1   1  0      0    0 0    0 (0)
But I've come to show you pleasure before I pass away!

5   6   3   2    0 4      2 (4)
Make room, make room, my gallants, room,

    1   1   1 1     2 2 (1)
    And give us space to rhyme;
```

```
3    26   1 1    190    1        1 (1)
We've come to show Saint George's play

      4    14   60         1 (60)
      Upon this Christmas time.                                    10

62  143 144 131    0      0 0      0 0       0    0   1   0 (0)
And if  you don't believe my words, I straight call out, Walk in,

Q    2   0 37     1        0   0       0   0 (0)
Walk in, O Valiant Soldier, and boldly now begin!

             37   15   14 22   37        5 (37)
Valiant Soldier:  Here come I, the Valiant Soldier,

       39       25 26 15 (47)
       Slasher is my name,

20    30    28   29      35 24 24 (44)
With sword and buckler by my side                                 15

       32 29   39 33  2    2 (39)
       I hope to win the game.

2    0   0   0        0   1   0 (1)
One of my brethren I've seen wounded,

       1        0    0    0 (0)
       Another I've seen slain,

0   31 2    0     0    0    0 (0)
So I  will fight with any foe

       0    0   1       0 (1)
       Upon this British plain.                                   20

0    35   22 0     21  2    0  0 (2)
Yes, with my sword and with my spear

       0    0   0   0     0    0     2 (0)
       To 'fend the right, I'll battle here!

             37   18   19 34  86        11 (86)
Turkish Knight:  Here come I, the Turkish Knight,

11   10   32       30   15 15 (30)
Come from Turkish land to fight;

2    15   190   11     0   0   0   0 (0)
I'll fight Saint George and all his crew,                         25

0    0          0   0       0
Aye, countryfolk and warriors too.

0    0   0    3   7    69       10 (69)
Who is this man with courage bold?

13 13  11     5    5    23   0  2 (23)
If his blood's hot, I'll make it cold!

             0  0    0   0     34  86     0 (86)
Valiant Soldier:  If thou art called the Turkish Knight,

5    23 35  0     0   0   0  0 (0)
Draw out thy sword, and let us fight!                             30

0 0  0   0      2  2    190    0 (190)
I am the friend of good Saint George,
```

```
0    0      0   0    0   0 (0)
I've fought men o'er and o'er,

1   6   4   2    2 2     190   0 (190)
And for the sake of good Saint George

0   2    2 2        0 (2)
I'd fight a hundred more.

0  0   0    0     0      0   0 0 (0)
To slay this false Knight did I try--                                      35

 0   0   0   0     0 0    0  0 (0)
'Tis for the right I have to die!
```

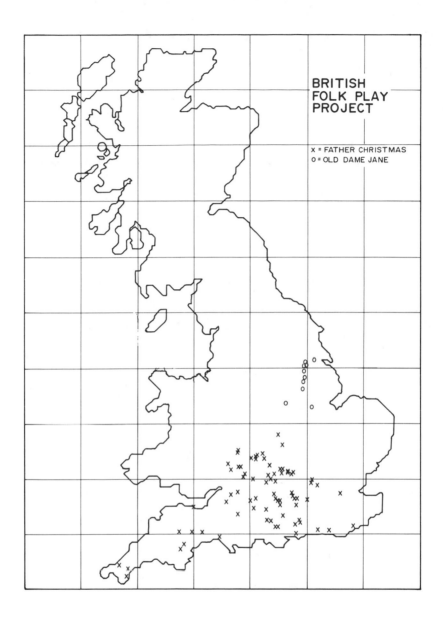

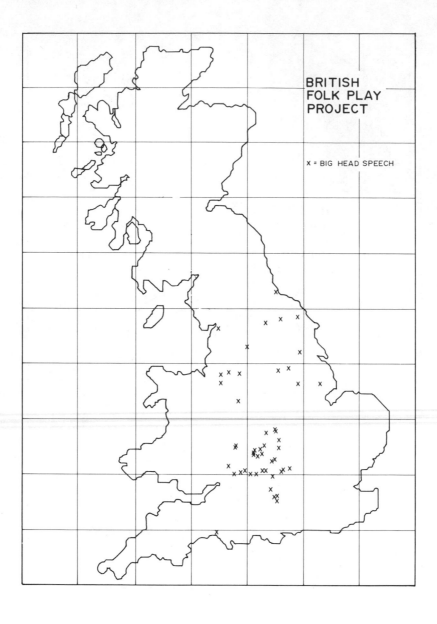

5
History

Coding of the Testimony of Prisoners in the Trial of the Templars in the Papal States 1309-1310

A. Gilmour-Bryson

The suppression of the Military Order of the Knights Templars at the Council of Vienne in 1312 is one of the most highly debated acts in religious and political history. Henry Lea calls it "the great crime of the Middle Ages".[1] That this act was carried out by Pope Clement V, first Avignon pope, with the active help and encouragement of Philip IV, King of France, is sure. What is much less sure is precisely how much real evidence existed to prove their guilt. For more than half the historians who dealt with this subject, the Templars were saintly men innocent of most or all the wrongdoing imputed to them.[2] Their Order was abolished by a wicked avaricious king with the collusion of a weak, credulous, greedy pope. To most of the rest of the scholars who have studied this question, the Templars were guilty of some, though not of all, the crimes with which they were charged.[3] Most agree the Order had little reason to exist, once the Holy Land had been lost with the fall of St. Jean d'Acre to the enemy in 1291. To these writers, the Templars appear as monks who have become money-loving and corrupt. The king and the pope simply did their duty.

It is not my intention here to enter into the hazardous area of Templar guilt or innocence. In order even to begin to consider that problem, in an active fashion unlike the polemic writers of the past, it would seem that an analysis of all the testimony taken at their trials needs to be made. One trial must be compared with another; all of them with each other. Work has been done on the evidence gathered at these trials, but most often one country at a time or one trial at a time, without attempting to consider the evidence as a whole or to consider the anomalies present in the testimony of individual witnesses.[4] It is the need to be able to consider all the evidence together which led up to the computer study of all the testimony begun this year.

Let us consider how the trials operated, under what conditions, and with what sort of documentary evidence remaining for us to use. It is not possible to know how many Templars existed in Europe in 1307, the year of their arrest. Informed estimates vary from a few thousand to twenty thousand.[5] Templar documents listing the members have disappeared. At this moment it is possible only to make an approximation of their numbers from the quantity and importance of their possessions in France, England and Ireland, Spain, Italy, and Germany. The pope stated that two thousand Templars had been interrogated between 1307 and 1311. The testimony of about nine hundred of these men exists in the form of contemporary manuscripts taken down at the interrogations by judicial notaries and authenticated with their seals. It is obvious that in some areas at least the vast majority of Templars escaped capture. In many regions such as southern

Italy documents attest to the existence of several hundred com-
manderies, preceptories or properties, but only a small number of
Templars were interrogated.

The Order, and its members, were charged with various acts of
blasphemy, idolatry, heresy, and assorted improper practices. These accusations, numbering 77 in some trials, or with the addition of 50 more
totalling 127 in others, were written down and sent out by the papal
chancellery to be used by the inquisitors in the interrogation of
prisoners. These trials provide an excellent opportunity to undertake a
comparative study of testimony or trial procedure in the early 14th
Century. It is possible to compare the depositions of several hundred
witnesses answering the same questions in various parts of Europe at
the same moment. We have complete manuscripts for the two largest
trials: those of London-York and Paris.[6] The fact that all the trials were
written down in Latin, even though the questions were explained in the
prisoner's own language if necessary, helps in the analysis of the
answers. Certain other trials are available in an abridged form in
Konrad Schottmüller or in manuscripts to be found either in the
Vatican Archives or the Archives of the country concerned.[7]

The trials operated under precise directives from the pope. Bishops
and other inquisitors were named in each area where Templars were
presumably to be found. They were to delegate other inquisitors in each
part of that area to carry out the investigation and to report back to the
bishop, who would in turn send a report to the pope. One may take as
an example of how the instructions were carried out throughout
Christendom the following message by the bishop of Paris in 1309:

...We, William...bishop of Paris...and the delegated inquisitor...having received from the
holy father the Lord Clement...sealed letters...instructing us to make an inquiry concerning the Templars living in our city and diocese...regarding the articles sent to us by the
most holy father, articles set forth in this document...[8]

These articles or accusations were always set forth in full in the trial
document, allowing us to compare the answers of prisoners in different
trials one with another knowing that, all over what is now Europe, men
were answering the same questions with their answers written in the
same language. In the case of trials using 77 accusations and not 127, it
is of course necessary, for purposes of analysis, to compare only those
allegations the trials have in common. I have listed in appendix one the
usual list of 127 questions with which we had to work.

Why the computer rather than the traditional methods of analysis in
handling these depositions? We have access to at least 900 of them
covering 77 to 127 responses each. We have to evaluate, therefore,
almost 100,000 statements if we wish to consider each person's
testimony and its relation to some or all of the other testimony. If only
one trial, preferably one numbering fewer than twenty prisoners, were
to be considered, the task could by done by making out a checklist for
each prisoner and crosschecking one with another. Even in a small trial,
however, the mere fact that each person answered 127 questions means
that the analyst usually chooses various key questions and correlates
the answers to them while ignoring all the others.

It is possible that what may emerge from a consideration of all the
witnesses and all the testimony is that some meaningful pattern exists.
There may be some correlation, hitherto ignored, between divergent
facts such as the prisoner's age and place of origin and the man who

received him into the Order, or the prisoner's status in it. There may be a correlation between the answers of two questions of unequal importance, such as whether or not the Grand Master could absolve the members from sin, and whether or not the Templars worshipped an idol. I was, and still am, not sure exactly what will emerge from a consideration of all the testimony. It is largely this uncertainty that makes the statistical analysis the most rational way to proceed. By coding and entering all the answers to all the questions, a bank of data is formed which can be later analysed regarding an almost unlimited number of criteria in order to find out whether these answers form a pattern, whether the pattern is regional, or instead clustered according to a completely different set of common factors such as age or social status.

As well as knowing which answers turn out to be usual in any particlar area – in England little if anything was admitted by prisoners with the exception of receiving absolution from the Grand Master; in Italy references to the existence and worship of idols are more frequent than elsewhere – it will be enormously helpful to know which responses are atypical in any particular prisoner's deposition.

The basic material with which to work is the trial manuscript itself. Relying on published editions often means having only an abridged version of the testimony to consider, which in turn furnishes less complete information than the manuscript itself. The answers of one person could not be compared with those of another if the full text were entered in its normal form. Semantic analysis could not be undertaken automatically unless the testimony were transformed into a code: identical in form for each prisoner in each trial. Each question must be coded separately in order to be able to compare persons with each other regarding only the questions which these persons answered in common. Unfortunately the manuscripts themselves are extremely wordy and contain much extraneous material. The trial I am editing in the Papal States 1309-1311 contains 60,000 words yet covers the interrogation of only seven persons.[9]

The wording used in the answers varies considerably. The simple response of guilty or innocent or yes or no, which could be compared without recourse to a code, rarely occurs. Often as many as six or eight questions are asked or answered in one block. This practice is responsible for the number of blank spaces in the coding sheets (appendices 2 and 5). The witness specifically answers only some of the six or seven, saying nothing definite about the other parts of that group of questions.

The decision was made to enter each answer for the first two trials to be treated. For comparative purposes the trial of Pisa-Florence *(Vat.Lat. 4011)*, which interrogated six prisoners at about the same time using the full list of 127 questions, would be used initially compared with D-207. If it is found that some questions and answers are definitely not necessary in analysing the results, they may easily be eliminated, more easily than adding questions originally omitted but later found to be essential. All questions are shown in the appendix in order to indicate the complexity of some of them, complexity which led to the difficulty in elaborating a code suitable for all the questions. One person's testimony, requiring up to 325 lines in the manuscript or 500 lines in print, was to be reduced to 127 groups of not more than eight symbols each.

The first code used may be seen in Appendix 2. The questions were numbered one to a line on graph paper, leaving space for an X to be

placed in a choice of six squares denoting: yes, no (or guilty and innocent), does not know, vague hearsay, specific hearsay, yes concerning
others but not the witness himself. Any question left out by the inquisitor would be indicated as missing. Questions asked, but not
specifically answered, would be left blank. The system was relatively
easy to use, demanding about thirty minutes to code each witness. It
would be easy to enter using a fixed format.

After coding all testimony in D-207 there were still some insoluble
problems. The code did not express with sufficient precision all the data
potentially required. Certain questions contained in reality two separate
ideas and needed to be divided into two parts: Question 1 included the
denial of Christ either at reception or later; 30 included both innocent
and improper kisses; 39 discussed frequent suspicion but some answers
mentioned only one incidence of it; 97 discussed both charity and
hospitality offered, while different answers were given each of these
matters.

A serious drawback to this first method of coding demanded the constant return to the list of questions or to the testimony in order to interpret the coded answer. The code was not sufficiently self-
explanatory. It was not possible to code in an unambiguous fashion the
many compound answers: the witness is innocent, Brother John guilty,
Brother Peter may have been guilty, but the witness knows nothing
about the Order as a whole.

It seemed that it was necessary to have more information about the
possibilities of guilt involved. It was vital to know exactly who might be
guilty in a positive (yes or guilty) answer to any particular question. For
that purpose a study was made of the possibilities inherent in each
question as to the person deemed to have been guilty. See examples in
Appendix 3. It appeared that eleven persons or groups of persons could
be considered guilty according to the sense of the question itself.

Professor Evergates of Western Maryland College indicated to me
the existence of an article entitled "Quantitative Studies of the French
Revolution."[10] by Shapiro, Markoff, and Weitman. This article proved
most helpful in the formulation of a new and better coding scheme to
handle the testimony under consideration. While the material being
analysed by them, the *Cahier de Dolèance*, had little in common with
my material, in both cases sheer volume of data indicated the need for a
code which would describe this data for reference purposes or analysis
in the fullest yet shortest and simplest possible form.

The authors called their system "Concrete Analytic Coding." This
term refers to the content analysis undertaken:

Content analysis is any research technique for making inferences by systematically and
objectively identifying specific characteristics within text.[12]

As Shapiro, Markoff and Weitman have pointed out, most often the
same categories are used for coding as for the analysis to be undertaken
later.[13] This practice in turn, presupposes that one can analyse the
material in an unambiguous way, that one knows at the beginning all
the possiblities for analysis to be encountered later. That idea implies
the need for the coders to consider the material in an interpretive
fashion rather than a literal one. All the implications of the data might
not be covered in the naturally self-limiting terminology employed, so
recoding would be necessary were a field of interest to be found which

did not form part of the original plan. My own study is at the first stage of the process: the coding of a mass of data for entry. The conditions for analysis must nevertheless be provided. The form and scope of that analysis will be worked out later when preliminary treatment indicates which areas need further analysis.

The coding scheme described in treating the *Cahier de Doléance* furnished the nucleus of the system which proved much more precise as well as easier to interpret in my own case. It used a succession of letters to describe the subject matter involved, beginning from the most general category and finishing with the smallest category into which that piece of information might fall.[14] Their system included the vital references to the text for each item. They provided a means to include other data not covered by the code.

In my case I needed to enter the places where illicit acts took place, the names of Templars mentioned in the document and other pertinent proper names. As these items are of unknown number until the end of the entry process, they will be entered in prose form accompanying each coded testimony. I have omitted these details from the sample sheets in the Appendix.

The actual coding system used began with the broad category corresponding to the *type of answer given:* G for guilty, I for innocent. For many purposes a simple total of these two letters would provide the requisite information. Y and N were used to represent yes and no. There must be no possibility in analysis to confuse an expression of guilt or innocence with a mere statement of fact, in itself not necessarily reprehensible. G to question 9 means that the receivers made those received spit on the cross. Y to question 35 means only that those received were considered to be full members without undergoing a period of novitiate. The difference in significance of these two answers indicates that they should not be coded in the same way even if the witness responded with the same words to each. K was used for does not know, a very frequent response *(nichil scire).* P was used if the witness stated that he felt that the question had in fact been answered previously. Whenever possible, that is, when the witness had specifically answered the question before, the code for that answer was added after the P appearing later. If, as unfortunately happens, the witness had at no time made any definite responses, the P was left to stand alone. The existence of P would permit a total to be made of the number of times witnesses felt the questions to be repetitive as, for example, question number 36, that receptions were clandestine, and 106, that receptions were secret.

The second category established concerned the *type of testimony* given. It was much more significant if the witness had seen an illicit act take place than if he had merely heard of the act in a vague and unreliable fashion. W indicates that the individual testifying witnessed the act described in question. S, on the other hand, means that the witness has heard that a certain person or persons committed the offence but did not see it occur. One step removed from specific heresay is the answer indicating vague heresay: the witness has heard the act was committed by someone somewhere in the Order. This response was coded V. Two other possiblities seemed to have direct bearing on the type of testimony: the presence of threats forcing the witness to commit the said act, coded T, and the witness's belief that the act was not illicit, coded A.to have been illicit. Idolatry committed under the menace of a naked sword held by the receiver cannot fairly be considered as the same offence as idolatry committed under the simple verbal suggestion of someone in the Order. T would enable a count to be made of the number of times witnesses referred to direct threats made against them. Ignorance of the gravity of the offence needs to be indicated, since it constitutes a valid excuse in heresy trials.[15] These two letters need not be considered in every analysis accomplished, but may be used selectively in compiling statistics.

The information derived from the coding up to this point, as it could be read from the code sheet itself, was already far more complete than it had been in the case of the first coding attempt. It was not yet as complete as it might be. In any later assessment of guilt or innocence one must know who performed the act in question. Did one person adore a cat or did everyone in the Order adore a cat (question 14)? The answer of guilty to an allegation does not indicate whether the act had been performed by the witness himself or by some other person alone, or by one entire group, several groups, or indeed the Order in question. Many of the suitable letters needed to designate these persons or groups were already in use in the code. Although numbers are less easy to remember than letters, numbers 1 to 11 were used to differentiate between the categories of persons performing the act (see Appendix 4). Numbers 1, 2, 6, 7, and 8 indicate one specific person or category of person; 3 and 4 indicate one group or preceptory in the Order, 9 and 10 indicate specific groups of persons, 11 isolated persons, or one person who does not fall into one of the other categories, 5 was used only when the entire Order was implicated in the answer.

The use of these numbers will enable an assessment to be made, with the minimum of difficulty, as to how many of the answers within any group of answers, however large or small, implicate the Grand Master (6), the priests or the receivers (10 and 2), or all the officials of the Order together (2,6,7,8,9). It will be clear in how many instances the witness himself performed the act (1), or as it often happens, testifies that he himself is innocent but that others were guilty (variety of numbers possible, excluding 1). The syntax was made as simple and as economical of symbols as possible. Any symbol from the first category governed the entire set of symbols unless another letter from that category were to appear. Consider 35 in Appendix 5: the witness himself was guilty; he saw others in the act, hence they are guilty; by means of vague hearsay he considers the Order in general guilty.

On occasion, as in 76 for example, two letters from category 1 may be used, both G and I. In this case the witness declares himself to be innocent while testifying by means of specific hearsay to the guilt of someone else. Similarly, in number 118 the witness answered affirmatively regarding himself, negatively concerning someone else.

Anyone even moderately familiar with this simple code can read and interpret each answer without recourse to the long list of questions or the even longer confession of the witnesses. Once the system has been thoroughly understood, coding of each witness' testimony can be done in about the same length of time as it could using the more primitive and less complete earlier coding scheme.

It is too soon to think that this code is the final one or the perfect one. In a free format such as the one used, other letters or numbers can be added if it is found that some vital detail from the evidence is not there in the coding used up to this point. It does seem, however, that the simplifying of some 20,000 words down to 889 short jumps of symbols, in a form the computer will handle, will undoubtedly make the task of analyzing the testimony of the Templars easier as well as making the result more precise.

I would like to thank the Computer Centre of the University of Montréal for making its facilities available to me, the Governments of Canada and of Québec who provided funds for my research, and most especially Professor Serge Lusignan of the Institut d'études médiévales who has guided every phase of this study and provided invaluable help with the analysis and coding of the data.

Appendix 1

The official list of 127 questions to be asked of each Templar prisoner. Translation by the author from the trial manuscript (Vat. Arch. D-207), crosschecked with several other trials to insure that the list is in fact the standard one. Words in brackets are not in the manuscript but have been added for clarity.

In spite of the fact that the order was supposed to be a sacred one approved by the Holy See, at the moment of reception of brothers into the Order, or sometimes later, the brothers carried out the following acts:

1) Namely that each one at his reception or after, or whenever it suited the receiver, denied Christ, or sometimes Christ crucified, and sometimes Jesus, sometimes God, and sometimes the Blessed Virgin, sometimes all the saints of God, led or ordered by those who received him.
2) Commonly the brothers did so.
3) Most of them (did so).
4) Even after the reception sometimes.
5) The receptors said and thus taught those received that Christ, or sometimes Jesus or Christ crucified, was not the real Lord.
6) They told those whom they received that he was a false prophet.
7) That he did not suffer, nor was he crucified, in order to redeem mankind, but for his sins.
8) Neither the receivers nor those received had any hope of salvation through Jesus and thus they told those received, or something similar.
9) They made those they received spit upon the cross, or on a replica of the cross or on a sculptured cross and on the image of Christ, although sometimes those received spat beside it.
10) They were ordered to trample that same cross.
11) The brothers sometimes trampled that same cross after they were received.
12) They sometimes urinated upon the cross and trampled it and made others urinate on that cross. Sometimes this happened on Good Friday.
13) Some of them, on that day or another of Holy Week, used to meet together to trample (upon the cross) or urinate upon it.
14) They adored a cat which sometimes appeared in their meetings.
15) They did this to revile Christ and the orthodox faith.
16) They did not believe in the Sacrament of the altar.
17) Or some of them (did not).
18) Most of them (did not).

19) Nor in other sacraments of the Church.
20) The priests of the Order omitted the words of consecration of the Host when saying mass.
21) Or some of them (did so).
22) Most of them (did so).
23) The receivers so ordered them.
24) They believed, and this was said to them, that the Grand Master could absolve them from sin.
25) Or the Visitor (head of a province within the Order) could.
26) Or the Preceptors (head of a house in the Order), although many of them were laymen.
27) This they did in fact.
28) Some of them (did this).
29) The Grand Master of the aforesaid Order confessed in the presence of very important persons, even before his capture.
30) In reception, or about that time, the receiver and the one received kissed each other on the mouth, navel or stomach, the anus or at the base of the spine.
31) On the navel or the nude stomach.
32) On the anus or at the base of the spine.
33) Or sometimes on the virile member.
34) In the reception they made those they received swear not to leave the Order.
35) They took their final vows at once (at reception).
36) Their receptions were clandestine.
37) No one was present except brothers of the Order.
38) Because of this, there was strong suspicion against the Order for a long time.
39) Commonly this suspicion was held.
40) The brothers were told that in turn they could commit carnal acts with each other.
41) It was indeed licit to do so.
42) They ought to do this to each other and to suffer it.
43) It was not a sin to do this.
44) They, or several of them, did in fact do this.
45) Or some of them (did).
46) In every province they had idols, namely heads, of which some had one face and some three faces, and some a human skull.
47) This idol or idols they adored especially in their grand chapter meetings and gatherings.
48) They venerated it.
49) As God.
50) As their Saviour.
51) Some of them.
52) Most of them who were in the chapter meeting.
53) They said that the head could save them.
54) It could make them rich.
55) All the riches of the Order were owed to it.
56) It could make trees flower.
57) It could make the earth germinate.
58) They tied cords around the head of the idol, or touched the cords to them, then tied the cords around their shirt or against their skin.
59) During the reception each brother was given the aforesaid sashes or some part of them.

60) They did this in veneration of the idol.
61) It was commanded to them that the aforesaid sashes be tied around them and worn at all times, even at night.
62) Commonly the friars in this Order were received according to the aforesaid methods.
63) Everywhere.
64) For the most part.
65) Anyone not wishing to do the above things at his reception or after was killed or put in jail.
66) Some of them (were).
67) Most of them (were).
68) They were ordered under oath not to reveal the aforesaid (acts).
69) Under pain of death or imprisonment.
70) Nor might they reveal the mode of their reception.
71) Nor did they dare discuss this among themselves.
72) If anyone was found out to have revealed (the above) he suffered death or imprisonment.
73) They were ordered not to confess to any but priests of the Order.
74) Brothers of the Order knowing the above errors did not correct them.
75) They neglected to warn Holy Mother Church.
76) They did not cease committing the above errors and communing with their brothers even though they had the opportunity of doing so.
77) All the above took place and was observed overseas in places where the Grand Master and Council of the Order stayed for a certain time.
78) Sometimes the denial of Christ took place in the presence of the Master and his Council.
79) The aforesaid took place and was observed in Cyprus.
80) Similarly on this side of the sea, in all regions and places in which brothers were received.
81) The aforesaid was commonly observed throughout the Order in general.
82) Generally observed for a long time.
83) By ancient custom.
84) Through statute of the aforesaid Order.
85) The aforesaid observances, habits, ordinances and statutes took place and were observed in all the Order overseas and at home.
86) The aforesaid was among the rules of the Order introduced through error after (the Order's) approval by the Holy See.
87) Reception of brothers commonly took place according to the above mode throughout the aforesaid Order.
88) The Grand Master of the aforesaid Order made it so and thus commanded it.
89) The Visitors (similarly).
90) The Preceptors (similarly).
91) Other senior members of the Order (similarly).
92) They themselves so behaved and ordered that it take place and be observed.
93) Or some of them (did so).
94) Another mode of receiving brothers in the Order was not used.
95) No living member of the Order remembers in his lifetime any other mode of reception.

96) Anyone not wishing to observe the above mode of reception was severely punished by the Grand Master, the Visitor, the Preceptors and other Masters of the said order.

97) Charity was not offered in the Order as it should have been nor was hospitality observed.

98) It was not considered to be a sin in the Order to acquire possessions by good or evil means.

99) They swore an oath to increase the material goods of the Order by good or evil means.

100) It was not considered a sin to perjure oneself in this regard.

101) The chapter meetings were held in secret.

102) Secretly, at the hour of the first sleep or in the first vigil of the night.

103) Secretly, that is, with all the family expelled from the house and the doors of the house being closed, and others of the family sent outdoors on the nights on which they held chapter meetings.

104) Secretly, since they close themselves inside to hold chapter meetings: that is to say, all doors of the house and of the church in which they hold chapter meetings are firmly closed that no one might come near them nor might anyone see nor hear anything that takes place.

105) Secretly, even to the extent of placing a guard on the roof of the house or church in which the chapter meeting is held so that no one may come near the building in which they hold their meeting.

106) Similar clandestinity took place and was usual in the reception of brothers.

107) The error exists, and had existed for a long time in the Order, that the Grand Master could absolve them from sin.

108) Even more serious, an error which existed and had existed for a long time was the notion that the Grand Master could absolve brothers of the Order from sins, even those they had not confessed, which they feared to confess through shame or fear of the penance which would be inflicted upon them.

109) The Grand Master confessed the aforesaid errors before his capture, spontaneously before worthy clerics and laymen.

110) In the presence of the major Preceptors of his Order.

111) The aforesaid errors were held not only because of the Grand Master but also because of certain Preceptors and Visitors and other important members of the Order.

112) Everything which the Grand Master, along with his councillors, ordered or legislated, all the Order clung to and observed.

113) This power he had held and did hold for a long period of time.

114) These errors had gone on so long that the members could in fact have been reformed not only once but twice since the beginning.

115) All those in both parts of the Order who knew of these errors refused to correct them.

116) They neglected to inform Holy Mother Church.

117) They did not give up the observance of the aforesaid errors or communion with their brothers even though they had the opportunity of doing so.

118) Many brothers of the aforesaid Order left that Order because of the crimes and errors, some of them entering another Order, others returning to secular life.

119) Because of all the aforesaid (practices) a great scandal arose in the hearts of the most important persons, even those of king(s) and prince(s) and almost all the Christian people.

120) Each and every one of these things was well-known amongst brothers of the aforesaid Order.

121) All this was public knowledge, common opinion and notoriety as much among the brothers as in the outside (world).

122) (Among) most of the aforesaid (persons).

123) (Among) some (of the aforesaid persons).

124) The Grand Master of the Order, the Visitor, the Grand Preceptor of Cyprus and of Normandy and of Poitiers, as well as many other Preceptors and some other brothers of the aforesaid Order, confessed the above items before justice as elsewhere, in front of official personnages as well as in several public places.

125) Some brothers of the Order, knights as well as priests, even in the presence of our Lord Pope and the Lord Cardinals, confessed to the above or to a large part of the aforesaid errors.

126) Under oath taken by them.

127) Even in full consistory they recognized the aforesaid items.

Appendix 2

First attempt at coding testimony, 1st witness, Ceccus D-207

	yes no	does not know	vague hearsay	specific hearsay	yes or others
1)	X				
2)			X threatened		
3)		see 1			
4)	X threatened				
5)	X				
6)	X				
7)					
8)					X
9)		X			
10)		X			
11)		X			
12)		X			
13)		X			
14)		X			
15)					X
16)					
17)					
18)		X			
19)					X
20)		X			
21)		X			
22)		X			
23)		X			
24)		X			
25)		X			
26)	X				
27)					
28)	X				
29)		X			

Line	1	2	3	4	5	6
30)	X mouth				X	
31)		X	X			
32)		X	X			
33)		X	X			
34)	X					X
35)	X					X
36)	X					X
37)	X					X
38)						
39)	X					
40)		X				
41)		X				
42)		X				
43)		X				
44)		X				
45)		X				
46)	X threatened					
47)	X threatened					
48)	X threatened					
49)	X threatened					
50)						
51)	X					
52)						
53)						
54)	X					
55)						
56)						
57)						
58)			X			
59)	X					
60)		X				
61)	X					
62)	X	X				
63)		X				
64)		X				
65)		X threatened				
66)						
67)						
68)	X					X
69)		X				
70)	X					
71)	X					
72)			X			
73)	X		X			
74)		X		X		
75)		X		X		
76)		X				X
77)			X			
78)			X			
79)			X			
80)			X			
81)			X			
82)			X			
83)			X			
84)			X			
85)			X			
86)	X					
87)			X			
88)			X			
89)			X			
90)						
91)	for 90-93					
92)	see previous					
93)						
94)		X				
95)		X				

```
 96)          X
 97)  charity yes hosp) does not know
 98)       X  X
 99)       X
100)       X  X
101)  X
102)                          X
103)          X
104)          X
105)          X
106)       X  X
107)  see 20-8
108)  see 24-26
109)
110)  for 110-111
111)  see 24-27
112)  X
113)  X
114)
115)  for 114-117
116)  see 74-76
117)
118)  X          X
119)  X
120)  X
121)          X
122)          X
123)          X
124)  X
125)  X
126)  X
127)  X
```

Appendix 3

Possible guilty party implicated by each question:

1) the witness.
2) the receiver
3) his group of brothers (the witness' group)
4) another group in the Order
5) the Order in general
6) the Grand Master
7) the Preceptor(s)
8) the Visitor(s)
9) the senior members of the Order
10) Priests of the Order
11) one other or isolated persons in the Order

Question	Principle Responsibility or Guilt	Secondary or Potential Guilt
1	1,2,11	3,5,7
2	3,4,5	1,2,7,11
3	3,4,5	1,2,7,11
4	1,2,11	3,5,7
5	2	1,3,4,5,7,11
6	2	1,3,4,5,7,11
7	2	1,3,4,5,7,11
8	1,2,3,4,5	7,11
9	2,1,5,11	3,4,7
10	2,1,5,11	3,4,7
11	1,3,4,5,11	2,7
12	2,1,3,4,5,7,11	
13	3,4,5	1,2,7,11
14	1,3,4,11	2,5,7
15	1,2,11	3,4,5
16	1,2,5,11	3,4,7,10
17	1,2,7,10,11	
18	3,4,5	

Exceptions in individual testimony in which the witness implicates someone other than the person ordinarily implicated are coded according to the individual answer: if the Grand Master adored a cat, that answer would be coded with a G and a 6.

Appendix 4

The coding adopted in testimony in D-207 and Vat. Lat. 4011

I) Type of answer given: G – Guilty
  I – Innocent
  Y – Yes
  N – No
  K – does not know
  P – question previously answered

II) Type of testimony: W – witness of act done by other(s)
  S – secific hearsay
  V – vague hearsay
  T – act commanded or accomplished under threat
  A – ignorance that act is illicit

III) category of person(s) performing the act:
  1 – the witness himself
  2 – the receiver of novices
  3 – witness' own convent
  4 – another group(s) in the Order
  5 – the Order in general
  6 – the Grand Master of the Order
  7 – the Preceptor(s)
  8 – the Visitor(s)
  9 – Senior members of the Order
  10 – priests of the Order
  11 – person(s) in the Order

Appendix 5

New coding for testimony of 1st witness Ceccus, servant, D-207.

1a I	41 I	85 K
1b G T 1	42 I	86 Y S 5
2 P	43 I	87 K
3 P	44 I	88 K
4 G T 1 S 11	45 I	89 K
5 G W 2	46 G T 1 W 11	90 P G W 7
6 G W 2	47 G T 1 W 11	91 P
7	48 G T 1 W 11	92 P G W 2
8 G W 2	49 G T 1 W 11	93 P G W 2
9 K	50	94 Y 1 W 11 K 5
10 K	51 G S 11	95 K
11 K	52	96 G W 2 K 5
12 K	53	97a I W 4
13 K	54 G W 11	97b K
14 K	55	98 I 1 K 5
15 G S 2	56	99 I
16	57	100 I 1 K 5
17 G S 2 I 1	58 K	101 G S 3
18 K 5	59 Y	102 G V 3 K 5
19 G S 2 I 1	60 I	103 K
20 K	61 Y 1 W 11	104 K
21 K	62 Y 1 W 11 K 5	105 K
22 K	63 K	106 P I 1 11 K 5
23 K	64 K	107 P G W 2
24 K	65 N T	108 P
25 K	66	109 K
26 G W 7	67	110 K
27	68 G W 2	111 P
28 G W 7	69 K	112 G V 6 9
29 K	70 G W 2	113 G V 6 9
30a Y 1 W 11	71 Y 1 Y 11 K 5	114 P
30b I 1 W 3 4 K 5	72 K	115 P I 1 G S 11
31 I 1 W 3 4 K 5	73 Y W 2 K 5	116 P G 1 V 11
32 I 1 W 3 4 K 5	74 G V 11 I 1	117 P I 1 G S 11
33 I 1 W 3 4 K 5	75 G 1 V 11	118 Y 1 N 11
34 G 1 W 11	76 I 1 G S 11	119 Y V
35 G 1 W 11 V 5	77 K	120 Y 5
36 G W 3 11	78 K	121 K
37 G W 2 3 4	79 K	122 K
38	80 K	123 K
39a Y	81 K	124 Y V 6 7 8 9 10 11
39b	82 K	125 Y V
40 I	83 K	126 Y V
41 I	84 K	127 Y V

References

[1]Henry Lea, *A History of the Inquisition of the Middle Ages* (New York, 1888), III, 238.

[2]On the innocence of the Templars see Henry Lea, *A History of the Inquisition of the Middle Ages* (New York, 1888), III; George

Lizerand, *Le Dossier de l'affair des Templiers* (1923; rpt. Paris, 1964); Charles-Victor Langlois, "L'affaire des Templiers," *Journal des Sauvant* (1908), p. 417 s.q..

[3]Pierre Dupuy, *Histoire de la condamnation des Templiers...* (Brussels: F. Foppens, 1713); Jules Michelet, *Le Proces des Templiers, II* (Paris, 1841-1851), introduction; G. Legman, *The Guilt of the Templars* (New York: Basic Books, 1966).

[4]Konrad Schottmuller, *Der Untergang der Templerordens* (Berlin: Mittler and Co., 1887); Hans Prutz, *Entwichlung und Untergang des Templherrenordens* (Berlin: Grote, 1888); Louis Lavocat, *Proces des Freres et de l'ordre du Temple* (Paris: Plon-Norrit et Cie., 1888); as well as general histories of the order.

[5]Lea, III, p.238 gives an estimate of 15,000 members; Schottmuller, I, pp. 236, 695 estimates up to 20,000; Thomas Parker, *The Knights Templar in England* (Tucson: University of Arizona Press, 1963) states that 150 were arrested in England and that no information exists on the number who escaped.

[6]Wilkins, *Conciliae Magnae Brillaniae et Hiberiae* (London, 1737), II, 328-401 and Juliet Michelet, *Le Proces des Templiers*, 2 vols. (Paris, 1841-1851).

[7]Konrad Schottmuller, *Der Untergang des Templerordens* (Berlin, 1887), II.

[8]Translation by the author from the *Livre de Guillaume le Maire, Eveque d'Angers*, who published the instructions of Guillaume de Baufet, bishop of Paris, from Lizerland, p.138.

[9]This edition was carried out with the help of the computer both to establish the text and to reconstitute the missing portions. See article by the author to be published soon in *Manuscripta* (St. Louis) for the procedure followed and benefits derived.

[10]Shapiro, Markoff and Weitman, "Quantitative Studies of the French Revolution," *History and Theory*, 12 (1973), 163-191.

[11]Shapiro, Markoff and Weitman, p. 172.

[12]Stone, Dunphy, Smith and Ogilvie, *The General Enquirer* (Cambridge: M.I.T. Press, 1966), p. 5.

[13]Shapiro, Markoff and Weitman, p. 172.

[14]Shapiro, Markoff and Weitman, p. 174.

[15]Leon Garzend, *L'inquisition et l'heresie* (Paris: Beauchesne, 1912), p. 89.

Sur le traitement automatique de données biographiques médiévales: le projet RESEDA

G.P. Zarri

Le projet RESEDA a été lancé en octobre 1975 grâce à la contribution financière du Centre National de la Recherche Scientifique (C.N.R.S.) et de la Délégation Générale à la Recherche Scientifique et Technique (D.G.R.S.T.) – contrat no. 75.7.0456. Il se propose la construction d'un système de question-réponse qui prenne en charge une base de données biographiques. Les informations contenues dans cette dernière se réfèrent aux 'personnages' – publics ou privés – qui se sont trouvés mêlés aux débuts du mouvement humaniste en France (fin du 14e siècle – première moitié du 15e siècle). On pose au système des questions formulées de façon rigoureusement formelle; les réponses, qui sont données dans le même format, sont obtenues par recherche directe sur le contenu de la base de données ou par des procédures d'inférence. Dans ce denier cas, on arrive par le cheminement de l'inférence à établir de nouveaux liens, des 'raccourcis', entre les données. Ces liens, après validation par l'opérateur humain, pourront être mémorisés de façon permanente par le système. Les difficultés inhérentes au codage des données très complexes dont on doit tenir compte et la complication des opérations d'inférence nécessaires expliquent que l'on ait négligé – du moins pour le moment – le problème d'une interrogation en langage naturel (Bozzolo et al. 1976a, 1976b; Ornato, Zarri 1976a, 1976b).

RESEDA est loin d'être une tentative isolée pour adapter des techniques d'intelligence artificielle aux exigences du repérage de l'information (*Information Retrieval*); il suffit de se reporter ici au recensement à l'échelle mondiale des travaux portant sur des systèmes interactifs évolués de documentation automatique, tel qu'il nous est fourni par un des derniers numéros du *Sigart Newsletter* (Waltz 1977). Ce système possède toutefois une originalité propre qui le différencie nettement des autres et qui dérive d'une double spécificité des données employées. Condsidérons d'abord leur aspect 'diachronique': il ne semble pas en effet qu'il y ait eu jusqu'à ce jour de tentative d'utilisation des techniques d'intelligence artificielle dans le but d'effectuer des recherches documentaires en histoire. De plus, ces données ne sont qu'en partie de ce type 'concret' habituellement traité en intelligence artificielle documentaire ou en histoire quantitative. Nous nous heurtons à la complexité d'éléments bien plus abstraits comme les croyances, les intentions et les attitudes mentales de nos personnages.

Mon intervention sera donc divisée en deux parties. Dans la première, je m'attarderai encore sur cette singularité des données et sur les difficultés qui en découlent en vue d'un traitement automatique. Dans la deuxième, je fournirai quelques éléments pour juger de l'efficacité et de l'intérêt général des instuments – métalangage et procédures d'inférence – élaborés pour répondre à ces difficultés et qui donnent finalement à RESEDA son caractère particulier.

aspect 'statistique' d' 'état civil', mais sous l'aspect des attitudes, des croyances, de l'idéologie politique ou religieuse des personnages qui nous intéressent. Cela implique que le type de codage adopté doit être à même d'exprimer des idées et des processus intellectuels, et que les algorithmes d'inférence ne peuvent pas se limiter à une logique manichéenne du type de celle du calcul des prédicats du premier ordre. On peut illustrer ce dernier point par un exemple naif. En face de l'affirmation "Comme Guillaume est partisan des Anglais, il trouve qu'il faut brûler Jeanne d'Arc," tout le monde conviendra qu'on a une relation de cause suffisamment stricte entre les deux moitiés de la phrase. La relation de cause est marquée du point de vue formel par 'comme'. Mais une telle relation ne pourra jamais être réduite à la simple implication matérielle car son inverse: "Puisque Guillaume trouve qu'il ne faut pas brûler Jeanne d'Arc, c'est qu'il n'est pas partisan des Anglais" ne serait pas nécessairement vrai.

On nous a déjà dit que nous étions en train d'élaborer une nouvelle 'logique des attitudes'. Je me permets de faire remarquer que nous n'avons pas choisi le moyen le plus simple de contribuer nous aussi au développement de la Science.

Métalangage et inférences

Par souci de clarté, je vais traiter en deux sous-sections différentes les deux thèmes annoncés dans le titre, malgré la stricte association fonctionnelle des outils qu'ils désignent.

Le codage des informations

En ce qui concerne le métalangage, je voudrais surtout illustrer la recherche de souplesse et d'exhaustivité qui a été notre souci constant dans sa construction. Je me limiterai ainsi à rappeler brièvement quelques-unes des options fondamentales prises dans ce domaine.

Le codage de chacun des 'épisodes' qui constituent les étapes fondamentales d'une biographie est réalisé en effectuant séparément la transcription des informations qui composent le cadre circonstanciel ou 'thématique' et celles qui concernent la description proprement dite. Par exemple, la traduction de l'épisode "Après la semaine de Pâques 1395, les trois ducs de Bourgogne, de Berry et d'Orléans prirent la voie d'eau à Châlons pour se rendre auprès de Benoît XIII à Avignon, où ils arrivèrent le 22 mai" comportera une partie thématique du type:
/après-11-avril-1395/22-mai-1395//Châlons/Avignon/   /Avignon/ //Bibl:Valois/
(Je donnerai toujours par la suite la représentation 'externe' du codage, c'est-à-dire celle dont se sert manuellement l'opérateur pour analyser un épisode; pour les détails sur la représentation numérique 'interne', voir p.e. Bozzolo et al. 1976b, pp.45-48). Sans approfondir davantage, on voit que la thématique prend en charge les références de temps et de lieu de l'épisode et les références bibliographiques (Bozzolo et al. 1976b, pp.3-4). Cette forme de présentation permet d'alléger le codage en évitant – dans la transcription de la partie plus proprement descriptive de l'épisode – l'introduction de 'corrélateurs' particuliers pour la datation et les localisations.

Dans la forme de présentation retenue, les indications de temps fournies en thématique se réfèrent obligatoirement à un *seul* 'état' du ou des

L'incertitude de l'histoire et la logique des attitudes

Examinons d'abord les problèmes liés au caractère historique de nos données. Les informations dont nous pouvons disposer sont incomplètes, vu l'impossibilité manifeste d'arriver à connaître tous les détails pertinents concernant une certaine période. Cela implique la nécessité de 'combler les trous' par des procédures d'inférence et fournit déjà une justification à la décision de nous aventurer sur le terrain de l'intelligence artificielle. Mais devoir tirer quelque enseignement nouveau des éléments très dispersés que nous avons à notre disposition rend encore plus évident – par rapport par exemple aux applications de l'intelligence artificielle dans l'analyse automatique du langage naturel – le caractère exclusivement 'probable' de nos inférences et de nos réponses. Il s'agit là d'une véritable caractéristique de notre système.

Une deuxième propriété 'historique' de nos données consiste en leur incontestable manque de stabilité. Déjà, au niveau de l'ensemble des données, un informateur, historien moderne ou source contemporaine (indiqué dans la section 'Bibl:' de nos 'plans', voir section suivante) nous raconte ce qui s'est passé à son avis. Cette information n'est pas, loin de là, nécessairement vraie (toutefois, nous disposons aussi de quelques 'vérités' que nous définissons comme 'générales' sous la référence 'consensus' en bibliographie).

Mais cette précarité de l'information peut aussi revêtir des formes particulières. Par exemple, nous sommes parfois obligés d'introduire expressément dans la base de données des informations que nous savons être fausses. Il peut s'agir, comme dans l'inférence de la section suivante, d'affirmations 'gratuites' de l'un de nos personnages à propos du comportement d'un autre: tout en marquant cette information de façon à pouvoir reconnaître son caractère très spécial, nous devons l'enregistrer, parce que porteuse de renseignements précieux à propos de l'attitude réciproque de deux personnages. Dans d'autres cas, nous avons des informations qui se contredisent ouvertement. Chacune des versions contradictoires est représentée séparément et une liste spéciale de ces contradictions doit être tenue à jour.

A la frontière des 'informations lacunaires' se trouvent enfin les propositions 'intentionnelles' – dont on ne sait pas si elles ont engendré des réalisations concrètes – et les propositions 'conditionnelles les' du type "si telle chose était arrivée, les conséquences auraient été ..." etc.

Nos données sont donc 'instables' en plus d'être 'incomplètes': en un mot elles sont 'incertaines'; c'est là une condition trop souvent oubliée par les partisans d'une mathématisation poussée dans les Sciences Humaines et les disciplines historiques en particulier. On en revient donc plus que jamais à constater le caractère probable des réponses du système: elles ne sont, très souvent, que des réponses plausibles fondées sur des inférences vraisemblables qui utilisent des données incertaines. Cela ne doit évidemment pas être interprété comme une excuse pour produire des résultats complètement démentiels: le système doit être capable de réaliser mécaniquement la démarche intellectuelle qu'aurait effectuée l'historien dans des conditions semblables, sans évidemment que soient simulées ni son intuition ni son érudition.

La deuxième difficulté présentée par nos données est due au fait que nous nous occupons d'informations biographiques non pas sous leur

personnage(s) mis en cause dans l'épisode. Pour l'exemple précédent, l'intervalle de temps indiqué couvre tout 'l'état de déplacement' (et seulement lui) des trois ducs entre Châlons et Avignon: c'est là le noyau de l'épisode relaté. Cela a comme conséquence d'obliger à détailler les biographies en épisodes qui ne comptent qu'un seul 'prédicat-état'; chaque biographie codée se présente finalement comme une succession plus ou moins serrée de 'flashs' historiques. Les effets bénéfiques de cette décision sur la cohérence interne de la base de données de RESEDA sont doubles. En premier lieu, l'obligation d'effectuer le codage selon une vision extrêmement analytique de l'histoire individuelle du personnage alourdit peut-être la tâche de l'opérateur mais donne comme résultat un matériel élaboré et très homogène. Deuxièmement, la réduction de la 'partie descriptive' de l'épisode aux éléments d'un noyau prédicatif unique diminue sensiblement le nombre de combinaisons de codes possibles, et donc la possibilité de codages parasites équivalents.

En ce qui concerne la structuration de la 'partie descriptive' qui compose le deuxième volet d'un épisode codé (les deux codages constituent ensemble un 'plan'), le principe déterminant a été de l'organiser selon une succession de cellules emboîtables ('corrélations') rigidement composées de trois éléments. L'élément-pivot central ('corrélateur') est chargé d'une double fonction, syntaxique d'une part, par rapport aux 'schémas' propres du prédicat, sémantique d'autre part, puisqu'il précise le rôle des deux éléments qui l'accompagnent dans la reconstruction du 'signifié' de l'épisode original. Examinons à ce propos le codage de la partie descriptive d'un épisode particulièrement simple comme "Clamanges a une correspondance avec un inconnu de Paris (*ANOM-1*) au sujet du Concile de Constance":
(*CLAMANGES* .SUJ. (((*ment+PRODUIRE* .OBJ. *lettre*) .DEST. *ANOM-1*) .ARG. *concile-de-Constance*))
où SUJ, OBJ, DEST, ARG sont des 'corrélateurs' (l'information 'de Paris' est évidemment rejetée en thématique). Pour être rationnel, ce type de codage n'en est pas moins souple: je me contenterai de citer à ce propos la possibilité d'emploi de la construction dite 'complétive', où un épisode entier constitue le deuxième corrélé de OBJ. Prenons par exemple l'information "En 1411, à Paris, Montreuil écrit à Clamanges, qui est sans doute à Langres à ce moment là, que les affaires personnelles de Jacques de Nouvion sont restées bloquées à Mâcon à cause de la guerre civile". Le codage suivant permet de ne rien perdre des éléments d'information ni surtout de leur succession logique:
1) /1411/ //Paris/ / /%Langres/ //Bibl:Ornato/
   (*MONTREUIL* .SUJ. (((*ment+DEPLACER* .OBJ. 2) .MODAL. *lettre*) .DEST. *CLAMANGES*))
2) /1411/ //Mâcon/Paris/ / / //Bibl:Ornato/
   (*VEDETTES* .SUJ. ((*neg+DEPLACER* .OBJ. (*biens-mobiliers* .QUALIF. *JACQUES-DE-NOUVION*)) .CAUSE1. *guerre-civile*))
où le deuxième 'plan' – désigné par son étiquette, ici '2' – entre comme 'objet' du 'transfert d'information' exprimé par le prédicat *ment+DEPLACER* contenu dans le premier épisode codé. On trouvera d'autres exemples semblables dans l'inférence décrite dans la sous-section suivante.

La construction complétive montre déjà que RESEDA dispose d'outils pour relier les informations contenues dans des plans différents.

Cette fonction d'association est pleinement réalisée par des 'corrélateurs-pointeurs' comme FINAL, CAUSE2 et COND qui montrent en outre avec une particulière évidence la superposition d'éléments sémantiques à la simple fonction syntaxique. C'est ainsi que FINAL a été réservé pour introduire certains épisodes qui – dans l'état des connaissances au moment du codage – apparaissent comme les visées, sans réalisation confirmée, du prédicat exprimé dans l'épisode premier corrélé de FINAL. Les rôles des deux corrélateurs FINAL et CAUSE2 trouvent une illustration dans cette suite de plans:

3) /après-11-août-1408/ //Paris/Cambrai/Paris/ / //Bibl:Valois/
   (*LOUIS-DE-SAINT-POL* .SUJ. ((*DEPLACER* .OBJ. *LOUIS-DE-SAINT-POL*) .SOURCE. *CHARLES-VI*))

4) /11-août-1408/ //Paris/Cambrai/ / / //Bibl:Valois/
   (*CHARLES-VI* .SUJ. (*contre+real+AVOIR-ATTITUDE* .OBJ. *PIERRE-D'AILLY*))

5) /après-11-août-1408/ //Cambrai/Paris/ / / //Bibl:Valois/
   (*PIERRE-D'AILLY* .SUJ. (*jur+ETRE-PRESENT* .SOURCE. *LOUIS-DE-SAINT-POL*))

6) /11-août-1408/ //Cambrai/Paris/ / / //Bibl:Valois/
   (*PIERRE-D'AILLY* .SUJ. (*neg+ETRE-PRESENT* .OBJ. *5ème-concile-Eglise-de-France*))

((3 .FINAL. 5) .CAUSE2. (4 .CAUSE2. 6)) .

Leur signification en langage naturel est la suivante: "Constatant l'absence de Pierre d'Ailly, le 11 août 1408, à l'ouverture du 5e concile de l'Eglise de France à Paris, Charles VI envoya le comte de St Pol l'arrêter à Cambrai". Les documents historiques en notre possession ne nous disent rien à propos de la concrétisation de cette arrestation (*PIERRE-D'AILLY* .SUJ. *jur+ETRE-PRESENT*). La fonction de COND peut être saisie par l'analyse des deux plans suivants:

7) / / //occident/occident/ / / //Bibl:consensus/
   (*catholiques* .SUJ. (*poss+fin+contre+AVOIR-ATTITUDE* .OBJ. *catholiques*))

8) / / // / / / / //Bibl:consensus/
   ((*papes-de-Rome* .COORD1. *papes-d'Avignon*) .SUJ.
   ((*ens+fin+soc+ETRE-AFFECTE* .OBJ. *papauté*) .SOURCE.
   (*papes-de-Rome* .COORD1. *papes-d'Avignon*)))

(7 .COND. 8)

En langage naturel ces deux plans ont la significance suivante: "Le schisme ((*catholiques* .SUJ. (*contre+AVOIR-ATTITUDE* .OBJ. *catholiques*)) pourrait (*poss*) prendre fin à condition que les deux papes, de Rome et d'Avignon, renoncent eux-mêmes (.SOURCE. (*papes-de-Rome* .COORD1. *papes-d'Avignon*)) à la tiare". On peut remarquer le 'consensus' en bibliographie qui, comme je l'ai déjà expliqué, indique une 'vérité générale': les deux plans 7 et 8 ne sont en effet rien d'autre que le 'nucleus' de la définition d'une des 'voies' pour résoudre le schisme, la 'voie de cession'.

Un excursus, même rapide, sur les possibilités 'expressives' du métalangage de RESEDA ne saurait être complet sans dire au moins quelques mots sur l'importance des 'modulateurs' dans l'économie générale du métalangage. Ils ont en effet comme fonction de restreindre au maximum la liste des prédicats en permettant de préciser leur domaine d'application par le biais d'un nombre limité de préfixes. On a par exemple rencontré jusqu'ici *ment* qui donne au prédicat associé la connotation générale 'd'activité intellectuelle'; *neg, contre, real* (ce dernier, obligatoirement utilisé avec les modulateurs *pour/contre*, fournit au prédicat *AVOIR-ATTITUDE* le caractère de 'réalisation concrète'); *jur* qui définit un 'lieu juridique' autour du prédicat avec lequel il est employé; *poss*, puis *fin* qui marque la fin de l'état défini par le prédicat; *ens* qui montre que l'état indiqué est commun à plusieurs personnages; *sac* qui ajoute un caractère officiel au prédicat. L'utilisation des modulateurs et de leurs combinaisons explique comment les cinq prédicats acceptés par le système dans sa version actuelle – *AVOIR-ATTITUDE, DEPLACER, ETRE-AFFECTE, ETRE-PRESENT, PRODUIRE* – sont à même de prendre en charge à eux seuls le codage de données biographiques assez complexes et variées.

Un aperçu sur les procédures de déduction de RESEDA

L'instrument de description esquissé ci-dessus est au service d'un ensemble de procédures de déductions naturelles qui permettent de répondre à des questions d'utilisateurs par l'instauration de connexions logiques nouvelles entre les données fournies au système (il s'agit là, comme je l'ai déjà souligné, d'une sorte d'accroissement automatique des connaissances). Je chercherai à en donner un exemple assez simple pour l'exposer ici en détail.

Supposons que nous ayons enregistré dans la mémoire du système les 'plans' correspondant à ce passage:

Les ambassadeurs de l'Université étaient porteurs d'une lettre pour Benoît XIII rédigée précipitamment par Clamanges, rédacteur habituel des lettres de l'Université depuis juin 1394, le jour même de leur départ (14 avril 1395). Cette lettre contenait presque une approbation des voies de concile et de convention. Il n'est pas étonnant qu'une lettre rédigée en toute hâte ait reflété les positions personnelles de son auteur plutôt que celles préconisées par l'Université. Ils avaient cru devoir la garder par devers eux. Quand ils furent de retour, l'Université elle-même prit soin de corriger cette épître en en retranchant tout ce qui ne tendait pas à l'éloge exclusif de la voie de cession – 26 août 1395 (d'après Valois 1891-1902, III pp. 70-71, Ornato 1969, pp. 25-26).

Pour ne pas trop alourdir mon exposé, je n'indiquerai ici que le codage 'externe' des plans qui seront effectivement utilisés dans l'exemple d'inférence:

9) /14-avril-1395/ //Paris/Avignon/ //Bibl:Ornato/
(*CLAMANGES* .SUJ. ((((*soc+ment+DEPLACER* .OBJ. 10) .MODAL. *lettre-officielle-1*) .SOURCE. *UNIVERSITE-DE-PARIS*) .DEST. *BENOIT-XIII*))

Le 14 avril 1395, Clamanges transmet au pape d'Avignon Benoît XIII, par une lettre officielle (dont la rédaction effective a été relatée dans un plan précédent), l'idée exprimée dans le plan 10 comme s'il s'agissait d'une idée de l'Université.

*10) /14-avril-1395/ //Paris/Avignon/ / / //Bibl:Valois/
(*UNIVERSITE-DE-PARIS* .SUJ. ((*pour+AVOIR-ATTITUDE* .OBJ. *BENOIT-XIII*) .ARG.*voie-de-convention*))

L'Université de Paris soutient le pape dans sa politique de compromis (*voie-de-convention*) entre Rome et Avignon (il s'agit d'une interprétation erronée de Clamanges, et le plan est marqué d'une astérisque comme 'faux').

11)/14-avril-1395/avant-26-août-1395//Avignon/   /Avignon/   /
   //Bibl:Valois/
   (*BENOIT-XIII* .SUJ. ((*neg+ETRE-AFFECTE* .OBJ. *lettre-officielle-1*) .SOURCE. *ANOMS-1*))

Benoît XIII n'a pas rec,u la lettre officielle de la part des ambassadeurs (*ANOMS-1*) dans la période comprise entre le 14 avril 1395 (départ de l'ambassade) et le 26 août (remaniement de la lettre par l'Université)

(11 .CAUSE2. (9 .COORD2. 13))

L'événement représenté en 11 – Benoît XIII n'a pas rec,u la lettre – est la conséquence du fait que Clamanges a faussement représenté (en 9) la politique de l'Université (donnée en 13)

12)/26-août-1395/ //Paris/ / /Avignon/ //Bibl:Valois/
   (*UNIVERSITE-DE-PARIS* .SUJ. ((*rep+PRODUIRE* .OBJ. *lettre-officielle-1*) .DEST. *BENOIT-XIII*))

Le 26 août, l'Université reformule (*rep+PRODUIRE* a le sens de 'refaire') la lettre officielle pour Benoît XIII

(12 .CAUSE2. (9 .COORD2. 13))

Cette reécriture (12) découle de la falsification effectuée par Clamanges (en 9) à propos de l'attitude de l'Université (13)

13)/26-août-1395/ //Paris/ / /Avignon/ //Bibl:Valois/
   (*UNIVERSITE-DE-PARIS* .SUJ. ((*int+ment+DEPLACER* .OBJ. 14) .DEST. *BENOIT-XIII*))

Le 26 août 1395, l'Université de Paris voulait (*int*) en effet informer Benoît XIII, à Avignon, de sa position réelle exprimée en 14

14)/1395/début-1408//Paris/Avignon/ / / //Bibl:consensus/
   (*UNIVERSITE-DE-PARIS* .SUJ. ((*contre+AVOIR-ATTITUDE* .OBJ. *papes-d'Avignon*) .ARG.*voie-de-convention*))

Entre 1395 et le début de 1408, l'Université de Paris s'oppose continuellement aux papes d'Avignon à propos de la politique 'voie de convention'.

Imaginons maintenant une question d'utilisateur du type "Pourquoi Clamanges, après août 1395, cesse-t-il toute activité de rédacteur officiel des lettres de l'Université de Paris?". La question sera ainsi codée:
   /après-août-1395/ //Paris/Paris/Paris/ / //
   (*CLAMANGES* .SUJ. (((*fin+soc+mult+ment+PRODUIRE* .OBJ. *lettre-officielle*) .SOURCE. *UNIVERSITE-DE-PARIS*) .CAUSE1. *?x*))
La 'multiplicité' de l'action de rédaction est indiquée par *mult* et son caractère officiel par *soc*.
   La réponse serait immédiate ('direct match') si on arrivait à trouver dans la base de données du système un épisode codé contenant les termes mêmes de l'énoncé de la question organisés de la même façon et proposant un plan ou un terme de lexique à la place de l'inconnue *x*.

L'impossibilité d'apparier la question avec une réponse nous force à avoir recours aux procédures d'inférence relatives au prédicat *PRODUIRE*; c'est toujours le prédicat présent dans la question qui détermine le 'programme' qui doit être sélectionné.

La recherche d'une 'cause' à l'interruption (*fin*) d'un 'rapport de travail' de type intellectuel (*ment*) nous aiguille – à l'intérieur du programme général qui définit le prédicat *PRODUIRE* – vers une sous-routine où l'on demande des renseignements sur le type de rapport en question. La présence de *soc* et de SOURCE permet de comprendre qu'on est dans un cas de 'délégation de pouvoir' de la SOURCE vers le SUJET de la question. On est donc autorisé à tester l'hypothèse suivante: "La rupture du rapport de travail – dans le cas d'une *délégation de pouvoir intellectuel* – peut être due au fait que le représentant, dans le cadre de sa charge, agit en contradiction avec la position officielle du représenté". Si l'on arrive à reconnaître en mémoire des épisodes codés qui s'adaptent à cette hypothèse, il faudra aussi – avant de les fournir à l'utilisateur comme réponse – vérifier, si possible, l'argument complémentaire selon lequel la cause d'interruption présumée est bien à l'origine de quelque action concrète – autre évidemment que la rupture explicite du rapport de travail – du resprésenté contre son représentant.

Tester l'hypothèse ci-dessus signifie – dans le cadre de notre 'logique des attitudes' – essayer de substituer à l'inconnue *x* de la question une série de plans présents dans la base de données et qui s'adaptent au schéma:

p) (*V1* .SUJ. ((*soc+ment+DEPLACER* .OBJ. q) .SOURCE. *V2*))

!q) (*V2* .SUJ. ((*pour/contre+AVOIR-ATTITUDE* .OBJ. *V3*) .ARG.*a*))

!r) (*V2* .SUJ. ((*contre/pour+AVOIR-ATTITUDE* .OBJ. *V3*) .ARG.*a*))

s) (*V2* .SUJ. ((*ment+DEPLACER* .OBJ. r) .DEST. *V4*))

Les 'vedettes' *V1* et *V2* sont le SUJET et la SOURCE de la question et *V3* – *V4* deux autres personnages qui peuvent ou non coincider; les 'points d'exclamations' devant les deux plans-objet signalent que ceux-ci sont contradictoires (si *pour* apparaît dans l'un des deux plans, *contre* doit apparaître dans l'autre). Les indications de temps portées par les thématiques doivent évidemment être cohérentes entre elles et avec celles de la question.

Dans le cas présent, *p* et *q* sont satisfaits par le couple de plans 9 et 10 vu précédemment (je n'insiste pas sur l'organisation en 'volumes' des plans dans leur représentation interne, qui ne présente pas ici d'intérêt immédiat; pour quelques détails voir p.e. Ornato, Zarri 1976a, 1976b). Le plan 10, je le rappelle, était marqué comme 'faux'; le plan 14, qui contredit brutalement le 10, rentre lui aussi dans le schéma puisqu'il satisfait le plan *r*. La forme particulière de la contradiction – une information fausse par opposition à une vérité établie ('consensus') – nous permet ici de nous passer de la recherche d'un plan *s*. En fait *s* doit être utilisé dans le cas le plus général, où les deux plans qui satisfont *p* et *q* sont simplement contradictoires, sans qu'aucun des deux soit carrément signalé comme faux. Dans ce cas, on doit retrouver une preuve (plan *s*) que *V2*, la SOURCE de la question, a informé quelqu'un de ce qui est indiqué en *r*. Mais si, comme dans notre cas, l'attitude de l' 'employeur' est bien connue, on n'a pas besoin de cette deuxième 'diffusion d'information' pour pouvoir constater la contradiction.

Le contrôle de vraisemblance, nécessaire pour montrer que l'initiative de Clamanges était suffisamment grave pour justifier une rupture des rapports entre lui et l'Université, n'est pas ici trop difficile. Il s'agit en effet de retrouver une réaction négative immédiate de l'Université à l'action de Clamanges. On doit donc chercher des situations où un corrélateur-pointeur CAUSE2 englobe p – c'est-à-dire le plan 9 – dans son corrélé de droite. Cela nous conduit aux plans 11 et 12 qui sont tous les deux provoqués par 9 (et par 13, mais ce dernier ne nous intéresse pas ici). Dans 12, *UNIVERSITE-DE-PARIS* apparaît comme SUJET, et la nuance de 'réprobation' associée au sens de 'refaire une lettre officielle' nous donne la vérification cherchée. Le plan 11 aussi aurait pu fournir l'attestation d'une réaction négative de l'Université (ses ambassadeurs n'ont pas donné la lettre au pape) mais évidemment au prix de manipulations bien plus complexes.

Le contrôle ayant donné le feu vert, on peut finalement fournir les plans 9, 10 et 14 à l'utilisateur comme réponse.

L'exemple que je viens de donner d'une utilisation de *PRODUIRE* montre suffisamment le degré de complexité et de raffinement qu'on demande aux 'programmes' des prédicats. Je préciserai toutefois que – dans la version actuelle de RESEDA – ces prédicats ont été en fait construits par simple juxtaposition de règles *ad-hoc* de résolution. Cela ne porte pas préjudice à leur utilité pratique, vu que leurs 'ramifications' sont suffisamment poussées pour couvrir un nombre élevé d'inférences possibles. Il n'en reste pas moins qu'avec ce premier modèle nous ne disposons que d'un système doté d'un nombre fini de structures d'apprentissage non évolutives, dont la capacité d'enrichissement – c'est-à-dire l'aptitude à trouver des rapports nouveaux entre les personnages ou les situations des personnages – est limitée à un nombre fini de contextes prédéterminés.

Nous avons ainsi commencé à envisager l'élaboration d'une nouvelle version de RESEDA où les structures d'accueil du métalangage seraient dotées d'une certaine capacité d'évolution. Une aide a été demandée à ce propos au C.N.R.S. dans le cadre de l'Action thématique programmée 'Informatique en sciences humaines'. Nous pensons aborder le problème de deux façons et donner un début de comportement évolutif à nos prédicats, en choisissant d'un côté l'approche traditionnelle des *production systems* (Newell, Simon 1972; Davis, King 1977; Davis et al. 1977) et de l'autre celle d'une généralisation au niveau de certains concepts comme le 'principe de contradiction' que j'ai utilisé – sous l'un de ses aspects particuliers – sans l'exemple d'inférence.

Conclusions

Je terminerai ici mon intervention par deux réflexions sur les centres d'intérêt que notre entreprise semble présenter. Le premier est que l'infrastructure générale du métalangage et des procédures déductives semble suffisamment souple pour pouvoir s'adapter sans changement important de la philosophie du système à l'exploitation 'évoluée' de n'importe quel corpus d'informations biographiques. On peut très bien remplacer nos rois et nos papes par des présidents de la république ou des secrétaires de parti politique modernes sans être obligé de procéder à un remaniement essentiel des structures du système. Cela explique l'intérêt de certains chercheurs pour RESEDA (en psychologie et en documentation juridique, par exemple) bien que leur sujet de recherche soit éloigné du domaine des études médiévales.

Un dernier point concerne enfin l'importance de ce projet sous un angle qu'on me pardonnera de définir comme 'épistémologique'. RESEDA contribue en effet à faire revenir sur terre quelques techniques d'une certaine sophistication employées en intelligence artificielle, dont l'importance et l'utilité théorique ont été plusieurs fois démontrées, mais dont les auteurs dédaignent très souvent les applications pratiques, à cause de leur conception étrange de ce qui est digne d'être considéré comme 'scientifique'. Même s'il s'agit là d'une considération plus abstraite que les précédentes, il ne faudrait pas négliger son importance dans le contexte de la discussion actuellement en cours sur les avantages et les limites de l'automatisation dans les Sciences Humaines.

Liste des ouvrages cités

C. Bozzolo, M. Ornato, G. Ouy, G.P. Zarri (1976a) *Projet RESEDA: Rapport sur les recherches effectuées du 1er octobre 1975 au 1er avril 1976* (Rap/CNRS/ERHF/1976/DGRST-1). Paris: Equipe Recherche Humanisme Français.

C. Bozzolo, M. Ornato, G. Ouy, G.P. Zarri, A. Zwiebel (1976b) *Projet RESEDA: Rapport sur les recherches effectuées du 1er avril 1976 au 1er octobre 1976* (Rap/CNRS/ERHF/1976/DGRST-2). Paris: Equipe Recherche Humanisme Français.

R. Davis, J. King (1977) "An Overview of Production Systems", dans *Machine Intelligence 8: Machine Representations of Knowledge*, Elcock et Michie, éds., New York: Wiley.

R. Davis, B. Buchanan, E. Shortliffe. (1977) "Production Rules as a Representation for a Knowledge-Based Consultation Program", *Artificial Intelligence*, VIII, 15-45.

A. Newell, H.A. Simon (1972) *Human Problem Solving*. Englewood Cliffs, N.J.: Prentice Hall.

M. Ornato (1969) *Jean Muret et ses amis Nicolas de Clamanges et Jean de Montreuil*. Genève-Paris: Librairie Droz.

M. Ornato, G.P. Zarri (1976a) "An Application of Artificial Intelligence in Information Retrieval: RESEDA Project for Medieval Biographies", dans *Proceedings of AISB Summer Conference*, M. Brady, éd. Edinburgh: AISB Society.

M. Ornato, G.P. Zarri (1976b) "RESEDA: A 'Semi-Intelligent' System of Information Retrieval from Medieval Biographical Data", dans *Proceedings of the International Symposium on Technology for Selective Dissemination of Information*, I. Cotton, éd. New York: IEEE Press.

N. Valois (1891-1902) *La France et le Grand Schisme*, IV vol. Paris: Picard.

D.L. Waltz (1977) ″Natural Language Interfaces″, *ACM Sigart Newsletter*, no.61, February 1977, 16-64.

6
Computer Assisted Instruction

MUSICOL: Musical Instruction Composition Oriented Language

P. Gena

MUSICOL, a computer language for composing music, was originally developed for composers with no previous knowledge of computer programming. A thorough description of the language and its use is found in *MUSICOL Manual, Version 1*. To facilitate the reader's understanding of the body of this paper, a sample MUSICOL program has been included in the appendix. The mnemonics table consists of conventional musical terms of up to ten characters (for example, VIOLA, FLUTE, D, G, PIZZ, MF, QUARTER, SULPONT, REST, 8VE4), and common punctuation marks which serve as non-arithmetic expressions (for example, / ( ) * - . +). Only zero and positive integer constants are used as operands after expressions.

MUSICOL statements (instructions) have a free format, and columns 2 to 72 of each card may contain as many of them as desired by the programmer. An incomplete statement continues on the next card providing no operation code is split. Expressions and blanks are recognized as delimiters. Any character in the first column of a card will allow fields 1 to 72 to be treated as comments. Similarly, the use of a comma in any column will render the remainder of the card free from compilation. Columns 73 to 80, which are ignored by the compiler, serve as the identification field.

The MUSICOL user has the flexibility to determine the process for choosing among strings of musical parameters (pitch, duration, range, attack, timbre, dynamics, and texture) in successive blocks of time, the lengths of which are variable. A total of sixteen different instruments can be used simultaneously. These are chosen from a list of common instruments stored in the mnemonics table (such as VIOLIN, FLUTE, PIANO, VIBRAPHONE), including non-pitched percussion. In addition, there are extra codes (INSTR1, INSTR2, etc.) available for assigning instruments not included in the table, or others (XTRA1, XTRA2, etc.) for timbres and attacks not contained. The contents for the strings of the individual parametric elements to be used in the compositional process can be declared by the composer, or generated by special routines. If no parameter string is indicated by the user, elements are randomly chosen from the appropriate collection in the mnemonics table. All of these features can be selected, changed, respecified, or eliminated at any point in the user's MUSICOL program.

Selection of Musical Parameters

Total randomness, stochastic processes, and literal selection are the three general methods presently available to generate parametric content. Various aspects of these techniques can be used alone or simultaneously within a time-block to achieve desired parametric configuration. A random generator is used to some extent in all decisions, with the exception of the literals declarations. Total randomness (zeroth-order) is assumed when no specific instructions are given as to how a choice, for an instrument or group of instruments, is made from the elements belonging to a musical parameter. Hence, the parameters affected are selected randomly from the pertinent list in the stored table. If a partial list of members in the table is desired for selection at equal probability, the mnemonics may be listed in a string within the time-block. During the compositional process, only those in the declared list will be eligible for inclusion. In addition, such a list of elements can be randomly generated, and the specific choice would, in turn, be impartially made. Furthermore, a parametric string, whether determined by the composer or generated, can be shifted about. This shuffling procedure can be called at any time, repeatedly, at the discretion of the composer.

A more interesting aspect of computer-aided composition constitutes the application of stochastic methods for parametric selection. Each element belonging to a parameter-class is assigned a rank order, that is, a hierarchy is established according to the percentage representing the probability of its occurrence. The most basic stochastic process in MUSICOL determines the texture of the composition by means of a play/rest ratio. Percentages of play/rest, derived from weighted probabilities, can be set inclusively for all instruments or for each individually. If a play probability of seventy-five percent is assigned, a twenty-five percent chance of rest is automatic. The elements of a declared parametric string can be subjected to stochastic selection by the use of rank ordering. These proportional percentages are chosen according to distributions as outlined in the following paragraphs.

To generate probabilities for parametric elements in a string, the basic random procedure can be weighted by merely repeating elements in accordance with their projected ranking. Since each element in a string receives equal distribution, repetition will increase its probability. In the following list:

(B A B-flat B C D-flat F B C B A C)

the pitch B (four occurrences) will have the greatest probability, that of 4/12 or 1/3, followed by C at 1/4, then A at 1/6. B-flat, D-flat and F will each have the same assignment, 1/12. This simple operation, of course, can be implemeted successfully for all parameter strings. The maximum list size of twenty-four elements allows a wide range of probability manipulations.

The third type of stochastic technique used for parametric selection is a simulation of an experimental result originally pointed out by George Kingsley Zipf. Zipf performed statistical studies on the English language where words from substantial texts were listed in order of frequency of occurrence, or rank-ordered. The results of these rank orders, plotted against the frequency, show relatively linear graphs. Therefore, each rank order has a probability approximately equal to the reciprocal of its number.

Example 1

       Rank order: 1,   2,   3,   4,   n

       Probability (P): 1/1, 1/2, 1/3, 1/4, ... 1/n

This empirical inverse relation between probability and rank became known as Zipf's Law. It is obvious that in order to hold the running sum of probabilities (P) at unity, it is necessary to multiply the inverse of each rank order by a constant (K), equal to the reciprocal of the sum of elements 1/1 through 1/n, that is:

$$K = 1/\sum_{i=1}^{n} P_i \qquad (1)$$

If $n = 5$:

      $(60/60 + 30/60 + 20/60 + 15/60 + 12/60) \times K = 1.0$

      $K = 60/137$

For individual probabilities:

$$P_r = 1/r \times K \qquad (2)$$

      $P_1 = .438$

      $P_2 = .219$

      $P_3 = .145$

      $P_4 = .11$

      $P_5 = .088$

In MUSICOL, the declared lists can be assigned rank order numbers. The programmer decides which element is to be the first. In the following:

      (PPP FT MP FF MF PP P)

if PPP is the first rank order, then:

      (PPP FT MP FF MF PP P)

rank: 1   2   3   4   5   6   7

The first element of the string need not always be the first order. Thus in the list:

      (PPP FFF MP MF FF PP P FT)

if FF is the first order, then rank will be assigned as:

      (PPP FFF MP MF FF PP P FT)

rank: 4   3   2   1   2   3   4 5

In the last case, elements sharing the same rank order number will also be equally probable.

Example 2

      (PPP FFF MP MF FF PP P FT)

Probabilities:

              $P(MF) = .438$

              $P(MP) = .11$

              $P(FF) = .11$

            $P(FFF) = .0725$

             $P(PP) = .0725$

           $P(PPP) = .055$

               $P(P) = .055$

             $P(FT) = .088$

To establish predetermined probabilities for elements, it may be necessary to repeat elements as needed.

  Example 3

      (MF FT MF PP P MP P MF)

rank: 4   3   2   1   2   3   4   5

Probabilities:

$$P(PP) = .438$$
$$P(P) = .1645$$
$$P(MF) = .2525$$
$$P(FT) = .0725$$
$$P(MP) = .0725$$

It is not required that all elements of a declared list be assigned rank order numbers for individual instruments. The instruction, FLUTE = C+ *5 will submit rank orders and select from the five pitches around C-sharp as follows:

```
      ( C+  D  F  A  E- B  D  C  F+  E)
rank:  1    2  3  4  5
```

Thus, the five rightmost pitches will not be chosen by the flute. However, instruments may divide or share elements in a list.

Example 4
Instructions: FLUTE = C+ *5, VIOLA = E*6 and OBOE = B*3 will yield:

```
          3  2  1  2  3                 – OBOE ranking
      ( C+  D  F  A  E- B  D  C  F+  E)
        1    2  3  4  5                  – FLUTE ranking
                   6  5  4  3  2   1     – VIOLA ranking
```

To increase programming flexibility, literal selection of parametric elements is available in MUSICOL. If a declared parametric string contains only one element, the element will be chosen exclusively. Also, an element can be designated as the first of only one possible rank order; its probability would be 1.0. Specific durational lengths within time-blocks can be specified for literals of any parameter for individual instruments. This frees the remaining time for the particular instrument to be controlled by other declarations pertaining to the required parameter.

Programming a composition in MUSICOL involves the logical implementation of continuous time-blocks where the previously described techniques are used to create a preconceived parametric content. It is hoped that such versatility in choosing musical parameters will allow the composer to implant his own personal style on a composition, eliminating the 'salt and pepper' effect often found in computer compositions that depend heavily upon stochastic processes to the exclusion of other controls.

Software Design

The language was originally designed to run on CDC 6000 or 7000 series computers, but can be altered to run on any medium to large computer with a FORTRAN IV compiler. The source program is constructed by means of four overlays: the main-line, the compiler, the simulator/executor, and the output routine. The binary source requires from 33,000 to 44,000 octal locations to load, depending on the CDC operating system. The majority of the routines are written in FORTRAN IV, excepting a small number of assembly language subprograms which can be easily translated. MUSICOL operation codes contain up to ten BCD characters. Obviously, the longer mnemonics must be reduced in length for computers with smaller word structure.

The word-packing of instructions, and so on, would also have to be adjusted accordingly. In the MUSICOL compiler, each instruction is assembled into a CDC 60-bit word, which is divided into five or six fields of a combination of six or twelve bits, depending on the instruction type. Instructions are stored as they appear in successive time-blocks for entry into the simulator. The simulator constructs a core memory for the program's MUSICOL source instructions, so that the execution of the compositional process is determined by the programmed specifics. The compiled code for each time-block remains in the simulated memory until the composing is completed for the set length, as specified in the block. Output is stored on a file as each block is processed.

Three stages of printed output result from submission of a program in MUSICOL. The source-code listing is followed by a compilation map, complete with mnemonic code cross-referencing. A loader-execution map tabulates all instrumental or parametric declarations, deletions, changes, etc., and points to the respective locations of the responsible code in the source program. An extensive diagnostic system serves both the compilation and execution stages. In the event of errors incurred during execution, the working simulated-memory is dumped as an extra debugging aid. The actual listing of the resultant composition is clearly printed (in MUSICOL mnemonics) chronologically by measure numbers, beats and subdivisions. This type of output could easily serve as input to a music writing program. Currently at Northwestern, the output is being fed to SMUT (System for Music Transcription), a music copying program using a Calcomp plotter.

Future

Since an undertaking such as MUSICOL can never be completely satisfactory, plans for an improved version (2.0) are now being formulated. Though it is proposed that probabilistic techniques allow freedom to the programmer in choosing syntax, more variety is surely needed. Ideally, Markoff processes could be added to promote smoother syntactic structure, especially when using order approximations as an influence on subsequent choices. In addition, it may be desirable to cross parameters during selection, that is, certain choices in pitch may be used to prejudice those of rhythm, and so on. Other features such as *Iching* and stochastic processes used by Xenakis might also be implemented as options. Harmony in version 1 is essentially a by-product of the specified linear structures taken vertically. A composer is able to influence the selection of types of chords by carefully manipulating pitch and rhythmic distributions, but a new procedure must be developed to allow direct access to controlling vertical simultaneities. There are several existing MUSICOL mnemonics which are not yet active. Most of them depend on referencing material already composed. A search and store memory access program will be developed to make all output material recursively accessible.

It seems that a common goal of most composing languages or systems is to provide the user with a flexible base of directives which will insure artisitic individuality. Obviously it is impossible to create a language which remains impartial to the author's aesthetic, or void of any personal compositional bias. Indeed, MUSICOL is not without limitations in this respect, nor will future revisions render it totally objective. My philosophy behind the design is that simplicity of basic choice procedures will invite the user to re-evaluate his own musical ideas in terms of probabilities. This requires considerable pre-compositional thought, a tradition which is clearly as necessary when using automated systems as it is before sitting down at a piano with a pen and manuscript paper. To this end, not until the composer understands his process objectively, will he be able to establish a degree of personal uniqueness.

References

Byrd, Donald. *SMUT: System for Music Transcription.* Indiana University, July, 1975.

Cherry, Colin. *On Human Communication, A Review, A Survey, and A Criticism.* Cambridge, Mass.: The M.I.T. Press, 1966.

Gena, Peter. "MUSICOL Manual, Version 1," *Technical Report No. 7.* SUNY at Buffalo, New York, 1973.

Hiller, Lejaren. "Closed Subroutines for Musical Composition," *Technical Report No. 9.* SUNY at Buffalo, New York, 1975.

Hiller, Lejaren. "Information Theory and Musical Analysis," *Technical Report No. 5.* University of Illinois Experimental Music Studio, July, 1962.

Gena, Peter. "Programming the *I-Ching* Oracle," *Computer Studies in the Humanities and Verbal Behavior.* Vol. III, No. 3, October, 1970. p. 130-143.

Moles, Abraham. *Information Theory and Esthetic Perception.* Translated by Joel E. Cohen. Urbana: University of Illinois Press, 1966.

Pierce, J.R. *Symbols, Signals, and Noise.* New York: Harper and Row, Inc., 1961.

Xenakis, Iannis. *Formalized Music, Thought and Mathematics in Composition.* Translated by C. Butchers, G.W. Hopkins, and Mr. and Mrs. J. Callifour. Bloomington: Indiana University Press, 1971.

Zipf, George Kingsley. *Human Behavior and the Principle of Least Effort.* Cambridge, Mass.: Addison-Wesley Publishing Co., 1949.

Appendix

The following pages contain a sample of a complete test program in MUSICOL. Interpretation of instructions are outlined below according to expressions.

Expression	Example
- denotes range	FRQRANGE=3A−4F (general pitch range of 3rd Oct. A to 4th Oct. F#). VIOLIN=3G−7C (Violin range of 3rd Oct. G to 7th Oct. C).
* specifies rank orders and play/rest ratios	(See Example 4, page 5).
/ separates time signature values	TIMSIG = 3/4
( ) parameter-string and voice delimiters	(PP FF FT PPP MF) – dynamics string; VIOLIN(2) – 2 voices possible.
= sets all parametrical specifications for instruments; assigns extra op-codes; used for instrument deletion and replacement; used before all range instructions, etc.	VIOLIN(2) = 3C−5G+ = Arco*1 XTRA1 − SULTASTO (mnemonic for SULTASTO is assigned) VIOLIN = END (Violin deleted) FLUTE = RANDOM (all parameters for FLUTE will be chosen randomly)
, renders all code to the right as comments	
signifies multiple stop probabilites and literal lengths.	VIOLIN(2) .1 *2 (selection of 1-voice texture is twice as probable as 2-voice texture). RITARD = 40.122 (ritardando to over a period of 122, 32nd-note values. FLUTE = 16TH.96 (selects only 16th notes for flute for 96, 32nd-note values).

```
MUSICOL(SUNYAB) 1973. - VER 1.1  NU - P. GENA          14.29.38.       04/25/77                    PAGE   1
000000                          START     MUSICOL TEST DECK NUMBER 1, MUSIC COMPOSITION, 19 MEASURES          TEST001
                                  .                                                                           TEST002
                                  .     THE RANK ORDER PARAMETERS ARE BEING SET FIRST                         TEST003
                                  .                                                                           TEST004
000000                          ORDERS (PP PPP MP P MF FT FF FFF)  (NORMAL ARCO PIZZ COLLEG SLUR SFFZ         TEST005
000003                             SFZ)  RONGEN(0- 12)    (8VE1  8VE2  8VE3  8VE4 AVE5 8VE6 AVE7)             TEST006
000007                             (NORMALT SULPONT MUTED XTRA1  GLISS FLUTTERTGE )  (WHOLE HALF              TEST007
000011                             QUARTER EIGHTH 16TH 32ND  WHOLE+ HALF+ QUARTER+ EIGHTH+ 16TH+)             TEST008
000014                 TIME=1.00  XTRA1= SULTASTO                                                             TEST009
000016                           FRQRANGE=3A-4F+  DYNRANGE=PP-MP NTRANGE=WHOLE-16TH  HALF*1                   TEST010
000022                             PLAY* 85               NORMAL*7              QUARTER*120                   TEST011
000025                             FLUTE(1)=4D-7C =NORMALT*1                                                  TEST012
000030                           VIOLA(2) =3C-5G+ = ARCO *1   BASSOON(1) =2C-5A =NORMALT*1                    TEST013
000036                 VIOLIN(2)=3G-7C .1*2 =HALF*4 =SULPONT*1 =PP*2 =ARCO*1 =XTRA1.8A                        TEST014
000046                 TIME=6.9 NTRANGE=QUARTER-EIGHTH FRQRANGE=2C-5A+ DYNRANGE=MP-FF                         TEST015
000052                           FLUTE= 4E-7A =RANDOM =FLUTTERTGE *1  VIOLIN=XTRA1*1=PIZZ*3=FF.8A             TEST016
                       C----------------- VIOLIN SHOULD CRESC. UNTIL TIME=9.0                                 TEST017
                                  .                                                                           TEST018
000060                           BASSOON=EIGHTH*1=8VE2*1  VIOLA=COLLEG.8     SHUFFLE (ARCO 7)                 TEST019
000064                 TIME=9.0  CRESC=FF.122  RITARD=40.122 FRQRANGE=2C-7C NTRANGE=HALF-16TH                 TEST020
000071                           ORDERS(SULPONT MUTEN  XTRA1  GLISS FLUTTERTGE   NORMALT)                     TEST021
000073                           FLUTE =16TH.96   BASSCON =RANDOM =NORMALT *3                                 TEST022
                       .-----------------CLIMAX OCCURS AT BAR 13, QUICKLY DIMINISHES                          TEST023
                       .-----------AT TIME=13.00, VIOLA DELETED, BASSCON IS REPLACED BY CELLO                 TEST024
000076                 TIME=13.0  FRQRANGE=2C-4F+ NTRANGE=WHOLE - HALF  REST=*45  QUARTER=60                  TEST025
000103                           INSTR1(1)=VIOLA2=3C- 4F+=SULPONT*1=PPP*1=ARCO2*4=8VE3*2                      TEST026
000112                           VIOLA = END   BASSCON=CELLO(1) =2C=4C+                                       TEST027
000116                             WHOLE*1   DIMTN=PP.8A  VIOLIN=MUTED*1                                      TEST028
                       .----------PIECE ENDS AFTER 19 BARS                                                    TEST029
                                  .                                                                           TEST030
000121                 TIME=16.00  DYNRANGE=PPP-PPP VIOLIN=PIZZ*1                                             TEST031
000124                           FLUTE = NORMAL *1    CELLO =REST* 100                                        TEST032
000126                 TIME=17.00  .-----CLEAR RANK ORDERINGS FOR PITCH AND ATTACK                            TEST033
000127                           RONGEN=E 01  SHUFFLE(SFZ 0) FLUTE=SFZ*0=E*0 VIOLIN=SFZ*0=E*0                 TEST034
000135                           INSTR1=SFZ*0=E*0                                                             TEST035
000137                 TIME=20.00                                                                            TEST036
000140                                  END  MUSIC COMPOSITION        P. GENA                                 TEST037
```

```
MUSICOL(SUNYAB) 1973. - VER 1.1  NU - P. GENA              14.29.38.         04/25/77                    PAGE   2
         MUSICOL COMPILER VERSION 1.1. 1976................CALLED.........EXIT .........PROGRAM LENGTH
                                                              .064           1.129            000140


      NUMBER OF CARDS
        37

      NUMBER OF STATEMENTS
        96

      ASSIGNED MNEMONICS
         LOC DEF.  MNEMONIC  SYMBOL TAG  REFERENCES
                        A                000016  000034
                        B                000052
                        C                000026  000031  000034  000037  000050  000067  000067  000077  000105  000115

                        D                000026
                        E                000052  000127  000132  000134  000136
                        G                000037
                        P                000000
                        A+               000050
                        C+               000115
                        D-               000004
                        FF               000001  000051  000057  000065
                        FT               000001
                        F+               000016  000077  000105
                        G+               000031
                        MF               000001
                        MP               000000  000017  000051
                        PP               000000  000017  000043  000107  000117
                        END              000112  000140
                        FFF              000001
                        PPP              000000  000122  000122
                        SFZ              000003  000130  000131  000133  000135
                        ARCO             000002  000032  000044  000063  000110
                        HALF             000011  000021  000041  000070  000100
                        PIZZ             000002  000056  000123
                        PLAY             000022
                        REST             000101  000125
                        SFFZ             000003
                        SLUR             000003
                        TIME             000014  000046  000064  000076  000121  000126  000137
                        16TH             000012  000020  000070  000073
                        32ND             000012
                        8VE1             000005
                        8VE2             000005  000061
                        8VE3             000005  000111
                        8VE4             000005
                        8VE5             000006
                        8VE6             000006
                        8VE7             000006
                        CELLO            000113  000125
                        CRESC            000065
                        DIMIN            000117


MUSICOL(SUNYAB) 1973. - VER 1.1  NU - P. GENA              14.29.38.         04/25/77                    PAGE   3
                        FLUTE            000025  000052  000073  000124  000131
                        GLISS            000010  000071
                        HALF+            000012
                        MUTED            000007  000071  000120
                        VIOLA            000030  000062  000112
                        WHOLE            000011  000020  000100  000116
           000007       XTRA1   SULTASTO 000015  000045  000055  000071
                        16TH+            000013
                        COLLEG           000002  000062
                        EIGHTH           000011  000047  000060
           000103       INSTR1  VIOLA2   000135
                        NORMAL           000002  000023  000124
                        RANDOM           000053  000074
                        RITARD           000066
                        ROWGEN           000004  000127
                        VIOLIN           000036  000055  000120  000123  000133
                        WHOLE+           000012
                        BASSOON          000033  000060  000074  000113
                        EIGHTH+          000013
                        NORMALT          000007  000027  000035  000072  000075
                        NTRANGE          000020  000047  000070  000100
                        QUARTER          000011  000024  000047  000102
                        SHUFFLE          000063  000130
                        SULPONT          000007  000042  000071  000106
                        DYNRANGE         000017  000051  000122
                        FRQRANGE         000016  000050  000067  000077
                        QUARTER+         000012
                        FLUTTERTGE       000010  000054  000072


      TOTAL COMPILATION TIME
        1.065 SECONDS




MUSICOL(SUNYAB) 1973. - VER 1.1  NU - P. GENA              14.29.38.         04/25/77                    PAGE   4
         MUSICOL LOADER - SIMULATOR.....VERSION 1....................LOADER CALLED
                                                                        2.256

      EXECUTION CONDITIONS

         ROWGEN CALLED. LOCATION= 000004.     PITCH RANK ORDERS CHANGED AS FOLLOWS
            A          D          F       A-        C+        G-        G        A+        E        C
            E-         B

      NO INITIAL TIME SIGNATURE SPECIFIED. 4/4 ASSUMED

            FLUTE RANDOM-CLEARED. LOCATION 000053

         SHUFFLE CALLED. LOCATION= 000063.     ATTACK RANK ORDERS CHANGED AS FOLLOWS
            SFFZ       NORMAL         SFZ       PIZZ      SLUR      COLLEG     ARCO

            BASSOON RANDOM-CLEARED. LOCATION 000074

            VIOLA DELETED. LOCATION  000112

            BASSOON REPLACED BY      1 CELLO. LOCATION 000113

         ROWGEN CALLED. LOCATION= 000127.     PITCH RANK ORDERS DELETED

         SHUFFLE CALLED. LOCATION= 000130.     ATTACK RANK ORDERS DELETED


            TOTAL EXECUTION TIME = 1.960 SECONDS
```

MUSICOL TEST DECK NUMBER 1, MUSIC COMPOSITION, 19 MEASURES

APPROXIMATE DURATION =   1 MINS. AND 8 SECS.

POSITION	INSTR. NAME	PITCH	RANGE	DURATION	DYNAMICS	ATTACK	TIMBRE	SPEC 1	SPEC 2	SPEC 3	SPEC 4

```
**********************************
*   TIME SIGNATURE =  4/ 4   *
**********************************
*  M.M =   QUARTER =125       *
**********************************
```

POSITION	INSTR. NAME	PITCH	RANGE	DURATION	DYNAMICS	ATTACK	TIMBRE
BAR 1 BEAT 1 + 1	FLUTE	E	8VE4	HALF	PP	NORMAL	NORMALT
	VIOLA	D	8VE4	WHOLE	MP	ARCO	SULPONT
	VIOLA	C	8VE4	WHOLE			
	BASSOON	B	8VE3	EIGHTH	PP	SLUR	NORMALT
	VIOLIN	REST		16TH			
BAR 1 BEAT 1 + 3	VIOLIN	C	8VE4	16TH		ARCO	SULPONT
	VIOLIN	B-	8VE4	16TH			
BAR 1 BEAT 1 + 5	BASSOON	B	8VE3	EIGHTH		SFZ	NORMALT
	VIOLIN	A	8VE4	WHOLE		ARCO	SULPONT
BAR 1 BEAT 2 + 1	BASSOON	G+	8VE3	32ND	P	NORMAL	NORMALT
BAR 1 BEAT 2 + 2	BASSOON	B	8VE3	HALF		SFFZ	
BAR 1 BEAT 3 + 1	FLUTE	D+	8VE4	HALF	MP	NORMAL	
BAR 1 BEAT 4 + 2	BASSOON	F+	8VE4	HALF	PP		
BAR 2 BEAT 1 + 1	FLUTE	REST		WHOLE+			
	VIOLA	B-	8VE4	16TH+	P	ARCO	MUTED
	VIOLA	F+	8VE4	16TH+			
BAR 2 BEAT 1 + 4	VIOLA	G+	8VE3	EIGHTH+	PP		
BAR 2 BEAT 1 + 5	VIOLIN	C	8VE4	EIGHTH			SULPONT
BAR 2 BEAT 2 + 1	VIOLIN	A	8VE4	HALF			MUTED
BAR 2 BEAT 2 + 2	VIOLA	F+	8VE4	HALF	MP		MUTED
	BASSOON	REST		HALF			
BAR 2 BEAT 4 + 1	VIOLIN	B-	8VE4	EIGHTH	PP		SULPONT
	VIOLIN	G	8VE3	EIGHTH			
BAR 2 BEAT 4 + 2	VIOLA	A	8VE4	WHOLE+			NORMALT
	VIOLA	C	8VE3	WHOLE+			
	BASSOON	G+	8VE3	HALF	MP	NORMAL	
BAR 2 BEAT 4 + 5	VIOLIN	REST		HALF			
BAR 3 BEAT 2 + 2	BASSOON	E	8VE4	HALF	P	SFZ	
BAR 3 BEAT 3 + 1	VIOLIN	G+	8VE3	HALF	PP	ARCO	SULPONT
BAR 3 BEAT 3 + 1	FLUTE	D	8VE4	EIGHTH	MP	NORMAL	NORMALT
BAR 3 BEAT 3 + 5	FLUTE	F+	8VE4	HALF			
BAR 3 BEAT 4 + 2	BASSOON	B-	8VE4	EIGHTH		SFZ	
BAR 3 BEAT 4 + 5	VIOLIN	F+	8VE4	HALF	PP	ARCO	SULPONT
BAR 3 BEAT 4 + 6	BASSOON	G+	8VE3	HALF	MP	SFZ	NORMALT
BAR 4 BEAT 1 + 5	FLUTE	F+	8VE4	WHOLE+		SFFZ	
BAR 4 BEAT 2 + 2	VIOLA	F	8VE3	HALF		ARCO	MUTED
BAR 4 BEAT 2 + 5	VIOLIN	D+	8VE4	HALF	PP		SULPONT
	VIOLIN	C+	8VE4	HALF			
BAR 4 BEAT 2 + 6	BASSOON	B	8VE4	HALF		SFZ	NORMALT
BAR 4 BEAT 4 + 2	VIOLA	G+	8VE3	HALF	MP	ARCO	SULPONT
	VIOLA	E	8VE3	HALF			
BAR 4 BEAT 4 + 5	VIOLIN	C+	8VE4	HALF	PP		
BAR 4 BEAT 4 + 6	BASSOON	B-	8VE3	WHOLE		SFZ	NORMALT
BAR 5 BEAT 2 + 2	VIOLA	REST		HALF			
BAR 5 BEAT 2 + 5	VIOLIN	A	8VE4	HALF		ARCO	SULPONT
BAR 5 BEAT 3 + 5	FLUTE	D+	8VE4	HALF		SFZ	NORMALT
BAR 5 BEAT 1 + 5	FLUTE	D+	8VE4	EIGHTH		SLUR	
BAR 6 BEAT 2 + 1	FLUTE	D+	8VE4	32ND			
BAR 5 BEAT 4 + 2	VIOLA	C	8VE4	QUARTER		ARCO	SULTASTO
BAR 5 BEAT 4 + 5	VIOLIN	A	8VE4	QUARTER+			SULPONT
BAR 6 BEAT 2 + 1	VIOLIN	A	8VE4	32ND		SLUR	
BAR 5 BEAT 4 + 6	BASSOON	F	8VE4	QUARTER+	MP	SFZ	NORMALT
BAR 6 BEAT 1 + 2	VIOLA	E	8VE4	EIGHTH		ARCO	SULPONT
BAR 6 BEAT 1 + 6	VIOLA	E	8VE4	EIGHTH	PP		NORMALT
BAR 6 BEAT 2 + 2	FLUTE	E	8VE4	QUARTER+	MP	SFZ	FLUTTERTGE
	VIOLA	D+	8VE4	EIGHTH+	FT	COLLEG	GLISS
	BASSOON	D+	8VE2	EIGHTH	MP	SFZ	NORMALT
	VIOLIN	F	8VE4	EIGHTH	CRESC	NORMAL	SULTASTO
	VIOLIN	F	8VE4	EIGHTH			SULTASTO
BAR 6 BEAT 2 + 6	BASSOON	REST		EIGHTH			
	VIOLIN	C+	8VE4	EIGHTH	-	SLUR	SULTASTO
	VIOLA	F+	8VE4	QUARTER	MP	COLLEG	GLISS
BAR 6 BEAT 2 + 8	VIOLA	A	8VE4	QUARTER			
BAR 6 BEAT 3 + 2	BASSOON	G+	8VE2	EIGHTH	FF	SFZ	NORMALT
	VIOLIN	REST		16TH			
BAR 6 BEAT 3 + 4	VIOLIN	A	8VE4	QUARTER	-	COLLEG	NORMALT
BAR 6 BEAT 3 + 6	FLUTE	B-	8VE5	QUARTER	MP	SFZ	FLUTTERTGE
	BASSOON	REST		EIGHTH			
BAR 6 BEAT 3 + 8	VIOLA	A	8VE4	EIGHTH+		ARCO	SULPONT
	VIOLA	F	8VE4	EIGHTH+			
BAR 6 BEAT 4 + 2	BASSOON	B-	8VE3	EIGHTH		SFZ	NORMALT
BAR 6 BEAT 4 + 4	VIOLIN	C	8VE4	HALF	-	NORMAL	SULTASTO
BAR 6 BEAT 4 + 6	FLUTE	REST		32ND			
	VIOLA	E	8VE4	WHOLE+	FF	ARCO	GLISS
	BASSOON	C+	8VE2	EIGHTH	MP	SFZ	NORMALT
BAR 6 BEAT 4 + 7	FLUTE	C	8VE4	EIGHTH+			FLUTTERTGE
BAR 7 BEAT 1 + 2	BASSOON	REST		EIGHTH			
BAR 7 BEAT 1 + 5	FLUTE	E	8VE4	EIGHTH	FF	SFFZ	
BAR 7 BEAT 1 + 6	BASSOON	B	8VE3	EIGHTH		SFZ	
BAR 7 BEAT 2 + 1	FLUTE	E	8VE4	QUARTER+	MP	SFFZ	FLUTTERTGE
BAR 7 BEAT 2 + 2	BASSOON	E	8VE2	EIGHTH	FT	NORMAL	NORMALT
BAR 7 BEAT 2 + 4	VIOLIN	A	8VE4	HALF	-	PIZZ	SULTASTO
BAR 7 BEAT 2 + 6	BASSOON	F	8VE2	EIGHTH	FT	SFZ	NORMALT
BAR 7 BEAT 3 + 2	BASSOON	B	8VE3	EIGHTH	MP	NORMAL	
BAR 7 BEAT 3 + 5	FLUTE	F	8VE4	WHOLE		SFFZ	FLUTTERTGE
BAR 8 BEAT 3 + 5	FLUTE	F	8VE4	QUARTER+		SLUR	
BAR 7 BEAT 3 + 6	BASSOON	C+	8VE2	EIGHTH		NORMAL	NORMALT
BAR 7 BEAT 4 + 2	BASSOON	B	8VE3	EIGHTH		SFFZ	
BAR 7 BEAT 4 + 4	VIOLIN	D	8VE4	EIGHTH	-	SFZ	SULTASTO
BAR 7 BEAT 4 + 6	BASSOON	F	8VE2	EIGHTH	FF	SFFZ	NORMALT
BAR 7 BEAT 4 + 8	VIOLIN	D	8VE4	EIGHTH	-	PIZZ	SULTASTO
BAR 8 BEAT 1 + 2	BASSOON	E	8VE2	EIGHTH	FT	NORMAL	NORMALT
BAR 8 BEAT 1 + 4	VIOLIN	F	8VE4	HALF	-	PIZZ	SULTASTO
BAR 8 BEAT 1 + 6	BASSOON	A	8VE3	EIGHTH	FF	NORMAL	NORMALT
BAR 8 BEAT 2 + 2	BASSOON	REST		EIGHTH			
BAR 8 BEAT 2 + 6	VIOLA	F	8VE4	QUARTER		ARCO	MUTED
	BASSOON	C	8VE2	EIGHTH	MP	NORMAL	
BAR 8 BEAT 3 + 2	BASSOON	F	8VE2	EIGHTH	FT		
BAR 8 BEAT 3 + 4	VIOLIN	F+	8VE4	QUARTER+	-	COLLEG	SULTASTO
BAR 8 BEAT 3 + 5	VIOLIN	F-	8VE4	32ND		SLUR	
BAR 8 BEAT 3 + 6	BASSOON	F+	8VE2	EIGHTH	MP	NORMAL	NORMALT
BAR 8 BEAT 4 + 2	VIOLA	D	8VE3	EIGHTH+		ARCO	
BAR 8 BEAT 4 + 2	VIOLA	D	8VE3	32ND		SLUR	
BAR 8 BEAT 4 + 2	VIOLA	G+	8VE3	EIGHTH+			
BAR 8 BEAT 4 + 8	VIOLA	G+	8VE3	32ND			
BAR 8 BEAT 4 + 2	BASSOON	G+	8VE2	EIGHTH	FF	NORMAL	
BAR 8 BEAT 4 + 6	BASSOON	A	8VE3	16TH+	MP	SFZ	

Microcomputers and Computer Assisted Instruction

R. Hirschmann, G. Clausing, E. Purcell

Among the most interesting developments in computer technology in recent years is the introduction of microcomputers. What makes them interesting, and even exciting, is not that they are capable of performing any new logical functions that were previously unavailable on larger computers. It is their smaller size and lower cost that sets them significantly apart, both from the large computers and the minicomputers. Instead of the hundreds of thousands and even millions of dollars that a large computer installation costs, a microcomputer system will cost merely a few thousand dollars, and these prices are still coming down. The prototype system used for much of our development work can be purchased for less than $2,200.

With such a great cost differential one would expect significant differences between these two types of systems. The large computer's memory system will be much more capacious; it will be connected to a far greater variety and quantity of peripheral equipment, and in addition, it will have a far greater operating speed. Each of these factors increases the cost significantly, so in order to use such a machine effectively, it is not financially sensible to have only a few people using it at a time. Instead, many users simultaneously will want access to, and responses from, a large machine, for jobs submitted on punched cards for batch processing, for remote entry jobs or for an inquiry from a student sitting at a terminal in the language laboratory.

The astounding speed of that large computer, however, will not be noticeable to any of these users, since they are all in competition with each other for the computer's attention. Everyone who has worked on large computers knows about the problems of turnaround, and those who have worked with Computer Assisted Instruction (CAI) know what a dispiriting effect slow responses have on the student's attention and motivation.

The Promise of Microcomputers

Microcomputers can be used to overcome this shortcoming of conventional CAI, namely the slow and undependable response time of large systems, since microcomputers can be applied in a fundamentally different way. Their low cost makes it unnecessary to have so many users competing for one computer's attention; in fact, it is feasible for a language laboratory to have a microcomputer dedicated to the single function of teaching languages. The economic advantages of this approach should be significant, especially to the smaller colleges and high schools that do not have their own large computers. Instead of buying expensive connect time to a large commercial or university computer, they can own or lease the necessary microcomputer equipment themselves.

A natural question that arises concerns the number of terminals that can be connected to a microcomputer. This will vary considerably, depending upon the type of terminal and the type of microcomputer. If conventional Cathode Ray Tube (CRT) or typewriter terminals were used, most microcomputers could not support more than about a dozen of them before exhibiting the same problems of slow and unreliable response time that were to be solved in the first place.

The key to appropriate use of microcomputers in the language laboratory, however, is to use a microcomputer in the terminal, thereby preprocessing data, rather than to use just one microcomputer with conventional or 'dumb' terminals. Since the necessary microcomputer chips are available for thirty dollars and even less, it makes sense to use many of them, one in each of the terminals, thereby making them 'smart', and one or several in a central control computer. These are then linked in such a way that most of the processing is done in the terminals themselves.

Distributed Processing

In this type of computer architecture, known as distributed processing, there is not just one Central Processing Unit (CPU) working on a job or a set of jobs. Instead, the jobs are dissected into smaller segments and submitted to any of several processors, depending on the requirements of the job segment and on which processor is idle. Under the most general form of distributed processing, some processors are built to be particularly efficient in performing arithmetic calculations, others in doing string manipulations, still others in handling input and output functions, and finally, one in deciding how to segment all those jobs and how to submit the individual segments to the most suitable processor.

The situation encountered in the CAI laboratory is a special case, of course, and several of these logical functions are not required. The central computer in this instance will primarily have the function of controlling the access of each terminal to the materials needed to conduct a CAI session. These materials are stored in a bank of floppy disk mass storage units and include both the operating software that each terminal needs in order to be 'intelligent' and the actual language materials which will be displayed on the terminal to which the student will respond. The session itself will be conducted by the computer inside the terminal without the help of the central control computer. We will return to details of this scheme below.

Programmable Characters and Graphics

In addition to the benefits of lower cost and faster response time, microcomputer-based CAI (MCAI) offers the advantage of flexibility. The fact that each terminal is a small computer makes it possible to give each the characteristics uniquely suited to a certain application, be it a particular lesson or language. These characteristics can be changed to meet new requirements under software control simply by accessing a new program file on the floppy disks through the central control computer.

In CAI this permits the convenient display of the special characters in foreign languages, for with the addition of a programmable character generator developed by one of the authors, it is possible to display any repertoire of 256 symbols as long as each is definable in terms of a rectangle of eight dots in the horizontal and thirteen in the vertical direction. This means that the alphabets of German and Russian, as well as the International Phonetic Alphabet, can be displayed directly rather than through cumbersome graphemic substitutions. In addition, it will be used for simple pictorial illustrations, since the shapes of individual symbols can be changed and combined rapidly under software control.

The Structure of a Session

In order to illustrate the interaction of all these components, the progress of a typical session of the system will be described. The student chooses any of the thirty-two terminals that are in the laboratory and signs on by typing his name. The central control computer will use this information in order to search a disk file to determine the password, the language and level of progress of the student and also the most recently covered lesson materials. While the search is going on, the central control computer might give the student messages stored by laboratory personnel for transmission to all students and then ask for a password.

Under most circumstances the disk search will be completed by the time the student has typed the password. In the worst possible case, namely when students at all thirty-two terminals sign on simultaneously, the unluckiest of them will wait about one minute. Assuming that the password is correct, the central control computer can now send any messages intended specifically for this student, perhaps prepared by the teacher for all members of the class, then remind the student of what was accomplished in the last session and ask what is to be done today. While waiting for the student's response, the operating software, that is, the instructions that the terminal needs to conduct the session, will be transmitted to and stored in the terminal.

At any time after the password match has occurred, the language of communication can be switched to the target language. This is accomplished by the central computer in retrieving the character set of the target language from disk and transmitting it to the terminal. In fact, since a total repertoire of 256 characters can be stored in each terminal, a full character set, say, for Russian and English can be available at the same time. This is especially useful in the earliest lessons when English cues are still in order.

After the student has indicated the lesson to be covered today, this information is transmitted to the central computer. It then searches the disks to locate the material and transmits it to the terminal. This process typically will take two to five seconds, and during the search time any special messages can be displayed. When all of the lesson material has been received the central computer's task is done, and control for the session passes to the terminal where the student is sitting. Response time will now be very fast, since the student is the only one requiring the attention of the computer in the terminal. Response time will seldom be more than a fraction of a second.

The software now stored in the terminal guides the student through the lesson materials until a determination is made that new materials are needed. This may come about because the student has successfully mastered the materials, in which case a more advanced lesson will be requested from the control computer; or because the student has repeatedly answered incorrectly and the terminal's software requests that a remedial lesson be accessed; or because the student signals being bored and asks for new materials.

However the decision is reached, the request for new lesson materials is transmitted to the central computer together with a record of the student's performance on the previous materials. After the new materials have been sent to the terminal, the student's disk file is updated with the record of performance. When the student finishes the session, the file is again updated, and a line printer is used to write a profile of what materials were covered and, possibly, suggestions for topics to be studied at home. This sheet of paper is ready for the student at the door, and in the meantime, the terminal can be used by another student studying another language.

The Software

The foregoing discussion has described the hardware of the system and has touched only lightly upon the software. Two software systems are required to make the hardware work. The first is the computer software, which allows the terminals to interact with the central computer and which allows the central computer to do its job of file management. This software provides the operating intelligence of the system and remains the same, regardless of the language being studied.

The second software system may be called the 'courseware', for it consists of the language lesson materials. This will naturally vary from one language and one lesson to another. Each of these software systems must be compressed into small segments in order to fit the restricted memory capacity of the terminals. We will discuss only the prominent characteristics of the second of these systems, the courseware.

The courseware must be packaged into lesson units of eight thousand characters each, which is the equivalent of four double-spaced typewritten pages. This restriction is necessary to keep the cost of each terminal close to $2,000. At present prices this can be achieved by restricting memory size to 16,000 bytes and using one half for operating software and the other half for courseware. As the price for semiconductor memory continues to decline, it may become possible to increase these numbers by a factor of two, but our experience so far indicates that 16,000 bytes are adequate.

Pedagogical Strategy

Initially we will develop a series of exercises which quickly frustrate the student. Once it becomes clear that a particular student is lost, the system inside the terminal instructs the central computer to branch to a small tutorial on the relevant points, using English primarily. Once this is mastered, control passes back to the target language and to the start of the lesson that caused the frustration.

From the very beginning the emphasis will be on giving the student a realistic language experience. Although the lesson segments will incorporate a certain amount of retracing of past lessons, our main goal will be to teach the student to comprehend and produce *integrated* language texts. Thus rather than asking students, "Supply the ending in: Fritz sing... immer," our pedagogical approach asks, "Supply a word that fits the following sentence: Meine Frau singt immer ..... ." Such items naturally present much greater challenges to programming and response anticipation.

Individual lesson segments will be linked in such a way that the student's path is controlled. Access to more difficult segments will be restricted until easier ones have been mastered. In addition, there will always be a means for the student to indicate frustration or boredom and to terminate the lesson before its completion.

The sequence of lessons will lead from those tutoring the student in analysis and synthesis of simple strings (that is, sentences) on the basis of supplied ingredients (that is, words) to the more complex task of text analysis and comprehension. We will also experiment with synthesized phoneme discrimination and the automatic recognition of acceptable and unacceptable pronunciation of isolated sounds. While the hardware exists for such synthesis and analysis of speech, much effort in software development appears still to be required before speech recognition and synthesis can be used in the laboratory with ease.

Learning From the Students

Although systems may one day be developed that are self-contained and require no classroom contact, we see the role of our system as a complementary one. It will be used together with conventional written materials in a classroom setting to relieve the teacher of certain types of routine work. In order to make our system as useful as possible we intend to keep records of the following information: the number of attempts before a correct answer is given, in order to determine the difficulty of each question; unacceptable reponses to each item, in order to diagnose the source of misunderstanding; the lessons which caused students to become frustrated or bored; and indications from students as to what improvements they want to suggest, implemented by asking the student for an explanatory message before the signal of frustration or boredom is acted upon.

This information can be used to improve weaknesses in software and courseware, and to track the progress of individual students. It is also possible to divide students into various achievement groups, based upon speed of comprehension and regularity of attendance, and for the teachers to provide individualized messages of praise and encouragement or remedial tutorial materials for each group. Indeed, it is possible to assess the teacher's effectiveness by analyzing and comparing the progress of parallel sections of the same course. The possibilities extend into ethically questionable realms, but since most are still hypothetical, we are not troubled – yet.

Status

Our progress to date has been much greater in acquiring the hardware than in developing the software. We presently have a microcomputer laboratory in operation with two intelligent CRT terminals, one hard copy dumb terminal and a central control computer that can access two floppy disk drives. Nearly all of the hardware concepts discussed above have been tested and verified. For those interested in the details of our hardware, one intelligent terminal is a Processor Technology SOL 20 with 16k bytes of memory, the other is a terminal custom-designed by one of the authors. It includes the original programmable character generator. The hard copy dumb terminal is a DECwriter LA-36, and the control computer is an extensively modified Altair 8800. The floppy disk unit consists of two ICOM drives which can store a total of 500k bytes on line. Each of our CPUs is an Intel 8080 or equivalent, which is as close to an industry standard as is presently available. If a problem in response speed is to develop, it would probably occur only in the central control computer. In such a case we would either upgrade the CPU to a Zilog Z-80 or divide the various functions among several specialized processors.

Our present task is to develop the software capabilities that are outlined above. While some already have been implemented on our microcomputers, most of them have not, and while we have considerable experience with CAI on large computers, we are aware of many special problems in transferring that experience to microcomputers.

We believe, however, that the potential rewards are great. The system we have outlined will be replicable at low cost and will be suitable for use with any language and many other subjects. It will be more flexible than present CAI systems, with the possible exception of the PLATO system by CDC. However, it will be much more affordable than any of these, especially to the many schools that do not have large computers.

We want to thank the Humanities Division Development Fund, the LAS Faculty Academic Innovation Fund and the Graduate School Faculty Research Fund of the University of Southern California for helping us purchase the components of the microcomputer laboratory described above.

Computer-Assisted Instruction in Beginning Design

J.R. Truckenbrod

The computer is being used in the Design Area of the Northern Illinois University Art Department, to aid in the teaching of Basic Design principles. The computer graphics programs support specific aspects of the Basic Design program curriculum. Each of the programs discussed here focuses on a specific component of the Basic Design course content. The programs provide examples of the principles involved, and serve as a tool for the students to use to explore numerous alternative solutions to design problems. These computer-aided graphics are not meant to replace the hand-executed projects, but to supplement the class projects, and to provide an additional means of exploration and experimentation for the students. This exploration and experimentation is based on the theory and principles presented in class. As a result, the computer has become a successful teaching aid in these beginning design classes. These programs are written in Fortran IV programming language and use both a 663 CalComp drum plotter and the line printer for output. Northern Illinois University is currently operating an IBM System 360/65, OS Release 21.8, MVT, HASP Version 3.30.30.

Basic Design Curriculum

The Basic Design course is a component of the 'core courses' required of all Art students at Norther Illinois University. Each year there are about 400 students enrolled in this course. The Basic Design curriculum consists of basic design principles, problem solving methodology and the use of materials and equipment. The course outline includes the study of point, line and plane, spacial organization methods, and visual methods such as tension, compression, and movement. Gestalt principles of perception are discussed throughout the semester. Class projects involve symmetry operations, modularity, proportion, and grid structures. Studies in abstraction of form and in the systematic distortion or modification of a form, are carried out to explore a series of images, shapes, or figures. Basic concepts such as balance, harmony, and continuity are discussed and integrated into the class projects. Basic color and value theory are also presented during the course. The computer-assisted projects discussed in this paper aid in the instruction of these principles. These computer programs are tools for developing and exploring ideas. The student directs this exploration and makes the decision as to the success or failure of a design idea or an aesthetic image based on the principles involved and the criteria established by the professor. The following four programs are gradually being introduced into all sections of the basic design course: Symmetry Operations;

Systematic change, modification, or distortion of an image; Value studies; and Moire patterns.

Symmetry Program

The first Computer Graphics program to be introduced into this course was the Symmetry Operations program. This program was written by Marshall Chanzit, a Northern Illinois University graduate student. It is used in conjunction with the study of Symmetry relationships. Symmetry provides a means of organization. Symmetry operations describe the relationships between the parts of a whole. Use of these operations as a means of organizing a composition provide an inherent continuity and balance. This balance can be static as in a symmetrical composition, or it can be dynamic as in an asymmetrical design. There are four basic symmetry operations: translation, bilateral, inversion, and rotation. Translation is the parallel displacement of every point or line in a given figure, each being moved equal distances in the same direction. Bilateral symmetry is the reflection or mirror image of a figure. Inversion is a 180 degree rotation of the figure. Rotation is a periodic repetition of a figure around a fixed point at regular intervals, giving a kaleidoscopic effect. Each of these operations changes the orientation or position of a figure or image in a given format. By changing the orientation or position of a shape or figure, the perception of that figure changes, that is, it appears different. For more information concerning this phenomena, refer to the article "The Perception of Disoriented Figures" by Irvin Rock in the January, 1974 issue of *Scientific American*.

There are numerous variations of each of these four operations. More than one operation can be performed on a figure to create additional variations. A series of diagrams that illustrates the use of these symmetry operations individually and in combinations can be found in the book *The Geometry of the Environment*, by Lionel March and Philip Steadman. As these diagrams illustrate, by using symmetry operations to determine the repetition and positioning of a modular unit, or a series of images, a generating system is created that can produce a wide range of design possibilities. The continuity and balance exhibited in compositions created on the basis of symmetry operations is inherent in the compositions because the parts are the same but their positions in relation to each other and to the format are different. In his book *Visual Thinking,* Arnheim states, "The strong connection uniting the corresponding parts of a symmetrical pattern come about because these parts are identical in shape but opposite in spacial orientation." A complex, visually exciting image can be created by repeating and positioning an initial image, according to various symmetry operations.

The computer-assisted symmetry program has twenty configurations available to the student. Each of these twenty possibilities is a variation of one of the four basic symmetry operations. This program contains five variations of translation, three variations of bilateral symmetry, five variations of inversion, and seven types of rotations. This program also has scaling capabilities that are not used in this course. The student should understand the basic symmetry operations before working with this program in order to make some predictions concerning the design he will obtain, based on the design of the initial shape used in the

Figure 1. Symmetry Program

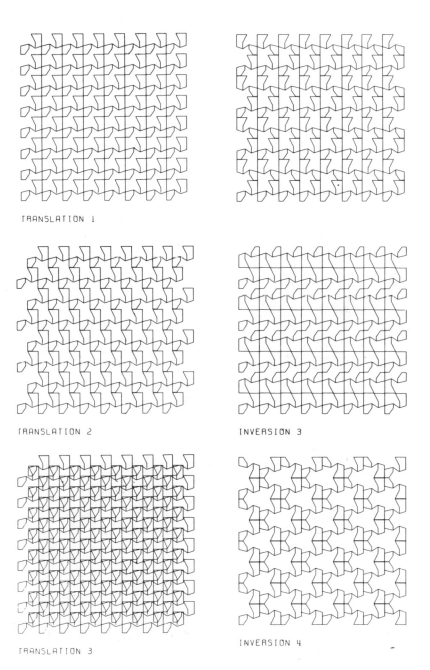

Figure 2. Symmetry Program

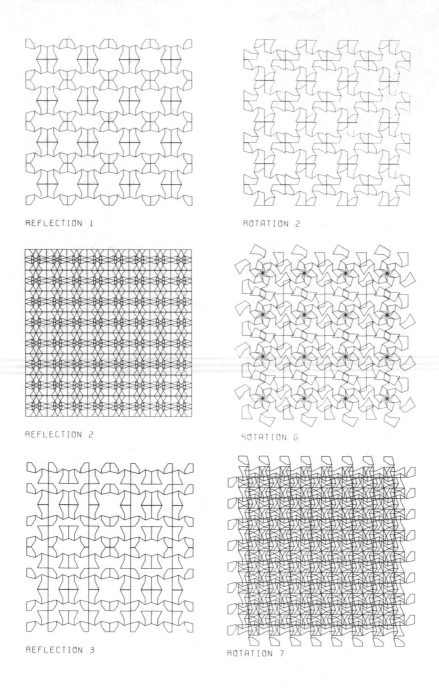

program. Initially the student creates a shape, figure, or module within a one inch graph divided into tenths of an inch. The location of each corner or vertex of this shape is identified with x or y coordinates between zero and one. The program connects these points with straight lines in the order that they are read in. The images or figures will be repeated and positioned a minimum of 64 times on an eight-inch square format in the patterns specified by the student. After the program is executed, the images are drawn by the CalComp Plotter. Complex figures are discouraged as the complexity of the composition will become evident as the figure is repeated by the program. The potential of this program for generating design ideas is unlimited. The patterns that are created by the program could be used for fabric design, package design, or the design of wallcovering. See Figures 1 and 2 for examples of twelve of the twenty design patterns that are possible with one initial design module. The variety of design patterns shown here illustrates the value of using symmetry operations.

Systematic Change Program

The author has recently completed the second computer graphics program that will be available to students in these beginning classes. This program provides a good contrast to the first program in that it systematically modifies an initial figure or image according to the user's directions, and creates a sequential series of images. This series of images is repeated and arranged in a sequential order. The student must design an initial image as in the first program, together with a plan for modification of that image in seven steps. Examples of the output of this program are shown in Figures 3 and 4. These designs have been drawn by the plotter and are eight inches square but have been reduced for illustration purposes.

The process of developing a series of figures or images by systematically changing, modifying, or distorting an initial image, is a valuable concept. This procedure is useful for exploring new shapes or forms. Many times it is the intermediate shapes in a sequential series of shapes that prove to be the most successful. By generating a series of images, a student has a number of alternatives to choose from in solving a design problem.

The development of a series of shapes or figures in a systematic manner is difficult because it requires a close regulation of the amount of change from one image to the next in order to create a smooth transition or rhythm throughout the series. If the series of images is used to create a composition, the gradual change of shape will create a smooth flow in the composition. Beginning design students are generally not able to make the fine discriminations necessary to maintain the same increment, or amount of change, in a shape from one step to the next. This computer-assisted program can be used to increase the student's perceptual awareness of the gradual, systematic change in a series of shapes, and to sensitize them to the feeling of the subtle, smooth transformation in a composition created with a sequential series of images.

In using the program, a student designs a shape in a one inch square and defines the shape on a graph with x and y coordinates between one and zero. This is the same format used in the symmetry program. The

Figure 3. Systematic Change Program

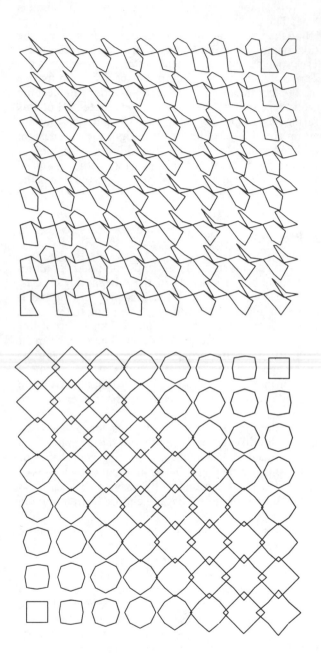

Figure 4. Systematic Change Program

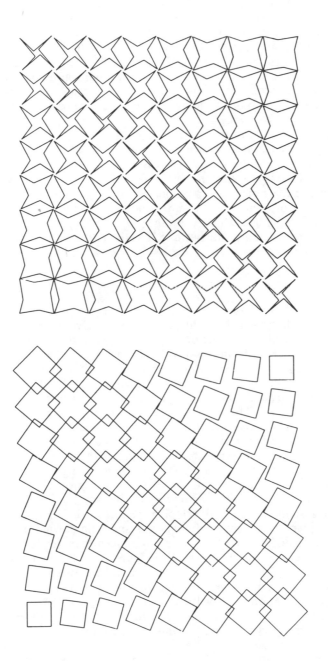

student then determines how that shape should be changed in seven sequential steps. The shape modification is done by systematically changing the locations of the various points by adding or subtracting a small amount to the x and y coordinates of any of those points. The increments will be added or subtracted to each step to create that next shape. See Figure 5 for a diagram of this procedure. When using this program, the success of the final design of this procedure depends upon the design of the initial image; the type of change or modification that is specified – literally the choice of points that are to be relocated or moved in the series; and the amount of change or the increment to be added or subtracted during each step.

Color can be added by hand to the design produced by this program. A color progression can be used to reinforce the progression of shape, or it can be used to disintegrate the shape progression. Adhesive color film can be adhered directly to the plotter drawing as one means of coloration. Additional arrangement possibilities for the series of shapes will be added to the program soon. Another addition to the program will be the use of parallel lines to shade in the shapes. This can be done by incorporating the CalComp subroutine SHADE. The current listing of this program is in Figure 7.

Value Studies

The third program being used in this course is the Symap/Symvu program from Harvard. The portion of the program that we use employs the line printer to fill in areas with different grey values. This program is generally used by geographers for various kinds of maps such as those illustrating population densities. The popularized computer pictures of Snoopy and others that are done on the line printer can be done with this program. However, it is very time consuming on our system, as all the points in an image must be identified and the location coded. To avoid requiring each student to locate and code all the points in a picture, we provide them with an abstract image that has already been coded. The students must decide how to distribute the grey values throughout the composition, based on the criteria given by the professor. To allow for a maximum number of solutions in a fixed image, a modular system is used in developing the image. This image is thirteen inches square with eight modules across and eight down. There are 64 squares, each divided into two areas. Consequently there are 128 areas that must be assigned grey values. See Figure 9 for the open grid given to the students in this project. Value refers to the relative lightness or darkness of a color, and is best understood by the study of a grey scale. The value graduations in this program are created by the use of various typewritten characters used singly or together in overprinting. See Figure 10 for the grey scale used in this project. The advantage of using greys rather than colors in projects involving value studies is that the emotional or connotative meaning attributed to various colors does not interfere with the study of value when grey is used. In this project, with 128 areas in the composition, and a choice of ten values for each of the areas, there is an unlimited number of patterns that can be created. This project affords a wide range of exploration in the study of value relationships, and can be used in the teaching of various concepts and design principles. Different criteria can be established for determining the distribution of the grey areas on the given modular design.

Figure 5.

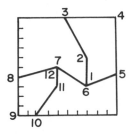

	X Coordinate	Y Coordinate	X Increment	Y Increment
Point 1	0.70	0.30	0.00	0.00
2	0.70	0.60	-.07	0.00
3	0.50	1.00	0.00	0.00
4	1.00	1.00	-.05	-.03
5	1.00	0.40	0.00	0.00
6	0.70	0.30	0.00	0.00
7	0.40	0.50	0.00	0.00
8	0.00	0.40	0.00	0.00
9	0.00	0.00	0.05	0.05
10	0.20	0.00	0.07	0.00
11	0.40	0.30	0.05	-.05
12	0.40	0.50	0.00	0.00

Figure 6. Input Format

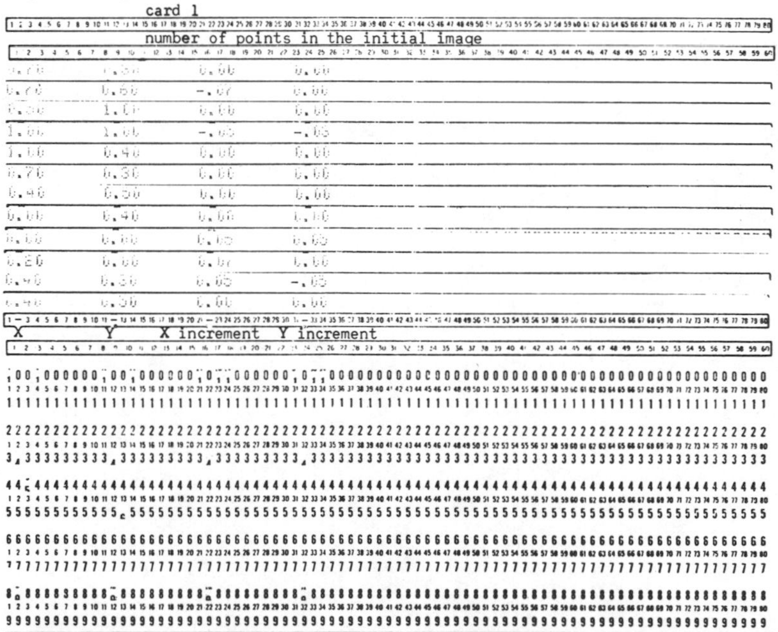

Figure 7.

```
FORTRAN IV G LEVEL  21          MAIN          DATE = 77114      16'40/21          PAGE 0001
                    C       SYSTEMATIC CHANGE, MODIFICATION, OR DISTORTION OF AN IMAGE
                    C       COMPUTED GRAPHICS PROGRAM FOR BASIC DESIGN CLASSES
                    C
                    C       JOAN TRUCKENBROD              NORTHERN ILLINOIS UNIVERSITY
                    C
                    C       THIS PROGRAM PROVIDES FOR THE SYSTEMATIC CHANGE, MODIFICATION,
                    C       OR DISTORTION OF AN INITIAL TWO DIMENSIONAL IMAGE.    THIS
                    C       MODIFICATION IS DONE ACCORDING TO SPECIFICATIONS GIVEN
                    C       BY THE USER.  A SERIES OF IMAGES IS GENERATED BY CHANGING EACH
                    C       IMAGE SEQUENTIALLY.  IMAGE 2 IS CREATED BY MODIFYING IMAGE 1,
                    C       AND SO ON.  THE SERIES OF IMAGES GENERATED BY THIS PROGRAM IS
                    C       ARRANGED IN AN EIGHT INCH SQUARE FORMAT IN THE FOLLOWING
                    C       ARRANGEMENT.  THE NUMBERS REPRESENT THE NUMBER OF THE IMAGE
                    C       IN THE SERIES.
                    C
                    C           8 7 6 5 4 3 2 1
                    C           7 8 7 6 5 4 3 2
                    C           6 7 8 7 6 5 4 3
                    C           5 6 7 8 7 6 5 4
                    C           4 5 6 7 8 7 6 5
                    C           3 4 5 6 7 8 7 6
                    C           2 3 4 5 6 7 8 7
                    C           1 2 3 4 5 6 7 8
                    C
                    C
                    C       VARIABLES
                    C       NPTS REPRESENTS THE NUMBER OF POINTS IN THE INITIAL IMAGE
                    C       X AND Y CONTAIN THE COORDINATES OF THE ORIGINAL IMAGE
                    C       X1 AND Y1 CONTAIN THE COORDINATES OF THE MODIFIED IMAGE
                    C       XINC AND YINC CONTAIN THE  THE INCREMENT TO BE USED IN MODIFY-
                    C       ING SPECIFIC POINTS IN THE IMAGE
                    C
                    C
                    C       INPUT FORMAT
                    C
                    C       CARD 1 - COL. 1 AND 2 - NUMBER OF POINTS IN THE IMAGE
                    C       THE REMAINING CARDS CONTAIN THE COORDINATE POINTS AND INCREMENT
                    C       THERE IS ONE CARD FOR EACH POINT IN THE IMAGE.
                    C       DECIMAL POINTS FOR X AND Y COORDINATES IN COL. 2 AND 12
                    C       DECIMAL POINTS FOR THE  THE INCREMENT OF CHANGE FOR THE
                    C       X AND/OR Y COORDINATES ARE IN COL. 22 AND 32
                    C
        0001            REAL X(12),Y(12),X1(12),Y1(12),XINC(12),YINC(12)
        0002            REAL BUF(1000)
        0003            INTEGER M,N,P,T,K,J,T,NPTS,FLAG/0/,L/6/
                    C  INITIALIZE THE PLOT ROUTINE
        0004            CALL PLOTS(BUF,1000)
                    C  ESTABLISH THE ORIGIN
        0005            CALL PLOT(0.0,-20.0,-3)
        0006            CALL PLOT(0.0,-0.0,-3)
                    C
                    C  READ THE INPUT DATA
        0007            READ(5,6)NPTS
        0008       6    FORMAT(I2)
        0009            DO 7 J=1,NPTS
        0010            READ (5,8)X(J),Y(J),XINC(J),YINC(J)
        0011       8    FORMAT(F5.3,5X,F5.3,5X,F5.3,5X,F5.3)
        0012            WRITE(6,9) J,X(J),Y(J),XINC(J),YINC(J)
        0013       9    FORMAT(' ','POINT NUMBER',2X,I2,5X,'X=',F5.3,5X,'Y=',F5.3,'X INCRE
                       1MENT IS',2X,F5.3,5X,'Y INCREMENT IS',2X,F5.3)
        0014       7    CONTINUE
                    C
                    C  DEVELOP AND PLOT EACH IMAGE SEQUENTIALLY
                    C  N REPRESENTS THE EIGHT ROWS
                    C  M REPRESENTS THE EIGHT BOXES IN EACH ROW
        0015            DO 10 N=1,8
        0016            K=N-1
        0017            DO 15 M=1,8
        0018            J=(M-1)+K
        0019            IF (J.GT.7) FLAG=1
        0020            IF (FLAG.EQ.1) GO TO 40
                    C  MOVE THE PEN TO THE FIRST POINT IN THE IMAGE
        0021            X1(1)=X(1)+J*XINC(1)+(M-1)
        0022            Y1(1)=Y(1)+J*YINC(1)+(N-1)
        0023            CALL PLOT(X1(1),Y1(1),3)
        0024            DO 20 I=2,NPTS
        0025            X1(I)=X(I)+J*XINC(I)+(M-1)
        0026            Y1(I)=Y(I)+J*YINC(I)+(N-1)
        0027            CALL PLOT(X1(I),Y1(I),2)
        0028       20   CONTINUE
        0029            GO TO 15
        0030       40   X1(1)=X(1)+L*XINC(1)+(M-1)
        0031            Y1(1)=Y(1)+L*YINC(1)+(N-1)
        0032            CALL PLOT(X1(1),Y1(1),3)
        0033            DO 45 I=2,NPTS
        0034            X1(I)=X(I)+L*XINC(I)+(M-1)
        0035            Y1(I)=Y(I)+L*YINC(I)+(N-1)
        0036            CALL PLOT(X1(I),Y1(I),2)
        0037       45   CONTINUE
        0038            L=L-1
        0039            FLAG=0
        0040       15   CONTINUE
        0041            L=6
        0042            FLAG=0
        0043       10   CONTINUE
        0044            WRITE(6,60)
        0045       60   FORMAT(' ','IMAGE COMPLETE')
        0046            CALL PLOT(20.0,0.0,999)
        0047            STOP
        0048            END
```

One project that can be done with this program is the creation of movement on a compostion. A feeling of movement can be created by placing the grey values in a sequential pattern – light to dark – on the given grid. This can be done in a horizontal, vertical, or diagonal pattern. If there is a subtle change in the series of grey tones used, the composition will exhibit a gradual movement or flow, with a regular rhythm, throughout the composition. A feeling of greater acceleration in the movement can be achieved by proportionately increasing or decreasing the increment of change in the grey value. This will create a more dynamic composition. This project facilitates the study of various aspects of movement in a visual composition, such as speed, acceleration, rhythm, flow, direction, and proportional increments of change. As the student becomes more sensitive to the effects of these various elements in a composition, he can better control the visual forces at work in a composition.

Another idea that can be explored using this program is that of creating a feeling of depth on a two-dimensional surface through the use of overlapping, transparency, and contrast in value – light and shadow. By distributing the values to create areas of high contrast, a feeling of light or luminosity is created. By carefully determining the areas to be shaded with various greys, the composition takes on a three dimensional character. Areas can gradually recede from view by gradually reducing or increasing the value of the grey. By using a great variation in the values, the surface of the composition will change abruptly with the contrast in values. See Figure 8 For examples of this program. The composition is actually thirteen inches square but has been reduced for illustration. The student assigns a grey value of one to ten to each area or space on the grid. He then punches that value onto a computer card. There is one card for each area, so there are 128 cards required for each composition that he completes.

Figure 8. Value Studies

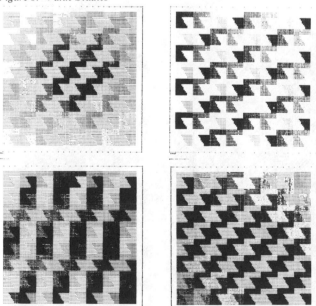

Figure 9. Basic Grid

Figure 10. Gray Scale

Figure 11. Moire Program

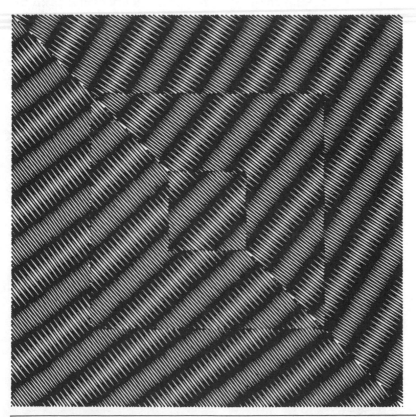

Moire Patterns

The final program is currently being worked out by the author. This program provides the students with a means of generating Moire patterns. The Moire effect is that of movement and visual vibration that results from overlapping series of parallel lines. It is the intersection points of the lines that create the visual vibration. In order to achieve this effect the variation of the angle of the lines in the different sets must be slight. See Figure 11 for an example of this program.

The computer is proving to be a very helpful tool in the teaching of basic design concepts. The programs discussed here directly support the basic design curriculum, and are expanding the scope of these beginning courses. In addition to providing a new way of teaching basic design principles, these programs allow the students to explore and develop numerous ideas in relation to a problem. This computer usage also helps the students understand the fundamental procedures necessary for working with Computer Graphics Programs. Hopefully a significant number of students will begin to realize the potential of computer-aided Design and Art. As they become familiar with these programs and develop the technical skills necessary to use the programs, they can apply them as aids in upper level design and art projects such as weaving, product design, graphic design, and interior design. It is important to illustrate the successful use of the computer as an aesthetic tool at the beginning of the students' careers, so that they will continue to use these computer programs in their advanced courses.

References

Arnheim, Rudolf. *Visual Thinking*. Berkeley: University of California Press, 1969.

Bevlin, Marjorie Elliott. *Design Through Discovery*. New York: Holt, Reinhart, and Winston, 1977.

California Computer Products. Host Computer Basic Software Library. Northern Illinois University.

Chanzit, Marshall. "Symmetry Operations." Dekalb, Illinois: Computer Graphics Program, Northern Illinois University, 1975.

March, Lionel, and Philip Steadman. *The Geometry of the Environment*. Cambridge, Massachusetts: MIT Press, 1974.

Metelli, Fabio. "The Perception of Transparency." *Image, Object, and Illusion*. San Francisco: W.H. Freeman Co., 1974.

Rock, Irvin. "The Perception of Disoriented Figures." *Image, Object, and Illusion*. San Francisco: W.H. Freeman Co., 1974.

Symap: Symagraphic Computer Mapping Program, The Laboratory of Spacial Graphics, Harvard University, Cambridge.

Truckenbrod, Joan R. "Moire Patterns." Dekalb, Illinois: Computer Graphics Program, Northern Illinois University, 1977.

Truckenbrod, Joan R. "Systematic Change, Modification, or Distortion of an Image." Dekalb, Illinois: Computer Graphics Program, Northern Illinois University, 1977.

7
Music

The Computer As Interdisciplinary Catalyst: Music and Psychology

A.J. Cohen, P. Issacs, S. Flores, D. Harrison, J. Bradley

Nothing really happens to a man except as it is registered in the subconscious. This is where event and feeling become memory and where the proof of life is stored. The poet – and we use the term to include all those who have respect for and speak to the human spirit – can help to supply the subconscious with material to enhance its sensitivity, thus safeguarding it. The poet, too, can help to keep man from making himself over in the image of electronic marvels. For the danger is not so much that man will be controlled by the computer as that he may imitate it. The poet reminds men of their uniqueness. It is not necessary to possess the ultimate definition of this uniqueness. Even to speculate on it is a gain. (Norman Cousins, 1966)

Music and psychology share problem spaces. Music exists by virtue of the human mind in its creation by the composer, execution by the performer, and perception by the listener. Psychology is the science of mental life and, as such, must share common ground with music, a product of mental life. It is difficult to imagine that an explanation of how music is composed and perceived could not either contribute to or, conversely, be derived from the psychological theories of how the mind works. Nevertheless, the two disciplines, music and psychology, have existed relatively independently.

The independence of music and psychology is not without reason. In contrast to centuries of musical history, psychology has just completed its first centennial. In actual fact, the first experimental psychologists did consider music important. The early interest of music declined when, in 1912, psychology resigned to study 'objectively observable behaviour', a category which seemed, at the time, to exclude music completely. Furthermore, psychoacoustics, that branch of psychology which most concerns hearing, concentrated almost entirely upon sine tone, as a result of limited technology. And while it was agreed that music could be decomposed into or synthesized from sine tones, the results of sine-tone psychoacoustics were not easily applied to music perception, especially to the understanding of higher-order musical structure. Thus, it is understandable that psychology, during most of its career, avoided consideration of music.

What about music's past interests? For the past four centuries, the music literature has concerned 'observables' but at a slightly different level: history, style analysis, form, performance technique, and acoustics. The extent to which such writing either assumes or implies how the mind works, that is, represents and organizes acoustic information, is far greater than is generally appreciated. Nevertheless, musicologists have not explicitly regarded the mental representation of music as a problem central to their concern. Hence, it is not fair to say that a theory of mind *has always been* part of the musicologist's problem space. We intend to argue, however, that today, as a result of progress in computer science, the problem of how sound is mentally

represented is very important to music theorists. Similarly, as a result
of progress in computer science, the mental representation is of great
but recent interest to psychology.

The term 'mental representation of the music' is an indication of the
convergence of music and psychology. In the first part of this paper, we
will describe three specific developments in computer science which
effect the convergence of music and psychology. Each development
brings to light a particular aspect of the overlapping problem space.
The second part of the paper addresses the solution. Answers to the
shared questions require quantification of the music-listening response.
The computer assists in the generation of experiments by providing independent access to musical stimuli, experimental paradigms, and
analysis procedures.

Computer Synthesis

Both music and psychology have always been concerned with the control of sound. The goals have differed for the two disciplines: for music,
sounds should be pleasing and of wide variety; for psychology, precision
(to the microsecond level) is desired. The digital synthesizer, or the
digital control of analogue hardware, satisfies both needs. Indeed, it
provides the musician with greater precision than necessary and the
psychologist with wider stimulus possibilities than are needed. These
'extras' suggest that synthesis systems are not optimized for the particular user, and user-oriented synthesis programs are in demand.[1] But
in articulating the demand, the following question arises: what level of
control is, in fact, necessary; that is, what differences in acoustic signals
or tone patterns make perceived differences? This has always motivated
psychoacoustic research. But the possibilities provided by computer
synthesis, for example, in the control (generation and timing) of complex functions, raises the problem to a higher power. Likewise, while
the 'ear' in music has always been appreciated, the definition of its
limits of resolution has never been so important to musicians.

Artificial Intelligence and Knowledge Representation

A second reason for problem-space convergence is slightly more subtle,
and results from concepts of artificial intelligence. In the context of artificial music intelligence – the capacity of the computer to carry out
any task related to music – the question of what is real human music intelligence takes on a new light. By virtue of this juxtaposition, both the
limitations and strengths of natural musical intelligence become more
pronounced.

Thus, the concept of artificial intelligence raises questions to
musicians concerning the nature of the human musical intellect. In
more general terms, the question illustrates the fact that the most important problem facing cognitive psychology today is the theoretical
representation of human knowledge.[2] For example, the failure of
artificial intelligence to meet its promises of twenty years ago in, for example, machine translation, forces psychologists to demand a (better)
theory of cognition. As Miller has argued, before we can program computers to do what we want, it is necessary for us to be able to implement

in them our own real-world knowledge, that is, to specify such knowledge and how it develops.[3] And music, particularly the representation of acoustic pattern information, is a part of that problem. The same question is important to musicologists and music educators as well. The latter are concerned with the definition of music knowledge, with teaching such knowledge and facilitating its creation.

An obvious omission in this discussion of artificial intelligence, music and mind, is the role which information processing has played in recent perceptual-cognitive theory.[4] Inevitably, modellers of mind are influenced by the most advanced technology of the day. Thus, perceptual-cognitive theories have emphasized similarities between mental and computer processes. We emphasize in our discussion another significant aspect of artificial intelligence – that music mental processes are not music computer processes, at least as far as computer processes are presently conceived. Rather, artificial intelligence highlights the idiosyncratic properties of the human intellect and calls for explication of human musical knowledge.

Computer Music Composition, a Challenge to Music Theory

The computer promotes an interaction between music and psychology in a final way. This is the result of the apparent incongruence between the 'new' music made possible by the computer and the 'old' music theories. In the past, music composition was constrained by the listening experience of the composer, his originality, and the instrument available. Music theory described the music produced under these constraints by various symbols such as triads, chord progressions, or interval patterns, which applied to redundant sound patterns. The symbols worked. They facilitated communication among those who knew them, and that was sufficient. The success of the symbols in application to most music made it unnecessary to consthat is their derivation, that is, whether the symbols derthat is from the musical notes, or whether they derived from the (ideal) listener's experience.

Traditional Music and Music Theory

Music theorists would be hard pressed to specify which of the possible domains, notational, acoustic, or psychological, the music symbols referred to. The three domains of possible reference are characterized in Figure 1.

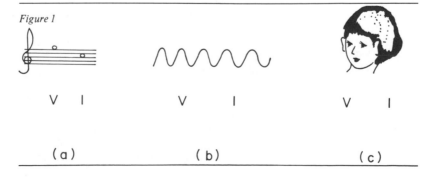

Figure 1

V   I   V   I   V   I

(a)   (b)   (c)

It is useful to begin with this illustration symbolizing traditional music before moving the argument to the ground of computer music composition. At (a) is the score, the notes themselves; in the example, the dominant (V) tonic (I) relation is notated; (b) represents acoustic fundamental frequencies generated by an instrument performing the score. Their frequency ratio 3:2, that of the dominant to tonic, is therefore specified as shown, V I. Finally, (c) represents a listener either receiving the acoustic signal at the ear, or imagining the sound of the score.

The figure raises two questions: to what extent is (c), the mental procedure, isomorphic in some sense to either (a), the score, or (b), the sound waves, and to what extent can the mental process at (c) be described as V I? Suppose music theorists assume that music symbols such as V I describe mental processes. If so, the symbols are poor descriptors, for indeed, the limits of their applicability are undefined. For example, does V I describe a process in every listener, or in the average listener, or in the ideal listener? If not in every listener, then what distinguishes those listeners who will represent V I from those who will not? The question is even more complex than this, given the almost infinite combinations of notes to which V I could theoretically apply. What combinations will most reliably generate the V I mental procedure? Which of these combinations are better described by VII I or V7 I, rather than by V I? As Babbitt has noted, what constitutes a 'best' musical analysis is unclear to music theorists.[5] He suggests that the answer will come from psychology, in that psychology attempts to describe the limits and propensities of mental processing (specifically he mentions Miller's classic 'magic number' paper).[6]

Typically, music theory makes the assumptions about mental processes. Consider just one example from the Oxford Harmony:

The notes C E G sounded together have practically no musical significance unless they are preceded or followed by some other combination of notes, and this progression in turn does not attain its full musical effect until it can be related to some key center.[7]

To what does the term musical significance refer if not to the listener's mental processing of C E G ? Is Andrews not making the psychological hypothesis that C E G will be perceived in a certain way when placed in a particular context of notes, especially if the context notes are perceived as related to a particular reference tone or key center?

A further interesting example is the work of the music theorist Schenker which is blatantly psychological in its orientation.[8] For example, he entitles sections of his *Harmony* "On the psychology of contents and of step progression" and " On the psychology of chromatic alteration." His notion of hierarchical structure, foreground, and background, and of basic operations for generating music at various levels, are hypotheses about the mental structuring of acoustic information. But they are seldom recognized as psychological hypotheses by either psychologists or music theorists.

Why psychology never took hold of traditional music theory by the horns and said, "hey, here's a lot of good ideas about how the mind structures complex tone patterns" can be accounted for by a number of reasons. As we noted in the previous section, the representation of real-world knowledge is of very recent interest in psychology. Secondly, awareness of the potential of music theory requires knowledge of music theory. The majority of psychologists do not have this familiarity.

Finally, music theorists did not encourage the attentions of psychologists. Music theory was surviving nicely without any help from psychology. Music theorists neither needed psychology, nor saw their own relevance to psychology. The climate was not right. But, we believe, the advent of computers changed this. It provided both a new context and a need for the question: What is a music theory? We show in the following discussion that the answer involves psychology.

Computer Music and Music Theory

Prior to the advent of computer music, the important question "What is really to be expected of a music theory?" was bypassed with statements that music theory (a) has the purpose of illuminating music, or (b) goes hand in hand with the study of composition. But, given that the symbols of traditional and atonal music theory (a) do not illuminate our understanding of the sound patterns determined by formulae input to computers, (b) do not apply to the greater part of formalized music made possible by computer technology, the questions of what actually is to be expected of a music theory, and what are its basic assumptions, can no longer be avoided. The formulation of the question in this context of computer-generated sound provided an answer – the unavoidable answer that many of the assumptions underlying music theory are assumptions about human listeners and that music theory is a theory of how the listener hears.

The triple isomorphism encompassed by the problem space of music theory is illustrated in Figure 2 where (a) is the 'score file', a set of commands to the computer, specifying (b) the resulting sound waves which are subsequently mentally represented by the listener at (c).

Figure 2

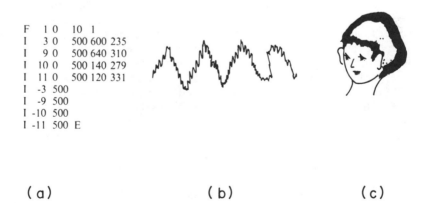

```
F    1 0    10  1
I    3 0    500 600 235
I    9 0    500 640 310
I   10 0    500 140 279
I   11 0    500 120 331
I   -3 500
I   -9 500
I  -10 500
I  -11 500  E
```

(a)   (b)   (c)

It is apparent to anyone dealing with computer-generated sound, that
one cannot predict completely the phenomenal outcome (c) from the
specifications entered at (a). And which parts of the process does music
theory concern itself with: input or output? Well, certainly not input
alone, that is, the mathematical description. Not that mathematics is
out of place in music theory. Music theory must seek to be computational, but the computation of interest here is the mapping of the
physical description of the sound onto the mental sound space. This is
also a psychophysical problem, a search for the functional relation
between physics and mind. But unlike psychophysical theory developed
from *objective* data on human perceptual performance, music theory
has been based upon subjective notions about how sound patterns are
heard. The student of perception is quick to learn that subjective impressions are often illusory. Both music theory and cognitive-
psychological theory require code of the relation between illusions and
physical sound parameters.

Quantifying the Mental Representation of Music

In the previous section we have argued that an overlap in the problem
space of music and psychology has been created by an all purpose tool
for sound synthesis, concepts from artificial intelligence, and computer
music. These developments raised three questions, respectively: what
acoustic differences are discriminable? what is the human music intelligence? and what is a music theory? It seems apparent that answers
to these questions will be stated in terms of a quantification of the mental representation of music. Broadly speaking, the general question,
then, is to define the relevant dimensions of the physical musical
stimulus and to measure a behaviour which is dependent upon the encoded mental representation of those dimensions. Referring again to
Figures 1 and 2, the problem is to define the function relating the music
stimuli at (b) and their mental representation at (c). The ultimate complexity of this function is almost inconceivable, as it must take into account the music acquisition process, past effects of musical experience,
individual differences, and all music sources. Nevertheless, simply the
concept of a precise systematic relation between music stimuli and
perceptual procedures is important, and, if fully appreciated, is half the
battle won in answering questions shared by music and psychology.

After having accepted the importance of measurement, where does
one begin? Simply in terms of the number of possible response
measures, the scope for research is enormous. The research space is
multiplied by considerations of age variables, individual differences and
effects of experience. As previously noted, neither the music-theoretic
attempt to describe structure in music nor the psychophysical attempt
to relate elements of sensation to mind alone will lead very quickly to an
adequate description of the mental map of music. A general approach
which can include features of both will be most successful; a psy-
chophysics of music at all its levels is in order. In the absence of a
general theory, it seems reasonable to encourage individual experimenters to test predictions based on their own intuitions about
music perception. Accumulated data should be stored in some transmit-
table form, for it is upon such data that an eventual cognitive theory of
music can be built. For two reasons, experimenters would be urged to

take advantage of numerous stimulus possibilities and experimental paradigms. First, this may prevent a too sudden acceptance of a theory. Second, numerous experiments will permit the separations of effects attributable to the stimulus (what we are most interested in) from those attributable to the task demands. The idea of multiple response measures for individual stimuli has been urged by the cognitive psychologist Garner, and is called 'converging operations'.[9]

Experimental Structure

The context for measurement of the music listening process is the psychology experiment. The goal of the experiment is to provide data which reflect the functional relation between music stimuli and their cognitive representation. In general, experiments consist of blocks of trials presented to listeners. Trials are subdivided further into the music-stimulus presentation and the listener's response possibilities, which are dependent upon the task demands, for example, to press the correct button as quickly as possible. Although the term experiment may be foreign to musicians, the resemblance between ear-training test structure and standard psychological paradigms is often seen (see Figure 3).

The experiment can be further conceptualized as three stages: set-up, control, and analysis. During the set-up stage, the experimenter is on his own. He chooses the sounds he will use in the experiment, the hardware requirements for stimulus presentation and response collection, the temporal characteristics of the trial structure, the number of trials, and of blocks of trials, the order of presentation of stimuli, and the manner in which the raw data should be stored. During the control stage of experiments the listener is presented with the blocks of trials. The analysis stage permits the computation of statistics describing trends in the listener's behavioral response, as, for example, in mean number correct responses. When all listeners have carried out the experimental task, statistical analyses of all data are computed. The choice of statistic depends upon the experimenter's aims (see Figure 4).

Figure 3

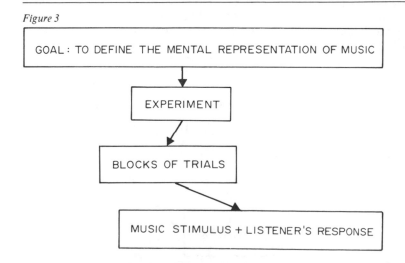

The results of the experiment are interpreted within the context of broad experimental question: how is the music stimulus mentally represented? For example, low scores on the discrimination between two tone sequences might indicate either that the stimuli had identical mental representations or that memory for their mental representations was poor. Subsequently, experiments would be carried out to test whether stimulus confusion resulted from encoding, memory, or both. On the basis of the new results, the original theory would be refined, and future performance predictions made. Thus, the relation between theory construction and experiment design is dynamic. The results accumulated from many studies would lead to increasingly more encompassing and precise theories of music perception and a wide variety of research paradigms.

A System for Generating Music Experiments

Progress in data acquisition is facilitated by a system for experiment generation. Ideally, such a system combines infinite varieties of musical stimuli, experimental paradigms, and analysis procedures. In addition to this flexibility, the system is fast and accurate. A computer helps to satisfy these requirements.

With our particular PDP-11/40 based system under development, stimulus control is accomplished via digital synthesis or analog-to-digital conversion. Selected stimuli are stored digitally in a library on a computer disk for retrieval and digital-to-analog conversion during the experiment. The computer controls all aspects of the trial structure, including data storage. Complex data analyses are transferred to the maxi-computers on the campus (see Figure 5).

Attention has been directed to making a wide variety of stimuli equally accessible. This has involved the implementation of a sophisticated sound synthesis program, MUSIC-11, Barry Vercoe's fixed-point assembly language adaptation, which had its origin in the early MUSIC-V and MUSIC-360 programs. The latter have relatively long histories of use in computer composition and psychoacoustics. Thus, not only does the program provide a limitless source of sound possibilities, but also a body of knowledge upon which to build, and a language familiar to most people involved with music and computers for easy communication.[10]

Figure 4

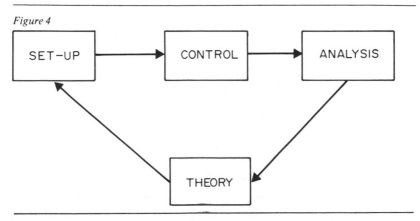

The distinction between sound-synthesis systems and music-structure generating systems applies to the goal of generating experiments to reveal the relation between music and mind.[11] What is known as sound synthesis can be handled fairly straightforwardly by MUSIC-11. Generation of musical structures is handled in two ways. First, programs are written to generate quickly examples of particular structures of interest. One such program generates tone patterns on the basis of independent information about scale structure and sequential characteristics. This permits the study of the independence of scales and sequential characteristics in mental representation of music. The other important source of real music structure is derived from analog tapes of recorded music. By means of a sophisticated sound editor, the sections of the music are extracted and stored in the sound library. Barring limitations of disk space, sounds from almost any source can be used in experiments.

Figure 5

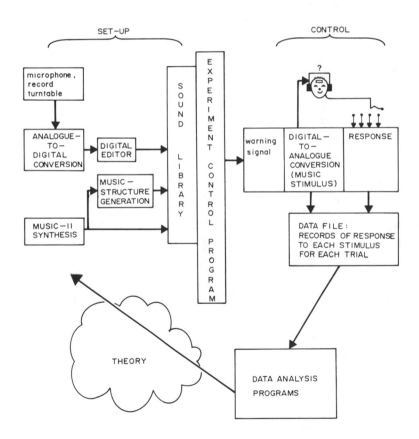

Psychology research over the last ten years has made increasing use of the computer for control of all stages of the experiment. In our case the computer takes over as much as possible (with the exception of those studies run off-line, using computer-generated stimuli reproduced on a tape-recorder). After the experimenter creates his sound library for the experiment, the basic program prompts the experimenter for such information as number of trials, duration of warning signal, stimulus, response interval, inter-trial interval. Because it is as easy to present pure tones as to present excerpts from classical music, a wide variety of research can be controlled from a single program. For example, studies on the perceived tonality in the music of Bach, the perceived duration of tones differing only in frequency, and the absolute identification of tones from different scales can be controlled by the same basic program.

There are a number of similarities between the system we describe and those found in music composition studios, psychoacoustics or ear-training labs. We draw attention, however, to a few essential distinguishing features of our system. First, the goal of our system is to reveal the functional relation between music and mind. The goal is not inconsistent with goals of psychoacoustics, ear-training, or music composition, but it is broader, and encompasses them all in the sense that they all depend on the mental representation of music. Each of our functional units, that is, each experiment, ends with a number reflecting some aspect of the relation between music and mind. Second, the equal accessibility of both digitally synthesized sound and analog sound allows the experimenter to consider a wide variety of music, and keeps a broad perspective for research. Finally, we emphasize the ability to produce countless varieties of experiments as a result of the independent access to music stimuli, experimental paradigms, and analysis procedures.

We have said that the development of sound synthesis, artificial intelligence, and computer music raised the following questions for music and psychology: what acoustic differences make psychological differences, what is the nature of the human musical understanding, and what is music theory. In the second part of the paper we have argued that these questions may be answered through the quantification of the functional relation between music stimuli and the listener's mental representation procedures. As an aid, the computer can control a wide variety of musical material, experimental paradigms, and analysis procedures while at the same time affording both speed and accuracy. The resultant data will provide a foundation for a psychologically-based precise music theory, a theory applicable to both traditional and contemporary music, a theory which can clarify current internal inconsistencies in musicology, and a theory which is relevant to the understanding of cognition in general. And for those who may still be skeptical about the role of computers in the humanities, we remark that it is the mindless computer which draws our attention to the role of mind in both music and psychology and forces us to consider more carefully our own human nature.

References

[1] B. Truax, "The Inverse Relation Between Generality and Strength in Computer Music Programs," Paper presented at the First International Conference on Computer Music, M.I.T., 1976.

[2] J.R. Anderson and G.H. Bower, *Human Associative Memory* (Toronto: Wiley, 1973).

[3] G.A. Miller, "Needed: A Better Theory of Cognitive Organization," *Transactions of I.E.E.E. Man, Systems and Cybernetics* (1974).

[4] A. Newell and H.A. Simon, *Human Problem Solving* (Englewood Cliffs: Prentice-Hall, 1972).

[5] M. Babbitt, "Contemporary Music Composition and Music Theory as Contemporary Intellectual History," *Perspectives in Musicology*, eds. B.S. Brooks, E.O. Downes and S.V. Solkema (New York: Norton, 1972), 151-184.

[6] G.A. Miller, "The Magical Number Seven, Plus or Minus Two," *Psychological Review*, 63 (1956), 81-97.

[7] D. Andrews, *The Oxford Harmony* (London: Oxford Press, 1950), II.

[8] H. Schrenker, *Harmony*, ed. O. Jones, trans. E.M. Borgese (Chicago: Chicago University Press, 1954).

[9] W.R. Garner, *The Processing of Information and Structure* (Toronto: Wiley, 1974).

[10] Our use of the synthesis program for both psychoacoustic work and computer music composition makes the study of contemporary-music perception relatively straightforward.

[11] W. Slawson, "Input Languages Affect System Design," Paper presented at the First International Conference on Computer Music, M.I.T., 1976.

[12] This work was supported in part by the National Research Council of Canada, Grant No. A0266 to the first author. The second authors of the present work were indispensable contributors and the order of their names was assigned arbitrarily. Special thanks is given to Dr. L.L. Cuddy and Dr. D.J. Mewhort of the Department of Psychology of Queens University. The help of Dr. M.E. Alexander, Mr. C. Knowles, and Mr. R. Melen, University of Waterloo; Dr. M. Taylor, Defense and Civil Institute of Environmental Medicine; Mr. B. Buxton, University of Toronto; and Professors L. Braida and B. Vercoe, Massachusetts Institute of Technology is acknowledged. We also thank the Department of Psychology of the University of Waterloo for generously providing facilities for this project.

Models of Interactive Computer Composition

B. Truax, J. Barenholtz

A question we may seriously ask in looking over the last two decades of computing applied to the humanities is, "in what way has the computer actually proved itself useful?" By asking this question, we risk an argument as to what each of us considers worth doing with a computer. If we substitute the question, "what does the computer allow us to do that couldn"t or wouldn"t have been done otherwise", we seem at first to get somewhere because one can immediately conjure up a problem that was so large, expensive, complicated or tedious that a computer alone served to bring about a solution. And although a few will still linger over this answer in arguing whether such a demanding task was in fact worth doing after all, and others will point out that the same amount of time was spent simply in getting a program to perform the task correctly as in doing it oneself, and still others will object that the computer became a substitute for exploitative cheap labour with little associated risk of revolution, many of us are inclined to pass over this answer and look for a deeper significance.

As an alternative, we might object to posing the question in this manner at all, and suggest that the importance of the computer is not that it can or cannot solve this or that problem, but rather that its generality, its celebrated ability to be programmed to solve any problem which can be suitably represented numerically or symbolically, is its crowning achievement, and one cannot ask more of it. After all, it is a general purpose machine, and perhaps the first of its kind in that respect. As intellectually satisfying as this seems, many of us return from the epiphany of that realization to our daily lives, searching for the practical results that will make it all seem to be true. In the meantime, the computer has hit the home hobbyist market with all the economic force of any expensive fad, and we as professionals watch as our own experience and questioning over these problems gets translated into the public arena where every and any application is eagerly snatched up and packaged, and the ideal of the general problem-solver now becomes a sales promotion line.

Ignoring for the moment the vast literature of reports of other people's programs, and declining to try to infer from the mass of detail (most of which just reflect computer language needs and not problem-oriented needs), just what has proven useful to others (which from these accounts is by no means obvious) we turn to our own experience for an answer. One of us is a composer whose creative work centres almost entirely around the use of the computer, the other is a musician-programmer whose major interest is in computer animation and music composition and their inter-relation. We each do our own programming (that is, we are not an arts-technology interface), and both of us have worked with other artists in assisting them with the realization of their own goals. Somewhat independently we came to a similar conclusion, that what we wanted to do could only be done within a machine environment. Neither of us is in the position of Edgard Varèse, who in 1917 foresaw that non-existent means would be required to realize his ideas, and in 1950 had those means become available. Instead, our working methods have gradually evolved such that our goals and the working methods themselves have become influenced, and to a large extent shaped, by what our experience with the computer has taught us. Although results are important, and one could go back and say only with a computer could one have achieved this, results for an artist are always in the past, and what emerges as having the greatest significance is that new kinds of thought, of organization and design, of methods and techniques, of learning and knowledge have become possible.

What characterizes the crucial elements that create this situation? One of those which is the most central is that of the interactive program environment. interactive program environment. The programs we regard as most valuable are those that participate in whatever process is going on, particularly when it is a design process. On the other hand, the vast majority of computer music programs are those where the machine enters only at the end of the compositional process to realize the structure in actual sound. Others seem to participate in the compositional process by using the input data to produce a given scored result, or set of results. The output is arrived at by an algorithmic procedure, but unless that result is deemed unsatisfactory, the use of the program seems to have little impact on the actual compositional process itself. In this type of process, it may be more accurate or simply more convenient to use a machine, but does the machine actually influence the process, re-direct or re-shape it? More generally, we may even ask, what role or image of the composer/artist does this use of computers continue to support?

The interactive program environment, we will argue in this paper, is at least one of the more significant achievements which the use of computing in the humanities has produced. We will discuss its significance in terms of composition and animation, but with reminders that parallels may be drawn in many related fields. We will argue from the basis of process, rather than results. However, from an artistic point of view, the results must also be convincing, and this we believe to be true as well. To argue backwards from the results is also a plausible approach, but it leads us back to the value-laden debate over whether the result was worth doing anyway, and whether the ends vindicated the means. Instead, we will concentrate on the particular implications of interactive programming on process, including the possibility that our notions of process may be entirely re-formulated through the use of such systems.

Learning Systems

The most obvious and perhaps farthest reaching characteristic of interactive systems is that they create a unique learning situation with rather interesting properties. This is particularly striking when the machine is programmed to produce sounds that are the acoustic realization of the structure being worked with. The user of the system has an actual sounding output that can influence future strategy and behaviour. Plans can not only be verified and optimized in this way, but also the acoustic output may suggest relations, such as timbral, colour relations, that will shape the course of the structure. Individual sound qualities may also be worked on interactively, that is, one may spend as much time designing the sound as the structure, and both may benefit from the feedback of results.

The underlying principle being evoked here is, as suggested by Piaget, "to know an object is to act upon it," that is, to transform it, mold and experiment with it, and thereby, to understand it. Interactive systems allow one to participate in this activity systematically, precisely, and in some cases very quickly as well. Interactive systems are best aided with what is called 'real-time synthesis' techniques, that is, the situation where the sound is calculated at the same time as it is heard, with no intervening storage. With the speed of modern hardware, the points of the acoustic waveform can be computed quickly enough that when those numbers are passed to a digital-to-analog converter, the output filtered and amplified through a loudspeaker, the sound may be heard immediately. Although there is a limit to the complexity of calculations performable in real time, and therefore to the acoustic complexity generated in this way, the advantage of the immediacy of the sound, and the ability to control precise variables of a given sound tend to outweigh the limitations, which are also growing less severe with newer generations of hardware. Immediate feedback of results clearly enhances the learning potential at any level of operation.

It may be argued that the piano was also an effective interactive learning tool for composers of the past who tended to try out their ideas on it first, and later to score or orchestrate the piano version. However, several important differences exist in what can be called the communicational aspects of each system. First of all, the use of the piano in this way was largely as an aid to memory. The composer could reasonably be expected to have memorized all of the actual acoustic properties of the instruments which would eventually play the notes; the piano tended to emphasize the harmonic and other relations, whereas the timbral variable remained fixed. In the twentieth century, timbre has come to assume a much larger role in composition than before. The sound repertoire has been enlarged enormously, and as often as not, the composer is dealing with new sounds. Hence there is no mental image of these sounds, and one is actively involved in shaping the acoustic repertoire. The interactive system not only allows one to hear the sounds being worked with, but also, in the best situation, gives one strong methods for controlling them. Unlike the piano, the computer has memory and can perform operations transforming every aspect of the sound.

We have described the relative importance of strong, specialized methods as opposed to weak, general ones, for interactive programs. General methods are weak in that they require a great deal of user input with little guarantee of a solution, or in this case, a well-formed sound or sound structure. However, their generality ensures a wide possible range of output. Strong methods essentially give the user 'handles' on the output in the sense of applying specialized knowledge in the form of effective control variables. For example, specifying an acoustic pressure function requires a great deal of information, typically ten to forty

thousand samples per second. Although it is technically true that any
sound may be produced by specifying the correct numbers, one clearly
needs strong methods that reduce the amount of user data to a
reasonable size. This is generally done through acoustic knowledge that
describes how particular sounds may be produced by using only a small
amount of data. Although any such technique necessarily restricts the
range of output, some methods become very useful because they give
the user a powerful control mechanism which essentially brings the output within easy reach of the user in terms of how much information is
needed, and how long it will take to specify it. Strong methods which
retain a sufficient degree of flexibility are particularly appropriate to an
interactive environment because they may be quickly utilized by a composer to optimize a result, and because. they tend to guarantee a
reasonably well-formed output corresponding to the acoustic model being used. Musical instruments may also be thought of as embodying
strong acoustic methods to produce basically well-formed results; with
digital models, however, the range of output from one such programmed 'instrument' may be even greater, and will certainly be more accessible to both the novice and expert.

Compositional Models

Similar to the advantages of strong acoustic models in the interactive
environment, strong compositional models have a particular importance as well. The environment in effect is a testing ground for such
models, because they are put to actual use in compositional tasks where
their advantages and limitations will become immediately obvious.
Models, then, do not remain restricted to textbooks to be tried out on
novice theory students. Rather, they can be tested within actual working situations. In fact, as has been already described, interactive
programs tend to call for strong compositional methods in order for
them to be of best use. In the past, few such methods have been implemented on the computer. This lack has been particularly evident in
systems which require the composition to be fully specified as the input
to the program, which translates the input into sound. Such a system
implies a great deal about what kind of compositional process will be
used, and to some extent even what kind of role the composer will be
playing; such systems do not generally exhibit any compositional
facility, and therefore compositional knowledge.

Although there are many features of compositional models which
could be discussed, and in other publications already have been, one
point in particular can be singled out here as a feature shared by the
programs of both authors. That is specifically the ability of compositional programs to handle architecture, and the user's involvement
with it, in rather unique ways. Architecture, or the design of structural
units and relations, is a problem of particular importance to composers
and artists in this century, partly because new materials and techniques
often involve new forms as well. To date, the tape medium and
electronic sound-generating equipment have greatly expanded the
acoustic repertoire, and even influenced ways of putting sounds
together, but at the level of larger units, the composer has tended to
have to rely on what amounts to manual means that are then imposed
on the working method.

Although in many computer programs, the composer is still working with individual notes and note relations, there are now programs, such as those of the authors, which take what might be called a 'top down' approach in emphasizing structural control right from the beginning. The user is expected to work with a variety of control levels, including that of structural units, not simply with individual details. As well, in the POD program for composition and synthesis, the specific details are determined by various statistical algorithms or selection procedures available to the user. These allow a working method that differs significantly from previous ones, and that only makes sense within an interactive environment. The computer can work with general or specific relations between units other than notes, and leave the details to be worked out according to some other procedure such as that of a statistical distribution. The details of the specific events are controlled, but from higher levels of constraint. Some contemporary musical scores are termed 'indeterminate' because some of the details are left up to the performer, and even traditional scores give performers certain liberties, mainly dependent on the performer's sense of the appropriate style or idiom. However, in general, composers have always had to specify all aspects of a structure before it could be heard. It is not surprising then that there has been a tendency to 'over control' various aspects of the music, that is, to be making decisions that look specific, such as a particular pitch at a particular time, when in fact a number of interchangeable possibilities would also suffice, such as any pitch within a certain range. A compositional model that allows one to have various degrees of control over a parameter, from random to highly determined, offers the facility that in working on a specific structure, control may be applied selectively only where and when it is perceived to be necessary. One may proceed from rather simple, general specifications, hear what a possible implication or instance of that might sound like, and then impose greater control, variety or restraint where it is thought to be needed. All decisions at the specific level do not have to be made by the composer, and all do not have to be made at once in order to hear any result. This facility inevitably changes the way a composer will tackle a problem, and offers a wider range of possibilities within the same system. The interactive aspect may prove valuable to develop an idea from the start, or else to optimize an already complex structure that has been worked out beforehand.

Many aspects of interactive systems with strong compositional models that have already been presented are features of the POD program for synthesis and composition. This program runs on various mini-computers and therefore is quite accessible in terms of time and cost. The program is tailored to suit the particular hardware configuration of any given system, though in most to date, the user issues commands and gives data via a CRT terminal, and receives information back on that terminal, on a line printer, and most importantly as sound from a D/A converter. Use of a graphic input terminal is also being considered. The compositional strategy, however, remains the same in each system, and to a large extent this is also independent of the particular synthesis method used; that is, the same compositional strategy may be used with different synthesis 'instruments'. Similarly, the program can be used to produce sounds that will be recorded on tape, or else to have the sound structure translated into a simple representation of conventional music notation which may then be performed.

The structure aspects of the compositional model may be shown in the following way:

Composition Section and Variants
Performance Variables
Distribution of Events
Sound Object
Event

Although the basic unit of sound is classed as an event, the user works with distributions of events and their performance interpretations and variants. The user is also concerned with defining 'sound objects,' which are the descriptions of particular sounds that may be synthesized by the program. They differ from the event by describing only the timbral dimension of the event, leaving specific pitch, loudness and point of entry in time to be determined by the distribution itself, that is , a sound object may be transposed in pitch, attenuated in loudness, and, optionally for the user, scaled in time relative to some percentage of the time available between events. By treating the sound object in this way, the compositional model emphasizes what might be called the 'mapping' of the timbral domain onto a syntactic field of the pitch-time structure. Timbre was earlier regarded as constant for a given melody, and that which distinguished one instrumental line from another. It is treated in this program in a way that is consistent with the greater emphasis placed on it by composers in this century. Note also that the computer program allows these variables to be separated and treated systematically in a much more powerful and convenient way than was possible before.

A second aspect of the compositional structure listed above is that the user may work at the various levels listed and control their interrelationship. Differing degrees of control, for instance, may be imposed at each level. The program already shifts the emphasis from control at the event level to control at the level of the distribution. At each level, however, a simple control may interpret or change all of the units at a lower level. The performance variables are powerful examples of these. A simple change at this level re-inteprets how, for example, the time structure of the section will be treated, without the user having to go back and adjust individual event durations. Finally, the ability to make systematic variants is a possibility only with a computerized system. A simple change of random start number, for instance, will produce a different set of random numbers in a statistical selection process. The result will follow the same general structural rules, but be different at the level of specific events.

This facility for deciding exactly what aesthetic possibilities to control, and when to apply this control is also a key feature of GRAX, an animation system. In GRAX, the animator may describe individual segments of an animation, each in its own time/space framework, and then specify how the segments are to be put together in the overall 'viewing space '. Or, a fully 'top down' approach may be used. Here, the animator will specify that some yet-to-be-defined process is to start at a particular time and place in the viewing space, and then is to proceed along some path, or through some set of visual transformations. Several unspecified processes can be simultaneously choreographed in the viewing space, and the relationships between the processes can be worked out in great detail. At this level, each process would be represented by some simple visible token, like a small square or triangle on the computer's display screen.

Then, the animator can go back and define what each of the unspecified processes is to be. The triangle token might, for example, be replaced with a detailed animation sequence of a person running, while the square might be replaced by a puppy dog trotting. Alternatively, abstract visual patternings, or herds of dots moving through visualizations of the physicists' wave equations, or randomly sequenced images selected from some existing library, could be substituted for the process tokens. In any case, the overall structure of the piece will be that imposed by the relations between process at the top level (that is, before the substitution of sequences for tokens).

The significance of this ability to work top down, or bottom up, or to combine the two styles, lies in the fact that the artist is now free to put his or her energy where he or she feels it should go. The tendency to 'over-control' the animation is minimized.

Before computers were introduced, the animator did not really have even the equivalent of the composer's piano to help him or her visualize the implications of decisions. As a result, time factors and cruel economics forced the artist to get the animation 'right' the very first try. The real-time playback facilities and flexible control and editing capabilities which characterize interactive computer environments thus allow, indeed encourage, a level of visual experimentation never before practical in animation.

Thus, in both composition and animation, the interactive nature of computerized systems, the fact that these are learning environments promotes the growth of new ways of approaching the art forms. New experimentation with sounds and graphics, with structures and methods of organization and interaction of objects in their sound or visual spaces, are not only made possible, but also promoted by the very nature of the medium.

These new possibilities come at a very opportune time in terms of the current state and goals of art. Over the last century or so, composition and performance in music have grown to be more and more separate activities, in the sense that composers no longer see their work solely in terms of providing new music for themselves or their groups to perform. Many of today's composers see composition as a means of exploring the possibilities intrinsic to a set of sounds, or as experiments in the structuring and organization of groups of sounds. The key words here are 'exploring' and 'experiments.'

The 'underground' film-makers and the 'experimental' video artists also define much of their work in terms of aesthetic explorations, or if you prefer, as aesthetic research. One can see Picasso's work with perspective, Vasarelli's work with colour, and Barth's work with narrative story forms, in this same light. Expense usually prohibits animations from being very explorative, but many of the short (cheap) animations shown at the festivals are clearly experimental in intent.

And so we find that the computer systems employed by some artists and musicians are quite apt to the general directions that art and music are taking today: they are research-oriented, interactive learning environments, well suited to experimentation and exploration.

Users' Communities

Throughout the history of art, whenever, a new approach or a new technique was being developed, a group of artists formed around it. These groups were held together by some shared aesthetic vision primarily, and secondarily by such factors as working in the same medium and in the same town, or studying from the same people, or being perceived as similar by the public or by the critics. Occasionally, a manifesto or some such document would appear, in which an attempt was made to articulate what bound the members of the group together. But more often, the work of the artists was the only medium for recording the binding energy. What is more, the only ways that the various members could communicate their insights and discoveries to one another was by example (the works of art) and by discussion. These methods of communication obviously have considerable value, but they also have limits. Referring back to Piaget's concept of knowing, example and discourse are weak methods at best for sharing knowledge.

One possibility which computers have created is that of sharing knowledge by adding something to the system itself. As has been mentioned above, a computer system is an embodiment of a model of whatever process it is applied to. Thus, if a user of the system adds something to it, the model itself has been expanded. By the nature of computers, any new facility is available to all the users of a program, and thus the new idea embodied in the new facility is rendered knowable (in the sense of Piaget) to all the users.

Thus we see computer systems taking on a new role: they are a medium for knowledge storage and exchange (as opposed to their conventional role as a medium for information storage and exchange). An analogy may make this point clearer and help to underscore its importance. Consider a woodworking collective, where each member has his own tools, but all work in one large shop. Suppose a member invents a new way of joining two pieces of wood, and builds a specialized set of clamps and jigs for the purpose. He can then bring into the shop some examples of his new type of joint, or some photos of furniture which use it, thereby sharing the information that the new technique exists. Or, he can bring in the clamps and jigs, and explain how to use them, in which case he is offering to share the techniques and knowledge he has gained.

While it is not uncommon for computer systems to grow in response to suggestions from their users, it is a somewhat new situation for models of animation or composition to grow in this way, since there has been no medium in which these models were previouly embodied. The authors' experiences with the growth of both POD and GRAX suggests that this type of growth is going to be one of the more exciting and positive aspects of computerized systems in the arts.

Another important aspect of a users' community is its implications with respect to the social role of composers, and the nature of composition itself. Over the last century or so, the variety of styles of compositions has grown enormously. Some composers score only for conventional instruments, others on tape, others with computers, and yet others with a mix of the media. Some composers seem interested almost exclusively in structural aspects of music, others in timbral aspects, yet others in the spatial possibilities created by multi-channel, multi-speaker arrangements. Some composers are exploring the theoretical aspects of the performances per se, while others use performers in a traditional way, or not at all.

The apparent diversity of styles has so impressed most of the listening public, the critics, and even some of the musicians, that the composer is being seen more and more as an eccentric, working on his or her own, in a vacuum maintained by the esoteric nature of the music itself. Music as a whole is seen by many as being directionless. Many find it difficult to compare the works of any two composers, because they do not see anything in common in the compositions.

Elsewhere, we have summarized these views as "the notion of the composer's activity as irrational, non-generalizable, non-teachable, and non-programmable." However, the authors' experiences with their programs challenges the correctness of this notion. The POD system has been used in compositions by more than a dozen composers with highly varied backgrounds over the last few years, and has been used with good results in teaching composition to a large number of students. The fact that many composers with different styles have found POD useful points to the fact that the model of composition which it embodies is shared. At least to some extent, there is a general (that is, non-idiosyncratic, generalizable) model for musical composition. Likewise, the value of POD in teaching demonstrates that some principles of composition are more general than the whim or invention of a single individual composer.

GRAX, like POD, is a 'strong' system in that it embodies one specific conception of the process of animation. The implementation of GRAX is not yet complete, and so there have been no animations which make more than trivial use of the program per se. But even in its incomplete form, it has served well as a teaching tool, making it possible to communicate its model of animation to students, and to more experienced artists. Several people have been delighted to find a shared medium for expressing some of the ideas with which they have been working, and on the basis of the model have proposed a number of projects within animation, such as animated concrete poetry and interactive image processing. Whether GRAX as a program will prove as successful as POD has in realizing projects remains to be seen. But the fact that GRAX as a paradigm for animation – for the organization and control of visual events – is attractive to a variety of people indicates that there are some deep principles of organization which underlie the art form; that the form is not in fact, "irrational, non-generalizable, non-teachable, non-programmable," and generally speaking, idiosyncratic.

Thus, our experience has shown that, appearances notwithstanding, the existence of users' groups points to the existence of general principles of organization and structure in both music and animation. Furthermore, interactive computer systems and the users' communities which grow around them provide a good environment for exploring, learning, and teaching these structures, as well as for using them in one's own artistic work.

The Effects of Micro-Computers

The computer industry has been making small machines and cheap memory available in the last year or two, and the enthusiastic response of hobbyists more or less guarantees that this will continue. In the not very distant future, one may expect composition or animation systems of varying degrees of sophistication which will be priced in the $1000-$2000 range (less than half the cost of a car or a good piano). These machines will be capable of running any one of a number of composition or animation programs, or of allowing their purchasers to develop their own.

Periodicals like the newly started *Journal of Computer Music* will probably take on the role of distributing, or at least indexing, new programs or extensions to existing ones. This will effectively extend the 'user community' of any given system to include virtually everyone. Without any doubt, this will be of great value to the serious, 'professional' users of these systems. In particular, knowledge (as opposed to information about knowledge) will become more easily - transportable from place to place, and therefore from individual to individual.

One may also anticipate a few less delightful prospects. The same micro-computer technology which *could* turn a T.V. set into an interactive graphics display device has already found wide-spread commercial application in T.V. games like pong. As more and more people become involved with micro-computer technology, more and more such devices may be heaped onto the market. It is entirely possible that the same interests which have been adding more and more complex automatic rhythm generators to electronic organs, and promoting Muzak, will turn their attentions to what can be done with cheap digital technology. The mind boggles at the possibilities.

It is a matter still hotly disputed whether art can live through the ravages of a technological culture. We can expect the micro-computer technology to heat the dispute a bit more.

Throughout this paper we have been arguing that computers are providing at least one unique and important contribution to the humanities and the arts through the implications of interactive program environments. The focus has been on the behaviour of the user/program system within the framework of design and architectural work in music and animation. Although the results of such systems may reflect the impact of the new technology, we have been pointing to the new aspects of the working process which we feel are unique to this use of the technology. These centre around the advantages of the system as a learning situation within which strong compositional models may be implemented, shared, optimized and used. The computer participates not only by producing technical results of greater complexity and precision than before, but more significantly by creating a compositional tool that allows the very question of process to be addressed, influenced and re-directed.

When a new working technique begins influencing the composer or animator at such a basic level, as opposed to being simply a stylistic influence, it seems inevitable that certain traditional notions of the role and image of the composer or animator may change as well. It is doubtless too soon to see the full impact of this change, but most of the points raised in this paper have some bearing on this question. An interactive system pre-supposes that all users are novices at some point. The distinction between the student and the professional becomes blurred; all have access to the same means, and each has an opportunity to grow in personal expertise. It may well become more difficult to maintain the notion of the 'personality cult' among artists or the competitiveness which it breeds. The composer's work may start to have more connection to that of the music student, since the means for the sharing of knowledge have been improved. Moreover, music may become less isolated as it links to other processes of thought and as its design becomes clearer and more developed.

References

Barenholtz, J. "An Artist's Animation System for Modest Computers." *Proceedings of the Northwest ACM/CIPS Pacific Regional Symposium*, 1976.

Barenholtz, J. "Towards a New Technology for Computer Animation." Unpublished thesis, University of British Columbia, Vancouver, 1977.

Truax, B. "A Communicational Approach to Computer Sound Programs." *Journal of Music Theory*, 20, No. 2 (Fall 1976).

Truax, B. "Computer Music in Canada (1975)." *Numus-West*, No. 8 (1975).

Truax, B. "General Techniques in Computer Composition Programming." *Numus-West*, No. 4 (1973).

Truax, B. "Some Programs for Real-Time Synthesis and Computation." *Interface*, 2 (1973).

Truax, B. "The Computer Composition-Sound Synthesis Programs POD4, POD5 and POD6." *Sonological Reports*, No. 2, Utrecht (1973).

Truax, B. "The Inverse Relation of Generality and Strength in Computer Sound Programs." paper delivered to the First International Conference on Computer Music, Boston, 1976.

Truax, B. "The POD System of Interactive Composition Programs." *Computer Music Journal*, 2 (1977).

A Computer Aided Analysis
of Canadian Folksongs

J. Wenker

During the past twenty years, several thousand folksongs have been collected in the province of Ontario. Many of these have been published with their tunes. Because these transcriptions have been made by conscientious, capable musicians specializing in folksongs and working from tape recordings of the songs, these tunes are faithful representations of the music. Any analysis of the music of a collection of folksongs is, of course, dependent upon the reliability of the tune transcriptions. With the recent publications of reliable transcriptions, it is now time to analyze the music of these folksongs.[1]

Many techniques for the analysis of the music of folksongs have been developed by folklorists, ethnomusicologists, musicologists, and anthropologists. Most of these techniques have been used on a limited basis because they involve a substantial amount of repetitive labor. The repetitive labor which in the past has constrained the analysis of folkmusic, encourages the use of the computer.

In order to perform a preliminary detailed analysis of the music of folksongs, ninety-two folksongs of Ontario were selected for the analysis presented here. Once this data has been thoroughly analyzed, and each analysis technique evaluated, then additional folksongs can be included in a larger study of folkmusic.

One of the problems in the analysis of folkmusic is that most existing forms of music analysis have never been evaluated to determine what useful information they provide. Some techniques have been used to gather and publish data for a single collection of songs without any comparisons with other collections of folksongs. What is needed is to have the same type of data gathered from two or more collections of songs, followed by a comparison of the results, using statistical analysis where appropriate. Fortunately, some of the same forms of music analysis used here were applied to a collection of 100 United States Negro spirituals by Portia Maultsby.[2] Therefore, some comparisons of results have been made, including some preliminary evaluations of certain analytical techniques.

The computer processing required to support the amount and types of music analysis described here is substantial. The music processing system used to develop the tools, utilities, and analysis programs needed for this project is called the MUSTRAN System.

The Central MUSTRAN System

The basic approach used in the development of the MUSTRAN System is that the input source data should be a mnemonic human-oriented keypunchable representation; and that this notation should be read only once by the computer. Thus, the first and most complex component of the system is a compiler or MUSic TRANslator which reads the music as keypunched and produces as output a binary table which is much more suitable for machine processing. It should be mentioned that, while the compiler is being used for folkmusic here, it is capable of processing (subject to temporary size restraints) any music from the renaissance through Bach, Beethoven, Brahms, Brubeck and the Beatles, and non-western music as well. After a piece of music has been compiled, a subroutine is used to write the binary table produced into a sequential data file which could be tape or mass storage. This file containing one or more pieces of music is the input data file for all other components of the full MUSTRAN System.[3]

As the compiler converts the input source notation into the binary table for future processing, it also produces a printout of the translation, including error information. The MUSTRAN compiler contains substantial error detecting and correcting capabilities. It will flag any notation which it has difficulty in evaluating and produce an interpretation of that erroneous data. As an aid to the human, the compiler uses the final binary table (produced as output) to re-generate input notation, and this 'back-translation' is included in the printout. Thus, if any errors are detected and flagged by the compiler, the user can easily compare the input notation with the resultant notation. In many instances this comparison will show that the compiler produced the desired output and the piece of music will not have to be recompiled.

Once the compiler has produced the input data file for the MUSTRAN System, the user will need human-oriented means of accessing this file. This has been implemented by a library of MUSTRAN subroutines which the user calls upon to read items of music, search for specific music symbols, and unpack individual symbols for ease of analysis. Because of the availability of this library, the user does not need to know any details of the format of the binary table. All analysis programs and all utility programs are written using these library subroutines, as is the compiler itself.

The last component of the central MUSTRAN System to be discussed is the set of utility programs which simplify the handling of files of translated music. The following utility programs have proved to be very useful and should be available for any music processing system.

1) XFTOC – lists the identification title and size of each piece of music in a data file.
2) XFMRG – uses one input file containing a base set of pieces of music and a second input file containing corrected pieces of music and/or additional pieces of music. It merges these two files to produce an updated output data file. For example, if a data file was produced containing ten pieces of music and one was in error, that one could be re-compiled and, by use of XFMRG, replaced in the datafile. Without XFMRG (or an equivalent utility) the entire ten pieces of music would have to be re-translated.
3) XFSEL – uses control card data to select items of music from an input datafile and write them to an output datafile.
4) XFSRT – uses control card data to read an input datafile, reorder the items and write an output datafile.
5) XFREN – uses control card information to read an input datafile, rename one or more items of music, and write an output datafile.

The analysis programs have been excluded from the central MUSTRAN System because they are only one use of that system. Other uses of the system include programs to print music, and programs to perform music (via the MUSIC V program). This brief description of the central MUSTRAN System exemplifies the tools needed for computational musicology (in the broadest sense). Now that the basic tools have been mentioned, the actual music analysis functions implemented under the MUSTRAN System can be discussed.

Several of the individual music analysis programs were designed to gather data on more than one analytical function. This was done because it is easy to gather data on several related topics at the same time. It has also been found that data gathered for one analytical function has provided additional information helpful in other analytical functions. For these reasons, and to avoid unnecessary discussions of the computational details of individual analysis programs, it has been decided that only the various analytical functions and the results of the analysis will be included here.

The following discussion of the various analytical functions includes information on the function (when appropriate) and the results of the analysis of the full 92 tunes. When equivalent information on the spiritual collection is available, it will be included. By combining the two analyses, it will be possible to do a preliminary evaluation of the analytical function at the time that it is being presented. An additional advantage is that the Canadian results do not have to be presented more than once.

Scales

The 92 Canadian folksongs utilize 23 different scales and the individual scales have from five to nine different pitches (excluding octave duplications). Comparable data exists for the spiritual collection as shown in the following table.

Table 1.

| | Number of Pitches | | | | | | | |
	3	4	5	6	7	8	9	Totals
Canadian Scales	0	0	3	6	7	5	2	23
Number of Tunes	0	0	5	22	40	20	5	92
Spiritual Scales	1	1	6	9	5	4	0	26
Number of Tunes	1	2	25	41	23	8	0	100
Shared Scales	0	0	2	4	4	3	0	13
Canadian Tunes	0	0	4	17	34	16	0	71
Spiritual Tunes	0	0	17	32	22	7	0	78

This table shows that, for the most part, the Canadian singers use seven-pitch scales (plus or minus one) while the spirituals use six-pitch scales (plus or minus one). Four possible reasons for this difference can be suggested:

1) Pentatonic (five-pitch) scales are very common among White singers in the south-eastern portion of the United States;
2) Pentatonic scales are assumed to have been common in 18th century Africa;
3) Functional difference between group and solo singing could account for the more complex Canadian scales; and
4) The spirituals were transcribed during performance while the Canadian tunes were transcribed from tapes, thus making it possible for the transcriber to obtain more details.

The results given here suggest additional research would be desirable.

The values in rows 2 and 4 of the table given above were statistically tested and are significant at the 0.1% level. Thus, this analytical function produces results which are mathematically meaningful, and this function should be used in future work. Since all, or part, of this function is commonly used in folkmusic publications, it would probably be retained for historical purposes even if it were not productive of solid, comparable results.

Notice that although the two collections have only thirteen scales in common, these thirteen scales account for more than three quarters of the tunes in each collection. The most common scale in each collection is Ionian (major); the other scales which are common in one collection appear infrequently in the other collection and this distribution of the common scales is also statistically significant.

General Range Analysis

The ranges of the Canadian tunes can be separated into three distinct groups which account for 82 of the 92 tunes. These groups, the ranges involved, and the historical names for the groups are as follows:

Table 2

Name	Low Pitch*	High Pitch*	Total Range (Semitones)	Number of Tunes
Authentic	F, F#, or G	G+, A+, B-flat+ or B+	13-18	47
Plagal	D	D+, E+, or F+	12-15	26
Mixed	D	G+	17	9

*All of these values are determined after the tune has been transposed (within the analysis program) to end on G. The plus sign indicates a pitch in the octave beginning with C above middle C.

If the remaining ten tunes are forced into the three historical categories, the counts then become: Authentic – 50, Plagal – 29, Mixed – 13.

For the spiritual collection, range information has been supplied for 78 of the 100 items. Using this information the following table comparing the Canadian tunes with the spiritual tunes has been produced.

Table 3.

| | Range and Counts | | | | | | | | | | |
	7	9	10	12	13	14	15	16	17	18	All
Canadian	0	0	0	11	7	29	10	15	17	3	92
Spiritual	2	11	4	24	1	16	6	4	10	0	78

The results in the above table are statistically significant. The average range of the Canadian tunes is 14.8 semitones while the average range of the spiritual tunes is 12.7 semitones. This difference is probably related, at least in part, to the difference in the scales (as discussed above), since scales with a range of less than an octave usually have fewer than seven pitches.

Interval Analysis

The interval between the pitch of one note in a tune and the pitch of the following note has, in the past, been shown to be a unit worth analyzing. Thus, counts of which intervals are used, and how often a particular interval is used in a collection of tunes produce significant results.

In comparing the Canadian tunes with the spiritual tunes, the following short table includes several interesting results.

Table 4.

| | Size of Interval (Semitones) | | | | |
	0	1	2	3	4 or More
Canadian	1115	572	2045	665	987
Spiritual	1685	272	1236	680	898

The first result is that the spirituals use far more repeated notes than the Canadian tunes (35% versus 20%). Next, the spirituals use few intervals of a single semitone (6% versus 10%). This second result is to be expected because the spirituals include many tunes with five or fewer pitches and these scales, in general, do not have pitches close enough for single semitone intervals to be permissable. The third interesting result is that both collections use about the same percentage of intervals larger than three semitones (about 19% in each case), thus indicating that, for comparative purposes, only small intervals may be worth investigating.

When ascending intervals are analyzed separately from descending intervals, the Canadian tunes show, for each interval size, fairly equal counts in both directions, with slightly higher usages of an ascending semitone and a descending minor third (three semitones). The spirituals are distinctly non-symmetrical, with large counts for ascending intervals of four or more semitones and descending intervals of two or three semitones. This result indicates that the spirituals have a tendency towards melodic patterns involving an ascending jump followed by a descending series of steps.

In the Canadian collection, the analysis of intervals with the songs grouped by performer or by textual category show statistically significant results. The meaning and interpretation of these differences in interval usage will require additional analysis.

Interval Patterns

Another form of analysis which can be done is to investigate the patterns which result when two or more consecutive intervals are considered. Early studies in this area have concentrated on searches for a limited number of specific patterns simply because of the amount of labor this search involves. The computer makes it practical to count all patterns of a desired number of intervals and then investigate more thoroughly selected patterns known to be present in a collection of music.

The preliminary work on interval patterns has been concentrated on patterns of two and three intervals. As the analysis looks at longer patterns, the number of patterns that occur more than a few times becomes very small. Thus, with the Canadian collection of 92 tunes the only three-interval pattern which occurs more than 75 times is the repetitive monotone (the same pitch repeated for all notes in the pattern) and that pattern occurs only 126 times. For four intervals, the repetitive monotone is again the most common pattern with only 56 occurrences. When a pattern occurs less frequently than the number of tunes being analyzed, it probably is not characteristic of that group of tunes. The current programs will allow patterns of up to twenty-four intervals, which could prove useful in searches for parallel phrases.

The repetitive monotone is the most common two-interval pattern in both the Canadian collection (358 tunes) and in the spiritual collection (686 tunes). Other common two-interval patterns in the two collections are as follows:

Table 5.

| | First Interval, Second Interval (Semitones) | | | | | | |
	−2,−2	2, 2	2,−2	2,−3	−2, 2	0, 2	0,−2
Canadian	234	232	220	195	189	172	170
Spiritual	145	*	136	*	*	143	177

* = not a common interval in the spiritual collection

The other common intervals in the spiritual collection and their frequency of occurrence in both collections are as follows:

Table 6.

| | First Interval, Second Interval (Semitones) | | |
	−2, 0	0,−3	3, 0
Canadian	134	64	60
Spiritual	193	156	132

These tables show that, for the most part, the most common interval patterns in the Canadian collection are not the most common patterns in the spiritual collection and vice versa. Notice also that in the spiritual collection the most common intervals usually involve one interval of zero; this is to be expected from the very high use of repeated pitches, as mentioned above in interval analysis, and as re-emphasized by 686 occurrences of the repetitive monotone as a pattern of two intervals.

Similar results occur in the analysis of three-interval patterns. The only result worthy of comment is the repetitive monotone, which occurs 126 times in the Canadian collection and 323 times in the spiritual collection.

The comparison of interval patterns in the two collections is statistically significant, showing, as expected from the interval analysis results, that there is a distinct difference in interval pattern usage between the two categories of songs. Thus, this analysis function is also one that can and should be used in any future analysis of single voice music. With minor alterations in the program this same analysis function could be applied to any voice in analyzing multiple voice pieces of music.

The Canadian collection has been sorted into groups based upon performer, and the number of occurrences of each common interval pattern have been calculated for each group. These results are also statistically significant, implying that performers differ in terms of which interval patterns they prefer. However, further analysis is required due to the limited number of songs analyzed. When the songs were sorted on textual grounds, differences which require further investigation were also found.

Rhythm Analysis (Duration Pairs)

One of the new analytical techniques which has been made practical only through the use of the computer is an analysis of rhythmic sequences. This analysis function tabulates all duration pairs, thus identifying, for each duration used in a tune, which durations follow it and how often. Thus, it is easy to determine how often a quarter note duration is followed by an eighth note, an eighth followed by an eighth, and so forth. Because all of the tunes in the Canadian collection were transcribed by the same musician, there is no question as to the validity of comparing rhythm values from one tune to the next. The most common rhythm pairs in the Canadian collection and their number of occurrences are: eighth followed by eighth – 1165; fourth followed by fourth – 909; eighth followed by fourth – 757; and fourth followed by eighth – 732. The next most common duration is eighth followed by dotted quarter, with 227 occurrences. The tunes have been sorted by performer and by textual type and the counts for the various common patterns have been calculated for each group. These counts differ significantly and this will require additional analysis.

Rhythm Analysis (Rhythmical Complexity)

Another form of rhythmic analysis consists of determining the number of different rhythms which occur in each tune. For the Canadian collection this number ranges from two different durations in a tune to nine different durations in a tune. Most tunes use three (18 tunes), four (23 tunes), five (25 tunes) or six (16 tunes) different durations. While further investigation appears to be necessary, it appears that this level of rhythmic complexity is not related to the performer.

A second level of rhythmic complexity analysis consists of dividing the number of note-note duration pair combinations which occur in a tune by the square of the number of valid durations in that tune. This value is equal to the percentage of the total possible duration pair combinations for the tune. For example, if a tune consists of quarter-note and eighth-note durations and the duration pairs, quarter followed by eighth, eighth followed by eighth, and eighth followed by quarter occur in the tune, the percentage value is 75% (three divided by two squared). If the tune also included quarter followed by quarter, then the percentage value would be 100%.

The current analysis of these percentage values reveal that the higher the number of different durations in the tune, the lower the percentage which actually occurs. There is enough variation in this general curve that it is possible that this aspect of rhythmic complexity may be worth analyzing by performer and textual categorizations.

Phrase Numbers and Durations

Sixty-three of the ninety-two Canadian tunes consist of a four phrase verse with no chorus. Thirteen of the remaining tunes consist of a four phrase verse with a four phrase chorus. The remaining fifteen tunes have from five to nine phrases of verse or have a chorus of one to five phrases.

The phrase durations of all four phrase verses and all four phrase choruses is also under investigation. A verse or chorus can be defined to be "regular" if it has four phrases and the individual phrase durations satisfy one of the following three criteria:
1) all four phrases have the same duration;
2) three phrases have the same duration while the remaining phrase differs from the others by no more than 10%; or
3) the phrases consist of two phrases of one duration, and two phrases of a second duration, with the difference between the two phrase durations being no more than 10%.

Using this definition of "regular", the Canadian collection includes 40 regular verses and choruses, 57 non-regular verses and choruses and 18 verses and choruses which were not four phrases long. Notice how much variation there is at this level of analysis, while the full collection consists of mostly four-phrase units.

While further investigation of this analytical function is necessary, it should be stated here that this function should only be applied where the majority of items in a collection fit into a limited number of common phrase structures.

Range Placement Analysis

Dr. Bertrand H. Bronson has made a study of many Anglo-American folksong tunes as sorted into the three range groups called 'authentic,' 'plagal,' and 'mixed.' (See 'General Range Analysis' above for details).[4] The Canadian collection consists of 50 authentic, 29 plagal and 13 mixed tunes. These values (as percentages) are similar to Dr. Bronson's counts. He has also studied the last pitches for the first two phrases of each tune (when sorted into these three categories and transposed to end on G). The results obtained for the Canadian collection do not seem to parallel his results; further investigation is necessary.

Melodic Movement

Preliminary investigations concerned with the direction of movement of the tune (is the last pitch higher, lower, or equal to the first pitch?) have been made. At present, it appears that for the Canadian collection the results show no significant correlation with either performer or textual category. The values for the whole collection are: ascending – 30; descending – 43; and same pitch – 29.

Time Signature Analysis (Manual)

Data on all time signatures used in the Canadian collection has been gathered manually. The amount of labor required to automate this data gathering is relatively small but not warranted for the analysis of only the Canadian collection. The 92 Canadian tunes have been placed in three groups based upon the time signatures used throughout the tune (including variations). The first group includes all tunes with only duple time signatures (2/4, 4/4, 2/8, and so on). The second group includes all tunes with purely triple time signatures (3/4, 6/8, 9/8, and so on). The third group consists of all tunes that include both duple and triple time signatures. Using these three groups the tune distributions are: duple – 28; triple – 33; and mixed – 31.

A second sort of the tunes into one group with fixed time signatures (only one time signature appears in the tune) and another group with multiple or changing time signature produced the results: fixed – 52 tunes; and variable – 40 tunes. In comparing this result with the previous paragraph it is obvious that there are relatively few tunes which have multiple time signatures and which change from duple to triple or vice versa.

Additional Developments

Additional analysis functions are in the process of investigation. These include the following topics:
1) A study of tune range versus number of pitches in the scale along with other forms of range analysis.
2) Interval pattern analysis in which the patterns are grouped together (thus all interval patterns of +3, +4 and +4, +3 semitones could be combined as +third, +third).
3) The common interval patterns are expected to appear very frequently in each tune. If the percentage (common patterns divided by total patterns) is abnormally high, the tune could be said to be 'trite', while if this percentage is low the tune would use many uncommon interval sequences and would then be 'strange.' This index of 'common' versus 'strange' is being investigated.
4) The size of the interval between the first pitch of a tune and the lowest pitch of the tune appears to be worthy of investigation (at least for the Canadian collection).
5) The range of each phrase of each tune is being analyzed to determine the ranges of tunes on a phrase by phrase basis.

It has been found that the process of evaluating and documenting one analysis function frequently results in suggestions for new forms of analysis. When these new forms require data which has been previously collected by an existing analysis program, then these new functions can easily be included in the full scale study of the Canadian collection. Otherwise, these new suggestions are saved for future investigations.

Because the development of new analysis forms remains a continual factor, it is not currently possible to state that the techniques to be applied to the Canadian collection are limited to the ones mentioned or discussed here. As new techniques are developed and included in the study of the Canadian collection, the analysis becomes more thorough.

One of the advantages of the use of the computer in an extended analysis of a collection of tunes is that as new forms of analyses are suggested, they can frequently be tested with a minimum of labor. This can then result in a rapid growth in analysis programs and analytical functions. The MUSTRAN System is a major contributor to this process by greatly simplifying the design and implementation of new analysis programs.

In summary, the MUSTRAN System is being used in the analysis of a collection of 92 Canadian folksongs. The resultant study includes an analysis of the full collection, a comparison of the Canadian tunes with a collection of Negro spirituals from the United States, and additional analysis of the Canadian tunes in terms of performers, textual categories of the songs, and the scales of the songs. These last three analyses are ones that have not previously been attempted on any significant level due to the labor required by manual analysis. The analysis includes both standard and new forms of folkmusic analysis and the analytical methods themselves are also being evaluated.

Some of the topics being investigated, and selected results of the analysis have been presented here to give an overview of computer-aided music analysis, the analysis of folkmusic, and selected characteristics of some Canadian folksongs.

References

[1] Most of the tunes included in this study appear in the following two publications: E. Folke, ed., *Traditional Singers and Songs of Ontario* (Hatboro, Pa., 1965), 62 tunes; and E. Folke, ed., *The Penguin Book of Canadian Folk Songs* (Harmondsworth, England, 1973), 23 tunes. All 92 tunes used were transcribed by Peggy Seeger.

[2] The spiritual analysis is part of the following Ph.D. dissertation: P.K. Maultsby, *Afro-American Religious Music: 1619-1861* (Wisconsin, 1974).

[3] The MUSTRAN notation is presented in articles in the following two books: B.S. Brook, ed., *Musicology and the Computer* (New York, 1970), pages 91-129; J.L. Mitchell, *Computers in the Humanities* (Edinburgh, 1974), pages 267-280.

[4] Dr. Bronson's work is presented in: B.H. Bronson, *The Ballad as Song* (Berkeley, 1969), pages 79-91.

8
Dance

Computer Interpretation of Dance Notation

J. Barenholtz, Z. Wolofsky, I. Ganapathy, T.W. Calvert,
P. O'Hara

Dance must be regarded as an illiterate art. A number of movement notation systems have been invented, but only a few have been developed and are in substantial use. Movement notation systems are inherently complex and are therefore difficult to master.

The aim of our work is to develop a computer system which can aid choreographers, dancers, students of movement notation and historical researchers in dance to make use of movement notation as a tool in their work.

This has been achieved by producing a computer system which can accept movement notation symbols (Labanotation) entered with a light pen on a computer graphics terminal; convert these symbols into numerical representations of the body positions; and display the output as a computer driven movie.

While the input and output involves sophisticated technology there are no conceptual problems. The translation of notational commands into movement of the body involves a form of artificial intelligence since the dancer fills in the details of movement not specified by the notation. The measure of success we have achieved must be judged from the accuracy and naturalness of our synthesized movies of dancing stick figures.

The Need for Dance Notation

Notation are extremely complicated because they must be capable of recording the many possible variations of movement that bodies can perform. Thus it is difficult to gain literacy. A number of notation systems are available – we have chosen to use Labanotation since it is relatively well known, in use and fully developed, and since it is a general movement description system as opposed to one which notates only specific styles such as movements in ballet.[1]

Formal training in the use of notation is quite arduous, typically taking two years, so it is not surprising that many dancers and choreographers are unwilling to invest the time to learn to read or write a notation. In spite of the difficulties there are obvious advantages in increasing the literacy of the art. These include:

a) increased knowledge and performance of choreographers' work, with higher standards of choreography and dancer education being achieved by this increased exposure;

b) decreased time spent by dancers in learning a role and increased repertoires of individual dancers;

c) ability for comparative or historical study of dances through a universally understandable vocabulary; and
d) stricter control of copyright protection for choreographers.
The goal of this study is to use computer technology to increase literacy. One way is to develop a system which would accept notation as input and produce 'movies' of the notated dance as output.

The usefulness of such a system would be three-fold. For choreographers, the ability to visualize movements, without dancers, would be realized. The computer would be a type of 'electronic notebook'. There are also education benefits to such a system. For students of notation, an aid to learning notation and checking the accuracy of their notation exercises, using an objective system, would be available. To dancers, whose knowledge of notation might be very limited, access to the library of notated dances (with the subsequent learning of these dances) would widen their repertoire and that of their audiences. The computer would provide a cursory glance at the general statement and movement patterns of the dance, and might be an aid in the reconstruction of difficult notation passages. A third use might be in the verification of notated dances. Notators have had no method of verifying their notation other than by reconstruction. This type of system could provide an alternative.

Although the major interest of this study is in dance, the notation system and its automation by computer should have value for others who study body movement. There is no comprehensive system which is used to describe clinical abnormalities in movement. Another application which we are planning is the production of educational movies to aid in teaching human biomechanics.

Computer Interpretation

There are three components to the problem: input of the notation, translation of the notation into the changing co-ordinates of body parts and the display of output as a computer driven movie. There has been work done on all three components. Eshkol *et al.* showed that kinematic descriptions of movement could be derived from Eshkol/Wachman notation although they limited their work to a single complex limb.[2] The input of Labanotation using computer graphics has been implemented in a limited way by Shapiro.[3] Recently a proposal to implement the computer interpretation of Benesh notation has been made by Arcner in the United Kingdom.[4] Our work is a continuation of the research conducted by Montgomery and Wolofsky between 1971 and 1974.[5] Our approach to each of the three components of the problem will be discussed in turn.

Input

Initially an alphanumeric code was used to represent the Labanotation symbols. This has been replaced by an approach which utilizes the light-pen on the GT40 graphics terminal to select, position and control the size of the Labanotation symbols. As shown in Figures 1 and 2, two Labanotation staffs of 2 beats each are permanently drawn on the left.

On the right are the symbols and devices to adjust their size, position and shading. The user first 'nits' the WR (write) spot on top of the screen. Then a symbol is selected by touching it and its position is determined by touching any spot on the staff (this process will also work if the staff position is selected first and then the symbol). The vertical position of the symbol is chosen in this way and its horizontal position and size are adjusted by applying the light-pen to the appropriate Light Potentiometer. The shading of the symbol (to indicate level of the movement) is selected by touching the appropriate shading box. When the symbol has the correct position, size and shade the WR spot is hit again and a new symbol selected. Another spot DE allows deletion and the spot ED is used for editing. In fact the notator frequently produces the notation by first setting only the symbol lengths for each side of the body for a number of beats. Then the notator comes back to fill in the details. This is easily achieved with our edit facility. As the score is built up and the staffs are filled, the light spot ST (store) is hit to move the score down and produce blank staffs, however the notator can later recall and revise the whole score.

The complete score is stored in memory and on the disk of the GT40. We are currently designing a system to transmit the score to the IBM 370 and have it drawn out on paper by the Calcomp plotter. In this way a written record would be available for archival purposes, for checking and for publication.

Translation To Body Co-ordinates

Labanotatian commands are either destinational or motivational. The destinational commands, which are also called gestural, specify the position in space of a body segment at the end of a specified time period. Thus the position in space of the end of each body segment can be

Figure 1 Entering a Labanotation score with a light-pen on a GT40 graphics terminal.

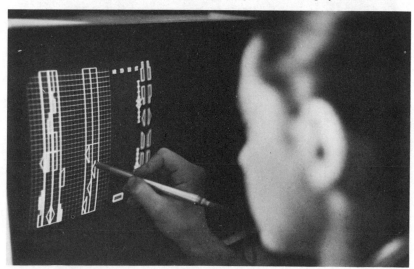

calculated by applying linear transformations to rotate the body segment about its 'fixed' end. The velocity profile with which the body segment moves is not specified and must be chosen to reproduce the natural acceleration and deceleration patterns of human movement. Wolofsky implemented a FORTRAN program which translates Labanotation gestural commands and gives as output the co-ordinates of the ends of each of 21 body segments in space as a function of time.[5]

The interpretation of motional commands is much more difficult. The dancer can easily interpret the rather simple commands to walk, run, or jump in a specified direction at a specified rate. But each dancer interprets the command in the light of past learning and imparts his or her own style to the movement. Thus for computer interpretation it is necessary to build in a form of artificial motor intelligence. The motor intelligence of the brain is often ignored by the psychologist but the engineer must be impressed by the size and complexity of the cerebellum, which apparently is devoted to the co-ordination and control of fast movement but has about as many nerve cells as all other parts of the brain combined.[6] The program to interpret motional commands is under development.

Computer Generated Movies as Output

The interpretation program generates the co-ordinates of body segments in three-dimensional space. After a position for the viewer is specified a two-dimensional projection is produced. These projections can then be displayed on a graphics terminal at any desired frame rate. A display rate of 12 frames per second has been found to be satisfactory for a GT40 graphics terminal. Two typical stick figures are shown in Figure 3.

Figure 2 A view of a partially completed score.

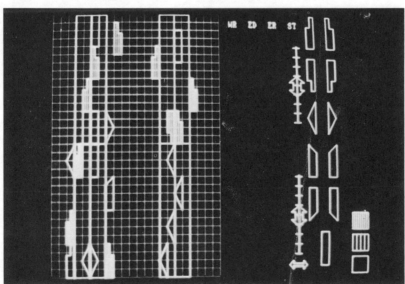

System Operation

The Labanotation score is entered into a GT40 graphics terminal with the aid of a light pen as described above. It is stored on a floppy disk and later transmitted by telephone to the Simon Fraser University IBM 370/155, where the interpretation program accepts an alphanumeric representation of the symbols as input. The interpretation program produces a 370 disk data set sufficient to produce Calcomp Plotter drawings which sample the movement on the desired frame rate. The Calcomp plots are generally not produced but the data set is read by an

Figure 3 Two stick figures from a Tektronix hard-copy unit.

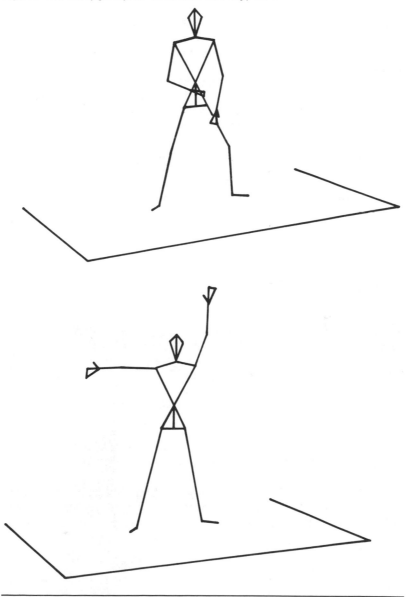

APL-SV program and transmitted to the GT40 by telephone. The GT40 APL handler makes the GT40 compatible with a Tektronix 4013 graphics terminal. At the GT40 the display frames are stored on floppy disk. The display movie can be produced at any desired frame rate up to 60 per second. One floppy diskette can store a dance sequence of approximately 2.5 minutes at 12 frames per second. The system has been assembled in this way as a research tool. It should be quite feasible to implement it as a stand alone system based on a GT40 with its integral PDP-11.

System Evaluation

Wolofsky compared a stick figure dance sequence synthesized from Labanotation by computer with the same sequence interpreted by a dancer from a Labanotation score. To make a realistic comparison the dancer was filmed performing the sequence, her film frames were reduced to two-dimensional co-ordinates with a Vanguard Analyser, and from these co-ordinates a dancing stick figure movie was produced. Students in a dance class were asked to compare the two movie sequences; the overall conclusion was that the two stick figure representations of the dance were equally natural.

The system could be improved by embellishing the stick figures to make them appear more natural, although this would involve algorithms for the hidden line problem. The existing displays are certainly of high enough quality to be used in the education of notators. Whether they can aid in the creative process remains to be shown.

References

[1] A. Hutchinson, *Labanotation,* New York: Theatre Arts, 1970. 2nd Edition.

[2] N. Eshkol, P. Melvin, J. Nichl, H.V. Foerster, and A. Wachman, *Notation of Movement* (Urbana, Ill: University of Illinois, 1970).

[3] M. Shapiro, Personal Communication.

[4] L.B. Archer, *A Study of Computer Aided Choreography,* (London: Royal College of Art, 1975).

[5] Z. Wolofsky, "Computer Interpretation of Selected Labanotation Commands," *MSc* Thesis, Simon Fraser University, 1974.

[6] T.W. Calvert, and F. Meno, "Neural Systems Modelling Applied to the Cerebellum," *IEEE Trans. on Systems, Man and Cybernetics,* Vol. SMC-2 (1972), pp. 363-374.

Computer Choreography and Video

J. Lansdown

The growing use of computers in the arts has resulted not only in an increase in the numbers of those engaged in devising works of computer art but also, and more importantly, a considerable widening in the scope of activity. In the history and prehistory of the subject (up to about 1968), there was a tendency to see the role of the computer in art as restricted to graphics and music but, in more recent times, the work of such as Edward Ihnatowicz, John Lifton, Colin Emmet, Robin Shirley, and others has expanded the role to embrace virtually the whole field. [1]

The performing arts have not been neglected in the expansion and, since 1969, the author has been using computers to choreograph a large number of dances which have been successfully performed in Britain and Europe by modern dance groups, particularly the London-based, Another Dance Group. [2] The dances, some of which have been described in writing and on film, illustrate an approach to creativity different from the conventional and, significantly, make use of a technique now so familiar to some ballet critics in Britain that they rarely find it necessary to comment on the fact that a computer has been used. [3]

This paper deals with both my methods of computer choreography and a development of them applied to television arising from some experiments carried out over the last two years under the sponsorship of an Arts Council of Great Britain Bursary. In order to set this development in context, it is necessary to outline the differences from conventional choreography.

Conventional and Computer Choreography Compared

A choreographer wishing to devise a dance by conventional means would, starting from some basic concept, develop his ideas intuitively, either by dancing himself or by building up the movements in collaboration with dancers. He may record the movements either by means of one of the standard dance notations[4] or by one of his own invention.[5] It is likely that he will have chosen the music in advance , that the movements would be developed to relate to it, and that the particular ideas, problems and skills of the dancers would influence the final form that the dance would take. On the other hand, it is possible – though unlikely – that he could completely *pre-write* the work, presenting the dancers with a finished score as a composer of music might, leaving only the limited interpretation of the work to the performers. No conventional case where this happens is known, but it is feasible and, for reference purposes, we can term the first of these methods, *open* and the second, *closed.*

Although the author has devised a pre-written score, the method is termed *open* for it requires much more creative cooperation of dancers for its success than is customary in any conventional method. Indeed, the problem is approached from an entirely different viewpoint to the conventional, starting not with ideas about the final form that the dance will take, but with sets of abstract *procedures* which, when embodied in computer programs, produce performance instructions for dancers. Often these procedures have nothing to do with dance as such and may simply be, for example, ways of generating patterns of numbers. It is only when the patterns are incorporated into computer programs designed to convert them into written, notated, or drawn instructions for performers that they can be seen as valid in the context of dance. In some of the works, too, the same procedures are used to compose the attendant music as to devise the dance.

Once the procedures are determined and correctly embodied in the programs, no further ideas are imposed on the dancers, who are to interpret and compose the dance within the scripted conventions.

Numbers, Computers and Art

Much of this work derives from the assumption that it is possible both to describe and to generate art works by devising suitably ordered sets of numbers which are to be interpreted in some way by a computer program. In the case of music, for example, these sets might be either a musical score presented as a sequence of numbers, or a digital description of the sound wave forms themselves: both are in current use in computer music. It is not difficult to *describe* an existing work by means of a number pattern, but to *generate* a new work by similar means is a matter of considerable complexity.[6]

Central to the concept is the idea of the program: the set of instructions which the computer has to follow in a step-by-step fashion to produce its work. The program has two basic features: a *vocabulary* and a *grammar,* both words having connotations slightly different from their normal meanings.

The *vocabulary* is the particular set of data elements which the program uses and manipulates. These elements might, for example, be words or phrases in the case of poetry programs, notes or chords in the case of music programs, or representations of movements, combinations of movements or positions in the case of ballet programs.

The way in which the elements of the vocabulary are used depends not only on the form of the work but also on the way in which the results are to be presented after processing takes place. For example, a program to produce a notated musical work for performance by players uses very different elements of vocabulary from one whose output is direct from the computer to an electronic device for synthesising the sounds.

The *grammar,* on the other hand, is the set of rules which regulate the allowable or desirable combinations of vocabulary. In a dance program these rules will, as a minimum, prevent physically dangerous or impossible moves arising.

An essential feature of any grammar will be a 'stopping rule' which determines the point at which the work is considered to be complete.

This can vary from a simple rule telling the computer to stop after a given elapsed time or a given number of instructions, to a much more sophisticated rule taking into account 'completeness' as defined by some special combination of circumstances. Even in *avant-garde* music or dance, it frequently happens that the passages which end a work have to have an air of finality about them. Therefore, it is often convenient to program the computer to determine the end of the piece first and then to work backwards to the beginning.

Built into the grammar will be a 'selector', that is, a method for choosing those elements of the vocabulary and grammar on which the computer is to operate at any given time. Such a method might be *deterministic*, so that once started, the program follows an inevitable, and theoretically predictable course; or *probabilistic,* so that the course followed depends on the outcome of some chance happening. It must be realised that artistic intuition, as we understand it, cannot be programmed and that the selector is in part the substitute for this.

In common with the general trend in computer art at that time the author's earliest attempts at computer dance in 1969 explored the use of chance procedures to generate closed sets of numbers which were interpreted by the computer as movement paths, stage positions, directions, tempo, and so on. While streams of random numbers were used to activate these procedures, the grammar in which they were manipulated produced dances which were far from random in appearance. However, the unusual relationship between one group of movements and the next brought about patterns which were sometimes too difficult for dancers to remember in performance. Although part of the *raison d'etre* for such work was to create these challenging patterns, the performance problems arising were such that the chance approach is now minimized. Recent work has been more concerned with the development of deterministic procedures, the generation of simpler patterns and the open, interactive cooperation with the dancers. This, too, reflects the trend in other areas of computer art.

The Process

In summary, the process of choreographing dances by computer can be broken down into steps in the following way:
– Devising the initial concept and the relevent procedures to be incorporated;
– Establishing a suitable vocabulary;
– Inventing a grammar which correctly embodies the concept, procedures and physical restraints;
– Devising a means of presenting the computer output to the dancers in a manner which they can understand;
– Rehearsing and interacting with the dancers.
Although, for the purposes of description, the steps in the process are set out in order, it must not be assumed either that they are independent or that they need necessarily follow one another in the sequence given. As in any creative process, each part is closely bound to the rest, and both influences and is influenced by it.

Concept and Procedure

An art work begins with an idea: some initial concept that an artist
thinks worth exploring. Conventionally, ballet, painting, literature and
(to a very much lesser extent) music, derive their initial concepts from
some narrative or descriptive theme that channels development along a
coherent line which is fairly easily related to human experience. On the
other hand, procedural and computer artists do not generally devise
narrative works: their interest lies more in exploring non-literal,
abstract ideas. As in conventional art, the success of a particular piece
of computer art depends both on the quality of the initial concept and
on the way in which this is expressed in the work.

We can distinguish between concept and procedure by saying that the
concept is what the work is about and the *procedure* is one of the means
by which the concept is made manifest.

Vocabulary

Dance deals with such things as movement, gesture, rhythm, spatial
position and so on and hence it is likely that any vocabulary used in a
dance program will embody elements which express this concern. Just
as words in the vocabulary of a natural language are symbols which
stand for such things as external objects or actions and may be grouped
into classes such as nouns, verbs, adjectives, and so on, so in a dance
program, elements of the vocabulary might represent choreographically
relevant features which may be classified in a manner which helps determine the way they are used.

A typical vocabulary, for instance, could comprise representations
(in the form of words, numbers or symbols) of groups of movements for
particular limbs, gestures, rhythmic patterns or joint angles. However,
it would be unnecessarily restricting to assume that a vocabulary need
be confined to representations which have such an obvious and direct
relationship with dance. A perfectly valid vocabulary could, for example, be built up from geometric figures: squares, circles, triangles,
stars and so on, which, after manipulation by a grammar, are to be
presented to the dancers for *interpretation* in movement.

Such a vocabulary was used in the dance *Touching 2* (Figure 1),
where the elements were simply items in a geometric notation specially
created for this single purpose and were devised to represent sequences
of actions which the dancers composed in detail themselves.

Grammar

Just as in order to make meaningful sentences, we have to choose words
which not only fit the grammatical structures of a language but are also
consistent with the logic of the real world, so too, in computer-
generated dance, we have to ensure that our grammar allows only those
combinations of vocabulary which make choreographic and physical
sense. Natural language and computer choreography are analogous in
respect of this need for rationality but, as pointed out earlier, one of the
reasons for using the procedural approach is the possibility of achieving
combinations of movements, patterns of gesture, and so on, which

might not have occurred by the use of more conventional means. It would seem logical therefore that any grammatical restrictions we place on the arrangements of vocabulary should be the minimum consistent with the needs of the original concept, safety and physical feasibility. It is clear that the difficulty in devising a grammar satisfying these requirements depends very much on the type of vocabulary employed. The grammar which helped generate Figure 1, for instance, was extremely simplistic because virtually all the choreographic decisions other than those given in the guidelines by the script were to be made by the dancers themselves. Figure 1 thus probably represents the most minimal contributions that any computer-generated score could make to a dance. Incidentally, it was not very successful.

On the other hand, when the computer is to give more detailed instructions to the dancers, the grammar is bound to be more complex. So for successful outcome, much creative effort needs to be spent at this stage of the work.

Figure 1. Vocabulary of Touching 2

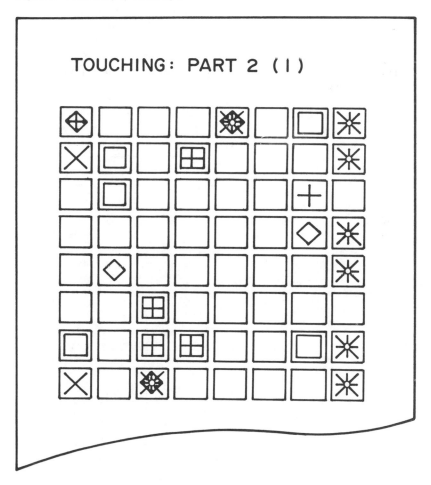

Presentation

Depending on the grammar and vocabulary used, there is a large range
of possibilities for presenting instructions to the dancers. Although, in
theory, one of the existing ballet notations should be adequate for all
occasions, in particular cases they may not be appropriate. In addition,
there are three practical difficulties which militate against the use of the
established notations: firstly, they are by no means universally understood by dancers; secondly, because of their inevitable complexity, the
task of computerising them is a major one which has not yet been fully
achieved, and thirdly, but perhaps more importantly, each notation is to
some extent embedded in, and coloured by, the concept of dance
favoured by its inventor.[7] Descriptions in words can be used in a
surprising number of cases, particularly in situations where only outline
instructions are needed. Indeed, in some cases, it is difficult to see what
other form of instructions could be appropriate. For example, Figure 2
shows part of the script for a dance entitled *Phases*, in which visual
emphasis is placed on the repetitive movement of certain joints by three
groups of dancers moving in unison or sequentially.

The script is in two sections: a Repertoire of Movements and a Table
of Repeats. The Repertoire lists twenty sets of instructions in a
shorthand form, covering the body joints to be used, the manner of
usage (whether symmetrically or not, whether jerkily or smoothly), the
general body configuration (standing, moving, kneeling, lying) and a
figure indicating, in beats, the length of time the movement is to last.
Although these instructions are not always precise, they are sufficiently
detailed to circumscribe the range of available options, and it is intended that they provide a framework within which the dancers are to compose simple patterns of movements.

Figure 2. Script for dance Phrases

REPERTOIRE OF MOVEMENTS

I. ELBOW ASYMMETRICAL	HIP STANDING	BACK JERKY		4 BEATS
2. ELBOW ASYMMETRICAL	WRIST STANDING	ANKLE SMOOTH	BACK	6 BEATS
3. KNEE SYMMETRICAL	ANKLE STANDING	JERKY		9 BEATS
4. HIP ASYMMETRICAL	KNEE LYING	BACK		

TABLE OF REPEATS

DANCER ONE		DANCER TWO		DANCER THREE	
MOVEMENT	REPEATS	MOVEMENT	REPEATS	MOVEMENT	REPEATS
I	I4 (56)	I	0 (0)	I	0 (0)
2	I0	2	I0 (60)	2	0 (0)
3	I2 (224)	3	I3 (I77)	3	I I
4	I0 (3I4)	4	I I		
5	6				

The Table of Repeats indicates, for each of the three groups, how many times each of the movement patterns is to be repeated. As the number of repeats is likely to be different for each group, the movements pass in and out of phase: at some times, all the groups move in unison, at other times all have the same movement pattern but are at different points in its cycle and, at yet other times, the groups are performing the patterns sequentially.

While words and numbers are the elements most conveniently output by computers without the use of special equipment, a more exciting potential for presentation lies in the computer-production of drawings. In order to do this, a choreographic technique had to be devised which seemed appropriate to the idea, so the animated cartoon was used as a starting point.

When an animated film maker designs his cartoons he first of all draws in sequence the chief positions of his characters. When he is satisfied with these drawings, called key frames, he passes them to other artists, appropriately known as *in-betweeners,* who create the drawings in-between the key frames, hence achieving an illusion of smooth movement. It seemed to me that I could parallel this process by setting the computer to produce the key frames and the dancers to carry out the in-betweening.

In order to test the validity of this idea before embarking on the quite difficult task of programming the computer to devise the key frames, it was necessary to simulate the process. Dancers were asked to provide forty unrelated poses for one, two or three performers, using the criteria that the poses should be varied and visually interesting, technically challenging, or simply unusual in the context of dance. The poses were then photographed for record purposes and classified into seven sets which graded them by the 'energy' required to hold, get into and out of the pose.

Using various procedures, experiments were conducted with computer programs to select and arrange the poses in sequences as well as to determine the spatial positions and facing directions of the dancers on stage.

From the resulting numerical computer output, were prepared, initially by hand, but later by computer, illustrated scripts in the form of *story boards* (Figure 3) which gave dancers the basic information necessary for them to compose their own linking movements between one key frame and the next. The information given included timing counts, which were derived from an analysis of the music (if this was already composed) or by the computer if it was not. The amount of composition required by the dancers is controlled by the time allowed between one key frame and the next.

It immediately became clear that this was a promising line of approach which would not only justify further computing effort but which, more surprisingly, could also be used as a technique in its own right. Since the initial experiments, a large number of dances have been computer-choreographed using this method.

Two problems needed solution before it was possible to achieve the long-term plan to computer-generate the initial poses. These were first, to devise a mathematical model of the human body that the computer could manipulate which would need to take into account such things as the length of limbs, permissible joint movements, balance, centre of

Figure 3

Profiles: Sue's Dance
Dancer: 1

gravity and so on, and second, to devise a suitable technique for display-
ing the generated poses.

Considerable research had to be carried out in order to derive an
appropriate mathematical model and, although much of the basic work
on computerising human body data had already been done by
American Airforce Scientists in connection with the US Space
Program, this work was of a nature not immediately applicable to the
problem at hand. Thus, even after two years of study, only partial
success was achieved but it did become possible to derive a
suitable – though limited – model and hence create, within certain
restrictions, the ability to generate poses for a small number of related
dancers.

To deal with the second part of the problem it was necessary to invent
a method of illustrating the poses in a way comparable to that used in
the simulation. Again, the US Aerospace Industry had done some work
in this direction by devising a very realistic and anatomically correct
computer-drawn mannequin which would have been ideal for the purpose but, unfortunately, the programs were not readily available and required computing resources beyond our means.[8]

Accordingly, the present form of output for computer-generated
poses is in the form of stick figures having some of the attributes of
mannequins and some of notation (Figure 4). Clearly, considerable
work needs to be done before this form of presentation is as clear as the
photographically derived drawings, and efforts in this direction (Figure
5) are as yet fairly limited.

Figure 4

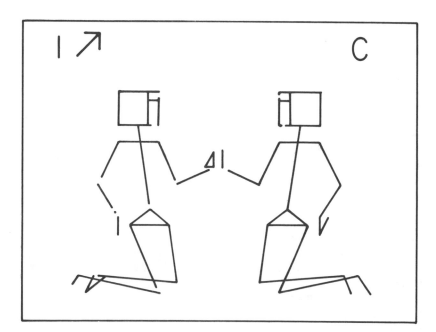

Figure 5

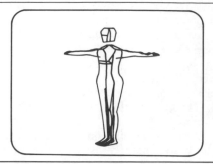

Rehearsal and Interaction

When this work first began, the plan was to provide computer scripts which would be handed to dancers for them to interpret without further instructions. In many ways this was a consequence of a commitment to the procedural approach and the belief that, once the procedures and their manifestation in scripts were devised, there should be no further influence on the way in which the dances were produced. This concept turned out to be too difficult to embody in practice. Dancers needed further guidance and reassurance on the way they were to interpret the instructions.

While still attempting to minimise the author's creative contribution, work is done closely with dancers, noting their reactions to scripted ideas and cooperating with them to improve the results of further developments.

Computer Generated TV Direction

Early in the development of these ideas it became clear that, as the computer knew where a dancer following its instructions should be on stage at any moment, in which direction she was facing, and basically what she was doing, it would be comparatively simple to get the machine to output a timed shooting script for television cameras covering the scene. Better still, it could generate both performance and camera instructions to realise a set of compositions, devised either by itself or a choreographer, solely in terms of what is seen on the screen. In 1975 a Bursary by the Arts Council of Great Britain purchased TV studio time in order to experiment with this idea, and work began in black-and-white at the studios of the Inner London Education Authority and later, in colour at the Royal College of Art.

The purpose of the black-and-white work was three-fold: firstly, to test the basic assumptions of the method in the cheapest possible way; secondly, to train a TV crew in the technique; and finally, to create a set of videotapes which could be further processed by colour synthesiser, again under computer-devised instructions.

Essentially the steps in the process of generating instructions for this work were:
– Devising the initial concept and procedures;
– Establishing a vocabulary for the screen compositions and the dance;
– Creating a grammar which related the screen compositons to the physical constraints on the dancers, the camera positions, movements

and lenses, and TV treatments;
– Devising a means of presenting the computer output to the vision
mixer, cameramen, and dancers;
– Rehearsing the TV crew and dancers.

Image and Reality

When considering the processes involved in computer-generated TV
direction, it is advantageous to consider the action as it appears on the
screen at any moment as *image* and all other activities as *reality*. In the
case where the computer itself determines the image, it begins by
creating a set of 'snapshots' at time intervals chosen by procedure or by
musical requirements. If these snapshots were to be displayed (as they
would need to be if a choreographer wished interactively to create or
modify them) they would appear as rectangles of various proportions
and sizes in different parts of the screen. Using very simplistic techi-
ques, the program then sorts out from its repertoire of poses a subset of
potential candidates for matching the image. It will appreciated that, if
the composition requires a large rectangle almost filling the TV screen,
then virtually all the poses are available if photographed in close-up but,
if what is needed is a thin horizontal rectangle at the bottom of the picture, then perhaps only one or two poses would fit the bill.
    The matching of reality to image is, of course, not only determined
by the overall shape of the pose at the snapshot moment, but also by the
position of the dancer on stage, the way in which the cameraman com-
poses the picture in his viewfinder, and which of the cameras and lenses
is being used.
    Even with so many degrees of freedom, it is not always possible to
match reality with image. For example, in the interval allowed between
one snapshot and the next, it may not be possible for a dancer to move
from a prone position at one part of the stage to a kneeling positon
some distance away. In such a case, the program backtracks to create a
new image. Between each snapshot, the program must decide at which
point to switch from one camera to another to ensure (if this is indeed a
requirement) that the action is always completely covered.

The Scripts

When the foregoing process is complete, information for three types of
script is available: (1) similar to Figure 3 for the dancers; (2) for the
vision mixer, giving the shot number, the time of change, and the type
of transition (cut, mix or superimposition); and (3) for the cameraman,
giving the standard information they get in normal work (shot number,
type of shot, camera position and so on). The vision mixer's script is
dictated onto one track of the music tape and relayed both to him and
to the cameramen (for complicated dances, also to the dancers, who
find that it helps them to remember timing and which camera they are
on). In this way, the instructions are always in correct synchronisation
with the music, no matter how many times the work is rehearsed.
    The video work described here is in its very early stages and, as it
progresses, new techniques and procedures suggest themselves. With
the increasing introduction of computerised vision mixing, for instance,

it would be possible to dispense with the vision mixer's script altogether and to program the mixing console direct from the composition program. The vision mixer would then be relieved of the nerve-racking process of real-time manipulation of the equipment and could concentrate his skills on the quality of the treatments and transitions. It must be emphasised that, while the various scripts give full instructions to all concerned, great scope is left for interpretation and compositional skill. None have felt that the use of the computer has diminished the contribution that they make to the image.

Finally, I must thank all who have helped me in these experiments and, my son Robert, without whose assistance in programming, sound recording and vision mixing, this work would have been very much less enjoyable.

References

[1]Edward Ihnatowicz, "Le Senster," *IBM Informatique*, No. 13, p. 55; John Lifton, "Cybernetics and the Restructuring of Aesthetic Perception," *Proceedings, International IEEE Conference on Systems, Networks and Computers* (Mexico, 1971); Colin Emmett, *Bulletin of the Computer Arts Society* (October, 1972), p. 26; and Robin Shirley, "Poet and Program," *Bulletin of the Computer Arts Society* (October, 1972), p. 25.

[2]John Lansdown, "Computer Art for Theatrical Performances," *Proceedings, ACM International Computer Symposium* (Bonn, 1970).

[3]Clement Crisp, "No Need to Fear Computer Ballet," *Parade*, No. 153 (London Press Service); Robert Parslow, "Computer Aided Art," *Computer Aided Design* Vol 2:3 (Spring, 1970), pp. 22-28; *Tomorrow's World*, BBC TV Film; and *Computer Choreography*, ILEA Schools Film.

[4]M. Causley, *Benesh Movement Notation* (London: Max, 1967); A. Hutchinson, *Labanotation* (New York: Theatre Arts, 1954); and N. Eshkol and A. Wachmann, *Movement Notation* (Tel Aviv: Israel Music Institute, 1969; London: Weidenfield and Nicholson, 1968).

[5]Roselee Goldberg, "Performance: the Art of Notation," *Studio International* (July/August, 1976), pp. 54-58.

[6]J. Lansdown and P. Friedman, "Procedures for Artists," *CAS Interact Conference* (Edinburgh, 1974).

[7]Zella Wolofsky, "Computer Interpretation of Selected Labanotation Commands" (Unpublished MSc Thesis, 1974); and N. Eshkol, P. Melvin, J. Michl, H. Von Foerster and A. Wachmann, "Notation of Movements," *Biological Computer Laboratory Report*, BCL 10.0 (University of Illinois, 1970).

[8]W. Fetter, "A Human Figure Computer Graphics Development for Multiple Applications," *Proceedings, Eurocomp Conference* (London, 1974).

Using the Computer for a Semantic Representation of Labanotation

S.W. Smoliar, L. Weber

Labanotation, also known as Kinetography Laban, is a two-dimensional graphic notational system for recording movement. Rudolf Laban originated the system, describing it in the treatise *Schrifttanz*, first, published in 1928.[1] Since then the system has been revised and extended by Laban and his colleagues, and it is now maintained by a 'standards organization', the International Council of Kinetography Laban. One of the major applications of Labanotation has been the recording of both classical ballet and modern dance, and an extensive library of Labanotation scores is currently maintained at the Dance Notation Bureau in New York.

Though usage of Labanotation has been expanding at a rapid rate, most dancers and choreographers tend to isolate themselves from the system. For the composer of music, notation is a unilateral medium of communication to the performer. It is the means by which the performer understands how to realize the creator's conception of a composition. Choreographers do not, as a rule, communicate with their performers through a notational medium. They are more inclined to build their compositions on their performers during rehearsals. The act of creation involves interaction between the choreographer and the dancers. The goal of notation is to have a means by which the finished product may be recorded for purposes of reconstruction at a later date, thus eliminating the need to repeat the entire interactive process.

In such a situation the notator must serve as a 'third party' to the creative process in a role similar to that of a court stenographer. All information passed from the choreographer to the performers must be collected, eventually to be organized in the form of a final score. Furthermore, in most cases the performers are no more likely to be literate in Labanotation than is the choreographer. For this reason, reconstruction also involves a 'third party' – someone who understands the notation well enough to be able to demonstrate all notated material to the dancers.

We believe that the computer may provide the best means to narrow this gap between Labanotation and the people it ultimately serves. We are currently developing a compiler whose source language is Labanotation and whose object code will be a sequence of commands to a graphic processor. This processor will produce an animated display of the movement represented by the source code, thus enabling any individual to *see* the actual movements recorded in a Labanotation score. Like most compilers, this translator can be described as a sequence of three computational stages: lexical analysis, syntactic analysis, and semantic analysis. The first stage is concerned with the graphical structure of the elements of Labanotation, the second involves the extraction of movement description primitives from this structure, and the third involves the interpretation of these primitives in such a way as to produce an effective display. We shall discuss the structure of these stages in greater detail.

Lexical Analysis

The first problem in writing a Labanotation translator is finding a suitable input representation for the notation itself. A rather halfhearted attempt has been made to represent a subset of Labanotation in terms of a conventional character set, but we find this a rather unpromising approach.[2] In the first place, the restrictions which define the subset tend to preclude certain notational practices found in most Labanotation scores. A more significant problem, however, is that while a character string is a readily accessible input data structure for almost any computer, its usage forces the presence of many structural complications which do not exist in the notation itself. Thus, any program concerned with Labanotation input would first have to unravel the character string to build a data structure which resembles the actual structure of Labanotation more closely. (It might noted that a similar problem exists in using character strings to represent input recorded in music notation, for example, DARMS.[3] The solution to this problem is to allow for input directly in Labanotation through a graphics editor.[4] The data structure for the source input then becomes the internal data structure used by the editor. At the same time, such an editor will serve as a valuable tool for the preparation of Labanotation scores. With the assistance of such an editor, a notator is in a position to maintain clean copies of notation recorded at each rehearsal, as opposed to notes frantically scrawled in pencil. Alterations by the choreographer no longer imply extensive rewriting of the pencil drafts; they are simply conventional updating operations. Finally, the need for an independent, final stage, in which the score is autographed for publication, is no longer necessary. The editor is always in a position to produce copy of final-draft quality.

Unfortunately, the editor designed by Brown is not a very adequate solution to the lexical problem in Labanotation. It is based on a one-to-one correspondence between a subset of the ASCII character set and a set of basic Labanotation symbols, with the provision that a Labanotation character may be qualified by additional data concerning its size, shading, orientation, and position. Owing to the limitation of the ASCII subset, certain Labanotation symbols must be composed by superimposing two or more of these qualified characters. The editor, unfortunately, does not recognize that the *purpose* of the superposition is to define a single symbol. It simply modifies the character it recognizes and places them where the user wants.

We have observed that while full Labanotation uses a rather large number of symbols, these symbols may be formed from a more limited set of graphic primitives and a set of rules of composition – operators which assemble primitives to form symbols. In this respect, Labanotation is rather like an extensible language; in fact, it is theoretically possible to apply these rules to form new symbols. (The acceptability of new symbols is one of the major concerns of the International Council of Kinetography Laban.)

Let us give an example of how different Labanotation symbols are constructed from graphic primitives. In referring to the body of the performer, a filled in circle, ● , stands for the center of gravity. An empty square, □ , is the basic sign for an area. By placing the center of gravity symbol inside the area sign, we obtain the symbol which stands for the pelvic area: ◧ . It is also possible to draw a rectangular area sign: ▯ . This indicates a larger area, delimited by two areas given in the upper and lower halves of the rectangle. For example, the head is represented by the sign: C. Consequently, ▣ represents the area from the head to the pelvis, regarded as a single unit. An area box may, in turn, be modified by a short line which designates a surface of the area. For example, ⊶◧ designates the middle left side of the pelvic area.

A related use of the center of gravity symbol is in establishing orientations. Superimposing the center of gravity symbol on a cross of axes (+) forms the notation of the Standard Cross of Axes: ✛ .. Any movement may be described by a vector whose dimensions are determined by one of several crosses of axes located in the body. The Standard Cross of Axes establishes a particular set of conventions regarding the orientation of these crosses of axes. Other levels of complexity can be obtained with additional primitives. By adding a space hold ◇, a further limitation is placed on those crosses of axes associated with *twisted* parts of the body. The interpretation is that the *untwisted* orientation of the cross of axes is to be maintained. This particular specification, known as the Stance Key, is written: ◈.

In a conventional compiler lexical analysis serves to scan the initial string of characters which forms the source module and to isolate and classify all those substrings which function as symbolic primitives in the programming language.[5] For example, in FORTRAN the character string 19761.25E+1 is a single symbolic unit which represents a real constant (equal to 197612.5).[6] In Labanotation, instead of a string of characters, we have a well-defined structure of graphic primitives. The role of lexical analysis now becomes one of isolating and classifying all those substructures which stand for single symbolic primitives in the notation.

Syntactic Analysis

What *are* the symbolic primitives of Labanotation that may be combined to form a score? What are the rules by which they are combined? These are questions of *syntax*. Before considering them in greater detail, let us take a look at a typical example of a Labanotation score.[7]

Let us begin by viewing this score with respect to its graphic layout. The
notation is written on staves read bottom-to-top, the staves proceeding
left-to-right. Below the staves are floor plans which indicate the pattern
of movement on the stage. The staves are divided into measures, each of

Figure 1. Measure 1-4 Introduction offstage

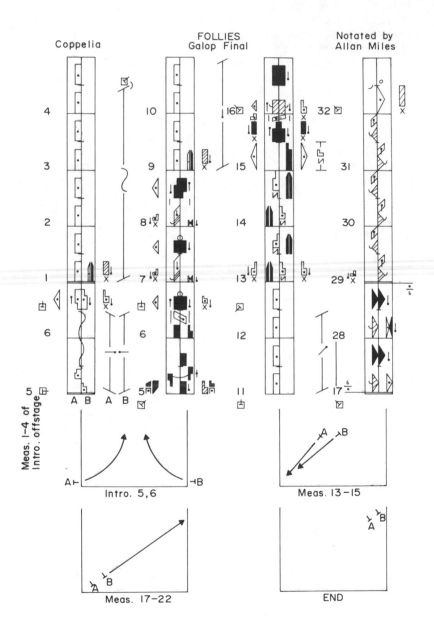

which is divided into beats by small tick marks. The measures are numbered for correlation with the floor plans and with the accompanying music. Each staff is divided into columns, within which the movement symbols are written. A single symbol indicates a movement *direction* (by its shape), *level* (by its shading), and *duration* (by its size). The *part of the body* performing the movement is determined by the column in which the symbol appears. The following chart summarizes the meanings of the basic symbols.

Figure 2. Labanotation basics

Labanotation Basics

directions are indicated by the shape of the symbol :

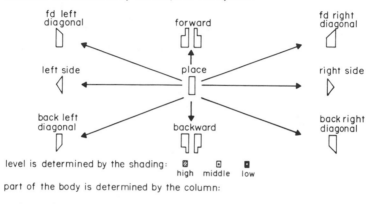

level is determined by the shading: high   middle   low

part of the body is determined by the column:

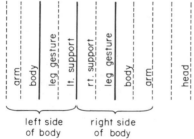

timing is determined by the relative length of the symbol :

The way these basic symbols are interpreted depends on the presence of several modifying symbols. In measure 6, for example, the 'X' sign below the forward middle sign in the right arm column indicates that the arm should be slightly bent. The pin next to the symbol specifies that the hand (that is, the free end of the arm) is to be placed in front of the center line of the body. The placement of the hand without this modifier would be in front of the right shoulder joint. In measure 7 the symbol in the left support column indicates a clockwise pivot turn on the left foot, beginning on the toe and ending on the whole foot, a full turn from the previous orientation. While that is happening, the right leg is gesturing so that the knee is to the side of the hip and the leg is bent with the ankle in front of the center line of the body. The turn takes one beat. The leg gesture is reached in the first quarter of the beat. Beginning at the same time, the left arm takes half a beat to move to the forward bent position. The symbol to the left of the staff at the end of the measure 6 indicates the dancer's facing with respect to the room prior to the turn. This particular symbol indicates a downstage facing.

In summary, we have been modifying symbols used for the following purposes: indication of bending (they can also be used for contracting, shortening, or, conversely, extending), indication of placement with relation to the body of the performer, indication of turns (both direction and amount), indication of orientation. Other modifiers refer to the surface of a body area (as we saw in the preceding section), establish alternative systems of reference within which directions are established, and provide details concerning the path traversed by the movement. Finally, there are modifiers to indicate contact of body parts with other body parts, with other performers, with the floor, with the performer's costume, or with props. These symbols may be further modified to indicate if a contact is receiving or providing support.

We may now turn to the question of what constitutes a syntactic analysis of a Labanotation score. Let us regard the human body as an elaborate parallel processor in which each part of the body is a component sequential processor. A single Labanotation symbol may be regarded as a command to one of these processors. This command will be interpreted with respect to certain *environmental properties* which characterize that processor. Modifying symbols may be regarded as a part of a *symbol group*. This symbol group contains commands which may change the environmental properties of the processor which executes it. It may also change the environmental properties of other processors, as well. From this point of view, a 'parsing' of a Labanotation score amounts to composing an ensemble of parallel programs, one for each body part whose movement is specified, in such a way that each program instruction corresponds to a Labanotation symbol group. All that remains is to characterize the architecture of the processor which will interpret these instructions: the problem of *semantic analysis*.

Semantic Analysis

In establishing a representation of the human body as a parallel processor, we have been particularly influenced by certain aspects of the SIMULA language.[8] Most useful is the SIMULA concept of a *class*. This is a program block which has its own set of locally declared data structures and procedures. The most important attribute of the procedures is that they may be regarded as executing as co-routines with procedures local to other classes. Classes may exchange data via pointer variables. Under this model each part of the body capable of movement is represented by a class. Each class is, thus, a processor unto itself. A command to be passed to a particular processor will be defined primarily with respect to the local variables of the class – the environment of the processor. Thus, the direction of movement of the arm (in the arm class) will be judged with respect to a cross of axes placed at the shoulder. The Cross of Axes component of the environment gives the method of finding the orientation of this cross of axes. (Where is front? Is it determined by the front of the room, the front of the dancer as a whole, or the front of the upper torso? Where is up? Is it against gravity, or is it 'headward', that is, body oriented?) The environment must provide a method for retrieving the necessary information to establish 'front', 'up', and 'left', either from the data local to the arm class or through pointers to other classes. At a higher level the environment establishes such properties as the connectivity of the body and the interrelationship among centers of gravity of the parts of the body (and thus, the center of gravity of the whole body) and the base of support (for maintenance of stability).

To outline the executive cycle of the entire parallel processor, we see every basic movement command specifying a direction and a duration. Also, certain changes to the environment, such as rotations, will have associated durations. Other environmental commands, such as establishing a new system of reference, may be regarded as having zero duration. Thus, execution will depend upon a *master scheduler* capable of determining the times (with respect to the entire movement sequence) at which individual commands must be initiated.[9]

At certain key moments, selected procedures within specified classes will begin their execution. This execution will depend upon the values within the local environment. It may also depend upon certain values within other environments (in addition to forcing certain compensatory alterations to other environments – for example, a notated movement of the torso carries with it an implied movement of the head). Thus, we may express execution in terms of a three-stage process:
1) Fetch – collect all instructions which initiate movements
2) Compensate – schedule all secondary movements which are consequences of the initiated movements
3) Perform – indicate how all parts of the body will move.

As we have mentioned, we shall be using this semantic model for the translation of a Labanotation score into an animated display. Thus, the actual output of the class procedure and the actual data to be produced during the 'perform' stage will be a frame-by-frame specification of a two-dimensional projection of the body on a display screen. For now, we are assuming an essentially linear interpolation (with smoothing) to represent a movement across a sequence of frames. However, we wish to explore the possibility of non-linear interpolations as a means of representing certain subjective movement qualities. These are qualities which Laban studied in conjunction with his development of a theory of 'effort'.[10]

Future Considerations

A compiler capable of translating Labanotation into an animated display allows for a wide range of applications. The most important of these is the ability to bring Labanotation closer to those people who are most influenced by it, choreographers and dancers. An animation would allow the choreographer to have a more direct hand in the process of recording a dance. He could review the animated display of the notation with the notator and point out where a passage has been incorrectly recorded. At this stage, the notator could benefit from a flexible interactive debugging aid, allowing for the animation to be interrupted to accept changes in the source code. At a somewhat more advanced stage, one could envisage the choreographer giving corrections directly to the system in English and having his statements processed into modifications of the Labanotation source code. As an aid to the performer, the animation would allow an individual dancer more opportunity to learn his part. A properly designed display file would allow for observation from several points of view and at differing levels of detail. It could also assist an individual dancer's understanding of how he relates to his partner or to an entire ensemble.

The next step in terms of basic research, however, is a *decompiler*. Using techniques of pattern recognition and scene analysis, we envisage the possibility of recording position of the human body on successive frames of a film of a moving person. Such an analysis would yield data very similar to that produced by the Labanotation compiler. In this case, however, the problem would be to work backwards to the original source code, thus obtaining a Labanotation score of the filmed movement. Because of the limitations of film, such a score might not be a perfectly faithful recording of the original movement: dancers do make mistakes during filming. Nevertheless, it would be an invaluable aid to the notator with a Labanotation editor as a means to get the desired movement data into the system for subsequent editing.

Finally, there is the potential for research into style analysis. Labanotation has the ability to be quite exhaustive in recording a movement. However, practical Labanotation scores involve many implicit assumptions concerning the stylistic vocabulary of the choreographer. Thus, a simple passage in Labanotation might admit of different realizations in movement, depending on whether the choreographer is Balanchine or Graham. For example, when ordinary walking is written, does the toe or the heel lead? These assumptions will involve certain decisions in the design of the local procedures in the classes for body parts. We ultimately envisage an interface between the user and these specifications through which one could characterize a particular choreographer's style and 'teach' it to the semantic processor. Such characterizations could be stored away and invoked during the interpretation of the appropriate scores. This would allow one to obtain a complete display from an essentially partial specification. But, more interesting than that, it would force us to determine rigorously a means by which stylistic attributes could be accurately described.

References

[1] A. Hutchinson, *Labanotation: The System of Analyzing and Recording Movement* (New York: Theatre Arts Books, 1970). Revised and expanded second edition.

[2] J. Keen, "Movement," (Sydney: Basser Department of Computer Science, University of Sydney, 1973).

[3] S. Bauer-Mengelberg, "The Ford-Columbia Music Representation," (unpublished report).

[4] M.D. Brown and S.W. Smoliar, "A Graphics Editor for Labanotation," *Computer Graphics*, Vol. 10, No. 2, (Summer, 1976), pp. 60-65.

[5] D. Gries, *Compiler Construction for Digital Computers* (New York: John Wiley & Sons, Inc., 1971).

[6] *IBM System/360 FORTRAN IV Language* (IBM Systems Reference Library, File No. S360-25, from C28-6515-4, 1967).

[7] P. Hackney, S. Manno,, and M. Topaz, *Elementary Reading Studies* (New York: Dance Notation Bureau, 1970).

[8] O.J. Dahl and C.A.R. Hoare, "Hierarachical Program Structures," in O.J. Dahl, E.W. Dijkstra and C.A.R. Hoare, *Structured Programming* (New York: Academic Press, 1972), pp. 175-220.

[9] S.W. Smoliar, "A Parallel Processing Model of Musical Structures," (Boston: Massachusetts Institute of Technology, 1971), Artificial Intelligence Laboratory, report AI TR-242.

[10] M. Davis, *Towards Understanding the Intrinsic in Body Movement* (New York: Arno Press, 1973).

9
Literary Data Management

The University of Manitoba Computer Braille Project

P.A. Fortier, D. Keeping, D.R. Young

The Braille system for tactile representation of written text uses a basic cell having six positions, which may or may not contain raised dots, as in Figure 1. Thus the maximum number of characters which can be represented is sixty-four. This small character set can represent the full range of information found in a printed text by using two or more Braille characters to stand for a single printed character when needed, such as capital letters or numbers, or by having flags to signal typographical features like italics or bold face type.

Given the size of Braille cell needed for easy recognition, a page of Braille can contain only a maximum of one thousand characters – less than 40% of what is found on a standard printed page. This fact has led to the development of two distinct systems for Braille representation. Grade I or uncontracted Braille uses one or more Braille characters to represent each printed character. Grade II or contracted Braille is highly abbreviated. Infrequently used characters stand for frequently used groups of letters within words, and short mnemonics stand for longer and frequently used words.

Both Grade I and Grade II Braille have been produced traditionally using a device with six keys, one key corresponding to each position in the Braille cell. The operator reads the text to be transcribed, and depresses the appropriate keys to produce Grade I or Grade II Braille, as desired. After the text is transcribed, it must be proofread by a Braille reader before corrections can be made. This work requires both good manual dexterity and constant mental agility. Training to transcribe Grade II Braille usually takes six months, and after training average output is two pages per hour.

Figure 1 The Braille Alphabet

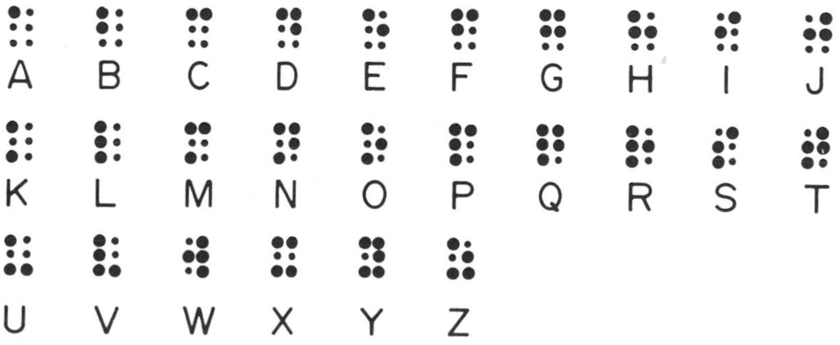

In 1973, we faced two cases in which traditional production methods did not fulfill a pressing need. On examination, we realised that there were three bottlenecks in the system: the training required for manual keying, the slowness of this operation, and the necessity to proofread after the Braille has been produced.

We were able to set up production of Braille avoiding these bottlenecks. Texts were input to a standard disc-editing system. Proofreading was done on listings of the input, and corrections made before the text was transcribed. This eliminated one bottleneck – proofreading. We produced uncontracted French, German and Spanish Braille using a simple reformatting program which we wrote, and Grade II English Braille using an existing program, DOT-SYS III. Translation into Braille codes was done at machine speeds, and actual production via a 120 character per second Braille embossing terminal. This eliminated the bottlenecks caused by manual keying of the Braille characters.

With computerized Braille production humming along quite satisfactorily, we turned our attention to the programming side of the activity. We expanded the capacities of the existing English Grade II Braille translation system, adding to it features for producing mathematical notation, phonetic transcription, and uncontracted French, German, Latin and Spanish texts.

Development of a Bilingual Grade II Braille Production System

Our development research was aimed toward improving Grade II English Braille production, and devising a system for computer production of contracted French Braille. On considering existing systems, like DOTSYS III, we were struck by the fact that they emulate the steps of the process whereby a human being transcribes Braille, moving one word at a time along the stream of text, determining the contracted or Grade II version of a given word, and outputing it.

We knew that for grammatical tagging of texts good results had been obtained from the approach of dividing the text into its component words, sorting them to put multiple examples of the same word in adjacent positions, and processing the sorted file. This approach allows multiple occurrences of a single type of word to be treated once per type rather than once per occurrence, and fosters the use of an archive of already tagged forms. Such advantages are important because the process of translating a word into its contracted or Grade II Braille form necessarily involves extensive rule testing, and is the most expensive part of the process. Already in DOTSYS, less than total perfection in English Grade II Braille had to be accepted, in order to keep the cost of the program within reason. The French contracted Braille system – which can be defined as having fifty rules and about 5,000 exceptions – is considerably more complex than the English one.

These considerations led to the development of the system structure shown in Figure 2. We shall sketch, in the following paragraphs, our experience in transforming our ideas into working programs.

BRAILE1 and BRAILE5 are the input and output modules respectively of the system. We decided to implement them first, because elegant and easily readable output is a *sine qua non* for a successful system in this type of application, and, of course, an output module presupposes an input module which supplies data to it.

So we started by developing BRAILE1, which produces Grade I or uncontracted Braille, and checks the validity of format control commands before passing them on for further processing. Experience developing BRAILE5 dictated modifications to BRAILE1 on many occasions. Development of these two programs proved to be the most meticulous and demanding part of the task and we were glad that we accomplished it at the beginning of the project.

We had originally planned to add to BRAILE1 a routine which would translate multi-word expressions and those hundred or more very frequent words which make up 50% of any natural language text. For simplicity, and in order to keep the memory requirements of BRAILE1 within reasonable limits, we decided to put these functions in a separate program, BRAILE2, which also divides the text into three files. One contains format control words, words and expressions already

Figure 2 The Braille System

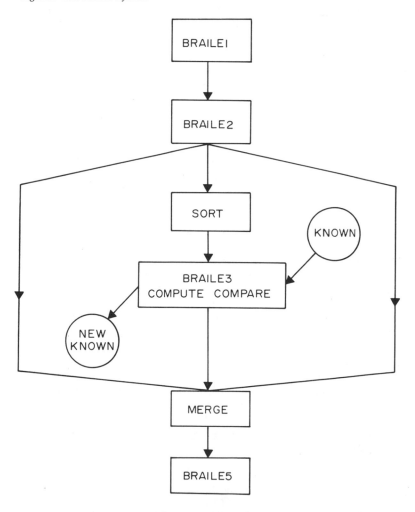

translated, mathematical expressions, punctuation, and words signaled to be left in Grade I or uncontracted Braille codes. This file goes directly to the merge step preceding BRAILE5, since it requires no further processing. Words flagged as French and not yet translated go into a separate file; they are sorted into alphabetical order, and translated into contracted Braille codes by BRAILE3. Words flagged as English undergo similar processing, which is not explicitly shown in the flowchart.

BRAILE4, which translates English words, is a small PL/1 program using equivalency tables taken from DOTSYS. It was virtually impossible to modify these tables, because they have approximately 5,000 entries, or conversion rules, expressed in a highly symbolic manner. We were thus facing a complex special use computer language – one with sketchy documentation and no built-in debugging aids.

With our knowledge of DOTSYS firmly in mind, and realising that the historic trend is for machine costs to decrease and programming costs to increase, we decided to make BRAILE3 as easy as possible to maintain or modify, while keeping operating costs within reason. The basic element of this program is a relatively simple routine which determines the abbreviated version of a word by comparing the file of known contractions to the text file. Since both files are in alphabetical order, this process is quite fast and cheap. When a text word is in the file of known contractions, a straight substitution is made as many times as the word occurs, and the entry from the known contractions file is passed on to a new file of known contractions. At this point garbage collection is also performed to remove from the file contractions which have not been used in a specified number of runs of the program. When a word is not in the file of known contractions, the above process is carried out virtually unchanged, except that control branches to the largest section of the program, which computes the valid contraction for the word.

The first thing is to compare the word to a list of 795 possible endings. These endings are classed by length – from 2 to 19 characters – so that a check of the length of the word permits limitation of the number of possible endings which need to be examined. Once this is done, the uncontracted part of the word is processed for syllable contractions. We do this using the INDEX function in PL/1 to determine if a contractible string is in the word. If it is, control branches to a labelled position in the program, where tests are made on the environment of the string to see if it can indeed be contracted. After appropriate action has been taken, testing of the word continues until the whole array of 48 possible syllable contractions has been compared to the word.

To facilitate debugging and subsequent maintenance of the program, we have written into it a trace feature which can be turned on or off using a run-time parameter. When this feature is turned on, BRAILE3 produces a file ready for output through the Braille terminal. Each different word in the text produces one record in the file. This record is a

Figure 3 BRAILLE3: Printed Output

```
OBJET,,,OJ              ** KNOWN CONTRADICTION **
ORATEUR,,,ORAT.         ENDING(EUR) (1)OR
ORCHESTRE,,,:(ESOE      (*)(1)OR (1)RE (*)(1)TR (1)ES (*)(1)CH
```

line of Braille containing a word in uncontracted Braille codes, three commas, and the same word in contracted Braille. Parallel printed output contains the same information plus identification of words found in the file of known contractions, identification of endings computed by the program, and a list of possible syllable contractions found. When the contraction actually has been made, an asterisk signals this fact, as shown in Figure 3.

The first material run through the program was a data base of 42,283 forms drawn from 1,191,627 words of literary and school texts recorded for other purposes, plus a second data base of 25,367 forms originally recorded for theme study. This latter file contains a large number of learned and specialised words. The results produced by the trace feature of BRAILE3 were sent to the Reverend Rolland Campbell, Director of Les Editions Braille du Quebec, for checking and comment. This exercise proved both dismaying and gratifying.

We were dismayed to discover that a few dozen input errors, which had escaped all previous checking, were still cluttering the files. We watched with dismay as the basic file of known contractions – containing word abbreviations defined by the Braille system, as well as anomalies or exceptions beyond the capacities of the program – grew from an original 1,500 entries, past the estimated maximum of 2,600 to a total of 3,125. We were also disappointed that it was possible to reduce the endings list only from a maximum of 2,000 to a final size of 795 entries.

We were touched and gratified by the endless devotion and hard work expended by Father Campbell and his staff in checking Braille output. This checking process also allowed a practical solution of the 'ient' ending problem. This ending is abbreviated 'i-ent' or 'ien-t', depending on its pronunciation. To handle this anomaly, we originally planned a hand update stage after BRAILE3. Our experience has now shown that virtually all words ending in 'ient' have only one possible abbreviation. We have found only two exceptions – "il convient, ils convient; un expedient, ils expedient". Thus it is possible to treat these two exceptions as material for flagging on input, and to avoid the necessity for human intervention in the midst of the system's operation.

Most gratifying of all is our certain knowledge that our French Braille translation program – which is the world's first – works accurately on an extremely large sample of text.

Figure 4 shows the cost of running the system. It was generated from information gathered from production runs on Camus' *l'Etranger* and Gide's *l'Immoraliste*. The overhead was estimated by passing a twelve word text through the system. The production costs have been normalised to 10,000 words. Thus the figures for BRAILE1 of 26.4 seconds of CPU time must be multiplied by 3.498, and the overhead of .42 seconds must be added to arrive at the total cost of running this program on the completed text. The verification of format control commands explains the relatively high cost of this program. BRAILE3 has a relatively low cost, even when one adds on the cost of sorting required by its design. It will be noticed that the Gide text is slightly more expensive per ten thousand words than the Camus text. This is because Gide's text has a considerably richer vocabulary than Camus'. On the other hand, the file of known contractions output by the Camus run was used as input for the Gide text. By doing this we reduced the CPU time requirement of BRAILE3 by 2.33 seconds per ten thousand words, vis-a-

vis the cost if the basic file had been used. The use of the updated file
thus produces a savings of roughly 25%. These figures justify our basic
strategy for the contraction process. We shall be doing some more experiments with the system with a view to further improving its cost
effectiveness.

Ancillary Developments

Parallel to the main work on a new contraction system for producing
Braille in French and English, work has been going forward in two an-
cillary areas. One of these areas is simplification of input protocols. A
program has just been completed which generates from text input in
standard print format, the format control commands used by the DOT-
SYS program which is still our mainline production program. Now, the
person inputting the text no longer has to remember the rather complex
set of DOTSYS format control commands; he or she simply types the
text as it appears. Thus we are able to save time in the training of personnel, in actually inputting the text, and in proofreading.

   A program has also been completed which produces texts in greatly
enlarged typeface, using a Versatec electrostatic plotter/printer.
Enlarged typeface is useful for people who are not totally blind, but
whose sight is so limited that they are not able to read ordinary printed
material. With the Versatec we are able to vary the size and shape of the
letters so that they precisely fit the needs of the individual handicapped
user. This program accepts precisely the same input format as the
DOTSYS Braille translation program. This means that we can produce
a text in Braille and in enlarged typeface from the same input file, which
should allow us to realise some economies in producing this aid for the
visually handicapped.

Plans for the Future

Our system, like the DOTSYS program for English Braille, has been
produced by an approach that can best be characterised as brute force.
Certainly, we knew what we wanted to achieve, and had in mind a basic
strategy. But inevitably, as testing was followed by revisions, and
further testing by more revisions, the clean lines of our programs
became convoluted, and the distinction between rules and exceptions in
the Braille representation system became fuzzy.

Figure 4   Cost Factors

	Memory k bytes	Overhead CPU secs	I/O	Camus CPU secs	I/O	Gide CPU secs	I/O
BRAILE1	120	0.42	251	26.40	188	26.80	194
BRAILE2	88	0.46	288	14.79	300	14.94	289
SORTS	256	1.73	565	1.75	646	1.87	654
BRAILE3	180	3.17	528	8.39	140	9.13	168
BRAILE5	116	0.39	216	5.15	125	5.22	124
Total		6.17	1848	56.48	1399	57.96	1429

Now, however, we have on tape – thanks to the extensive testing which we performed – a data base of more than 50,000 representative French words, showing both their contracted and uncontracted Braille form. It thus becomes possible to run a computerized analysis of the French contracted Braille representation system. We also have at hand material for a similar analysis of the Grade II English Braille system. Such analyses should produce both more concisely expressed rules, and smaller exceptions lists. The results of these analyses in turn could be used to construct more compact and more efficient Braille contraction programs. In fact, such programs could well be compact and efficient enough to run on a mini-computer system – a development which would move computer Braille production out of universities or large central facilities, and down to the level of local services to the blind, where it belongs. It is to this aspect of Braille production that we hope to turn our attention in the near future.

Acknowledgments

The authors would like to thank the Reverend Rolland Campbell, Director of Les Editions Braille du Quebec, who encouraged us to undertake work on computer production of French Braille, and selflessly aided us throughout the work on the project. We would also like to thank Dr. Michael S. Doyle, Director of Computer Services, University of Manitoba, for his continuing and enthusiastic encouragement and support, without which the work reported here would not have been possible. Basic expertise in manipulating natural language data was acquired by Professor Fortier thanks to Canada Council assistance. Braille production at the University of Manitoba has been funded by the Dean of Arts and by the Group for Academic Innovation within the University, by the Mrs. James A. Richardson Foundation, Winnipeg, Manitoba, and by the Province of Manitoba, through its STEP Programme, and the Special Education Division, Department of Education. Work on the Bilingual Braille Production System was also funded by the Canada Council.

SPINDEX II: A Computerized Approach to Preparing Guides to Archives and Manuscripts

S.E. Hannestad

Archival institutions in general, and the National Archives and Records Service in particular, are faced with an increasingly complex problem of providing guides or finding aids to the enormous quantity of documents in their custody. The extent to which guides and finding aids are prepared, however, depends on the resources available and the importance of the collection. All collections do not warrant the same level or detail of description. Small but extremely important collections warrant the time and cost involved in document-by-document cataloguing and detailed indexing. Larger collections with high research activity may justify file-level cataloguing, with the index restricted in scope. Large collections with only moderate research activity probably do not warrant cataloguing below the series level, using only a broad topic index. While all archival institutions agree on the need for guides and finding aids, few have the staff available to produce descriptive material by traditional manual methods. The number of reference requests have been increasing, but the ratios of staff-to-records and staff-to-researchers have been declining. Within the past ten years it became apparent that an alternative to the traditional manual procedures for preparing finding aids had to be found that would allow archival institutions to continue producing finding aids without either a large increase in staff or a reduction in the quality of reference service.

In 1967, information retrieval specialists at the National Archives of the USA undertook the task of developing a system for producing computer-indexed finding aids to archival and manuscript materials. At the beginning of the project, certain guiding concepts were developed. The resulting system would have to be available at a reasonable cost to all archival and manuscript holding institutions. The system would have to meet the needs of small institutions as well as large national institutions, and would require sufficient adaptability to handle both extremely detailed finding aids and general guides to large collections. The Council on Library Resources, Inc. supported the early development by providing a $40,000 grant.

Sixteen institutions (nine university archives, four State archives or historical societies, the Public Archives of Canada, American Institute of Physics, and the Mystic Sea Port Library) cooperated during the design phase by contributing some 125 published finding aids for our analysis. Some of the descriptive approaches used by depositories appeared at first glance to be incompatible, but it was found that most of the seeming inconsistencies were actually variations of a single descriptive approach. Analysis of the finding aids provided by the cooperating institutions enabled the preparation of detailed specifications for a final system design. Early in 1968 representatives of the cooperating institutions attended a planning conference in Washington. Basic data elements to be included in the system were agreed upon, and many of the cooperating institutions furnished the National Archives test data for detailed testing of the system design.

Development of SPINDEX II led the National Archives into uncharted waters, and it is fair to say that the system was not an overnight success. As we were new to the system development process, overly optimistic expectations prevailed in the early years. When the desired results did not arrive on schedule, optimism turned to pessimism, and high level management began having second thoughts. When system design work began in 1967, NARS anticipated that it would take roughly two years and $60,000 to design the entire system. By the end of 1970, a rather primitive sub-system was available for testing, but is was not until 1974 that the full system was working satisfactorily. The cost of developing the system had also multiplied.

Over the years, several initial design concepts had to be modified. The goal of making the system hardware independent was an early casualty, when it became apparent that compiler or interpreter-level languages could not efficiently handle the complexities of both the variable length fields/variable length record format and the flexibility in report format we desired. These requirements necessitated the use of an assembler-level language, thus the system was programmed in IBM Assembler Language. The system is somewhat machine dependent, in that it will operate only on IBM 360/370 mainframes. Within this limit, the system is fully transportable. Operating system variations are accommodated by separate DOS-DOS/VS and OS-OS/VS versions of the system. Considering the general availability of IBM 360/370 computers, this limitation has not proven to be a serious problem

Another of the original design concepts that was abandoned was the institutional exchange of catalog data on magnetic tape, with consolidated guides to several institutions' holdings being produced by merging master files. As a first step in the development of this project standard data elements were selected, and field assignments were developed. In practice the standard format is rarely used, as the institutions currently using SPINDEX II have determined that it is more appropriate to their needs to produce customized finding aids specifically tailored to their own descriptive practices, than it is to produce interchangeable master files. Even within the National Archives and Records Service projects, each project uses its own set of data elements and field assignments.

System Features

The SPINDEX II master record format is variable in length (up to a maximum of 7,000 characters) and consists of a control field and up to 50 data fields. Data fields are variable in length and can include up to 1,-000 characters per field. Each data field is identified by a three character tag. The first two characters of the tag identify the type of data element contained in the field, and the third character controls field sequence within type of data element. For example, if a user wishes to enter three implied subject terms to further identify material described in a particular record, he may enter the first term under tag 200, the second under tag 201, and the third under tag 202. The '20' identifies the type of data element, 'supplied subject', the final character identifies the specific field within the record. The record contains both a record directory and field directories to facilitate handling of the variable length data.

The record control field is fixed in length, and consists of three elements. The first element, containing three characters, is used to identify project/repositories within combined master files. The second element, of 18 characters, provides the means of selecting an individual record when updating, correcting, or deleting, and is also used as the sort field for arranging the file for the register printout or catalog. The final element, one character, identifies the hierarchical level of the record. The control number element must contain at least two alphanumeric characters and may contain up to 18. If fewer than 18 characters are used, the program supplies the right blanks to reach the fixed subfield length of 18 positions.

As most depositories gather and classify their material in a hierarchical arrangement (for instance, items within folders within boxes), the record control field provides for up to eight hierarchical levels. Only the most complex arrangement schemes require using all eight hierarchical levels. Most applications use five or less. The hierarchical level indicator may be used for selecting or restricting certain levels when indexing.

Data fields are variable in length and can contain numeric or alphanumeric characters. The system fully supports lowercase alpha characters. Each field is identified by a three character tag. In addition to sequencing fields within the record, the tag identifies the type of data element. Data elements can be selectively included or excluded from both the register listing and index. In addition, the tag permits the selective assignment of index functions to each field. Each data element type can be assigned one of the following indexing functions: (1) nonindexing field; (2) field permuted word by word, each word generating an index term (normally used for the title and descriptive fields); (3) field indexed as one term (normally used for personal name fields and supplied subject fields); and (4) four-position numeric words – years – indexed (normally used for date fields).

Each application requires a basic data base design unless the 'standard' format is used. Data base design includes developing the record control format – assigning the hierarchical levels and the sequencing of records. It also requires selecting the data elements to be used, and assigning each type of data element a tag. The appendix distributed with this paper illustrates the standard format. While the system presumes the standard data format has been used unless parameter cards define a special data format, the system fully supports unique data base designs.

The system uses parameter cards in various programs to create customized report formats and indexes. These parameter cards control both the selection of data elements to be included in a printed report, and the positioning of that data element on the printout. In addition, they permit generation of index terms from fields that were not printed in either the register listing or the index listing (such as supplied subjects or inverted personal names). The parameter cards are also used to modify both the contents and position of column headings. Applications using the standard data base design and the standard report formats require a minimum amount of parameter card coding.

Custom data base designs and special report formats can require extensive parameter card coding. However, even the most complicated parameter card coding can be accomplished by an archivist or manuscript technician with no data processing experience, as parameter cards are coded on special forms that guide the user in English to make the correct entries.

SPINDEX II currently consists of 11 programs divided into three modules: (1) an input and files management module; (2) a register lister module; and (3) an indexing module. The input and files management module supports punched paper tape, punch card, and two different forms of magnetic tape input. This module includes four specialized input programs, a format and edit program, a formatted transaction sort program, and a merge and update program. The merge and update program permits new records to be added to the master file, deletes existing records, and corrects existing records. Existing records may be modified by adding a new field, deleting an existing field, or replacing an existing field. Two edit/error listings are produced by this job stream.

The register-lister module controls the production of the register or basic finding aid. Selected data elements from the master file are printed in control number sequence. Automatic indentation, based on hierarchical level, is provided to display the data in proper relationship to other data.

The indexing module consists of three programs: (1) the keyword generator; (2) the keyword sort; and (3) the index print program. The keyword generator interrogates selected fields for indexing terms, and produces an output record for each term found. There are options provided in the program for determining which hierarchical levels and which fields of the record are to be indexed. In addition, the user has options of indexing a field by permutation (each word in the field), by field (entire field as one indexing term), by four-position numeric words (normally year dates), or by any combination of the three. SPINDEX II offers flexibility in keyword length and secondary sort field length. It also permits the secondary sort field to be created either from the title field or from the date field. The combined keyword length and secondary sort field length cannot exceed 150 positions. Within that limitation, the keyword length and secondary sort field length can be varied from 5 to 99 positions. When permutation is used, the program automatically suppresses 38 words (such as 'about', 'concern', 'general', 'record', 'sent') that are commonly used in archival and manuscript finding aids. Using a stopword deck, the user can suppress additional terms so common to their application that they become meaningless index terms.

The keyword sort program sorts the master keyword file on disk by keyword and selected secondary sort field.

The index print program selects up to six specified fields from the sorted master keyword file for inclusion in the printed index. All printing elements can be repositioned and field lengths changed by parameter card action. Standard column headings can be repositioned or replaced, and additional column headings can be inserted and positioned by parameter card options.

Indexes may be produced by subject, personal name, date, or combinations of any of these. Alternatively, alphabetical listings by title

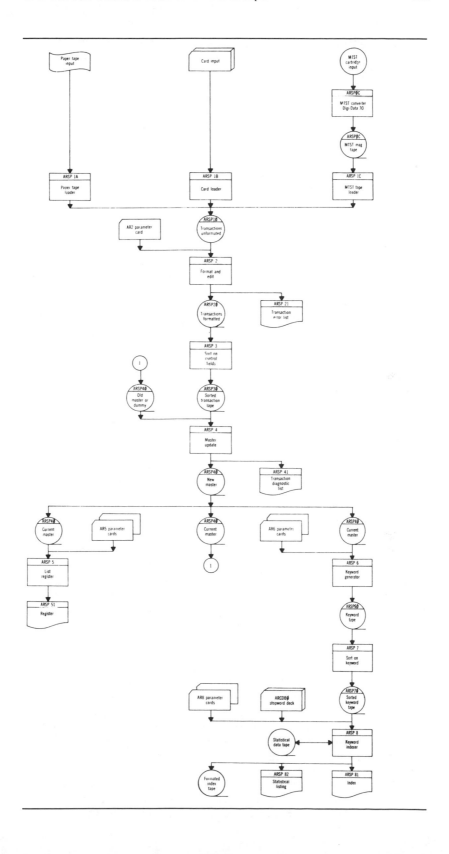

may also be printed. The following index formats are available: (1) subject and/or personal-name keywords, sorted thereunder by title; (2) subject and/or personal-name keywords, sorted thereunder by date; (3) year date keywords, sorted thereunder by month and day; and (5) alphabetical listings by title.

The optional features built into the system provide considerable flexibility in printed formats. The established print position of an entry may be changed to any position on the page, and the established line length of a field or element may be shortened or lengthened as desired within the limits of page width. Fields normally printed may be suppressed, and new fields may be introduced. Even the number of line-printed per page can be changed.

The adaptability of the report formats is limited by the characteristics of the line printer – a single type style, font, and size, and the limitation of 132 print positions per line. Certain SPINDEX II applications at the National Archives require greater sophistication in report layout than the basic system can provide. Therefore, on an application-by-application basis, we have developed specialized interface programs to utilize electronic photocomposition instead of lineprinter output. As these interface programs are limited to a particular data base design, they are not included as part of the basic SPINDEX II system. Using electronic photocomposition, NARS has produced SPINDEX II reports in various type styles, fonts (bold, regular, italics, caps and small caps), and sizes (6-point to 18-point). Use of photocomposition also permits significant reductions in the size of the report: one photocomposed page contains as much data as four lineprinter-produced register pages or six lineprinter-produced index pages.

Major SPINDEX II Projects at the National Archives

In honor of the American Revolution Bicentennial, the National Archives is producing an item-by-item index of the Papers of the Continental Congress. The largest part of this collection, the *Papers of the Continental Congress, 1774-1789,* has been published on 204 rolls of 35mm. microfilm. These records were catalogued into 194 record series by a clerk of the State Department in 1835, and that catalo is still the basic finding aid for the collection. An additional nine rolls of 35mm. microfilm published the uncatalogued 'miscellaneous' papers of the Continental Congress. Some of the material contained in the microfilm publications has been published in book form. In addition, copies of the microfilm are available for research at eleven regional archives branches and at most major research libraries. Various portions of this material were separately indexed, but there was no consolidated index to the entire collection. Each separate index used a different indexing philosophy, and the depth and quality of those indexes varies greatly. This collection is typical of the small, but extremely important, collections that warrant in-depth cataloguing and indexing.

Each document was carefully reviewed by specialists in early American history, and a data sheet was prepared. The data sheet included the document identifier (used as the SPINDEX control field); either the traditional title of the item or a coined descriptive title; the date of the item (estimated by the specialist if necessary); the names of the sender(s) and recipient(s); the length of the document; and list index terms. These data sheets were then transcribed on MT/ST magnetic cartridge typewriters using the SPINDEX format. Initial indexing was done without a thesaurus, but as work progressed rough indexes produced by SPINDEX were used to aid in the development of a project thesaurus. After the thesaurus was developed, the early entries were updated to comply with the terms in the thesaurus.

This procedure produced a SPINDEX master file containing a detailed, comprehensive calendar with associated index terms. A final index was produced, containing nearly 500,000 entries. Its massive size (approximately 5,000 pages in a three column, 8-by-10½ inch page format) necessitated the use of electronic photocomposition, since lineprinter output would have produced an unusable 30,000 page index. The indexing project, begun in 1971, will result in publication of the five volume index by the end of 1977.

The Captured German Records Microfilmed at Alexandria, Virginia, comprise nearly 14,000 rolls of microfilm. The records concern German Government agencies, military affairs, and the Nazi party, as well as records and papers of some private businesses, institutions, and persons. The period covered is chiefly from 1920 to 1945. Sixty-five manually produced, unindexed guides to this collection were produced prior to 1974. When the project of producing additional guides was transferred from the old manual system to SPINDEX, we wanted to continue the same format. As the old guides had been typed, and reproduced by mimeograph or offset printing, lineprinter output could replace the typewriter. A SPINDEX data base and report format was designed so that the computer-produced guides would closely follow the formats established by the earlier manually-produced guides. The SPINDEX-produced guides, however, include indexes. In the near future we intend to produce consolidated indexes covering related material from the new guides.

While the Papers of the Continental Congress project produced a detailed index and calendar of a significant collection of records at the document level, and the German Guide project produced a series of indexed guides at the folder level, a third project illustrates the ability of SPINDEX to handle production of a national guide to historical materials at the collection level. The National Historical Publications and Records Commission provides leadership, guidance, and grants to archives and manuscript repositories at State and local levels in collecting, describing, preserving, compiling, and publicising documentary sources significant to the history of the United States. The Archivist of the United States serves as chairman of the Commission. In 1961 the Commission produced a *Guide to Archives and Manuscripts in the United States,* covering 20,000 collections of personal papers and archival materials in 1,300 depositories. The Commission has begun work, using SPINDEX II, to produce an updated *Guide to Historical Source Materials in the United States.* This new edition will consist of two publications – a *Guide to Repositories,* listing over 6,000 repositories, and a multi-volume, collection level *Guide to Historical Source Materials in the United States,* covering over 100,000 collections. Both publications will be fully indexed. As the data base will be computerized, updating the publications will be much easier. Electronic photocomposition will be used both to reduce bulk and to provide a more pleasing publication. It is expected that the *Guide to Repositories* will be updated and reprinted every 2 to 3 years, and the *Guide to Historical Source Materials in the United States* will be updated on a volume-by-volume basis, with one updated volume produced each year. In order to reduce costs, the *Guide to Historical Source Materials* will also be published on microfilm – each hardback volume will cost about $20, but the microfiche edition of the same volume will cost under $3. Sample pages of the text and index of the *Guide to Repositories* have been distributed with the printed version of this paper.

SPINDEX II was the National Archives and Records Service's first venture into automation for descriptive purposes. Since the development of SPINDEX, several other special purpose systems have been developed. We fully expect SPINDEX to serve most of our future requirements.

In addition to its applications in the National Archives, SPINDEX II is in use at several other institutions, including State archives, university libraries, and corporate archives in the U.S.A., Canada, and England. The system is available for use by other institutions throughout the world at a nominal service charge ($500 for non-profit organizations, $750 for other users). The documentation is separately available for $5 per copy.

Appendix A: Standard SPINDEX II Design Format

The SPINDEX II format permits inclusion of any type of data entry. Each separate application can have an independent data base design in terms of assignment of data elements to fields. For most applications using the system, however, the necessary data elements can be confined to a standard format. The data element to field assignment table below is the system's default option: unless the user designs a unique field assignment and report format, the system assumes that the standard format is being used. Several of the field assignments have reserved functions, and should not be used in custom designs unless that special function is desired. Reserved fields are identified by an asterisk placed beside the tag number. The following data elements with their identifying tags can be used in the system without resorting to parameter modifications:

000*   *Control field.* This field identifies each record and, using the standard SPINDEX II format, provides location data. It consists of a 3-digit repository identification code, an 18-digit control number subfield, and a single digit record action code. Standard control number subfield allocations are listed below.

100   *General heading.* If the title is of a general or nondescript nature and permutation is not desired, the title field should be entered under a general heading tag (100).

110   *Subject title.* If the title is other than a personal name and if permutation of the field is desired, the title should be identified with the subject title tag (110). All words appearing in the field will be permuted, with the exception of single characters and those words appearing in the stoplist. If compound terms are used, they should be linked by a hyphen or by an underscore.

120   *Personal-name title.* If the title is a personal name, the field should be identified by the personal-name tag (120). The surname is entered first, and the entire field is indexed as one word.

150*   *Index cross-reference.* This special field prints on the index listing in place of the title field but does not print on the register listing. For example, if a record contained a 100-field "Aachen. See Aix-la-Chapelle," the register entry would read:

Aachen. See Aix-la-Chapelle.

The index entry would read:

AACHEN
    See Aix-la-Chapelle.

If the 150 tag was not used, the index entry would read:

AACHEN
    Aachen. See Aix-la-Chapelle.

200   *Supplied subject entries.* If subject entries are unmentioned, but implied in the title, or specified in the abstract of the record, or known to the archivist or researcher, they can be entered in this field as an additional area to retrieve from. The subjects in the field should be separated by a space. If compound terms are used, they should be linked by a hyphen or by an underscore.

210   *Alternate personal-name entries.* If it is desirable to separate a name as author from a name as subject, the alternate personal-name field will provide the means for separating these entries. The field is indexed in the same manner as the personal-name title (tag 120).

250*   *Span dates.* Inclusive dates of a record can be entered in this field in any form, provided that the year is a 4-position numeric and that the field does not exceed 21 positions (limited for printing purposes). Four-position year dates can be permuted for chronological indexes. If the date field will be used to create chronological listings, exact dates should be entered year-month-day, as the computer sorts left to right.

300*   *Quantity of material.* The quantity of material identified by the machine record, if known, will be entered in this field. The code for identifying the unit of measurement being recorded will be entered as the first position of the field, followed by the amount reported. If the figure exceeds five positions, the amount should be converted by the cataloger, using standard abbreviations, K for thousands, M for millions: 100,000 to 100K, 32,000,000 to 32M. The following codes should be used when identifying the type of quantity:

    I   (items)
    F   (folders)
    B   (boxes)
    V   (volumes)
    M   (microfilm reels)
    C   (cubic feet)
    L   (linear feet)

400*   *Collection ID.* The name of the collection of which this entry forms a part will appear in this field. The indentification is limited to a maximum of 10 positions to allow for printing. This field can be individually entered in each record through the normal input procedure, or inserted on all records in the file by use of the ARSP2 parameter card.

410*   *Inclusive box numbers.* When the record entry pertains to more than one box number, the inclusive numbers will be entered in this field. In most instances, the entry will be made only at the series level (standard SPINDEX II level 2).

900   *Abstract.* If an abstract or a textual note is desired, it will be
        entered under this tag.

Non-reserved fields may be assigned different definitions in custom
designs. Tags 001 through 099 would not normally be used.

Appendix B: Standard SPINDEX II Control Number Subfield Allocations

Level	Digits	Description
1	1-4	*Collection/record group identification.* A four-position number from 0001 to 9999 assigned in any desired sequence that identifies each collection or record group in an institution's holdings.
2	5-8	*Series number.* Four positions identifying the series within the collection or record group.
3	9-12	*Box number.* Four positions identifying the box within the series.
4	13-15	*Folder number.* Three positions identifying the folder within the box.
5	16-18	*Item number.* Three positions identifying the item within the folder.

NOTE: Volumes are normally entered at the box level (3), chapters at
the folder level (4), and pages at the item level (5) for bound collections.

A Computer Archive of Language Materials

D. Sherman

This paper will offer a brief survey of the Stanford Computer Archive of Language Materials (CALM). The purpose of CALM is to collect and to archive (in a computerized data bank) a large body of primary observational evidence about language systems and language usage, in order to meet such research needs of humanistic disciplines as grammatical analysis, language universals, lexicology and lexicography, historical phonetics, language pedagogy, and child language development. Access to the material archived in the CALM data bank is provided by printed reference works such as handbooks, indexes and concordances, and on-demand information retrieval services. The CALM project, in different forms, has been in existence since 1971 and has received financial support from the National Science Foundation (for language universals), from the National Endowment for the Humanities (for historical phonetics), from the University of California (for dictionary conversion) and from Stanford University (for processing textual files).

Because its goals are to provide answers to research questions in a variety of fields, the CALM data bank accepts information from a wide range of data sources such as dictionaries, textual corpora, and manually encoded descriptions of linguistic systems. All the materials stored in CALM, regardless of their source or their contents, are formatted within the computational framework of a single data structure (called MARC) and are processed by a common system of editing, retrieval, analysis, concordancing and print programs.[1]

CALM currently contains three different categories of data files: typological, lexicographic, and textual. Of these three, the typological files (which cover phonetics and phonology) are the most fully developed; during the next three years, we plan to expand significantly the lexicographic and the textual components of CALM.[2]

Typological Files

The typological files in CALM consist of detailed descriptions of linguistic subsystems; the descriptions are based on extensive analyses of published grammars, and are computerized on a cross-linguistic basis in order to facilitate research on language universals, that is, on those characteristics (phonetic, syntactic or semantic) which are present in all human languages, regardless of areal distribution or genetic affiliation Examples of linguistic subsystems which *might* be archived in a data bank such as CALM, are: kinship systems, color terminology, word order, schemes of numeral classifiers, phonetic inventories, processes of sound change. Of these topics, the last two, phonetics and phonology, have been formally archived by the CALM projcct.[3]

From a computational point of view, typological data tends to be structurally complex and highly inter-related, although the data files themselves may not be very large. The CALM typological files include phonetic and phonological descriptions of 200 languages which were chosen to represent an areally and genetically balanced sample. The data structure of the records in these two files defines over twenty independent fields of information, and over fifty separate subfields, which may be used to describe the phonetic inventory or the phonological rules of a single language.

Typical research questions which have been put to the CALM phonology archive are: what percentage of the world's languages are tone languages, and is tone an areally limited phenomenon? (answer: about 20% of the world's languages are tonal, according to the archived sample, limited chiefly to the native languages of Africa, Southeast Asia, Australia and New Guinea, and Central/South America); what is the most common phonological result of the sequence /nasal consonant/ plus /non-nasal consonant/? (answer: most frequently, the

Leader	Record Directory	Control Fields	Variable Fields

A) *Leader – The leader is fixed in length for all records and contains 24 characters.*

B) *Record Directory – The record directory is made up of a series of fixed-length entries (12 characters each) which contain the identification tag, the length, and the starting character postiion in the record of each of the variable fields. The record directory will end with a field terminator code.*

C) *Control Fields – The control fields contain alphameric data elements, many of which have a fixed length. These fields end with a field terminator code. Each control field is identified by a 3-character numeric tag in the record directory and these tags will not be repeated in a logical record.*

D) *Variable Fields – The variable fields made up of variable length alphameric data, and all fields end with a field terminator code except the last variable field terminator code except the last variable field in a logical record which replaces the field terminator with an end-of-record code. Each variable field is identified by a 3-character numeric tag in the record directory, and tags may be repeated as required in a logical record.*

Outline of Record Directory Entries

Tag	Length	Starting Character Position		F/T

F/T = Field Terminator

Outline of Variable Fields

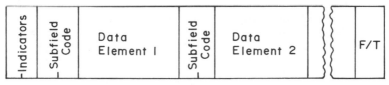

Indicators	Subfield Code	Data Element I	Subfield Code	Data Element 2		F/T

Figure 1. Summary of the MARC data structure

nasal consonant 'weakens' by assimilating in place of articulation to the following an consonant; occasionally, nasals cause voicing in following an otherwise voiceless consonant).

A reference handbook summarizing the contents of the CALM phonetics file is now being compiled and will be available in 1978 (for further details see section 5 of this paper). On-demand retrieval services are currently being offered and over 50 inquiries have been received thus far from linguists in the U. S. and in Europe.

Lexicographic Files

The lexicographic files in CALM are exactly what their name implies: computer counterparts of the full or partial texts of contemporary or of historical dictionaries. Dictionaries can be archived directly from photocomposition print tapes of recently published texts; historical materials require re-keying. In either case, the restructuring of raw input material into an appropriately defined MARC data structure is accomplished by programs which analyze the input text stream and identify significant fields of information and their constituent subfields.

The resulting file of MSRC structure records will reflect the traditional organization of lexicographic material into major categories of information such as orthography, pronunciation, definition, syntactic information, cross-references (synonyms, antonyms, etc.), and etymology. Many of these major data categories may be further subdivided into more detailed subfields of information, for example the identification of stress, syllable boundaries, and individual phonemes as the meaningful constituents of a lexical pronunciation data field. The CALM data bank currently contains the complete text of one contemporary American dictionary (*Webster's Seventh Collegiate*)[4] and the phonetic material from five 18th-century orthoepic (pronouncing)

MARC format for Phonetics and Phonology
(Record = Phone Segment or Phonological Rule)

Major subfield structures: (Sample Values)

$a Phonetic symbol (m, n, n-palatal, eng)
$b Segment class (obstruent, sonorant, vowel, glide, tone)
$c Place of Articulation (bilabial, dental, retroflex, palatal, velar)
$d Tongue height (high, mid, low)
$e Vowel backness (front, central, back)
$f Aspiration (aspirated, unaspirated, released, unreleased)
$g Voicing (voiceless, voice, ejective, implosive, glottal stop)
$h Tenseness (tense(+), tense(−))
$i Tonal pitch height (high, mid, low)
$j Tone contour (level, rising, falling, rising-falling, falling-rising)
$k Domain of tone (mora, morpheme, syllable, vowel, word)
$l Length (long(+), long(−), over-long, half-long, over-short)
$m Manner of articulation (stop, nasal, fricative, lateral, trill, flap)
$n Secondary articulation (nasalized(+), nasalized(−))
$r Lip-rounding (round(+), round(−), rounded-strong, rounded-weak)
$s Segment status (tag(−), tag(+), loan, allo, free)
$t Syllabicity (syllabic(+), syllabic(−))
$v Articulator (apex, blade, dorsum, slit, groove, concave, flat)
$y Click (click, click-affricate, click-lateral)
$z Statement of allophonic conditions

Figure 2.   Subfield structure for CALM typology file (Phonetic segment)

dictionaries.[5] In the near future, we hope to archive at lease one additional dictionary, preferably a British English text.

The purpose of developing a lexicographic archive is primarily to use computer-based techniques of storage, retrieval and analysis to explore the characteristics of dictionaries, both internally and on a comparative basis, and particularly to assess the relevance of dictionaries to the study of various linguistic problems. Some questions which may be investigated with the aid of an archive of contemporary and historical lexicographic texts are: the composition of the defining vocabulary of a dictionary in terms of the distribution and frequency of key terms and phrases; the logical and syntactic structure of definitions according to their traditional analysis into general (genus) and specifying (differentia) components. Historical texts can be used as evidence to document

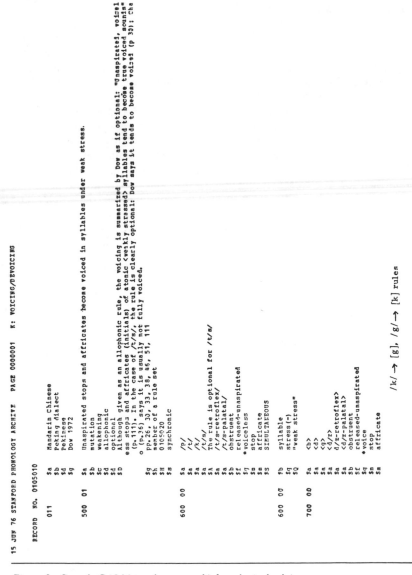

Figure 3. Sample CALM typology record (phonological rule)

the gradual change and diffusion of change in semantic or phonetic features, for example to trace the exact chronological course of phonetic processes such as the slowly increasing use of different stress patterns to distinguish noun-verb homographs *(su'bject* vs *subje'ct)* in English.[6]

A second purpose for having lexicographic files in the CALM data bank is to be able to link together textual and dictionary files for the sake of more precise and more efficient search and retrieval operations executed on the text file. By exploiting the possibilities of a lexical-textual interface, it is possible to relate (via indexes) some of the infor-

STANFORD PHONOLOGY ARCHIVE—INDEX: EJECTIVE/IMPLOSIVE STOPS

```
b=implosive' ───── KPELLE ── LOGBARA ── MAIDU
h=implosive-labialized ─────
b=prenasalized-implosive ─────
c=ejective ─────
d=implosive ───── LOGBARA ── MAIDU ── MAZUHUA
d=prenasalized-implosive ─────
d=retroflex-implosive ─────
d=retroflex-postglottalized ─────
g=implosive ─────
j=implosive ─────
l=postglottalized ─────
k=ejective ───── HUPA ── IZONAMA ── JAQARU
                 QUECHUA ── SOMALI ── SQUAMISH ── ZUNI
k=ejective-labialized ───── NOOTKA ── FICURIS ── PS SALISH
k=ejective-long ─────
k=ejective-long-labialized ─────
k=ejective-palatalized ─────
p=ejective ───── KWAKIUTL ── LAK ── MAIDU
                 TEWA ── TZELTAL ── WALAMO
p=ejective-long ─────
p=implosive ─────
q=ejective ───── NOOTKA ── POMO(SE) ── PS SALISH
q=ejective-labialized ─────

                                stop alternations
```

Figure 4. Sample typological index (to glotalized consonants)

mation coded in a dictionary entry, such as part of speech or syntactic pattern, directly to the words in a text, and therefore to formulate scarch requests such as the following: retrieve all text sentences which contain an intransitive verb preceded by an adverb (she *slowly walked* away); search for all phrases consisting of an adjective premodified by an adverb (extremely successful). A lexical-textual interface does not yet exist in CALM, but is planned during 1978, as described by Ferguson, noted above.

Textual Files

The textual files in the CALM data bank are the most extensive quantitatively and the least complex structurally. They are designed to be a mechanism for collecting a large variety of corpora of written and spoken English representing different sources, genres and linguistic registers. In spite of the recent criticism of corpus-based analysis which has resulted from the performance-competence debate in modern linguistics, it is still important for researchers to have convenient access to large files of citations and examples to supplement the insights of introspection and native speaker intuitions. The CALM textual archive aims to provide such a facility for linguistic research.

MARC format for Lexicographical Data
(Record = Lexical Entry)

Field and subfield structure (X digit of field tag used to code main vs run-on entry distinction; Y digit of field tag used to code primary vs secondary distinctions)

    1XY fields: Spelling data (Indicators are used to code part-of-speech)
        $a Spelled form of entry
        $b Hyphenation points
        $c Location of accent mark
        $l Status label

    2XY fields: Definitions (Indicators used to code part-of-speech of definition)
        $a Sense number
        $d Text of a definition
        $l Status label attached to the definition
        $s Synonymous cross-reference (used in lieu of a definition)
        $u Usage note
        $v Verbal example
        $w Type of directional cross-reference (see, see at, compare, called also)
        $x Directional cross-reference

    4XY fields: Pronunciation (Indicators used to code syllable length and stress)
        $a first consonant cluster
        $b first vowel cluster
        $c second consonant cluster
        $d second vowel cluster
        etc.

    500 field: Synonymy
        $a text of entire synonymy paragraph
        $w type of directional cross-reference

    600 field: Etymology
        $a text of etymology

    8XY fields: Partial pronunciation (Indicators are used to code which part of the pronunciation is missing)
        $a, $b, $c, $d, etc – see 4XY fields above

Figure 5.   Field and subfield structure for CALM lexicographic record

The core of this facility will be multi-million word files of non-literary printed data, plus a million-word archive of spoken English. Following the example of similar enterprises in other countries (such as Sture Allen's *Swedish Logotheque in Gothenburg*),[7] we plan to rely heavily on data which is already in machine-readable form, such as newspaper, magazine and textbook photocomposition tapes, and the results of previous research projects. Thus far we have archived (that is, converted to MARC-structure records) the well-known *Brown University Corpus of Present-Day American English*, and we have been promised access to several files of spoken British and American spoken English, including a large file of child language material as described in Ferguson, noted above. Archiving large files of printed data will depend in large measure on the willingness of publishers to co-operate on issues of copyright and data sharing.

The MARC data structure for CALM text files uses the sentence as the basic unit to be contained in a single record. Each field in a record represents all the data regarding a single word: its ordinal position in the sentence, its spelled form, and its contiguous punctuation.

Typical questions which can be investigated with the aid of the CALM text archive include the following: the semantic range of modal verbs (*can, may, could, might,* etc.), and the evolution of their use by children; the speech situations in which performative verbs (*promise, warn, demand,* etc.) are used; free and conditioned linguistic variation (*will* versus *shall* to express future time, *more* versus *-er* to compare adjectives, *which* versus *that* to introduce relative clauses); restricitions on the position of certain adverbs (*she arrived early,* but not **early she arrived);* restrictions on the intensification of adjectives (*a very tall man* but not **an absolutely tall man).* These questions are of theoretical in-

```
100 VB $AABIDE
101 VB $AABODE$I1$S1
102 VB $AABIDED$B4$I1$S1
103 VB $AABIDING$B4$I2$S1
110 N  $AABIDER$B4
120    $AABIDE BY
200 VT $A 1   $L&ARCHAIC$DTO WAIT FOR
200 VT $A 1   $SAWAIT
200 VT $A 2A  $DTO ENDURE WITHOUT YIELDING
200 VT $A 2A  $SWITHSTAND
200 VT $A 2B  $DTO BEAR PATIENTLY
200 VT $A 2B  $STOLERATE
200 VT $A 3   $DTO ACCEPT WITHOUT OBJECTION
200 VI $A 1   $DTO REMAIN STABLE OR FIXED IN A STATE
200 VI $A 2   $DTO CONTINUE IN A PLACE
200 VI $A 2   $SSOJOURN
220 N  $A 1   $DTO CONFORM TO
220 N  $A 2   $DTO ACQUIESCE IN
400 22 $E1* $YB1 $D0' $C15 $D1A $D2I $E1D $ZA0B1C1D2E1
500    $W9$XBEAR$W9$XCONTINUE$WS$XSTAY
600    $A¬M¬E &ABIDEN, FR. ¬O¬E &A?-BI?-DAN, FR. &A?--, PERFECTIVE PREFIX & &BI?-DAN
       TO BIDE; AKIN TO ¬O¬H¬G &IR-, PERFECTIVE PREFIX
601 11 $Y## $B0# $A1B $B1CW$C1D $ZA1B1C1
```

Figure 6. Sample CALM lexicographic record ('abide')

terest to many fields of linguistics (phiolsophy of language, sociolinguistics and variation theory, lexical semantics, child language development), and they also have a practical impact on language pedagogy in the formulation of teaching strategies, the allocation of priorities to alternative grammatical constructions, and the analysis of intelligence tests.

Published Reference Tolls

Accumulating a large archive of language materials would be pointless without a reasonable scheme for printing and disseminating reference works which summarize and provide convenient access to the major facets of the archived collection. Although these printed results will vary in form and in content according to whether dictionaries, texts or typological files are being summarized, the common strategy of CALM is to produce general purpose handbooks and concordances to begin with, and then to offer on-demand retrieval services to answer specialized requests for information. The results of specialized retrieval runs are saved and often can be used to answer future inquiries or to suggest additional kinds of general publications.

For typological material, a handbook with several selective indexes is the most efficient format for a published reference work. The first part of the handbook will contain a language-by-language summary of the

```
                             "The pair  whom Fatey is officially ccmmending for slapping
 acceptable alternative to Prince Souvanna Phouma,  whom it felt was too trusting cf Communists, it
     California journalist and reform politician,  whom he asked for his support.
  a liking; and the artillerist, Colonel Prevost,  whom the Count de Segur had persuaded to lend hi
   There were three other men within this prison  when Earton would have liked tc liberate, but th
                       <>The Serge Prokofieff  whom we knew in the United States of America was
   I say the late seventeenth century because Racine  (whom Lessing did not really know) stards on the
   once about an old friend of mine, S. K. Ratcliffe,  whom I had first met in London in 1914 and who a
                       <>The first royalty  whom Pama ever waited on in the White House was
   world: "The Lord is my light and my salvation;  whom shall I fear?
   on his name" Lord is my light and my salvation;  whom shall I fear?
   their grip: "The Lord is my light and my salvation;  whom shall I fear?
   of Junkerdom, to make room for the Polish Slavs  whom they had enslaved and openly planned to ext
                       <>These  whom I wish to address with this letter are for
   she would pass by all the outraged looks of these  whom the night approach.
   number of your profession heard, from those  whom we had the fortune to encounter, that we ha
   on the paper and brightens the lives of thousands  whom they have never known, and will never see.
   Then was it a final desperate plea from her, tc  whom?
                       <>Above all, he is a person to  whom a fledgling Representative can go to discus
   he knows "that an intellectual is not only a man tc  whom looks are necessary, he is any man whose re.
                       But the murderer tc  whom he clung had a tremendous advantage.
   during the depression, but the generous Broun tc  whom I wrote did not know his name and I somehow
   We will know, and He will know, tc  whom it is rendered, what the birds would ask: [!
                       Man, to  whom Fij gave endless attention and fealty, was !
   de Damas, three year's Littlepage's junior, tc  whom Nassau had taken a liking; and the artiller
   period to try to get in touch with a few people tc  whom cur dear friend Peppy had written.
   but consistently, was the portrait of a man to  whom serious thinking is alien enough that the m(
                       Each new teacher tc  whom the pupil goes is expected to study the inf(
   writers--- like Allen Tate, for instance, to  whom Valery was the last word in modern poetry a'
                       Tc  whom will the generals stay loyal?
   mania so deadly to Jews as well as to anyone upon  whom it happened to light, neither did it warn v(
   <>Every First Family seems to have one couple upon  whom it relies for true friendship.
   whom pressure is primarily directed, those upon  whom it may be permitted also tc fall, and those
   Nevertheless, like any other human being upon  whom the spotlight of the world plays continuall)
   deduced what had happened but did not know with  whom--- and didn't want to inquire.
   Pauel art dealer named Ernst Beyeler, with  whom he had long been trading pictures.
   or his uncle ffortescue in the exchequer with  whom he could more prevails than we".
   This is in contrast to the family with  whom he boards.
   , Warren G. Harding, Calvin Coolidge, FDR, with  whom he managed a social revolution.
   about new politicians and old men of letters with  whom he had been intimately thrown six decades be
   even suggested by Milton as those of persons with  whom he in any way consorted.
   <>Sound the roll of those with  whom he served and who preceded him in death.
   the help of White House aids in Washington with  whom he talked by telephone.
   and an American Jewish mother, long widowed, with  whom he lived in a comfortable home in Flushing.
   Woodrow Wilson, with  whom he began his years in Washington, Warren G.
   I never found it among any of the Chinese with  whom I spoke, though granted they were, almost al
   The lawyer with  whom I studied law steered re cff the Socialist t
   ), her son, Mr. Washizu (a prospective student with  whom I have been corresponding for more than a ye.
   label of un-American Jewish subversive on everyone with  whom it disagrees politically?
   having fellowship in the church with people with  whom, on the level of merely human agreeableness,
   and general expertise of the English professor with  whom cee attends the theatre.
   fact that he did see his niece and the woman with  whom she was staying.
   their way towards the hotel again, the hen, with  whom some sort of communication had been set up, :
   the mediums with  whom the Parapsychology Foundation is working in !
   each other as old people know the partners with  whom they have shared the same bed for many years.
   included Massa, jolly, generous, and pretty, with  whom they all fell in love, just as Papa had first
   strikingly in one pilot subject (the only one with  whom this technique was tried).
   meeting, "so it is good to know that those with  whom you get involved are not just dreary little
   looking at Simms Purlew, the only man in the world  whom he hated, he had seen the heavy, slack, best
   Pinders, for Stephens was one of the lost writers  whom Melville had seen in his childhood and when
```

Figure 7. Sample CALM left-context concordance (Brown Corpus)

primary topic covered in the file; in the case of phonetic descriptions, for example, the summaries will represent the entire phonetic inventory of a language, including its major phone segments, its allophonic and unconditioned variants, and all its marginal phones (such as those which occur only in loan words). All the members of this inventory will be arranged in their appropriate phonemic units.

The second part of the typological handbook consists of indexes which are primarily cross-linguistic and which list all the languages in the archived file in which a specific phone segment or a particular phonetic feature can be found. Such indexes would be consulted to find out, for example, which languages in the archive are tonal, which have distinctive nasalized vowels, which have rarely distributed phonetic segments such as the interdental fricatives (þ) or (ð), and so on. The CALM handbook of phonetic material is currently being compiled and will be available in 1978.

```
?0PAGE NUMBER 0351 W+ALKER 1791   DATE: NOVEMBER 6, 1974|*

DAINTY, DA1NE'TE1. S.|*

DAIRY, DA1'RE1. S.|*

DAIRYMAID, DA1'RE1-MA1DE. S.|*

DAISY, DA1'ZE1. S.|*

DALE, DA1LE. S.|*

DALLIANCE, DA4L'LE1-A4NSE. S.|*

DALLIER, DA4L'LE1-U2R. S.|*

DALLY, DA4L'LE1. V.N.|*

DAM, DA4M. S.|*

DAM, DA4M. S.|*

DAM, DA4M. V.A.|*

DAMAGE, DA4M'MA1DJE. S.{90}.|*

DAMAGE, DA4M'A1JE. V.A.{90}.|*

DAMAGE, DA4M'A1JE. V.N.|*

DAMAGEABLE, DA4M'A1JE-A4-BL. A.|*

DAMASCENE, DA4N'ZN. S.|*

DAMASK, DA4M'A4SK. S.|*

DAMASK, DA4M'A4SK. V.A.|*

DAMASK-ROSE, DA4M'A4SK-RO21ZE. S.|*

DAME, DA1ME. S.|*

DAMES-VIOLET, DA1MZ-VI1'O1-LE2T. S.|*

DAMN, DA4M. V.A.{411}|*

DAMNABLE, DA4M'NA4-BL. A.|*
```

Figure 8.   Sample input lexicographic record (DEPEP – Walker 1791)

For the contemporary lexicographic data in the CALM data bank, a concordance to the definitions in the dictionary is envisaged as the most significant kind of general purpose reference tool. Applying conventional KWIC concordancing techniques to dictionary definitions will provide a synoptic view of the distribution of terms and phrases in the defining vocabulary of a single dictionary, as well as across dictionaries (assuming that other dictionaries are added to CALM in the near future). In particular it will be possible to analyze the role of frequently used formulae such as: *of or relating to, used for, formed by, to become, to cause to, the act of, the art of.*

Ideally, analyzing the defining expressions of a dictionary should reveal a small but hierarchically organized vocabulary which is logically and uniformly applied to all definienda; in short, a definitional metalanguage built around a core of semantic primitives. Preliminary results with an Italian dictionary show that this is probably not the case however, and that there is in fact considerable stylistic and facultative variation in the choice and application of defining terminology within a single dictionary.[8] The CALM definition concordances will allow us to study this hypothesis with regard to English dictionaries. The concordances to the definitions in *Webster's Seventh Collegiate Dictionary* are currently being prepared and should be completed by early 1978; they will be available at that time, in microfiche form, if the publisher is willing to permit distribution for scholarly research.

The historical lexicographic data currently in the CALM data bank consists of 150,000 entries of phonetic material representing the contents of five major 18th-century pronouncing dictionaries: Buchanan 1766, Kenrick 1773, Spence 1775, Sheridan 1780, and Walker 1791. This material is being compiled as a part of the editorial work being done for the Dictionary of Early Modern English pronunciation (DEMEP), an international scholarly project under the general direction of Professor Bror Danielsson of Stockholm.[8]

Since each of the five source dictionaries in the archived DEMEP files uses a different system of phonetic transcription, the first requirement for editorial analysis is an exhaustive index to the phonetic symbols used in a given dictionary, especially to symbols used to transcribe vowels. When these indexes are completed, sometime in 1980, they will be unique compendia of the phonologies of the five source texts cited above.

For the text files in CALM, concordances will be the major format for printed reference works. Concordancing is by now a well established technique for constructing a detailed verbal map of a given text or a collection of texts, and needs no separate justification. The CALM concordances will differ from existing publications in several important respects. First, the concordances will refer to non-literary corpora, including spoken as well as printed sources: rather than illustrate the language of a single author/speaker, the CALM concordances will reflect the speech habits of a large community of adult and non-adult speakers. Second, the concordances will be designed for linguistic rather than for literary research, and consequently all the words in a text or corpus will be concorded, including frequently omitted classes such as pronouns, prepositions and auxiliary verbs. Third, microfiche will be used as the primary printing and distribution medium in order to minimize production and copying costs.

The basic arrangement of the CALM textual concordances will be based on the KWIC format, with a flexible range of options for sequencing citations according to the verbal contexts of the word being concorded. Currently available KWIC concordances, such as the recent Shaw compilation, use the right-hand context of the key word as the primary sequencing device; from the point of view of linguistic analysis, the results can be used as a concordance of phrases and (right context) collocations.[9] We plan to extend this technique by generating concordances which can be sequenced according to the verbal context to the left of the key word (as well as to the right), using either the normal or the reverse spelling of the key or the context words.

Left-context or left-collocate concordances are important tools for linguistic analysis because they can be used to study collocational questions such as: which nouns, verbs and adjectives can take 'that-complement' clauses (he *said that* he would go, there is *evidence that* he is guilty, we are *happy that* it rained); which adjectives commonly combine with *of (afraid of, ashamed of, aware of, confident of, conscious of,* and so on). By consulting left-context conconcordances of *that* and *of* respectively, the answers to the two questions posed above can be ascertained.

The implementation of the concordancing techniques described above, is currently in its final stage of testing; the largest experimental compilation to date is a left-context concordance to the four relative pronouns *that, which, who, whom* in the Brown corpus. The resulting 16,500 citations are printed on two microfiche cards. We plan to generate complete (microform) left and right context concordances to the Brown corpu 1978; if copyright problems do not prevent it, they will be available for distribution at that time.

Concordances and Microform

Concordances seem to be well suited for microform publication because of their sheer size and consequent prohibitive cost in hard-copy form. The economics of COM (Computer Output Microform) are currently such that a master fiche can be created (directly from a ordinary print tape) for about $2.50. Additional copies can be made from a master fiche for about ten cents per copy. Since a single fiche card can hold about 14,000 single-spaced lines of printout (the equivalent of 270 computer pages), a million-citation can be printed on 72 fiche cards.

The cost of producing the set of 72 master fiche is $180.00 and the cost of making 30 copies of each set is $216.00, or an average cost of $13.20 per set. Even if computer time and other overhead charges are figured into this calculation, the final cost to a purchaser should not exceed $30.00 for a million-citation concordance. The modest size and cost of a microfiche concordance can be contrasted with its nearest hard-copy counterpart, which is the previously cited concordance to the plays and prefaces of G. B. Shaw.[10] The Shaw concordance contains 725,000 citations, occupies 10 folio volumes, and sells for $275.00.

There are of course disadvantages to microfiche. Viewing is possible only with the assistance of a microfiche reader (the average price of a reader is currently about $200), and most scholars and students are unfamiliar with the regular use of microform readers. In addition, many of the usual browsing and scanning techniques used with printed material are somewhat altered in terms of microfiche grids and indexes.

Most of these difficulties are not insurmountable, however. University libraries usually have at least one, and frequently several, microfiche readers. At their current price it is possible for departmental libraries and even for individual scholars to own a small, portable reader, porvided there are enough important and valuable reference works in microform to justify such a purchase.

References

[1]Library of Congress, Information Systems Office *Manuals Used by the Library of Congress* (Chicago: American Library Association, 1969).

[2]C.A. Ferguson, *Constructing a Textual and Lexicographic Archive for Language Research* (Stanford, California, Linguistics Department, 1977).

[3]M.M. Vihman, *Reference Manual and User's Guide for the Stanford Phonology Archive* (Stanford, California, Linguistics Department, 1977).

[4]D. Sherman, *A New Computer Format for Webster's Seventh Collegiate Dictionary* (Computers and the Humanities, 8, 21-26, 1974).

[5]D. Sherman, *Computer Assistance for the Dictionary of Early Modern English Pronunciation*, DEMP Symposium and Editorial Meeting, ed. B. Danielsson (1976), pp. 121-135.

[6]D. Sherman, *Noun-Verb Stress Alternation: An Example of Lexical Diffusion of Sound Change in English Linguistics*, 159 (1975), 43-72.

[7]S.F. Allen, *The Swedish Logotheque*, Festschrift F. de Tollenaers (forthcoming).

[8]N. Calzolari and L. Moretti, *A Method for Normalization and a Possible Algorithmic Treatment of Definitions in the Italian Dictionary*, Reprints of the 1976 Computational Linguistics Conference (Ottawa, Mimeo, 1976).

[9]B. Danielsson, Proposal for DEMEP (Neuphil, Mitteil, 75 (1974), 492-500).

[10]E.P. Belvan, *A Concordance to the Plays and Prefaces of Bernard Shaw* (Detroit: Gale Research, 1971).

10
Programming for Literary Applications

A Comparative Evaluation of Fragment Dictionaries for the Compression of French, English and German Bibliographic Data Bases

V.L. Doucette, K.M. Harrison, E.J. Schuegraf

In some applications of computers in the humanities or social sciences large amounts of textual data must be processed. Conversion of certain material such as medieval texts or manuscripts into machine readable form presents difficulties and is often achieved only after substantial editing has taken place.[1] Frequently a researcher trying to process his valuable data may encounter one of two problems. On one hand the random access storage available to him may be too small to store all his data, and can for one of various reasons not be increased. On the other hand it may happen, that after using the data for some time and the initial enthusiasm has decreased, the researcher realizes that the cost of storing his data is too expensive for his limited funds. If a form of archival storage like magnetic tape is not available or too cumbersome to use, then the researcher faces one of three alternatives: abandon the project, process the data in small sections, or use a method to reduce the storage requirements of the data. Clearly, the first alternative is not acceptable, while the second may be ruled out by the particular application, since it may require that all the data be accessable during processing. Thus a method which reduces the storage space is the only viable alternative, if the reduced storage requirements are within the limits imposed on the researcher. In most cases, it is easier to prepare the data with the possible application of a data reduction method in mind, rather than trying to add one after the data has been prepared. Thus these so-called data compression or data reduction schemes deserve examination of their structure, operation and possible benefits. Of special interest are those methods suitable for textual data. A detailed survey of compression methods for non-numeric data bases has been described by E.J. Schuegraf.[2] It is necessary for the subsequent discussion to briefly describe the operation of a class of popular compression schemes, namely, those based on dictionary encoding.

The heart of such a compression scheme is a set of previously chosen language elements, commonly called dictionary. Selection of the dictionary is normally done after some kind of statistical analysis has been performed on the data or some sufficiently large sample thereof. Language elements may be defined to be a natural unit like a word, syllable or character, or it may be some arbitrary fixed or variable length character string, which is convenient for computer processing. In most cases, the dictionary is ordered such that each element can be uniquely identified by its position in the dictionary list. Figure 1 shows the structure and operation of such a system.

A record to be compressed, be it a sentence, or word, is scanned and all elements of the dictionary contained in the record are identified. A sequence of these elements is chosen in such a manner that the entire record is represented as a concatination of dictionary elements. For each of the dictionary elements in that sequence a code is substituted, generally of shorter length than the original language element. Normally the code represents the position of the element in the dictionary. The sequence of codes is called the compressed record and the collection of all these records is the compressed data base. Decoding is the reverse of the coding process and will reproduce the original record, provided the same dictionary is used as during coding. For each code a table look-up in the dictionary at the position specified by the code will produce a language element. If the sequence of language elements is the same order as their corresponding codes in the compressed record, then the original record has been reconstructed.

In many applications the data is coded initially, then manipulated in coded form or decoded before use. Under these special circumstances, where decoding is the more frequent operation than coding, it is imperative that the decoding process be very efficient. This aspect is especially crucial in retrieval systems where large amounts of data are stored and manipulated, and the frequency of access to individual records varies considerably.

Implementation Considerations

The problem of selecting a suitable dictionary for various data bases has been discussed extensively in the literature.[3] However, before a dictionary is selected two options available in any dictionary encoding scheme must be fixed before any actual implementation. Language elements can be chosen to be of fixed or variable length, as with syllables or words. In addition, codes may be of fixed or variable length. Each method resulting from a choice of different combinations of these options has its own advantages and disadvantages. A detailed discussion of the theoretical background and the merits of each scheme is beyond the scope of this paper, but can be found in the work of E.J. Schuegraf. A popular choice for a language element is a natural variable length unit like the word or syllable. A high degree of compression can be achieved if codes for these elements are chosen to be of variable length according to there probability of occurrence in the data.

Figure 1   Data Compression System

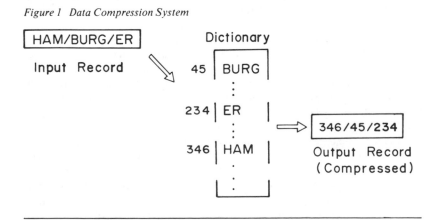

A reduction of storage requirements to 30% of the uncompressed data base has been reported by H.S. Heaps.[4] Two disadvantages are the large size of the dictionary and the manipulation of variable length codes by the computer. Normally, codes are generated from the probabilities of the language elements by a well known algorithm by D.A. Huffman, which associates short codes with elements of high probability and long codes with those of low probability.[5] Coding is relatively simple, but decoding is time-consuming, because most computers work with a fixed word length and processing of variable length bit strings is cumbersome.

Choice of fixed length language elements such as character, bigrams or the like, keeps the dictionary fairly small, but to obtain good compression it is necessary to employ a variable length code. Thus, the different choices of language elements do not eliminate the disadvantage of variable length codes. For these reasons a fixed length code should be chosen to represent a dictionary element. However, another problem appears. Information theory requires that in order to obtain good compression with fixed length codes the associated language elements must occur with equal probabilities.[6] Any deviation from this equifrequency requirement will result in a lower degree of compression, and thus more storage space is needed. If a fixed length code is chosen, the problem is transformed into finding a set of dictionary elements which occur with approximately equal frequencies in the data, and which can represent the entire data base by concatination of these elements. Obviously, natural units like words or syllables are ruled out by this approach, since it is well-known that their distribution is far from being uniform.[7] Even arbitrary fixed length character strings are eliminated, since it is impossible to find a set with equal frequencies. In order to reap the benefits of a fixed length code, mainly the easy decoding procedure, the natural units have to be abandoned. The dictionary will be a set of linguistically meaningless, variable length character strings, which have been called 'fragments' by Columbo and Rush.[8] However, they can be selected to possess the property of equifrequency, a suggestion first made by A.C. Clare, E.M. Cook, and M.F. Lynch, noted above. Other constraints on such a dictionary are discussed in detail in Schwartz.

Dictionary Selection and Data Compression Algorithms

Considerable freedom exists when a dictionary is to be selected, since various parameters can be chosen so as to make machine processing as simple as possible. For such reasons it is advantageous to restrict the maximum length of a dictionary element so that it is compatible with the computer's word length. It also proves beneficial to limit frequencies of those character strings which may be thought of as possible candidates for the dictionary. Their frequency of occurrence in the data base or sample should exceed a certain threshold value before they should be considered as dictionary elements. It is obvious that a character string which occurs only once or twice in the data base should not be included, since the savings in storage space are minimal. To assure a high degree of compression it is imperative that any method of dictionary selection maximize the average length of dictionary elements. Single characters must be included in the dictionary to guarantee a complete representation of the text by concatination of dictionary elements.

Selection of a fragment dictionary has been described in various papers, but one aspect has been somewhat neglected. After the dictionary has been chosen by some algorithm from a text sample, it will be used to compress the entire data base, not just the sample. When the complete data base has been compressed, all dictionary fragments should have approximately the same number of occurences, a property which may be difficult to obtain for two reasons. Firstly, the data sample may have been too small either to assure stability of the frequencies or to be representative of the total text. A second more serious reason may be the fact that the algorithm which was used to generate the compressed text did not preserve the equifrequency property. This can occur if dictionary selection and compression algorithms operate on different principles. A dictionary selection method which has as its objective the maximization of equifrequency may not be compatible with a compression algorithm which tries to maximize compression. When, during compression, all fragments embedded in a text record have been found, one of three algorithms can be chosen to build the compressed record. One is a so-called 'minimum storage form' algorithm, which uses the fewest number of fragments possible and thus achieves the highest degree of compression.[10] The second is the so-called 'longest fragment first' algorithm which removes recurrently the longest fragment until there are no more fragments to remove. The third and simplest is the longest match algorithm, which starts at the beginning of the record and tries to match the longest possible fragment to the initial characters. Characters covered by the matched fragment are replaced by the code for the fragment and the matching process continues recurrently with the next character not covered until the end of the record is reached. E.J. Schuegraf and H.S. Heaps provide a detailed description and a comparison of these algorithms in "A Comparison of Algorithms for Data Base Comparisions by the Use of Fragments as Language Elements."[11] When compressing data with the longest match algorithm it has been found that it uses approximately one-third of the time of the other two algorithms. However, savings in storage space are approximately 5% less than the other two, a loss which can be tolerated in most cases. Thus, the LM-algorithm appears as the most feasible one to use, since it makes the most of computer time and is easy to implement.

When comparing compression predicted by a dictionary with the one obtained after it has been used for coding, a significant discrepancy has been reported.[11] In some instances savings in storage space were only half of what was expected. When analyzing the results it has been found that equifrequency of dictionary elements was not preserved, which accounted for most of the discrepancy. To overcome this difficulty a dictionary selection algorithm had to be developed which was to match the operation of one of the coding algorithms and preserve the equifrequency property. For obvious reasons the LM-algorithm was chosen as the desirable coding algorithm and a selection method was designed which mimicked the operation of LM coding. A detailed description of the selection process can be found in the work of V.L. Doucette and E.J. Schuegraf, with experimental results showing very close agreement between predicted and actual savings in storage space.[12] This algorithm was used to generate dictionaries for the experiments with texts from three different languages.

Experimental Results

The purpose of carrying out experiments with three languages was twofold. On the one hand, they were set up to determine sample parameters, as well as the relationship of these parameters to dictionary characteristics such as size. On the other hand, the experiments were designed such that it could be determined to what degree these dictionaries of 'linguistically meaningless' character strings were independent of the original language. This hypothesis of language independence could be confirmed if dictionaries generated from various languages had a high proportion of common elements. The establishment of such a fact would be beneficial, since a single dictionary would be adequate for compression of different languages.

Bibliographic information was chosen as the textual data for the experiment, since it was readily available in three languages, and it could be assumed that the data would be similar to some degree. English text was taken from one issue of the MARC tapes, the cataloging information produced by the Library of Congress. French text was provided by the National Library of Canada from their CAN/MARC tape. German cataloging information was supplied by the Zentralstelle fuer maschinelle Dokumentation and represented two issues of the *Deutsche Bibliographie*. From these samples with cataloging data, author, title and subject heading fields were extracted and work frequency lists prepared. A detailed characterization of the three samples is given in Table 1.

It was decided that experiments would be carried out with word rather than text fragments, since the latter would have increased substantially the amount of computer time needed. Word fragments are character strings completely embedded in words, while text fragments may extend across word boundaries and may include blanks or punctuation symbols. The extra characters allowed with the latter fragment type increases the number of different fragments possible and thus needs more time for searching and sorting. Consequently the algorithm described in Doucette and Schuegraf was used to generate fragment dictionaries from each of the three samples.[12] Threshold frequencies were chosen to be five, ten, fifteen, and twenty, since a previous experiment with English text had shown that these choices produced dictionaries of manageable size. The thresholds picked are even multiples of the average word frequency, which for all three samples was approx-

Table 1   Sample Characteristics

	French	English	German
Author Fields	446	608	1099
Title Fields	467	494	1148
Subject Heading Fields	548	492	1517
Number of Word Tokens	5270	7241	8968
Number of Word Types	2030	2835	3569
Length of Sample (char)	32917	41551	53910
Average Word Length (char)	6.25	5.74	6.01
Length of Longest Word (char)	17	20	32

imately the same (2.5). Table 2 shows the important parameters of the dictionaries as a function of the threshold. The last column shows the compression obtained when coding the data base with these dictionaries. It may be seen that the best values are achieved when the number of elements in the dictionary is only slightly less than a number of the form 2^k, because k-bits can be used to code a dictionary element and all 2^k codes are utilized.

When analyzing the number of fragments common to two dictionaries with the same threshold but from different languages, it was found that approximately the same percentage of elements was shared between the two regardless of the threshold. A closer inspection revealed that for a low threshold a significant number of fairly long (between five and eight letters) fragments existed. However, for high threshold values the common fragments were made up of only two or three letter fragments. This can be seen in Figure 2, where the fraction of common fragments is plotted against their respective length. Table 3 shows the percentage of text covered by these common fragments and it is interesting to note that it increases with the threshold. As the threshold is raised the longer language dependent fragments become fewer and fewer, while the short, nearly language-independent fragments become more dominant. Table 3 also shows the coverage provided by those dictionary elements which are common to all three language dictionaries, and a small loss in the coverage is observed.

In order to discover possible relationships or connections between dictionary and sample size, various ratios were calculated. It was found that the ratio computed by dividing the number of elements in a dictionary by the number of characters in the respective sample was nearly constant, regardless of the source language. These ratios are displayed in Table 4 as a function of the threshold. The small variations are statistically insignificant.

Table 2   Results of Dictionary Generation

Threshold	Dictionary Size			Avg. Fragment Length in Comp. Data			Avg. Fragment Length in Dictionary			Compression (Percentage of Uncomp. Data)		
	Eng	Fr	Ger	Eng	Fr	Ger	Eng	Fr	Ger	Eng	Fr	Ger
5(15)	992 (10)†	766 (10)	1182 (11)	2.88	2.88	2.85	3.65	3.56	3.65	43.3‡	43.4	48.2
10(30)	578 (10)	454 (9)	652 (10)	2.42	2.38	2.46	3.02	2.96	3.10	51.6	47.3	50.8
15(45)	423 (9)	336 (9)	484 (9)	2.21	2.16	2.27	2.74	2.64	2.76	50.9	52.1	49.6
20(60)	338 (9)	285 (9)	398 (9)	2.05	2.08	2.19	2.49	2.39	2.61	54.9	54.1	51.4

† The number in parenthesis indicates how many bits are required for the code for one dictionary element.

‡ The values were calculated assuming an 8-bit character representation.

Figure 2   Common Fragments versus Length

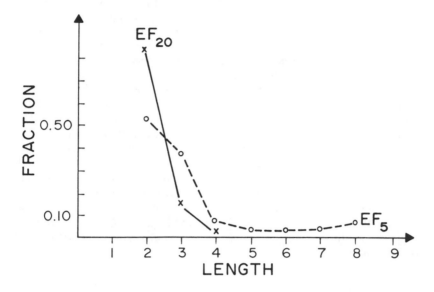

Table 3   Text Coverage by Common Dictionary Fragments

Threshold	EF	EF	FG	FE	GE	FG	E	F	G
	Common to Two Language Dictionaries						Common to Three Language Dictionaries		
5	33.4	39.5	33.8	40.8	34.4	22.3	24.0	30.0	20.1
10	37.7	45.3	41.1	45.8	37.1	29.3	30.2	37.1	27.1
15	40.3	50.3	43.3	48.5	40.8	29.9	33.0	39.4	27.7
20	45.7	52.0	47.2	54.0	41.4	32.9	37.9	44.1	31.0

EF_5 = Percentage of English text covered by common fragments. Threshold 5, Dictionary elements common to English and French fragment dictionaries.

Table 4   Dictionary-Sample Size Ratio as a Function of Language and Threshold

Threshold	5	10	15	20
English	.0871	.0402	.0278	.0202
French	.0828	.0408	.0269	.0206
German	.0802	.0376	.0247	.0193

Conclusions

The results above are sufficient to answer the two questions posed earlier. Dictionary size measured in characters is independent of the source language and only a function of the threshold frequencies, but is directly proportional to the number of characters in the sample. Dictionaries for two different languages possess a large number of common fragments, approximately 38%, but these common fragments cover approximately 40-50% of the text sample. The threshold is the critical factor in removing language dependencies: the higher the threshold the harder it is to identify dictionary elements with its source language. The number of elements common to dictionaries of three languages is smaller than for two, and they account for a smaller coverage of the text sample. It may be concluded that a dictionary generated by a high threshold from any one language will provide satisfactory results when used to compress text of another language. However, an extension to three languages produces less satisfactory results. Various other experiments were carried out, especially with dictionaries generated by merging the three samples, but space does not permit a description of these results.

Acknowledgments

Financial support for this research project was provided by the National Research Council of Canada and the University Council for Research of St. Francis Xavier University. The assistance provided by the National Library of Canada and the Zentralstelle für maschinelle Dokumentation in supplying the data samples is also gratefully acknowledged.

References

[1] R. Frank, and A. Cameron, ed., *A Plan for the Documentation of Old English* (Toronto: University of Toronto Press, 1973).

[2] E.J. Schuegraf, "A Survey of Data Compression Methods for Non-Numeric Records," *Canadian Journal of Information Science*, 2 (1976).

[3] See E.S. Schwartz, "A Dictionary for Minimum Redundancy Encoding," *Journal of the Association of Computing Machinery*, 10 (1963), 413-39; H.E. White, "Printed English Compression by Dictionary Encoding," Proceedings *IEEE*, 3 (1967), 390-6; J.P. McCarthy, "Automatic File Compression," Proceedings *International Computing Symposium*, (1973), 511-6, North Holland Publishing Company; E.J. Schuegraf and H.S. Heaps, "Selection of Equifrequency Word Fragments for Information Retrieval," *Information Storage and Retrieval*, 9 (1973), 697-711; F. Rubin, "Experiments in Text File Compression," *Communications of the ACM*, 19 (1976), 617-22.

[4] H.S. Heaps, "Storage Analysis of a Compression Coding for Document Data Bases," *INFOR*, 10 (1972), 47-61.

[5]D.A. Huffman, "A Method for Construction of Minimum Redundancy Codes," Proceedings *IRE*, 40 (1952), 1098-1101.

[6]F. Reza, *An Introduction to Information Theory* (New York: McGraw Hill, 1963).

[7]G.K. Zipf, *Human Behaviour and the Principle of Least Effort* (Addison Wesley, 1949).

[8]D.S. Columbo and J.E. Rush, "Use of Word Fragments in Computer Based Retrieval Systems," *Journal of Chem. Documentation*, 9 (1969), 47-50.

[9]A.C. Clare, E.M. Cook and M.F. Lynch, "The Identification of Variable Length Equifrequency Character Strings in a Natural Language Data Base," *Computer Journal*, 15 (1972), 259-62.

[10]R.A. Wagner, "Common Phrases and Minimum Text Storage," *Communication of the ACM*, 16 (1973), 148-53.

[11]E.J. Schuegraf and H.S. Heaps, "A Comparison of Algorithms for Data Base Compression by Use of Fragments as Language Elements," *Information Storage and Retrieval*, 10 (1974), 309-19.

[12]V.L. Doucette and E.J. Schuegraf, "Data Base Compression Using a Fragment Dictionary: A Dictionary Selection Method Matching a Coding Scheme," Submitted to *Journal of ASIS*.

Networks of Sound:
Graph Theory Applied to Studying Rhymes

J. Joyce

This paper studies rhyming words from the standpoint of mathematical graph theory. Representing a cluster of rhyming words as a graph has several advantages. It provides a construct for studying phonological similarities among rhymed words, and a construct for studying poetic choice in rhyming. The former principally concerns us here, though the latter is not without linguistic interest from the standpoint of semantic networks or topological modelling of language phenomena.[1]

In studies of the history of English (and other languages), words in rhyming postions within verse have canonically been used as evidence for historical pronunciation. Although rhyme words do not constitute the only source of evidence for pronunciation, they are major primary source indicating which words may have sounded alike, so enabling reconstruction of earlier states of a language. Since discussing or even listing all those who have used rhyme data in language reconstruction would exhaust the space I have here, I will limit my acknowledgement of previous work to that of three scholars: Miles Hanley, Helge Kökeritz, and John S. Kenyon.

In the 1930's Miles Hanley amassed a huge collection of rhymes in American and English poetry from 1500 to 1900. This collection is of 'direct rhymes', according to Hanley, and includes only "those [rhymes] which show peculiarities of pronunciation or those in which changes of pronunciation have occurred so that the rimes would no longer be considered 'good' ones."[2] The collection was published in microcard form in 1959, and the slips stored at the University of Wisconsin under the care of Professor Frederic Cassidy. Hanley's collection was consulted by Kökeritz in work leading to *Shakespeare's Pronunciation*, as he acknowledges in the preface. Appendix 3 of the book is "An Index of Shakespeare's Rhymes," prepared with the help of Mrs. Louise Hanley.

The Hanley collection was also consulted by Kenyon in work that was published in collaboration with Knott as *A Pronouncing Dictionary of American English*. The Hanley collection amply demonstrates the richness of data contained in rhymes.

Representing rhymes as graphs is a sufficient departure from the more traditional listing of rhymes (as exemplified by Hanley's *Index to Rhymes*) to warrant a theoretical rationale illustrated by examples.

Rhyme schemes in verse establish patterns of expected sound similarity; that is, when we read a Shakespearean sonnet we perceive the pattern

a b a b c d c d e f e f g g

in the final sound of the lines. If we read all 154 sonnets we find the pattern sustained in all but three, and even without the benefit of historical phonology we hear the end-rhyme pattern often enough that we know it must have been a structural reality. We may view the various end-rhymes for a given stanza as pairs of words associated under the relation rhymes with , as in: me rhymes with thee. If we know (or suspect strongly) that the words sound very much alike, we may indicate the relation 'rhymes with' is reflective: that is, 'me' rhymes with 'thee' implies 'thee' rhymes with 'me'.

However, in attempting to reconstruct phonology from rhymes we need not make so large an assumption regarding words in rhyming positions until it is needed. It appears to be enough to characterize the relation among rhyme words as 'is rhymed with' – this being a description of the relationship found in the rhyme scheme. Just how 'is rhymed with' differs from 'rhymes with' may be clarified by noting that 'is rhymed with' can be taken to imply a directionality in the relation: that is, 'thee' is rhymed with 'me' implies that 'me' occurred first, and 'thee' later in a rhyming position. This is illustrated in the couplet:

Make thee another self, for love of me,
That beauty still may live in thine or thee.
    Sonnets, x, 13-14.

Thus I wish to discuss rhymes from the standpoint that the rhyme scheme implies that the second rhyme word in a pair recalls the first word's final sound.[3] For this reason it seems appropriate[4] to graph the pair of rhyme words 'me' and 'thee' as:

me ← thee

Although the two words 'me' and 'thee' do make a graph, they do not make an interesting graph – one in which relationships among several rhyme words may be studied. An interesting graph, for example, exists within the rhymes of the first ten of the sonnets; it is the graph for all words linked by the rhyme scheme to 'me':

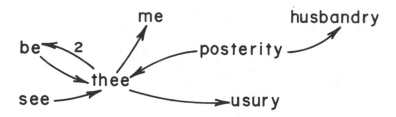

The number on the arrow from 'thee' to 'be' indicates there are two instances in which 'thee' is rhymed with (and thus recalls in sound) 'be'. Lack of a number indicates there is only one such instance; and lack of a line connecting two words indicates they are not linked as rhymes by the rhyme scheme[5].

This graph was chosen because it is the largest connected graph among all the end-rhymes in the first ten sonnets. The membership of 'husbandry' in this graph is through 'posterity', which in turn is a member through 'thee', which in turn is a member through any of the words 'me, be, see,' and 'usury'. The basis for membership in the graph is not that words rhyme with each other, but that they are associated by the rhyme scheme for the sonnets. Fortunately, in this case, in Modern

English they share the same final sound, /iy/, and we easily accept the graph as credible without having to argue the point.

The astute reader will note that by confining our attention to end-rhymes as identified by the rhyme scheme we have not represented all the final /iy/ sounds present in the first ten sonnets in the graph. 'Legacy' and 'free', for example, are not in the graph although they are rhymes in sonnet iv, lines 2 and 4. However, neither 'legacy' nor 'free' is connected to any of the seven words in the graph; thus though they share the same final sound in Modern English, they are not part of the connected graph. Such apparent errors are in part avoided by choosing a larger corpus from which to draw rhymes, though by relying on the rhyme scheme alone as the basis for associating words there will inevitably be groups of words that share the same final sound but are not linked by the rhyme scheme. I do not view this as a major drawback, but as a minor irritation.

The graph illustrates an interesting cluster of words (though limited because of corpus size). The word most often recalled in rhyme pairs is 'thee'; it has the most arrows pointing toward it: three. 'Be' has two arrows pointing toward it, but they are from the same word. Although repeated linking of the two rhyme words is undeniably important, a larger number of words linked with one word provides a broader-based network for study. An analogous result from sociometrics may help here.

Were we considering people rather than words, with the arrows indicating the relation 'admires', we would have what is known as a sociogram for a group. The most popular person in the group is the one the largest number of people in the group admire, and the leader of the group is the person the most popular person admires. In our rhyme sociogram 'thee' qualifies as the most popular, and given the obvious centrality of 'thee' to the other words in the graph, the choice is not inconsistent with what we deduce from visually inspecting the graph. However, since there are three different words pointed to by 'thee', this graph does not offer us a clear 'leader' rhyme word. Yet, we have identified the most popular rhyme word in the graph and should interpret what that means.

We could begin by noting that 'thee' refers to the young man to whom these ten sonnets are addressed. It appears from other rhyme graphs I have made that the most popular rhyme word in a graph is also an important word in the context of the piece. Of course, good poetic practice does not place unimportant words in rhyming positions, and subject matter does affect vocabulary choice, both on the level of individual poems and the era in which the writer lives[6]. But of the seven words in the graph 'thee' is clearly the most descriptive of the matter in the ten sonnets: the young man. Just why a major key word is 'recalled' rather than 'emphasized' – that is, is first in the rhyme pair rather than -second – is something that may perhaps be explained by consideration of what it means phonologically to say a word is the most popular word.

The basis for constructing the directed graph is the relation 'is rhymed with' among words at the end of lines in verse. As argued above, 'is rhymed with' implies that the second word in a pair recalls the first word. The most popular rhyme, containing the sound most often recalled, must embody the essential sound of the rhyme; in the case of 'thee', it is the sound we now pronounce /iy/. In mathematical terms, it is at least the result of the intersection of the phones for the most popular rhyme with the phones for all other words which recall it.

The qualification 'at least' is made because simple intersection of the sets of phones is an inadequate restriction on rhymes. To take a hypothetical example, if the most popular rhyme word and most of the words which recall it shared the cluster /tiy/ one would wish to study the graph and the words carefully before insisting the rhyme sound is only /iy/, especially if the remaining words end in /diy/, making the difference one of voiceless versus voiced.

The most popular rhyme sound, then, is the best embodiment in a word of the sound represented by the rhyme graph. This does not preclude the other words in the graph from also embodying the same sound; certainly in English poetry words directly connected to the most popular rhyme word may embody the sound of the entire rhyme word, or differ by only a single feature, as illustrated above. My point here is that the most popular rhyme word in a graph of rhymes should be the center for studying the rhyme group; the structure of the graph guides interpretation (literary or phonological) of the rhymes.

Having argued the phonological importance of the most popular rhyme word, I would like to advance a similar argument for why the most popular rhyme word is a major key word for the rhymes graphed. In good verse, rhymes are a pattern integrated with the whole of the work, that whole including the concept space shared by the poem or poems from which the rhyme graph was made.[8] Each of the rhyme words will be associated somehow (that is, not always directly) with the unifying concept. The most popular rhyme word, then, will represent at least the intersection of the words that recall it in the concept space; the intersection, or common ground, should be embodied in a word expressing the unifying concept. I would certainly not argue that the most popular rhyme word is the best embodiment of the concept unifying the verse, since rhyme is only one aspect of verse; as argued in note 4, the second word of a rhyme pair receives the greater emphasis of the two, and thus the word in that position would likely be a more meaningful word. I would not care to push this point too far, however, and will defer further comment until I have studied a larger number of graphs.

So far I have argued that representing rhymes as a graph, though a departure from the usual rhyme list, allows at least one interesting and useful result not available from a rhyme list. The next section of this discussion will present the concept of transitivity of the rhyme relation, and what the transitive property implies about rhyme graphs.

The largest connected graph among the first twenty stanzas of Chaucer's *Troilus and Criseyde* has as its most popular rhyme the word 'be':

Twenty stanzas were chosen as the text for investigation because the length is comparable to that of the ten Shakespeare sonnets, and Chaucer's stanza structure is more complex[7]:

a b a b b c c

Although the number of lines in the sample from Shakespeare is exactly that in the sample from Chaucer, the graph contains almost twice as many words. There is a word that is clearly the most popular rhyme word: 'be', which indicates the state of being Chaucer is establishing in this introductory section of the poem. There is also a leader in this rhyme graph, and that is the word 'auctorite'.

The most popular word, 'be', points to two words: 'he' and 'auctorite'. However, 'he' points to 'auctorite' by virtue of the fact that 'autorite' is the first b-rhyme in the stanza associating 'be', 'he', and 'auctorite'. In this instance (though not generally), 'be' recalls the rhyme sound in 'auctorite', and 'be' recalls the rhyme sound in 'he', which in turn recalls the rhyme sound in 'auctorite'. Thus, 'be' recalls 'auctorite' twice – once by direct linking of the rhyme scheme, and once by transitivity through 'he'.

A relation (such as rhyming) is said to be transitive if the relation has the property that

If 'be' is rhymed with 'he'
and 'he' is rhymed with 'auctorite'
then 'be' is rhymed with 'auctorite'

As has been noted, in this instance the statement of transitivity is literally true. But the same graph could have resulted from 'be' recalling 'auctorite' in one c-rhyme, and 'be' recalling 'he' in another c-rhyme, with 'he' recalling 'auctorite' in a third c-rhyme. We have selected our corpus for subjection to graph-theoretic analysis with the expectation that the rhymes for the most part are true rhymes, yet we must entertain the possibility that the transitive property may not hold unless it holds as literally as in *Troilus and Criseyde*.

Taken as a graph of three words, the most popular word is 'auctorite' – and if we apply the interpretation for the most popular rhyme word in a graph it must contain at least the intersection of the set of phones for all other words which recall it. Again, all of this must be qualified by how much we suspect the rhymes in the graph under analysis are true rhymes if we are to have a result that is meaningful. We also must note that the assertion of transitivity of the rhyme is in the direction of the arrows and not both ways[9]. The rhyme graph presents us with a long-standing problem in Chaucer studies: how often final 'e' is sounded. The two words for which this is a question are 'Troye' and 'joie' – and the question is not one I intend to answer here. Rather, I wish to indicate how study of a graph may frame the question in a way that is helpful for study. The graph here does not have a path from 'be' to either of the words 'Troye' or 'joie', nor to 'ye', which is rhymed with both of them. We may apply a transitivity argument to 'Troye' or 'joie', but it collapses because both are equally popular in the three-word section that constitutes the largest network flowing into either word. With the majority of the words being the ones we are asking questions about, the graph is simply inconclusive. A model that helps us avoid error is as valuable as one that helps us make conclusions.

The examples of graphs from Shakespeare and Chaucer have been for the purpose of illustration. The corpus from which they were drawn is small because a larger body of material would introduce a factor of complexity that might obscure the point of the examples. As a final illustration I wish to examine the graph for all words connected – no matter how distantly nor what direction the link is – with the word for 'jewel' in the Middle English poem *The Pearl*. The rhyme scheme for this poem is more complex than the rhyme royal stanza of Chaucer:

a b a b a b a b b c b c

It is sustained for 101 stanzas, except for stanza 5 of part VIII, which apparently is missing a line[10]. I chose the word for 'jewel' because the *Pearl*-poet refers to his loved-one in the poem as a jewel on several occasions. The graph for the word is given in Figure 3.

The first thing to notice is the complexity of the connections among the words, a complexity that is the result of the rhyme- scheme's multiple associations among the a-rhymes and the b-rhymes. This provides a rich network of rhyme, dividing neatly into two parts: double versus single 'l' rhymes; or, those words connected to 'juelle' and those connected to 'juele' / 'ieule'. I have also associated 'melle' and 'mele' for the purposes of this discussion, following the practice of Kottler and Markman in their concordance[11].

Interestingly, the Middle English word for 'jewel' is not the most popular rhyme word – either for 'juelle' or 'juele' graphs. The most popular rhyme words are 'melle' ('speak') for the 'juelle' graph, 'wele' ('precious thing') for the 'juele' graph, and 'melle' / 'mele' for the combined graph.

The popularity of 'wele' as a rhyme word in a poem for which the 'precious thing' [that is, the person who appears as the Pearl-maiden] is such a central concern is not terribly surprising. But 'mel[l]e', ('speak'), is another matter.

Although it is true that we view *Pearl* as the narrator's lament for a lost loved one, that is true because we read the poem from the narrator's point of view. The Pearl-maiden, however, is attempting through dialogue to direct the narrator's attention toward consolation for his loss. The medium for consolation is dialogue, but the narrator does not accept this, and thus at the end of the poem is still bitter. The audience of the poem has accompanied the narrator through the steps toward consolation, and realizes the narrator's error in not being consoled by what the Pearl-maiden speaks. Thus to speak is to approach understanding – from the point of view of the Pearl-maiden; thus, 'melle'.

The 'l' versus 'll' division in the rhyme graph is certainly provocative and deserves attention. Is the division a matter of chance, or does it indicate scribal or phonological practice? The double 'l' rhymes in the graph occur together in particular stanzas of *Pearl*; the same is true of the single 'l' rhymes in the graph. Such neatness of division is not beyond chance, but I suspect the scribe was simply doubling the 'l' to preserve the orthographic pattern in the other words. Another possibility is that 'juelle' has a longer, more sustained 'l' than 'juele'. Such questions would need to be asked in the context of all other rhyme graphs in the poem in which a word is spelled with a single and a double letter. My spot check indicates that orthographic uniformity was at least one of the scribe's considerations.

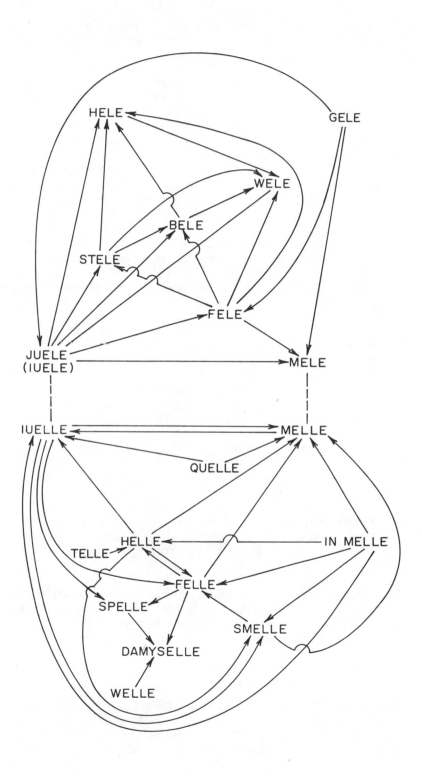

The example from *Pearl* shows several things about rhyme graphs: 1) the graph reflects the complexity of the rhyme scheme; 2) although the graph may be very complex, it can still yield interesting associations, such as the interpretation of the most popular rhymes and observations about the single versus double 'l'; 3) the graph is useful in that it indicates where further exploration should be done. There is much more that could be deduced from the rhyme graphs presented here, but the space limitation does not permit that luxury. Yet one further benefit from representing rhymes as graphs needs to be mentioned, that of a possible model for phonological change.

From each graph it is possible to construct a corresponding matrix. By constructing such matrices for certain word clusters over, say, thirty-year intervals, one may treat the matrices as representing the state of the rhyme relation at that time. By seeking the function that best describes the change from matrix to matrix we are also seeking a function that models phonological change over time. Ideas on how that might be done will have to await another opportunity for discussion. Nevertheless, I hope I have been able to show the usefulness of the technique and suggest how we may profit from exploring rhyme's network of sound.

References

[1] A theoretical discussion of topological modelling of language phenomena can be found in John M. Lipski, "Towards a Topology of Natural Languages," *Poetics*, 4 (March, 1975), 5-17.

[2] Miles L. Hanley, *Index to Rimes in American and English Poetry, 1550-1900* (Madison, Wisconsin: Microcard Foundation, 1959). All quotations from Hanley are taken from the introductory material reproduced with the *Index*.

[3] To simplify exposition here, I will use the term 'rhyme sound' to include rhymes of one or more phones and will not disrupt my remarks with constant reminders that 'rhyme sound' also applies to 'rhyme sounds'.

[4] The direction of the arrow could be argued to be first-word-to-second in that the second word of a rhyme pair receives more emphasis because it is the location at which we realize the phenomenon of rhyme. This can be seen in Pope's couplet

Know then thyself, presume not God to scan;
The proper study of Mankind is Man.

where emphasis is clearly on the second word of the rhyme pair. I suspect linguistic purposes are furthered more by modelling 'is recalled by' rather than 'is emphasized by' – though either way contains more information than the traditional list, and no doubt each merits study.

[5]However, lack of a line directly connecting two words is not a denial that they rhyme, and a line connecting them is no guarantee they do. As an illustration of this latter point we may consider Roethke's "Open House", which ends

Rage warps my clearest cry To witless agony.

The two words would be graphed as

cry ← agony

Here the rhyme is not true because the two words do not sound the same nor sound similar enough to rhyme in Roethke's idiolect. The pair (cry, agony) constitute a 'slant rhyme'. It should be evident that if one suspects the rhymed material being subject to analysis does not overwhelmingly consist of true rhymes the phonological evidence for sound similarity will be crude at best and probably misleading. Comic rhyme such as that in Byron's *Don Juan* can be relied upon, I suspect, because Byron derives his comic effect from juxtaposition of unusual or outrageous words ('new one' and 'Juan', for example), and for the comedy to succeed the words must sound sufficiently alike to be perceived as rhymes – though perhaps not very elegant ones. Much the same comment applies to the rhymes in the lyrics of Gilbert and Sullivan operettas ('strategy' and 'sat a gee' in the Major General's Song from *Pirates of Penzance*). To some extent these remarks imply one must prejudge the material to be examined. But in choosing the material to examine one must make at least a tentative decision regarding how reliable the rhyme scheme seems as one perceives what the rhyme scheme is; indeed, I find it difficult to separate perception of the pattern from reliability of the pattern, since we perceive pattern by its being reliable.

[6]Josephine Miles, *Eras and Modes in English Poetry* (Berkeley: Univ. of Calif. Pr., 1964).

[7]The fifth line of the stanza creates multiple associations of the b rhymes whereas the *Sonnets* generally are neatly divided into three quatrains and a couplet.

[8]Discussion of 'concept space' may be found in both Wallace Chafe's *Meaning and the Structure of Language* (Univ. of Chicago Pr., 1971), pp. 79-80, and in J. Joyce, "Fuzzy Sets and the Study of Linguistics," *Pacific Coast Philology* (1976). If the graph is constructed from a body of work without some unifying concept these remarks will undoubtedly be inapplicable.

[9]In work extending and generalizing the applicability of transitivity to the relation of 'is rhymed with' I expect to be able to relax the assumption of how true the rhymes must be. The key, I believe, is in regarding 'is rhymed with' as a similarity relation. For an extended discussion of similarity relations see Lotfi A. Zadeh, "Similarity Relations and Fuzzy Orderings," *Information Sciences*, 3 (1971), 177-200.

[10]E.V. Gordon, ed. *Pearl* (Oxford: Oxford Univ. Pr., 1953), p. 17.

[11]A. M. Markman and James Kottler, *A Concordance to Five Middle English Poems* (Univ. of Pittsburgh Pr., 1966). I am aware that the words are widely thought to be of different derivations; the *QED*, for example, lists 'mele' and 'melle' separately, and Gordon's Glossary to *Pearl* does also. However, the *Middle English Dictionary*, Part M.3, groups 'mele' and 'melle' together under 'melen', (to speak, talk). My purpose here is not to decide whether 'mele' and 'melle' are the same or different words, but to present a technique that may be of use in reconstructing pronunciation.

User Aids in a Lexical Processing System[1]

R.L. Venezky, N. Relles, L. Price

Over the past two decades, software designers have held a variety of images of the computer user. Initially, 'user' was synonymous with 'programmer,' and therefore few concessions were made for the naive, the forgetful, or the timid. Then came the era of the user as a competent, but slightly disoriented programmer, which gave rise to the gratuitous phrase 'user-oriented system,' and such *post hoc* and *ad hoc* features as *help* and *menu* statements. These were tacked onto a system after all else was implemented and generally supplied only token assistance, requiring the user to rely ultimately on a reference manual for further information.

Now we appear to be entering a third phase in which the user is seen as neither enthusiast nor programmer, but as bank clerk, reservation agent, or the equivalent, for whom on-line interaction with a computer is a daily requirement of employment. For this audience, systems are being designed with on-line documentation, extensive error diagnostics, and variable interaction modes as integral components of the initial system design. Many such features can be seen in systems like the New York Times Information Bank, the UNIX Time Sharing System for the PDP 11 and the PLATO Computer-Assisted Instruction System. Each of these reflects the newly recognized importance of simplified and humanized user interaction.

While the user is now, more than ever before, a focus of concern, no clear standards or specifications have emerged for either defining different types of user needs or designing protocols for user interaction. In a discipline that has yet to manage uniform design standards for terminal keyboards after almost 20 years of intensive use, this is perhaps not unexpected. Nevertheless, an attempt to develop design criteria for user aids, although perhaps premature, might serve as a focus for defining issues and alternatives. This paper is a modest attempt to do this by presenting the development of user aids in a particular software system which was implemented at the University of Wisconsin over the past four years.

The LEXICO System

Since the capabilities of this system, called LEXICO, are documented elsewhere, the emphasis in this article will be on the justification for the techniques which were implemented, with occasional discussions of alternatives which were considered.[2]

LEXICO is a mixed on-line and batch system that provides assistance in the construction of dictionaries. It is used primarily by lex-

icographers and students of stylistics, and supplies them with the following functions:
1) forming and maintaining a collection of texts (including text editing),
2) concording,
3) classifying text words by headword categories (lemmatization), and
4) generating a headword concordance and dictionary slips.

The users of LEXICO are not professional programmers; rather, they are editors, linguists, and the like, who are accustomed to non-mechanical techniques and will not convert to a computer system just for novelty. These users need to remain in constant communication with their data as it passes through the various LEXICO processes, since simple errors, if not corrected soon enough, could lead to intolerable expenses when large texts were involved. Therefore, facilities for constant monitoring of data are important components of the system.

In contrast with other attempts to classify computer users, our attempts found three types to be important for our design: the novice, the sustained user, and the occasional user[3]. Each of these has differing needs. The novice needs to know what functions the system can perform and the statements required for initiating these functions, in addition to learning how and when to create backup files, how to recover from syntax errors, and which servicing priority to select for particular cost and time requirements.

On the other hand, the sustained user who has acquired this knowledge wants to make requests as brief as possible. He neither desires nor needs extra documentation; because his errors are usually recognized quickly, they do not require extensive explication; and his servicing priorities are predetermined. Between the novice and the sustained users, however, is another class of users – the occasional users. These are people who have mastered the system once, but because of infrequent use, may have forgotten an essential item. They need some assistance, but their memories can often be jarred with a minimum of verbiage. Thus, while the novice may require a full page of explanation of a certain command, the occasional user needs only a sentence or two, and the sustained user desires at most an abbreviation.

With these users in mind, several design goals were established for LEXICO. These were:
1) the user should be totally isolated from the UNIVAC 1110 operating system and should be aware only of the data and tasks that are at his level of discourse;
2) the system should appear to the user as a single, unified entity, communication between user and system should have a consistent form that is independent of the required task, the formats for all commands should be similar and system responses should all have the same general style;
3) the means of requesting tasks should be flexible and easy to use and should minimize the chance of user errors;
4) to have a task performed, the user should be required to specify as little as possible;
5) the system should be very easy to maintain: in particular, it should be possible for programmers to implement new capabilities, modify the command language to accomodate new or revised capabilities, and trace system errors with minimal effort, facilities should be

provided for monitoring both user and system behaviour;
6) the system should not be too expensive to use, for in addition to demonstrating the feasibility of automating certain tasks, our goal was to provide a useful and practical alternative to other methods.

User Aids

Various types of user aids were designed and tested. To facilitate the discussion of these aids, two LEXICO interactive sessions are shown below. In the first, a user creates a collection for texts and enters some processing parameters. In the second session, a text is added to the collection. The bracketed numbers in the examples refer to sections of the following discussion.

Session 1

>lexico	*the user initiates interaction with LEXICO*
LEXICO VERSION 2.0 08/07/76 12:17:55	*LEXICO responds* (1)
COLLECTION NAME?	*LEXICO asks for a collection name*
>example	*the user enters the collection name*
NEW COLLECTION MAY BE CREATED	*LEXICO recognizes the user wants to work in a new collection*
TASK COMMAND?	*LEXICO asks for a task to perform*
>create	*the user wants to create a collection*
COLLECTION 'EXAMPLE' TO BE CREATED: YOU MAY ENTER COLLECTION DEFAULTS	*LEXICO acknowledges* (2)
>add stopwords del di e era negli nella >sul un 'c''era' cosi/ ma non aveva che	*the user enters the stopwords; c'era is entered as 'c''era' because*
>lo il ha agli su ti	*it contains an apostrophe*
COLLECTION CREATED	*LEXICO creates collection*

Session 2

Having created a collection, the user continues in the same interactive session, causing the text to be added to the collection as shown below.

TASK COMMAND?	*LEXICO asks what to do next*
>add john	*the user wants to add a text called 'john'*
TEXT CODE ASSIGNED TO 'JOHN' IS 1	*from now on the text may be referred to as 'John' or as '1'*
>input on card file 'test.material'	*the user tells LEXICO where to find the text* (3)

>end	*the user has no further specifications*
CREATE BACKUP IMMEDIATELY BEFORE THIS PROCESS? (Y OR N)	*LEXICO asks if a copy of the collection should be saved in case the computer goes down while the text is being added.* (4)
>n	*the user does not want a backup*
WHEN? (I, T, O, W)	*LEXICO asks for a run priority* (5)
>*equ	*the user requests an explanation of the question* (6)
THE CHARACTER YOU ENTER WILL DETERMINE WHEN THE RUN WILL BE INITIATED: I=>IMMEDIATELY T=>TODAY O=>OVERNIGHT W=>WEEKEND ANYTHING ELSE =>CANCEL RUN (FOR COST IMPLICATIONS, PRESS EXPLAIN-QUESTION AGAIN) WHEN? (I, T, O, W)	*LEXICO explains the options*
>*equ	*the user wants more detail* (7)
I=VERY EXPENSIVE T=LESS EXPENSIVE O=INEXPENSIVE W=LEAST EXPENSIVE (BUT NOT CHEAP)	
>o	*the user selects overnight priority*
RUN IDENTIFICATION: XD0848 (SAVERNO908*6122421)	*LEXICO tells the user how to identify the output at the computing center* (8)

Explanation

(1) One of the more difficult decisions to make in designing an interactive language is the mode of interaction. Most designers opt for keyword-oriented statements, entered by the user. For example, in the Burroughs 6700 System Editor, files are created, saved, and deleted through statements of the form 'MAKE newfile', 'SAVE', and 'REMOVE newfile', which are entered on-line. The other major options are *form fill-out mode,* and *interrogation mode.* In the former, which is intended primarily for CRT terminals, a form is projected on the screen and the user fills in requested information. In interrogation mode, the system requests information of the user in the form of questions or prompts.

In the initial design of LEXICO, all three modes were planned, with the user selecting whichever he prefers. A form fill-out mode was ultimately discarded because of its dependence on a unique type of terminal, which would have severely restricted the system's availability. In the end, both cost and training considerations led to a single mode which combined interrogation and statement modes, but at the system's discretion rather than that of the user. The cost considerations primarily involved implementation and maintenance, but also included the increased complexity of documentation.

Training considerations were based on the desire to have users learn the most efficient and flexible mode, which would have been statement mode. The other two modes, if always available, might discourage a new user from ever trying statement mode. Thus, a compromise was made: to ensure cost effectiveness, statement mode would be the primary means of communication, but some system interrogation would be included, particularly for those tasks whose specification would be most likely to confuse the user. The latter mode was also chosen in those instances where a single item of information had to be specified, such as a collection name or a processing priority.

In statement 1, the system asks the user for a collection name. If an existing collection is to be referenced, then that name is given. Otherwise, the user enters the name of the new collection he wants to create. For several other commands (for example, ADD, CONCORD), the user may enter either the full statement (for example, ADD text-name), or just the task specifier (for example, ADD). In the latter case, the system requests the text name.

(2,3) One of the most aggravating requirements of many computing systems is the need for continual specification of task parameters. The user of a typical concording system must specify such parameters as physical and logical record lengths, printing options, sorting options, and stopwords for each text to be concorded. For example, a user of BIBCON concording system must specify a minimum of 38 such parameters for each concordance generated.[4]

Many systems make a single concession to users: when not otherwise specified, a system-assigned default is used. This is, however, of little help to the user with non-standard parameters; these parameters must be re-specified each time a task is performed. The situation is even worse for a user with many differing sets of data. Managing the different task parameters may become more difficult than processing the data itself.

LEXICO avoids this problem by providing a hierarchy of default values. Built into the system are defaults for almost all system parameters; when a collection of texts is created, these values are assigned automatically. The user may declare those values that differ from system default values. All of the values specified by the user, together with the system defaults for other parameters, become *collection defaults* – they apply to every text in the collection and need never again be specified. However, the user may still specify that a particular text has different values. These specified values then become *text defaults* and need not be re-specified each time the text is used. Finally, some of the defaults may be overridden by explicit user declarations for a particular task.

In (2) of the example, the user enters a list of stopwords (words that are entered into a concordance listing with their frequencies of occurrence, but not their contexts). These stopwords become collection defaults and, unless overridden by explicit user declarations, will apply to all texts in the collection. In (3), the user tells the system which disk file contains the text input images. Since this statment is entered as part of a text-specific task, the file name becomes a text default.

Assisting users in minimizing the adverse effects of system errors is important for sustained processing, especially when interactive sessions tend to be very long and when large amounts of data are processed. LEXICO was originally designed without any recovery mechanisms.

But during the system's development it became obvious that protection was needed from software errors within LEXICO or the operating system, as well as from sporadic hardware failures (which occur at any computer installation). However, the trade-offs between the costs of generating and maintaining backup files, and the costs and aggravation when data is destroyed, vary among users. Therefore, no reasonable formula could be found for automatically generating backup files.

The solution was to provide a file recovery procedure through the creation and loading of backup files, but to leave to the user's discretion the employment of these options. Nevertheless, as shown in (4), LEX-ICO does interrogate the user at those junctures where backup files would most likely be created.

Increased system reliability has significantly reduced the need for backup and recovery procedures. But the rarity of system failures is of little consolation to that user whose data has been destroyed. All users must therefore consider the need to use backup facilities.

(5) The real world of computing runs on a cash basis; that is, real users pay real cost. This fact, plus the differential billing rates at the Madison Academic Computing Center where LEXICO is implemented, require assistance for the user in selecting run options. (5) is a request to the user to select a run priority. It is expected that after a suitably representative sample of statistics is gathered, the system will be able to estimate the cost of processing a given text at each of the available priorities.

(6,7) In this example, the user is not certain of the meaning of the request, so he uses one of the information aids built into LEXICO, 'explain question.' LEXICO responds with an initial explanation. But the user is still not sure which option to choose, so he requests and receives further information – in this case, a translation of run priorities into relative costs.

This seemingly simple feature, as well as other on-line aids, resolves a problem characteristic of many interactive systems: how to provide messages that are at the same time intelligible to the beginning user and not unnecessarily long and tedious for the experienced user. In addition to EXPLAIN QUESTION (*exq), available on-line aids include:

EXPLAIN ERROR (*err). If an error is made, the system displays a brief description of that error. In response to *err, a more detailed explanation is displayed. *err may be entered several times for progressively more detailed explanations.

EXAMPLE (*exa). Whenever the system solicits information or when an error has been made, examples of correct input may be obtained with this command.

MENU (*mnu). This command causes the system to display all commands allowed in the task which the user is requesting.

(8) One of the design goals of LEXICO was to isolate the user from the cryptics and protocols of the EXEC 8 operating system, using techniques similar to those implemented in the DUM system at the University of Maryland.[5] However, limitations on reaching this goal became evident quite early in the implementation of LEXICO and now, in retrospect, we have some reservations about the feasibility of the goal. In some situations, as shown here, the user needs to know certain system protocols to complete his processing. In this example, the run identification for retrieving printer output is given. Similar problems occur in file and error handling. (Some errors detected by the EXEC 8 monitor display unintelligible error messages over which LEXICO has

no control).

The degree to which we were ultimately able to isolate the user from the operating system has limited the system's portability. But because of the resulting benefits to a user, and because LEXICO is accessible from any remote terminal (and will soon be available through the EDUNET computer network), we feel that the sacrifice in portability has been worthwhile.

Assistance through Documentation

In addition to the aids shown above, the primary learning aids for LEX-ICO users are a series of seven user guides: an overview, and a guide for each of the six major processes. These guides replace a single, thick reference manual whose bulk might be a psychological barrier to prospective users. Each guide may be used relatively independently of the other guides, in case an application does not make use of all available capabilities, or when an individual user's responsibility is with a single task (for example, editing texts).

The multiple-guide approach has been well accepted and will be continued. Two problems remain to be resolved, however. The first, which will soon resolve itself, is the difficulty of maintaining up-to-date documentation on a changing system. Until recently, a guide more than a week old was an outdated guide. The availability of on-line aids, and the ease with which they may be updated, alleviates this problem to some extent.

The second problem is one inherent in all documentation, and that is the conflict created by attempting to make a single manual serve as both a reference manual, which is intended for experienced users, and a tutorial manual which is written for beginners. Expensive systems can afford both; for LEXICO, a compromise was adopted whereby explanations and examples were directed towards beginners, but format and summaries were directed towards non-beginners.

Programmer Aids

Several features of LEXICO were developed to simplify debugging and modification and to encourage more consistent, reliable programs. These are:
1) the ability to use LEXICO commands to perform system maintenance functions (such as updating system defaults and modifying the command language);
2) diagnostic features selectable by entering commands during interaction with LEXICO;
3) restriction of communication with the user to a set of routines incorporating the user aids;
4) a set of utility routines for command collection-related operations.

Implementation

User aids such as those described here require significant resources for implementation. In addition, they require a full integration into the .

system design.

During an interactive session, all LEXICO system routines must provide user aids to explain prompts, error messages, and user options. All such messages are specified on a system file and are therefore treated consistently by the interactive system. Messages are specified at increasing levels of detail; each successive level may be displayed at the user's request. An example of such a multi-level message (as specified by the programmer) is:

ESEQl3   ENTER CITATION:
ESEQl4   ENTER A NEW CITATION. USE AS MANY LINES
         AS NECESSARY; TRAILING BLANKS ARE
         IGNORED. TERMINATE WITH A CITATION
         DELIMITER.
EXEQl5   SEE USER GUIDE 5, SECTION 1.3

The Command Language Interpreter operates in conjunction with a context-free grammar and the file of user aids to communicate with the user. All collection-related data is maintained on several files that comprise a collection. To schedule tasks for later processing, LEXICO generates runstreams on files it creates and submits them to the operating system. The LEXICO user is totally unaware of any of these files and operations.

The operations performed by LEXICO in order to concord a text illustrate the interpretation of user requests and resulting file management. When a user enters a CONCORD statement, LEXICO retrieves from one data file all pertinent defaults and searches the directory to ensure that the requested text exists. If this is the first concordance to be generated in the collection, a concordance file and a word list file are created. When all declarations have been entered, followed by an END statement, LEXICO creates a system file to contain a runstream. Appropriate commands and data are entered in the file and the user is prompted for a scheduling priority. This is translated into a request to the operating system to schedule the task. The text directory (and possibly text defaults) are updated to reflect scheduling of the concordance. Later, when the operating system begins the actual task, a batch component of LEXICO ensures that the collection (and the text) still exist, and then begins to read citations from the text file. In addition to several intermediate system files (such as for sorting), the system generates a concordance file and a new list of words in the word list file (updating directories in each file). The collection directory is updated and the concordance is output according to the user's request (for example, on paper, magnetic tape, or mass storage). Finally, information about the task is logged on the system's statistics file for later analysis.

The design of user aids is clearly not a science; even to call it an art may be to grace it with a degree of dignity which it has yet to merit. Almost all on-line systems being developed today have some user aids, although none that we have seen have the variety and consistency of aids offered by LEXICO. But LEXICO was developed as part of a reasearch project in on-line computing; most of its components were tested, revised and retested over a four-year period. Therefore, it is difficult to generalize from LEXICO to other production systems. Compounding this difficulty of comparison are the complexities of lexicographic processing and the peculiarities of the EXEC 8 operating system, which was not originally designed for on-line interaction.

Nevertheless, the types of users considered by LEXICO, the integration of batch and interactive processing, the informational aids (such as explain error), the default levels, and the combination of statement and interrogation modes all seem applicable to a wide range of task specification languages. Perhaps the most severe test of LEXICO's success will be the degree to which these features are similarly integrated into other systems.

References

[1]The work reported here was carried out at the University of Wisconsin under support from the National Science Foundation and the Wisconsin Alumni Research Foundation.

[2]R.L. Venezky, N. Relles and L. Price, "LEXICO: A System for Lexicographic Processing," *Computers and the Humanities*, 1977, p. 11.

[3]J. Martin, *Design of Man-Computer Dialogues* (Englewood Cliffs, N.J.: Prentice-Hall, 1973). Martin, for example, divides on-line user ('terminal operators') into nine catagories, depending upon such factors as intelligence, training, programming ability, and 'ruggedness.' It is difficult to determine, however, how all these factors could influence software design.

[4]R.L. Venezky, *BIBCON: An 1108 Program for Producing Concordances to Prose, Poetry, and Bibliographic References* (Technical Report #113, Computer Science Department, University of Wisconsin, 1971).

[5]P.E. Hagerty, *The University of Maryland DUM System: Proceedings of the Univac Scientific Exchange Conference* (Paoli, Pa., 1972), pp. 29-80.

11
Sculpture

The BIRDS: Computer Controlled Sculptures

K.F. Lauckner

Intelligence is the essence of man! In fact, it is this distinguishing feature which has set man far apart from all other animals. His ability to think has been the concern of philosophers and many others for hundreds of years. The sculpture series entitled The BIRDS was motivated by this same curiousity: to better understand the phenomena of thinking and intelligence. The BIRDS have the unique purpose of simulating some aspects of intelligence, and in particular, human intelligence. This simulation of intelligence is preferably referred to as artificial intelligence, and it can be accomplished through the use of computers.

It is curious how The BIRDS series of sculptures got their name. The sculptor, while searching for some basic and simple demonstration of intelligence, noted a minor research report indicating that certain birds had the ability to count. It was reported that birds feeding in a field would leave the area when humans approached. They would perch in nearby trees until the intruders left. Curious about their ability to count, the researcher built a blind and then tried to confuse the birds into believing no one was in the blind. Up to five or six people could enter and leave the blind, singly or in groups. The birds counted all who entered and would not return to feed until all people left the blind. As the number of people became larger, the birds became confused. Many of the sculptures in the BIRDS series have a tree-like structure upon which the bird may perch after rising from 'feeding'. As concepts progressed, the connection with real birds became more abstract.

Before describing these sculptures, it is necessary to introduce a classification scheme for their actions. This scheme has two major divisions denoted as 'reflected intelligence' and 'internal intelligence.' The first, 'reflected intelligence,' refers to actions of The BIRDS which are only 'reflections' of the human viewer. If, for example, the viewer moves about the sculpture, this motion will be translated into some predetermined actions (for example, the 'reflections'). The second, which is concerned with 'internal intelligence,' would take the movements of the human viewer and respond with 'intelligent' actions. The response is not a simple 'reflection' of the viewer's movements, but it would appear as if the sculpture was being manipulated or controlled by some hidden person. Figure 1 summarizes the two types of sculpture.

To better understand this division, it is helpful to examine a 'non-computerized' hypothetical sculpture. Figure 2 shows the reflective case of a sculture (a piano) with a keyboard and sound output. The pianist's intelligent input is mechanically converted to sound and reflected back to him. An analogous intelligent sculpture could consist of a pianist, who hears the input sound from the viewer's piano and intelligently responds by playing the piano in a type of musical answer. The important feature in the latter case is that the second pianist, who is part of the sculpture, is making intelligent decisions to the viewer's sounds.

General Considerations

The most important design considerations used throughout The BIRDS is making the hardware and software 'upward compatible.' That is, efforts and ideas in designing electronics and writing programs should be usable by other sculptures in the series. In keeping with this strategy, it will be noticed that, with the exception of the very first sculpture in the series, all of the BIRDS have actions along vertical parallel lines. This gives the sculptures a similar 'output medium' for expressing their actions, thereby allowing great similarities in both their electronics and programs. One result of this arrangement permits the 'individual actions' on each of the vertical lines to form a surface. For example, two of the sculptures consist of columns of lights; if only one light in each column is 'on', then a surface of lights is formed. The surface appears to move when each light is turned off but an adjacent one is turned on.

Figure 1

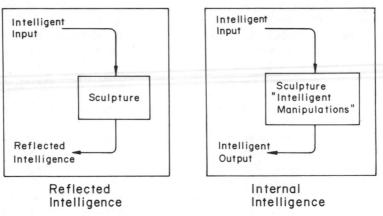

Figure 2

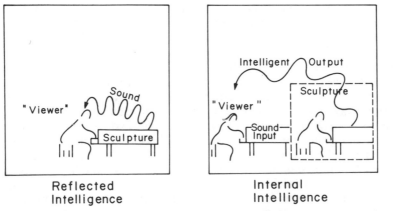

This surface motion, controlled by a computer program, could undulate as rhythmically as ocean surf or change suddenly from one position to another completely unrelated, or it could possibly disintegrate to a random array of flashing lights. This surface concept is carried to its extreme in the final sculpture of the series which occupies an acre or more of either water or land.

The main objective in The BIRDS is to create a meaningful interaction between the sculpture and the viewer. Whether this 'intelligent' interaction is to be of the reflective or internally intelligent type, it is still necessary to have a sensory system. Although only two types of sensors are currently in the designs, the fact that general purpose computers are being used makes it a rather simple problem to add other types of sensors. The simplest of the two sensors detects the movement of the people around the sculpture using the doppler shift phenomenon at ultrasonic frequencies. This sensor is essentially the same as the book-shaped burglar alarms which are currently being sold to homeowners for under $100. The basic system consists of an ultrasonic energy source which radiates from the sculpture. As an object moves in this ultrasonic 'field', reflections from it are at either a lower or higher frequency. This frequency 'shifted' energy is picked up by sensitive microphones, and indicates to the computer the presence of motion. The sensitivity of the system can be computer-controlled over a wide range: either so sensitive that air circulation from a furnace blower can activate it, or so insensitive that a large, fast moving object can barely be detected. The direction of a disturbance can be obtained by using several of the 'doppler sensors' each of which can only 'see' a certain region around the sculpture. By this means, the sensors could also sense the difference between a single viewer and a large group of people. But, the doppler-type sensor does not give as much information to the computer as does the second type of sensor used in The BIRDS. This sensor works in a manner quite similar to that of the solid state television camera. A lens focuses the image in its field of view onto a solid state image sensor which contains a 32 X 32 matrix of photo diodes; each photo diode can detect the brightness of the particular region it 'sees'. This means that the sculpture's sensor divides the scene into 1,024 cells. The computer can then store the brightness of each region and detect changes (such as movement) in the scene. Typically, a 'picture' of the view as seen from the sculpture would be 'taken' every two to four seconds. The computer would then analyze two consecutive pictures to 'see' if anything moved. Based on any movement or lack thereof, the sculpture would respond with an appropriate action, or modify a continuous action already in progress. For example, suppose the sculpture is currently outlining a 'surface' which is slowly undulating. Movement detected by a sensor could cause a 'ripple' in the surface starting at a position nearest to the disturbance. If the disturbance continues, this might cause the sculpture to ignore it and wait until it subsides. The computer may then try to evoke another disturbance from the viewer by repeating the earlier response. The sophistication of the interaction is a function of the programs and the power of the computer system used.

With the exception of the first sculpture, all of the series have various members of the PDP-11 family of computers, from the LSI-11 (a microprocessor-based system), up to the PDP-11/40. This family of computers are designed with compatibility as one of the most important features. In addition to compatibility, one of the most important reasons for using the PDP-11 family is maintenance. As art gallery directors know, electronic and mechanical art is usually a nuisance to keep operating. By using standard electronic equipment, maintenance becomes easier; therefore, because of the thousands of PDP-11's being used, there are many possible repair alternatives. Still another advantage of the PDP-11 family is the relative ease with which it can be interfaced to the large DEC System 10 Computer; this computer is commonly used in artificial intelligence research work. It is hoped that in the future, some of the 'fruits of labor' from these various artificial intelligence research projects can be applied to The BIRDS. The latter comment initiates the notion that in reality, The BIRDS will never be finished, but constantly changing as new programs are developed. With the exception of the first sculpture in The BIRDS series, all of them will have the capability to operate independently or via telephone lines to a DEC System 10 Computer. It should also be mentioned that several versions of the list processing computer language LISP are being implemented on the PDP-11. LISP is a very powerful language and happens to be quite common in artificial intelligence research.

It must be emphasized that the various sensors, physical forms, and computers are only the media (for example, the acrylic paints, brushes, and canvas) for the art. The real art is in the programs which cause the otherwise mechanically monotonous systems to respond intelligently to movements. Several characteristics of the software are considered desirable. The first of these characteristics concerns the 'learning ability' of the sculpture; the sculpture will take information from its sensors and use it to make changes in how it responds to the various disturbances. A good example of a learning program is available in a version of NIM, which is found in many university computers.

The game starts with three stacks of match sticks: the first pile has one match stick, the second pile has two, and the third pile has three. When it is your turn to move, you can take as many match sticks as you like from any one pile. The object of the game is to leave nothing for your opponent after your last move, then you win. The 'learning' version of NIM keeps a record of all the plays that it makes as it plays each game. When it is the computer's turn to play, the program will check all the alternatives and make the play which has lost the least number of times. As time goes on, the program will learn to play better and better. The BIRDS programs could vary the rate of 'learning' or 'change' from minutes to days or weeks. For example, the sculpture could regularly test the various modes of its operation and choose the the one which seems to produce the most viewer activity. A second feature of the software, randomness, if used sparingly, can produce very effective results. As an example, suppose the sculpture is responding to activity around it in a rather straightforward way, when suddenly, it starts 'acting' in an entirely different way. This is analogous to a conversation where one person suddenly changes the subject. The major philosophy in developing The BIRDS software is to implement only those programs which do not follow the same prescribed actions each time they 'run'. Instead, a great emphasis will be placed on heuristic algorithms (for instance, programs which use 'rules of thumb' rather than a definite set of rules to create the appropriate actions). These heuristic programs represent a great challenge to write efficiently for small computer systems.

Description of The BIRDS

The BIRDS sculpture series consists of six pieces with names whose forms symbolize our technological environment. All of the names have the prefix IS indicating Intelligent Sculpture and a suffix B from Birds. The number associated with each name indicates its complexity and sequence within the series. IS 50/B is the first member of the series. It started as a test of the multiplexed LED (Light Emitting Diode) system used in other sculptures in the series, and ended up as a multiple which will have approximately 100 copies. Its configuration, as shown in Figure 3, consists of a round polished cast metal base twenty-five centimeters in diameter with sixty-four parallel vertical rods, the highest of which reaches forty centimeters. At the end of each rod is a LED which is a tiny, very bright, red light. These lights are controlled by programs in a Motorola M6800 microprocessor with real time clock and related electronic circuitry. Each light can vary its intensity in sixteen levels from completely off to its brightest state. To achieve efficiency, a portion of the memory of the M6800 is accessible via Direct Memory Access (DMA) to a series of four registers which contain intensity information for the sixty-four LEDs; each register is responsible for sixteen LEDs in a multiplexed fashion. The prototype design has eight thousand words of Random Access Memory (RAM) and external connections for a terminal and cassette tape recorder used for mass storage. Later members of IS 50/B will have Erasable Programmable Read Only Memory, and terminal connections for testing and diagnostics. The program development for IS 50/B will be on a DEC System 10 Computer using a cross-assembler and M6800 Simulator.

Figure 3

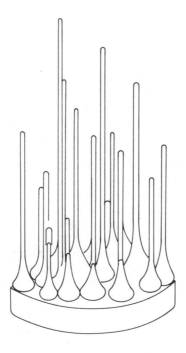

At this stage, programs will be written in the M6800 assembly language, cross-assembled, and then tested on the Simulator. After this, the program will be typed into the M6800 via terminal, then tested. Corrections and appropriate changes will be made and then saved on the magnetic cassette tape system. This means of software development is very tedious and difficult. A cross compiler (MPL) is available from Motorola and may be available for use on this project. IS 50/B will make use of the doppler-type sensor to detect motion.

Due to the flexibility of the input system of the M6800 microprocessor, a form of communication between several of the IS 50/Bs is being investigated. It would be possible to have several of them in a room; each would have its own sensory system and also be able to communicate with the other IS 50/Bs via low power radio. Programs could be developed to take movement sensed by one IS 50/B and relay the information to another IS 50/B which could, in turn, give an appropriate response by the pattern of lights that it flashes. The programming for this project is by far the greatest challenge.

The second member of the intelligent sculpture series shown in Figure 4 is IS 100/B. Physically, it consists of rectilinear blocks of polished stainless steel and has the dimensions 128 cm.×48 cm.×58 cm.. The main surface 24 cm.×106 cm. has four rows of poles, each row has sixteen poles of height thirty-two centimeters, and each of these poles has sixteen light emitting diodes. Behind the array of 1,024 LEDs is the mirror-like surface of a large polished stainless steel rectilinear block 106 centimeters long and thirty-six centimeters high. This surface serves to double the apparent number of lights. At the right end of the structure is a lens which has the obvious eye-like connotations. This eye is really the visual input to the computer. The visual information is fed to the computer for analysis; as movement occurs about the sculpture, the system will note these and make appropriate responses via changes in the lights. One type of action, reflectively intelligent in nature, would be an actual reproduction of the scene in lights (the scale is divided into 1,024 cells for analysis of gray scale and the eight levels of gray possible would result in eight levels of brightness in the lights). As a person moved about the sculpture, the lights would shift according to the motion. The 'internally intelligent' actions of the sculpture are considerably more difficult. In this regard, work is currently being done to design recursive programs in the language LISP which have interesting properties. These programs are for the DEC System 10 which immediately brings the hardware requirements of this sculpture into the discussion. The hardware planned for IS 100/B is the DEC Microprocessor System LSI 11/03. As the system grows in capability and in later members of The BIRDS series the larger DEC PDP-11 computers will have to be used. The model IS 100/B was essentially designed for development and testing purposes, although it is a legitimate sculpture in its own right.

The next member of The BIRDS series entitled IS 200/B consists of sixty-four poles, each two meters in height with sixty-four LEDs per pole. This large array of tiny lights, 4,096 in all, will stand on a floor level pedestal approximately two-and-one-half meters square, as shown in Figure 5. The software developed for IS 100/B will be readily adaptable. In addition, the structure lends itself to some additional features: because of its shape the viewer will be able to walk completely around the sculpture. This means additional visual inputs (eyes) to the computer are necessary, otherwise the sculpture would be blind to movements outside the range of a single lens system.

Figure 4

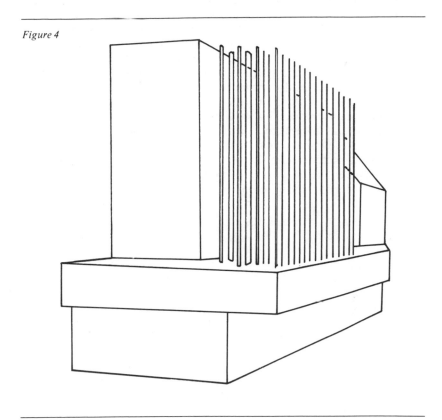

Figure 5

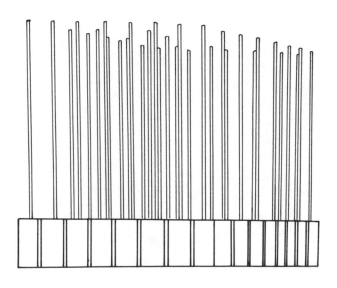

The fourth member of The BIRDS series of sculptures IS 300/B is a mechanical system. Physically, it consists of sixty-four stainless steel spheres suspended by very fine wires from a rectilinear structure approximately three meters above the floor, as shown in Figure 6. The length of each wire is controlled by an electric stepping motor. Again, the software developed for the earlier sculptures in the series would be readily adaptable. One interesting possible action for IS 300/B would be a constantly undulating surface which is disturbed by the motions of people around it. The disturbances could result in centers from which maverick waves would emanate.

The fifth sculpture in The BIRDS series IS 500/B (see Figure 7) is more traditional in appearance. But, this traditional nature is soon broken when the movements of the viewers are sensed by the same type of lens input system as IS 200/B. The abstract birds (approximately fifty centimeters in length) will move up and down their respective 'trees' according to the motions of the viewers.

Figure 6

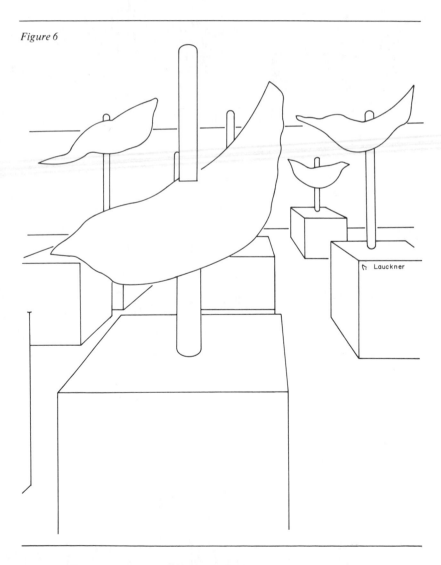

Finally, The BIRDS series culminates in a large public sculpture. IS 1000/B will cover at least one acre and can be located either over water (in a harbour or natural bay) or land. This piece consists of a large number of poles (the actual number depends on the location) which are approximately eight meters in height. The regularly spaced poles each have a rectangular-shaped surface which rides up and down the pole. These rectangular surfaces form a large surface which, under computer control, will undulate above the ground or water. The movement of the surface will depend on both visual and proximity sensors which feed information to the computer system. Spectators will be able to walk or paddle a boat around under this surface. It is obvious that this final effort would depend a great deal on the success of earlier work in the series. It is expected that several years of work will be necessary to complete The BIRDS.

The Future of The BIRDS

As the designs for the six BIRDS pieces described here are being worked upon, many new ideas will surely become evident. But, because of the high cost of these systems, only the IS 50/B and IS 100/B will be undertaken at the author's expense. It is hoped that some of the other works can be commissioned or possibly the sales of the IS 50/B multiple edition can finance other pieces in the series. In any event, the exploration of man's intelligence through his art is just beginning!

Figure 7

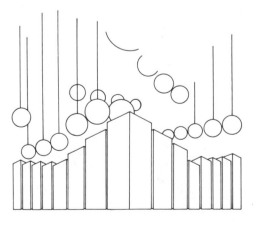

Figure 8

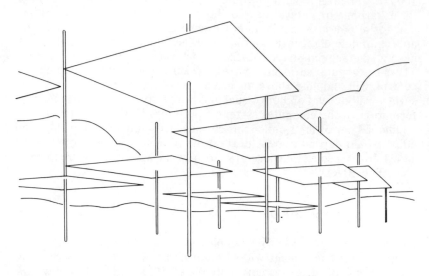

Index

Index

Contributors

Barenholtz, Jerry
The Leonardo Project
Faculty of InterdisciplinaryStudies
Simon Fraser University
Burnaby
British Columbia

Bender, Todd K.
English
University of Wisconsin
Madison

Bradley, John
Music
Wilfred Laurier University
Waterloo
Ontario

Calvert, Thomas W.
Interdisciplinary Studies
Simon Fraser University
Burnaby
British Columbia

Cameron, Angus
Robarts Library
University of Toronto
Toronto
Ontario

Clausing, Gerhard
German
University of Southern California
Los Angeles

Cohen, Annabel J.
Psychology
University of Waterloo
Waterloo
Ontario

Doucette, Virginia L.
Mathematics
St. Francis Xavier University
Antigonish
Nova Scotia

Flores, Sam
Computer Science
University of Waterloo
Waterloo
Ontario

Fortier, Paul A.
French and Spanish
University of Manitoba
Winnipeg

Ganapathy, I.
Kinesiology and Computer Science
Simon Fraser University
Burnaby
British Columbia

Gena, Peter
School of Music
Northwestern University
Evanston
Illinois

Gilmour-Bryson, Anne
Institut d'etudes medievales
Université de Montreal
Montreal
Quebec

Hannestad, Stephen E.
National Archives and Records Service
Washington
D.C.

Harrison, David
Integrated Studies
University of Waterloo
Waterloo
Ontario

Harrison, Karen M.
Mathematics
St. Francis Xavier University
Antigonish
Nova Scotia

Hirschmann, Rudolf
German
University of Southern California
Los Angeles

Isaacs, Paul
Psychology
University of Waterloo
Waterloo
Ontario

Joyce, James
Electrical Engineering and Computer
Sciences
ComputerScience Division
University of California
Berkeley

Keeping, Donald
French and Spanish
University of Manitoba
Winnipeg

Kenny, Anthony
Philosophy
Balliol College
Oxford
Great Britain

Lansdown, John
TLH Ltd.
London
Great Britain

Lauckner Kurt F.
Mathematics
Eastern Michigan University
Ypsilanti

Leavitt, Jay A.
Computer Science
University of Minnesota
Minneapolis

Mitchell, J. Lawrence
English
University of Minnesota
Minneapolis

Moreux, Bernard
Linguistique et Philologie
Universite de Montreal
Montreal
Quebec

Preston, Michael J.
Centre for Computer Research in the
Humanities
University of Colorado
Boulder

Price, Lynne
Computer Science
University of Wisconsin
Madison

Pringle, Mary Beth
Wright State University
Dayton
Ohio

Purcell, Edward
Slavic Languages and Literatures, and
Linguistics
University of Southern California
Los Angeles

Relles, Nathan
Computer Science
University of Wisconsin
Madison

Renaud, Jean
Linguistique et Philologie
Universite de Montreal
Montreal
Quebec

Ross, Donald
English
Universty of Minnesota
Minneapolis

Schuegraf, Ernst J.
Mathematics
St. Francis Xavier University
Antigonish
Nova Scotia

Sherman, Donald
Linguistics
Stanford University
Stanford
California

Smoliar, Stephen W.
The Moore School of Electrical Engineer-
ing
Computer and Information Science
University of Pennsylvania
Philadelphia

Spevack, Marvin
Englisches Seminar
Westfalische Wilhelms-Universitat
Munster
West Germany

Srinivasan, Desika
Dip. in Teach. German (Munich)
Baroda
India

Truax, Barry
Communication Studies
Simon Fraser University
Burnaby
British Columbia

Truckenbrod, Joan R.
Art
Northern Illinois University
Dekalb

Venezky, Richard L.
Educational Foundations
University of Delaware
Newark

Waite, Stephen V. F.
Kiewit Computation Centre
Dartmouth College
Hanover
New Hampshire

Weber, Lynne
The Moore School of Electrical Engineer-
ing
Computerand Information Science
University of Pennsylvania
Philadelphia

Wenker, Jerome
UNIVAC
San Francisco
California

Wolofsky, Z.
Kinesiology and Computer Science
Simon FraserUniversity
Burnaby
British Columbia

Young, David R.
French and Spanish
University of Manitoba
Winnipeg d

Zarri, Gian Piero
CNRS-ERHF
Paris
France